THE POPULAR
HANDBOOK *of*
ARCHAEOLOGY
and the BIBLE

THE POPULAR HANDBOOK *of* ARCHAEOLOGY *and the* BIBLE

JOSEPH M. HOLDEN
NORMAN GEISLER

HARVEST HOUSE PUBLISHERS
EUGENE, OREGON

Cover by Dugan Design Group, Bloomington, Minnesota

Cover photos © Helga, Martin Bache / Alamy

All uncredited interior photos are © Joseph M. Holden, 2013.

THE POPULAR HANDBOOK OF ARCHAEOLOGY AND THE BIBLE
Copyright © 2013 by Norman Geisler and Joseph M. Holden
Published by Harvest House Publishers
Eugene, Oregon 97402
www.harvesthousepublishers.com

Library of Congress Cataloging-in-Publication Data
The popular handbook of archaeology and the Bible / Norman Geisler and Joseph M. Holden.
    pages cm
Includes bibliographical references.
ISBN 978-0-7369-4485-4 (pbk.)
    1. Bible—Evidences, authority, etc. 2. Bible—Antiquities. I. Geisler, Norman L.
BS480.P645 2013
220.9'3—dc23
                                                        2012041424

13 14 15 16 17 18 19 20 21 / LB-JH / 10 9 8 7 6 5 4 3 2 1

To my two sons, David and Ian,
because of their youthful sense of adventure
and zeal for archaeology and the Bible.

—Joseph Holden

To my first teacher of archaeology,
who inspired me in the field,
the late Dr. Charles Shaw.

—Norman Geisler

ACKNOWLEDGMENTS

In a work like this one it is difficult to give credit to all involved, since so many contributed in their unique ways. Without them this book would never have come to fruition. It is our pleasure to acknowledge the staff and administration of our own Veritas Evangelical Seminary for their patience and encouragement throughout the writing of the book. Their support makes this work a team effort.

However, we would like to give a special word of appreciation to Andrew W. Pitts and Dr. H. Wayne House, whose research assistance has made the book better in every way.

Further, without the technical assistance of Sam Capshaw and the skill, professionalism, flexibility, and labor of Bob Hawkins Jr. and Steve Miller of Harvest House Publishers, this book would never have made it to the press. A special thanks also to Paul Gossard for his skillful editing and his attentiveness to the needs of the reader.

Most of all, we would like to thank our Lord Jesus Christ for the unadulterated privilege He has given us to share the unsearchable riches of Christ with our generation. We sincerely hope this book will glorify Him by being a small step toward casting some light on the historical reality behind His unconditional love for mankind.

CONTENTS

List of Key Charts and Tables 11

Foreword *by Dr. Walter C. Kaiser Jr.* 13

Preface: Facts That Support Faith 15

Part One: The Reliability of Old Testament Manuscripts

Introduction 19

1. The Masoretes and the Samaritans 21
2. The Dead Sea Scrolls and the Silver Scrolls 33
3. The Transmission of the Old Testament—Summary 49

Part Two: The Reliability of Old Testament History

Introduction 55

4. Moses, the Pentateuch, and the Major Prophets 57
5. Alleged Errors vs. Archaeological Discoveries 77
6. The Canon of the Old Testament 87

Part Three: The Reliability of New Testament Manuscripts

Introduction 97

7. The Transmission of the New Testament 99
8. The Manuscripts of the New Testament 111
9. The Accuracy of the New Testament Manuscripts 127

Part Four: The Reliability of New Testament History

Introduction 131

10. Historicity of the New Testament 133
11. Responding to Recent Criticisms of the Gospels 143
12. Criticisms of the Resurrection Accounts and the Epistles 159
13. The Canon of the New Testament 171

Part Five: Introduction to Archaeology

Introduction 177

14. Archaeology and the Bible 181
15. Keys to Understanding Archaeology in Biblical Lands 189

Part Six: Archaeology of the Old Testament

    Introduction 199

16. Creation and Flood, the Tower of Babel, and the Cities of the Plain . . . 203

17. Exodus and Conquest 221

18. The Amarna Letters, the Hittites, and the City of Megiddo 239

19. King David and His Dynasty 249

20. Nebuchadnezzar II and the Persian Kings 269

21. Old Testament Persons Confirmed by Archaeology 283

Part Seven: Archaeology of the New Testament

    Introduction 291

22. Jesus and Other New Testament Persons in Non-Christian Sources . . . 295

23. Jesus and Archaeological Sources 307

24. The Temple Mount 323

25. Herod, Pilate, and Caiaphas 343

26. More Fascinating Finds Relating to the New Testament 351

    Glossary of Key Terms 369

    Appendix A: New Testament Manuscript Papyri:
    A Descriptive List 373

    Appendix B: Ascertaining the Geography of
    the Cities of the Plain: 40 Points 383

    Appendix C: Expert Witness Opinions Regarding
    the Authenticity of the James Ossuary 389

    Notes 395

    Select Bibliography 409

    Index 413

List of Key Charts and Tables

Old Testament Manuscripts 52

The Historical Reliability of Genesis and Exodus:
Summary of Major Points 66

Archaeological Discoveries Supporting the Reliability of
Old Testament History 81

New Testament Manuscript Distribution
by Century and Manuscript Type 105

Papyrus and Codex Manuscripts of the New Testament: Summary Listing
of Key Early Witnesses to the New Testament's Reliability 118

Early Citations of the New Testament 125

New Testament Manuscripts Compared to Other Ancient Sources 129

Non-Christian Sources Within 150 Years of Jesus 141

Order of Resurrection Events and Evidence They Provide 159

The New Testament Canon During the First Four Centuries 175

Archaeological Ages and Israel 191

Understanding Archaeological Terms 193

Differences in Mesopotamian and Genesis Flood Accounts 210

Which Location of Sodom Accounts
for the Biblical Geography of Genesis 13:1-12? 219

The Book of Exodus and the Ipuwer Papyrus: Comparison 223

Scientific and Factual Errors in the Red Algae/Red Mud Theory
of the Exodus Plague of Blood and Ensuing Plagues 226

Seal Impressions of People in the Old Testament 261

Old Testament Persons Confirmed by Archaeology 283

New Testament Persons Cited in Ancient Non-Christian Sources 303

More Archaeological Discoveries Supporting New Testament Reliability 359

New Testament Manuscript Papyri: A Descriptive List 373

Ascertaining the Geography of the Cities of the Plain: 40 Points 383

Expert Witness Opinions Regarding the Authenticity of the James Ossuary 389

by Dr. Walter C. Kaiser Jr.

Among the newer generation of biblical scholars there is a strong but unnecessary sense of skepticism about the historical claims of the Bible. These leaders in the field call themselves "revisionists," but others regard them as "minimalists" or even the "new nihilists." They claim "it is no longer possible to write a history about any ancient person or event, much less about a biblical happening at all"!

Fortunately, this group is still not in the majority of biblical scholars by a long shot, but the corrosive effects of their persistent denials are arriving in the culture at the same time as the postmodern agenda is being offered as a view for all reality. Aspects of some of their reasoning and arguments have sifted down into all spheres of society—yes, even at times to those in the believing community!

Such a postmodern agenda includes some of the following traits: 1) a revolt against all authority, 2) a distrust of all that is universal, 3) the premise that "social constructs" set the bounds for all knowledge, 4) the belief that all truth is relative, 5) the idea that there is no "meaning" except the meaning each of us creates for ourselves, and 6) the notion that one ideology is just as appropriate as another; in fact, the more radical the idea, the more likely it will be accorded a gracious hearing and applauded by innovators in the culture.

When such an agenda is used to interpret biblical texts, the sense of the postmodern argument is that those texts should be "liberated from historical consideration." Therefore, it is against such an "antihistorical" movement that this volume has, in part, been conceived and written. The case for the reliability of the persons and events of the Bible becomes more needed and more necessary each day as the newer generation's antibiblical thesis takes a greater hold on the hearts and minds of its members.

Meanwhile, the evidence for the truthfulness and historicity of the Bible continues to mount up as never before. Just when skepticism seems to be making the most noise, we are being flooded with an overwhelming amount of real, hard evidences that demand a verdict opposite to what skeptics, revisionists, minimalists, and deconstructionists are clamoring for in their current worldviews and life views. Never has any previous generation seen the amount and significance of evidences that are now available to us today.

For all too many who have been touched by the acids of these negative forms of modernity, this book will seem "like honey from the rock," for it will lay out the opposite case in a most convincing and kind way. In a most delightful and truly readable fashion, one convincing argument after another will be set forth until the whole case for the reliability of the Bible and the truthfulness of its history strikes home to the reader with thunderous effects. There will be no need for anyone to be overwhelmed by current skepticism, for the biblical case is now weighted extremely heavily in favor of those who hold to the historical accuracy of the Bible. Enjoy this rare tour through the manuscripts, history, archaeology, and facts of the Scriptures.

Walter C. Kaiser Jr.
President Emeritus,
Gordon-Conwell Theological Seminary

FACTS THAT SUPPORT FAITH

In the twenty-first century, the previous century's debate over the historical reliability of the Bible has taken on a new face and has gained fresh momentum in light of recent discoveries unearthed through archaeological excavation of the Holy Land. Many of these findings relate either directly or indirectly to the people, places, events, customs, and beliefs recorded in the Bible. As a result, the assertion by critical scholars that the Bible's historical descriptions are a product of human invention can no longer be maintained without facing strong counterarguments. Because of these finds, many modern scholars have revisited the archaeological and historical data with fresh insight into the reliability question. However, much of this valuable material often languishes in the halls of academia, leaving the layperson unaware of the immense body of archaeological information at their disposal.

Over the years, it has been our privilege to teach apologetics and theology courses at various undergraduate and graduate schools and conferences throughout the world. In addition, we have had the opportunity to travel extensively throughout the biblical lands, including Israel, Egypt, Jordan, Turkey, Greece, and Italy, as well as participating in archaeological excavation. In the process of communicating this material in the classroom, it is common to draw upon archaeological and historical data in order to demonstrate the reliability of the Bible. In doing this, we have seen the need to share with the body of Christ the accumulating data that reinforces our confidence in the historical narratives throughout the Scriptures. For as C.S. Lewis once wrote,

> To be ignorant and simple now, not to be able to meet the enemies on their own ground, would be to throw down our weapons, and to betray our uneducated brethren who have, under God, no defense but us against the intellectual attacks of the heathen.

As we have engaged many thousands of students and laypersons over the years in defense of the faith once for all committed to the saints, we have become increasingly aware of the need for two important things: 1) to increase familiarity among the vast public of the basic archaeological evidence in support of the historical reliability of the Bible, and 2) to expand awareness that facts (that is, history) and values (that is, doctrine and morals) are inextricably connected. It is from recognizing these needs that this book was born.

This handbook offers a bridge that spans the gulf between higher academia and lay Christian readers. It provides a means of educating and equipping them for participation in the reliability debate, which has for too long been relegated primarily to journal articles and scholarly discussions. Moreover, this work is intended to fill the gap in knowledge that exists within the church between our readers and the historical events recorded in Scripture. This knowledge is crucial due to the role history plays—as the ground from which doctrine and spiritual significance grow. Jesus understood the relationship between history and doctrine when He asked Nicodemus a crucial question: "If I told you earthly things and you do not believe, how will you believe if I tell you heavenly things?" (John 3:12).

The time for compartmentalized thinking that separates history from faith is past, since it would align the church with the assumptions of negative higher criticism, which sees no connection between the Jesus of history (whom they consider a nonsupernatural cynic sage who lived in the first-century) and the supernatural Christ of faith worshipped as God in churches around the world. The implications of unified thinking become clear when we understand that the *historical* death of Christ on the cross is inextricably connected to one's *spiritual* forgiveness of sin (Romans 4:25); and the *historical* creation of "male and female" in the beginning, to one's view of marriage as existing only between a man and a woman (Matthew 19:3-8). The crucial link between history and doctrine cannot be broken lest we damage the apologetic structure supporting why evangelical Christians cherish and rely on these very doctrines (Matthew 12:40).

In view of these things, this archaeological handbook is offered as an introductory beginning that confirms the "earthly things" contained in Scripture, in hope that the reader will become intimately acquainted with God's redemptive history. After being acquainted with these discoveries, the skeptical mind can much more easily give the benefit of the doubt to the "heavenly things" offered in Scripture. Our threefold hope and prayer is that the reader would

1. recognize that the Christian worldview is holistic, viewing fact and value, faith and history, science and Christianity as complementary;

2. become familiar with the apologetic support offered by the field of archaeology as it relates to confirming the historical statements in the Bible; and

3. comprehend the height, depth, and extent of God's love for mankind as revealed through His redemptive plan—a love that can be verified in real time-space history.

The content of the book is not meant to be an exhaustive treatment of manuscripts or archaeological findings, nor a debate with the scholarly community. Rather, it is an introductory summary for the beginner who desires an understanding of the more significant artifacts and manuscripts relating to the historical and textual reliability of the Bible. Every attempt was made to offer commonly accepted facts concerning the data and its relation to the Bible, leaving the "technical" discussions for the professional archaeologist. It is our hope that our readers will grow in their interest, passion, and knowledge of the fascinating field of archaeology and the Bible. If this book piques the interest of our readers to further study, travel to Israel, or to get involved in archaeological excavation projects as a volunteer, it has been a success.

Joseph M. Holden, PhD
Norman L. Geisler, PhD

PART ONE

THE RELIABILITY OF OLD
TESTAMENT MANUSCRIPTS

The Bible is the most textually supported piece of literature from the ancient world. This is because thousands of biblical manuscripts offer scholars the best opportunity (in numbers of manuscripts, accuracy of the transmitted text, and earliness of manuscript dates) to reconstruct the English editions of our Old and New Testaments. This part will explore and describe the key manuscripts, the transmission, the canon, and the reliability of the Old Testament text. Part 3 will later offer a survey of New Testament manuscripts, transmission (copying process), and issues related to canonicity, and answer recent objections to the historical reliability of the New Testament text.

In this current part we will consider the biblical manuscripts (a *manuscript* is an ancient handwritten copy of a part or whole of a biblical book or corpus) of the Old Testament and survey the two major textual traditions (a *tradition* is a group or family of manuscripts to which a particular manuscript is related). One tradition is found mainly in the Hebrew Masoretic Text. The second, and much earlier tradition, is associated with the Dead Sea Scrolls discovered at Qumran beginning in 1947.

1

THE MASORETES AND THE SAMARITANS

The Hebrew text of the Old Testament was transmitted by a number of different groups within its history. The *Sopherim* (from Hebrew, meaning "scribes") were Jewish scholars who preserved and copied the text from the fifth to the third centuries BC. The *Zugoth* (meaning "pairs" of scribes) were entrusted with this responsibility in the second and first centuries BC. By AD 200, the *Tannaim* ("repeaters" or "teachers") took over this task until about AD 500.*

The Masoretes

From this point, the group of medieval scribes primarily responsible for transmitting (and introducing vowels into) the Hebrew text upon which all editions of the Hebrew Bible were based for centuries were known as the Masoretes, or Masoretic scribes (from *masora*, meaning "traditions"). Thus we call the text they produced the Masoretic Text.

There were two somewhat independent schools of Masoretes: the Babylonian and the Palestinian. The most famous Masoretes were the Jewish scholars living in Tiberias in Galilee in the late ninth and tenth centuries AD: Moses ben Asher (with his son Aaron), and Moses ben Naphtali. Though these two families are often considered to have formed separate traditions of textual preservation, they represent only a single textual tradition. The devotion and care with which the scribes copied the text is seen in the consonantal text—the pre-Masoretic text containing only consonants with no vowels. The versions preserved by the two families respectively contained a mere nine linguistic differences between them. The Ben Naphtali tradition eventually died out, while the Ben Asher tradition continued to flourish, representing the superior text.

The Ben Asher text is the standard text for the Hebrew Bible today and is best

---

* The work of the Tannaim can be found in the *Midrash* ("textual interpretation" of the Old Testament, a compilation of oral tradition), *Tosefta* (meaning "supplement" to the Mishnah, c. AD 240), and the *Talmud* ("instruction"), the latter of which is divided into *Mishnah* ("repetitions") and *Gemara* ("the matter to be learned"). The Talmud constitutes a commentary on the Mishnah—literally a commentary on a commentary. Comprising two collections of Talmudic literature—the Babylonian and the Jerusalem Talmud—the Talmud was slowly written between AD 450 and 650.

represented by *Codex Leningradensis* B19A (L). It is utilized heavily in both the *Biblia Hebraica* (BHK) and the *Biblia Hebraica Stuttgartensia* (BHS), edited by Rudolph Kittel, and the *Aleppo Codex*, used for the Hebrew University Bible Project. Other Hebrew manuscripts that reflect the Masoretic text include *Codex Cairensis* (also called the *Cairo Codex of the Prophets*), *Babylonian Codex of the Latter Prophets* (MS Heb. B3), the *Cairo Geniza* manuscripts, *Reuchlin Codex of the Prophets* and the *Erfurt Codices* (E1, 2, 3). These are each considered below as individual witnesses emerging from the Masoretic tradition.

The Masoretic Text

As we have seen, the Masoretic Text encompasses an entire group of manuscripts, not just a single one, being represented by an array of different codices (that is, bound manuscript copies). Because all ancient biblical texts originally contained only consonants without vowels, many of the words could be pronounced in more than one way, which could lead to different readings of the same text. For instance, the consonants *dg* could be read as *dig*, *dog*, or *dug*. This posed a problem—a uniform style of reading needed to be established. In order to standardize the biblical texts, the Masoretes developed the *Masora* (discussed below), which added vowel signs in order to establish a fixed meaning to each group of consonants (for example, in a particular context *dg* would only refer to *dig*, not *dog* or *dug*).

Soon after the authoritative consonantal text of the Old Testament had been established, it was obvious that a reading aid would be needed. Before the consonantal text was formed there was evidence of the use of vowel reading aids. While one could still read the text with some freedom, the proper reading would be indicated by the use of vowel words using *scriptio plena* (a Semitic alphabet that contained vowel points)—that is to say, by inserting vowel points at will. The Isaiah Scroll and the Samaritan text are both witnesses to this stage of development with their respective use of *scriptio plena*. After the authoritative text was put into use, the practice of using the *scriptio plena* eventually ended.

The end of this system provided the historical platform for a new system of vowel marking to emerge. One attempt to put such a vowel system into place incorporated the use of the Greek language, but the Jewish tendency to avoid anything Greek made it difficult for this solution to catch on. So, in the fifth to tenth century AD, a new system was adopted, one which implemented vowel markings written above and below the consonants of the Hebrew text. This system came to be known as "pointing" (that is, the vowel markings found within the Hebrew text from the fifth century on). Within the first stage of this development, vowel markings would be inserted only occasionally in the biblical text to make notations on proper pronunciations for liturgical purposes. This process eventually evolved into providing this pointing for the entire consonantal text.

Three different pointing systems were eventually developed in the east and west: 1) the Babylonian system, 2) the Palestinian system, and 3) the Tiberian system. The latter was created between the eighth and tenth century AD, and it dominated the other two traditions, supplanting them so thoroughly that the Babylonian and the Palestinian traditions were forgotten for hundreds of years until their rediscovery in the nineteenth and twentieth centuries.

Preservation of the Text's Integrity

On the basis of the Masora—the "tradition" the Masoretes had received—they codified and wrote down the oral criticisms and remarks on the Hebrew text. This Masora also became the foundation for an apparatus that the Masoretes created in association with their text, which then was transmitted in the margins of the text itself. The purpose of these marginal notes was to preserve the integrity of the Scriptures down to the minutest detail, so that nothing would be added or taken away from God's Word. This transmission tradition was born out of a high reverence for the Hebrew Bible, and especially the Torah, within Judaism. It served as the basis of their legal traditions, and thus there was a need to protect and preserve these sacred texts. Subsequent generations of Masoretes further developed the existing apparatus far beyond the marginal notes into separate volumes and handbooks of detailed observations of the biblical text.

During the fifth and sixth centuries AD it is believed that the Masoretes, having standardized the Hebrew text, systematically and completely destroyed all of the manuscripts that did not agree with their vocalization system and standardization. Although few early manuscripts exist, the quality of these manuscripts is quite exceptional. In fact, the very lack of the many early manuscripts attests to the accuracy of the ones we do have. When scribes made errors while copying a manuscript, or when errors were discovered in manuscripts, they were immediately destroyed. Also, even when accurate manuscripts eventually began to deteriorate, leaving portions of the text tattered, they also were destroyed. This was for the purpose of preventing erroneous and partial manuscripts from circulating.

Evidence for the integrity of the Masoretic Text can also be found in the comparison of duplicate passages within the Masoretic Text itself. For example, Psalm 14 occurs again in Psalm 53; much of Isaiah 36–39 is also found in 2 Kings 18-20; Isaiah 2:2-4 parallels Micah 4:1-3; and extensive portions of the Chronicles are found in Samuel and the books of Kings. Further examination of these texts and others show substantial textual agreement as well as, in some cases, an almost word-for-word identity. Consequently, the Old Testament texts, having endured years of transmission through the Masoretic traditions, have not undergone any sort of radical revision even if the parallel passages come from identical sources.

The witness of the Septuagint (LXX), the Greek translation of the Old Testament, is perhaps the best evidence for the reliability of the Masoretic Text. The Septuagint was translated during the third and second centuries BC in Alexandria, Egypt, and was for the most part a book-by-book, chapter-by-chapter reproduction of the scribal text of that day. A comparison of the two texts reveals only common stylistic and idiomatic differences. Moreover, it was the Septuagint Bible that Jesus and the apostles possessed, and it was from this Bible that the New Testament authors primarily drew their quotes. The Septuagint Bible from the third and second century BC closely parallels the Masoretic

Text dating to the tenth century AD, thus confirming the faithful and accurate transmission of the Old Testament Scriptures in the Masoretic Texts.

Attention to Detail

The Masoretes had as their primary concern the preservation of the sacred Hebrew Bible. Their attention to detail was remarkably evident within their work. They went to great lengths to develop the system of marginal notes with pronunciation marks and various instructions to make sure that the smallest detail of the text would not go unnoticed by the copying scribe. Every biblical book contained a "colophon" (that is, a scribe's notation of the details of his work, usually attached at the end of his manuscript) and a count of the total number of consonants. Moreover, scribal notes were taken identifying the middle letter of the book by location and stating the exact number of characters that preceded the letter and followed after it. In addition to these, the Masoretes' inclusion of accentuation notes in the Hebrew text was unique and most helpful. They served as punctuation marks, musical notes for the purpose of chanting the text in cantillation, and as accent marks to direct where the phonetic emphasis should be made on the various syllables of the words.

The Masoretes were reluctant to change or alter anything within the received consonantal text. They noted a handful of preserved corrections within the text while still preserving the original to call attention to a needed correction. A particular set of corrections were known as the *Kethib-Qere* variants. These notes occur when the traditional reading—that is, the traditionally accepted pronunciation—differs from the pronunciation the letters would normally suggest. The *Kethib* (Aramaic for "written") referred to what was written in the text itself, and the *Qere* (Aramaic for "read") referred to the consonants in the margin with the vowels found in the text of the Kethib.

Many manuscripts also contain various Masoretic lists of differences between the Ben Asher texts and the Ben Naphtali texts, either at the beginning or at the end of the biblical books. The books of the second Rabbinic Bible have lists even more extensive than the biblical manuscripts themselves, which were chosen from various sources by the editor of that edition. This collection was later known as *Masora Finalis,* or Final Masora. The Final Masora of the second Rabbinic Bible also counts the number of letters, words, and verses found within the different books of the Bible. For example, at the end of the book of Genesis, the Final Masora states that there are a total of 1,534 verses in the book. From the final Masora we also learn that the Torah contains 5,845 verses, 79,856 words, and 400,945 letters. It is the Final Masora that contains the information regarding the number of words in a book or section, the middle word of a book, and even the middle consonant of a book. For the Masoretes, the purpose of these statistics is to ensure accuracy within the textual transmission process. If a scribe completed a copy of his manuscript and it could not be coordinated with the counts in the Final Masora, then he would know something went wrong in the transmission process and would therefore know not to transmit the text that was in error.

The Hebrew Christian Jacob ben Chayyim (c. AD 1525) first edited and published the standard edition of the Masoretic Text. It was for the most part based on the text of the Masorete Ben Asher (c. AD 920). The Masoretic Text is now the greatest witness to the original Hebrew Old Testament text. It became the foundational text of all printed editions of the Hebrew Bible, including the critical editions used by scholars. It became the original-language basis for translations of the English Old Testament.

However, one important issue that confronts scholars today involves the vaunted role of "Masoretic" Text as the standard basis for the translation of the Hebrew Bible. Manuscript expert Frederic Kenyon posited a significant question when he asked whether the Masoretic Text truly represents the Hebrew text originally written by its authors. In order to answer Kenyon's question, careful consideration must now be given to the texts and manuscripts that make up the Masoretic Hebrew Bible. [1]

Manuscripts of the Masoretic Text

Codex Leningradensis (B19A)

In AD 1008, the *Codex Leningradensis* was copied in Old Cairo by Samuel ben Jacob (according to a colophon) from a previous manuscript (now lost) written by Aaron ben Moses ben Asher about eight years earlier. However, the testimony on this point remains conflicted since some (for example, Ginsburg) held it was copied from the *Aleppo Codex*. In any case, *Codex Leningradensis* represents one of the oldest extant manuscripts containing the complete Hebrew Bible. Rudolf Kittel employed this manuscript as basis for the third edition of his *Biblia Hebraica* (BHK), and the codex remains the major textual basis for *Biblia Hebraica Stuttgartensia* (BHS), where it is symbolized as "L."

Prior to the discovery of the Dead Sea Scrolls in 1947, the *Codex Leningradensis* was the oldest manuscript containing the entire Old Testament. Its challenger, the *Aleppo Codex*, is missing pages as a result of suffering damage during anti-Jewish riots. Further, L serves as the primary source of text in the efforts to recover the missing texts in the *Aleppo Codex*. Practically speaking, since the *Aleppo Codex* was not available earlier this century to scholars, the *Codex Leningradensis* was used as the textual foundation for the popular Hebrew texts of today. L currently resides in the Leningrad Public Library (Russia) and serves as a valuable witness to the Ben Asher text.

The *Codex Leningradensis* was used for the comparison of manuscripts from the first period of the development that led to the Masoretic Text. This first period, which is characterized by the internal differences within the textual transmission, has an uncertain beginning since it is not clear exactly when the Masoretic Text came into being. Although ambiguity surrounds this first period's beginning, its end can be confidently dated at the time of the destruction of the Second Temple in AD 70.

Within the Masoretic Text group during this first period of development, there existed many differences between manuscripts. These differences mainly pertained to the content and orthography, which were usually limited to particular words and phrases only. Because there are so few complete parallel sources from antiquity, what scholars will usually do is describe these differences by comparing them with later manuscript sources. The second Rabbinic Bible was used for this purpose at an early stage of research, and now in recent studies, the *Codex Leningradensis* is used.

When the early manuscripts of the Masoretic Text are compared with the *Codex Leningradensis* from AD 1008 it is apparent how closely the texts align with one another. These close alignments apply to the vast majority of the Dead Sea Scroll (DSS) texts, as well as the Masada and other early witnesses of the Masoretic Text. These discoveries attest to the fact that the consonantal framework of the Masoretic Text has not undergone any significant change over the course of 1300 years.

The second period of Masoretic transmission begins sometime after the destruction of the Second Temple. The dismantling of the temple and its systems, along with other changes in social, religious, and economic climate, led to the decline of the circulation of textual variations. Because of this trend, one of the characteristics of this transmission period is greater unity of the texts within the Masoretic Text family. Here again the *Codex Leningradensis* is used to compare manuscripts. Texts found in Nahal Hever and Wadi Murabba'at and other ancient translations written in the second period give evidence of the decrease in textual variations. Hence, these texts follow very closely with the text of the *Codex Leningradensis*. [2]

The Aleppo Codex

The *Aleppo Codex* is the oldest Hebrew text of the entire Old Testament. The manuscript was copied in Israel in about AD 925 by Shelomo ben Baya'a, heir of a well-known family of scribes who specialized in the copying of biblical manuscripts. The *Aleppo Codex* is considered to be the earliest and most important manuscript of the Ben Asher tradition. It identifies Aaron ben Moses ben Asher of the city of Tiberias (c. AD 930) as the writer of the vowel pointing marks, according to the colophon. This manuscript was preserved by key Jewish communities in and around Israel for over a thousand years.

Scholars have dated the *Aleppo Codex* indirectly based on Shelomo ben Baya'a's Pentateuch manuscript, which contains inscriptions indicating it was written in AD 929. This also points to the approximate time of the writing of the *Aleppo Codex*. Based on a comparative analysis of the handwriting found on both manuscripts, scholars have determined and confirmed that both manuscripts were indeed written by the same person, thus confirming what is written in the dedication of the *Aleppo Codex*. Mordecai Glatzer has suggested that the codex was the personal property of Ben Baya'a and was kept for many years as he continually corrected it, adding Masoretic commentary and editing spelling defects among other things.

The *Aleppo Codex* was known as the *keter* (crown) of Aleppo and is considered to be the most accurate existing manuscript of the Masoretic tradition we possess today. Because this manuscript was corrected by Ben Asher, whose reputation as an excellent scholar in his day was renowned, it was heavily relied upon as a standard text for the correction of books. Ben Asher was known to have put much effort in his work on the various details of the text, making many corrections on it for many years. Upon examination of the pre-Masoretic texts that were preserved among the much earlier Dead Sea Scrolls, it was discovered that the *Aleppo Codex* and the pre-Masoretic texts were practically identical. It is these factors and others that contribute to the fame of the highly regarded *Aleppo Codex*.

By the mid-eleventh century AD the *Aleppo Codex* made its arrival in Jerusalem, serving as an authorized source for the Hebrew Bible to both the Karaites and rabbinical Jews. At the end of the eleventh century, when the Crusaders had conquered Jerusalem in 1099, the codex was stolen from Jerusalem and subsequently taken to Egypt. The conquerors avoided damaging the codex because they knew it was valuable to the Jewish communities and could, therefore, command a high ransom to secure its release. The manuscript was eventually released from its captors into the possession of the rabbinical synagogue in Fustat, Egypt.

The journey of the codex from Egypt to Aleppo (Syria) is unclear. The manuscript was still present in Egypt at the end of the twelfth century AD, but the earliest record of its presence in Aleppo dates from the fifteenth century AD. There is no clear information regarding the intervening years in which the transfer from Egypt to Syria would have taken place. Some have speculated that it was transferred toward the end of the fourteenth century AD since it was known that the grandson of Moses Maimonides' great-grandson, Rabbi David ben Yehoshu'a, traveled from Egypt to his home in Damascus

The *Aleppo Codex* is a Masoretic three-column text written in the Hebrew language with vowel points/dashes beneath the consonant letters. It is currently on display at the Shrine of the Book Museum in Jerusalem. (Photo by Zev Radovan.)

and Aleppo in 1375. During this trip, Rabbi David brought along many manuscripts with him, one of which may have been the *Aleppo Codex*.

The Aleppo text originally contained the entire Hebrew Bible, but due to an anti-Jewish riot in 1947 at the synagogue in Aleppo, portions of the text were lost. Initially it was thought that the codex was completely destroyed. According to testimonies about the incident, rioters broke into the iron chest that contained the codex. Evidence shows that it was thrown around; the missing pages could be a result of this happening in the midst of the chaos, or of rioters intentionally tearing them out to destroy the codex, or a combination of both.

Most of what was missing from the *Aleppo Codex* comes from the beginning and from the end of the text, with a few isolated pages torn from the middle as well. Much of what was lost contained the Masora and many other important notes, such as its dedication and the inscriptions that provide information on its writing. The identity of the individual or group who rescued the manuscript is unclear, though it appears that it was passed on from one person to another for about ten years in order to keep it hidden and prevent further damage. In 1958, the codex was finally smuggled out of Syria to Jerusalem and delivered to the president of the State of Israel, Yitzhak Ben-Zvi.

When the *Aleppo Codex* arrived in Israel it was comprised of 294 parchment pages that were written on both sides. It was discovered, after further examination, that there were many pages missing besides what was mentioned above. Almost the entire Torah, with the exception of the last chapters of Deuteronomy, had been lost, as well as the final pages of the manuscript. In addition, portions of the Song of Songs, and all of Ecclesiastes, Lamentations, Esther, Daniel, Ezra, and Nehemiah were missing, as well as a few pages from the prophets. It was discovered that the codex had originally had approximately 487 pages.

In Israel scholars began an intensive study of the codex. It was found that the spelling contained in the manuscript and the comments in the Masora matched to an extent surpassing that of any other manuscript. All aspects of the text were examined, such as the vocalization signs, cantillation marks, and the Masora apparatus, with similar results. Much effort was made to reconstruct the missing portions of the text. However, these attempts unfortunately did not lead to many findings worthy of reproduction. These pages could have been burned, destroyed, or even hidden away. Subsequently, two important discoveries have been made: an entire page of the *Aleppo Codex* from the book of Chronicles was found, having been preserved by a family in the city of Aleppo. Another discovery yielded a portion of manuscript from the book of Exodus. This manuscript had been preserved in the wallet of a man who had used it as a good-luck charm.

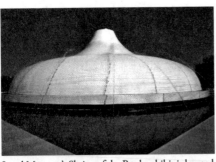

Israel Museum's Shrine of the Book exhibit is located in Jerusalem. The unique roof of the exhibit is designed in the shape of the clay jar lid in which the Dead Sea Scrolls were discovered.

The *Aleppo Codex* was revered by Jews and regarded as their most valued possession. It was strictly forbidden to remove it from the synagogue. It served as a model manuscript that was used liturgically only during the feasts of Passover, Weeks, and Tabernacles. The text is now displayed in Jerusalem at the Israel Museum's Shrine of the Book exhibit. The three-quarters of the codex that have been preserved are now published in an exact copy by M.H. Goshen-Gottstein as *The Aleppo Codex*. It also now serves as the foundation of the *New Hebrew Bible*, published by Hebrew University.

The *Aleppo Codex* has made a major contribution to the field of Old Testament studies. It has provided us with an authoritative manuscript that was faithfully transmitted and corrected by the renowned scholar Moses ben Asher, and it has been deemed a reliable and superior codex throughout history, being considered a model text to which all other texts are to be compared. Although doubts may arise regarding the missing pages, faithful efforts have been made to restore what was lost. Today, much of it has been restored through diligent research conducted by scholars. The existence of this codex has demonstrated the faithful transmission by scribes who were driven by duty and desire to make clear the testimony of the Old Testament Scriptures.[3]

Codex Cairensis

According to its colophon, the *Codex Cairensis* was written and vowel-pointed in AD 895 by Moses ben Asher in Tiberias while in Israel. It contains the Former Prophets (Joshua, Judges, 1 and 2 Samuel, 1 and 2 Kings) and the Latter Prophets (Isaiah, Jeremiah, Ezekiel, and the Minor Prophets). In the *Biblia Hebraica Stuttgartensia* it is symbolized by a C and is considered to be the most authoritative Hebrew text within the Masoretic Text tradition.[4]

Babylonian Codex of the Latter Prophets (MS Heb. B3)

The writing of the Babylonian Codex is dated to approximately AD 916. On occasion it is referred to as the *Leningrad Codex of the Prophets* (Kenyon) or the *St. Petersburg Codex* (Wurthwein). It contains Isaiah, Jeremiah, and the 12 Minor Prophets. What makes this manuscript significant is that the Babylonian school of Masoretic scribes was rediscovered through it. The *Babylonian Codex* is symbolized as V(ar)P in *Biblia Hebraica Stuttgartensia*.[5]

The Cairo Geniza Manuscripts

The *Cairo Geniza* documents were originally discovered in the storeroom (Hebrew: *genizah*) of the Ben Ezra Synagogue in Fustat (Old Cairo), Egypt. The manuscripts and fragments of this collection number in the tens of thousands and are now scattered throughout the world in various collections. Kahle has identified over 120 examples copied by the Babylonian group of the Masoretes. There have been 14 Old Testament manuscripts dating from AD 929 to AD 1121 discovered in the Firkovitch Collection in the Russian National Library in St. Petersburg. It is also contended that the 1200 manuscripts and fragments that come from the Antonin Collection in the Russian National Library are from the *Cairo Geniza* body of texts. (A list of 70 of these is published in the prolegomena to the *Biblia Hebraica,* seventh edition.) Some of the superior texts are housed in the United States (New York) as part of the Enelow Memorial Collection at the Jewish Theological Seminary, as well in the United Kingdom at Cambridge and Manchester Universities. [6]

Reuchlin Codex of the Prophets and the Erfurt Codices (E1, 2, 3)

The *Reuchlin Codex of the Prophets* has been dated to AD 1105 and now resides at Karlsruhe, Germany. It has been a valuable resource in the establishment of the fidelity of the Ben Asher text and contains a critical revision by the Tiberian Masorete Ben Naphtali.

The *Erfurt Codices* (E1, E2, E3) are currently listed in the University Library in Tübingen and are representative (more so in E3) of the Ben Naphtali tradition of the text and markings. E1 is a manuscript from the fourteenth century AD, E2 is probably from the thirteenth century AD, and the E3 is the oldest manuscript of the three and has been dated before AD 1100. [7]

The Samaritan Pentateuch

The *Samaritan Pentateuch* is an ancient text of the Torah that was written and preserved by the Samaritan community. After extended religious and cultural struggles, a radical division occurred between the Samaritans and the Jews during the fifth or fourth century BC. At this time the Samaritans accepted only the Pentateuch (the five books of Moses) as canonical, and they canonized their own version of these Scriptures for their community. The *Samaritan Pentateuch* is not considered a version of its own in the strict sense; rather, it is considered to be a portion of the Hebrew text itself.

Although the Samaritan text contains only consonantal characters, the Samaritans developed vowel signs later on, but only rarely did they insert them into their manuscripts. Only the more recent generations of Samaritans wrote manuscripts with full vocalization, for use only outside of their community. Shechem and Mount Gerizim are featured prominently; the text reflects only the religious principles of the Samaritans. Historical data on this scroll revealed that it was written in the twelfth or thirteenth century AD, contrary to the claims made by the Samaritan community that their scroll was an ancient text. Samaritan tradition claims that their community's origins come from the beginning of the Israelite nation, and that it is actually they who preserve the true Israelite tradition. The Samaritans believe it was not they but the Jews who strayed away from the orthodox tradition, during the time of Eli the priest in the eleventh century BC (see 2 Kings 17:24-34 for Samaritan origins).

Some scholars depart from both the Samaritan and Jewish traditions in their perspectives of the origins of the Samaritan community by asserting that the Samaritan community originated at a much later period. They base this view on the book of Ezra, where the Samaritans are seen as a group of people from Samaria who separated from the Judahites during the Persian period. Other scholars make their formulations on the origin of the Samaritan community based on the works of Josephus and other historians. Most are still unsure as to when exactly the *Samaritan Pentateuch* was written; some claim it could have been written prior to the establishment of the community itself or could have been created much later (though there exists no known manuscripts of the *Samaritan Pentateuch* earlier than the eleventh century AD). Evidence appears to support Samaritan origins sometime during the sixth to fourth century BC.

When the *Samaritan Pentateuch* and the Masoretic Text are compared, there appear to be approximately 6000 differences, which are considered to be a result of sectarian differences between the Samaritans and the Jews. Still others regard the *Samaritan Pentateuch* as a sectarian revision of the Masoretic Text itself. Because of these opinions, many scholars failed to give the text much attention upon its discovery in AD 1616, considering it useless in the realm of Old Testament textual criticism. However, upon further examination it was found that the *Samaritan Pentateuch* represented a textual tradition that preceded that of the Masoretic Text, offering insight into textual history.

The discovery of the texts that are now considered pre-Samaritan texts among the Dead Sea Scrolls has offered us much insight into the formation of the *Samaritan Pentateuch*, even though these pre-Samaritan texts are not Samaritan documents. The best preserved pre-Samaritan text contains large portions of Exodus 6 and 37 (4QpaleoExod^m). The pre-Samaritan texts are identified by the main characteristic feature of harmonization within the Pentateuch (discussed below). Though both the pre-Samaritan texts and the *Samaritan Pentateuch* have much in common, there are many instances where they diverge. The *Samaritan Pentateuch* deviates from the pre-Samaritan texts mostly in the Samaritan ideological changes that were inserted into the Torah. Though little can be said regarding the relationship between various pre-Samaritan texts, their overall agreement in important features seems to indicate a single common text from which subsequent varying manuscripts emerged. The pre-Samaritan texts give valuable insight into the development of the *Samaritan Pentateuch*, insight that was not available to scholars prior to their discovery.

The *Samaritan Pentateuch* also contains many linguistic corrections throughout its texts. Many of these "corrections" seem to be a result of attempts to smooth out the readings and to make the text more grammatically sound. Differences in content can also be found between the *Samaritan Pentateuch* and the Masoretic Text. These are minor changes that involve interchanging of single consonants and different words. Though many of these differences can be shown to be a result of the Samaritan stratum, it appears upon further inspection and comparison with the pre-Samaritan text that most of these differences are ancient and can be attributed to scribal errors that came into either the Masoretic Text or the *Samaritan Pentateuch*. Linguistic differences, in terms of morphology and vocabulary, can also be found in the text as well. Most of these are found in the pre-Samaritan texts.

The *Samaritan Pentateuch* has ideological elements interwoven throughout its text as well. However, these are only minor additions to the Torah. A few passages and wordings were altered in order to support Samaritan traditions, but the main ideological change made in the *Samaritan Pentateuch* concerns the Samaritans' central place of worship. An example of these alterations can be found in Genesis 22:2. In the *Samaritan Pentateuch* Abraham goes to build an altar for the sacrifice of his son Isaac on Mount Moreh near Shechem, which is a chief place of worship for the Samaritans. The Masoretic Text identifies the place Abraham goes to sacrifice his son as Mount Moriah. Another example is found in Deuteronomy 12:5. In this passage of Scripture Moses tells the nation of Israel that they are to "seek the place the LORD your God will choose"(NIV), alluding to Jerusalem in the Masoretic Text. Since in the Samaritan view the place of worship has already been chosen by Yahweh, the *Samaritan Pentateuch* changes the same passage from its future tense to past tense, portraying Moses as telling Israel to worship at "the place where Yahweh has chosen," alluding to Mount Gerizim.

Though many of the deviations from the Masoretic Text mentioned here are due to sectarian differences, most of the differences found in the *Samaritan Pentateuch* are neutral. That is to say, many of the differences were not for the purpose of altering the meaning of the text; rather, most were a result of attempts to popularize the text. The mere fact that the *Samaritan Pentateuch* followed the Septuagint and many of the Dead Sea Scrolls so closely attests to the claim that many of the differences with the Masoretic Text were not a result of sectarian differences. Scholars believe it is more likely that these textual variations are a result of the use of a different textual base that was widely used in the ancient Near East until well after the time of Christ.

It is no wonder that the *Samaritan Pentateuch* is considered a valuable text for its contribution to the field of Old Testament textual criticism. It offers a glimpse into a separate tradition of scribal transmission from an early period. Despite its alterations, the *Samaritan Pentateuch* is another witness to the reliability of the Masoretic Text. The majority of the Samaritan text follows the Masoretic Text tradition closely, with only relatively minor differences that are easily identified. The *Samaritan Pentateuch* also does much to illustrate the complexity that was present in the Old Testament textual tradition that existed before the authoritative textual standard of the Masoretic Text was established. It is in this way that the *Samaritan Pentateuch* can stand as a supporting witness to the Old Testament texts. [8]

THE DEAD SEA SCROLLS AND THE SILVER SCROLLS

Shortly after the conclusion of World War II, the Middle East reemerged as the center of political and religious attention when two significant discoveries that would revolutionize biblical studies were revealed to the world. The first was the Dead Sea Scrolls found in Israel, and the second was the Gnostic texts from Nag Hammadi, Egypt. The Gnostic literature greatly informed New Testament scholars of the mysterious sect's theology and apocryphal account of the life of Christ and His disciples.

However, nothing could compare with the accidental discovery of the Dead Sea Scrolls (DSS) in the limestone caves of Qumran. These finds consist of hundreds of the oldest biblical texts in existence: manuscripts and fragments of every book of the Hebrew Bible except Esther. The remarkable discovery of these Old Testament manuscripts led famed archaeologist William F. Albright to view them as the "greatest archaeolog-

The entrance to cave 4 is visible from the ruins of Qumran. This particular cave contained thousands of manuscript fragments that were discovered during excavations from 1951 to 1956.

ical discovery of modern times."[1] Most would agree with Albright—however, this agreement would only come after one has grasped and appreciated the scrolls' theological and apologetic value to the church.

The scrolls proved to be an important link in an unbroken chain of texts that contribute to establishing the textual reliability of the Old Testament Scriptures—a chain whose links date from 600 BC (the Ketef Hinnom Silver Scrolls) to AD 1008 (*Codex Leningradensis*). During this time period, however, the Dead Sea Scrolls (DSS) emerge as the most remarkable of ancient biblical texts. The Dead Sea manuscripts give scholars biblical texts that date over 1000 years earlier than any previously known Hebrew manuscripts. It is important to note that these texts come from a time where no authoritative standard text existed from which to transmit the Hebrew Bible, and therefore, greatly informed scholars of the process of transmission and the care with which the Hebrew Scriptures were copied through the centuries.

Discovery of the Scrolls

In 1947, during Israel's struggle to be reborn as a nation after nearly 2000 years of dispersion, Muhammad edh-Dhib, a Bedouin goat herder from the Ta'amirah Bedouin tribe, discovered the first of several manuscript caches in a limestone cave at Qumran overlooking the northwest shores of the Dead Sea. Eventually, edh-Dhib delivered seven scrolls to Khalil Sahin, a Christian antiquities dealer in Bethlehem, who in turn sold three of them to E.L. Sukenik of Hebrew University. In 1949, the remaining four scrolls were sold to Mar Athanasius Samuel of the Syrian Jacobite Monastery of St. Mark in Jerusalem, who shortly after traveled to America. On June 1, 1954, Samuel ran an advertisement in the *Wall Street Journal* offering the four Dead Sea Scrolls for sale. The ad was quickly brought to the attention of former Israeli military commander Yigael

The Habakkuk Commentary was among the first of seven scrolls discovered in cave 1 at Qumran. The manuscript contains multiple columns of Hebrew writing on leather that is sewn together between columns 7 and 8 (see stitching above). It was one of the scrolls purchased by the State of Israel in 1955 through an advertisement placed in the *Wall Street Journal*. It is currently on display alongside the other six scrolls at the Shrine of the Book Museum in Jerusalem. (Photo by Zev Radovan.)

Yadin, who was the son of Sukenik. Yadin, with the help of philanthropist D.S. Gottesman, purchased the four scrolls for approximately $250,000 and eventually returned them to Israel to be placed alongside the other three scrolls purchased earlier by Sukenik. Today, the seven scrolls are displayed on a rotating basis in the Shrine of the Book at the Israel Museum. These include two copies of Isaiah, Habakkuk Commentary, Thanksgiving Scroll, Community Rule, War Rule, and the Genesis Apocryphon.

Exploration and Excavation

After the initial discovery, Israel's war for indepen-
dence (1948) prevented the exploration of the Dead
Sea area until 1949. G.L. Harding and French Dominican Father Roland de Vaux (see photo) led the initial
investigation, which eventually brought the discovery
of some 30 more caves, 10 of which contained more
manuscripts, many of which were of extensive length.
The 11 limestone caves are in close proximity to the
ancient settlement of the Khirbet Qumran. Further
excavations from 1951 to 1956 by Roland de Vaux
revealed that the Qumran community was founded
in Maccabean times, under either John Hyrcanus
(135–104 BC), or Alexander Jannaeus (103–76 BC).
The small Qumran community served as an administrative center, assembly place, and burial site until its
destruction in AD 68 by Roman troops during the
First Jewish War (AD 66–70). It appears that Qumran later served as a Roman military post, and soon
after as a stronghold for Jewish rebels during the Second Jewish War (AD 132–135).

The initial excavation at Qumran
(1951 to 1956) was led by French
Dominican monk and archaeologist,
Father Roland de Vaux. (Photo by
Zev Radovan.)

The caves with manuscripts are numbered from 1 to 11 in order of their discovery.
Hundreds of leather scrolls as well as a few papyrus fragments were discovered in their
desolate and arid environments. Of the nearly 1,000 documents recovered, about 20
percent were of biblical books, while others were nonbiblical sectarian texts and commentaries. Of the 11 caves, cave 4 proved to be the most productive, providing fragments
of more than 380 manuscripts (both biblical and extrabiblical). Caves 1 and 11 added to
this cache by yielding the most well-preserved texts of all the caves.

During the excavations more than 190 fragments of biblical scrolls were located.
These fragments were small in size, representing no more than 10 percent of an entire
biblical book. However, one of the most heralded finds among the Dead Sea Scrolls is
two scrolls of the book of Isaiah found in cave 1: the complete St. Mark's Monastery Isaiah scroll (Isaiah A, or 1QIs^a), and the second scroll of the book of Isaiah, the Hebrew
University Isaiah (Isaiah B, or 1QIs^b).* Isaiah A is a popular copy that contains multiple
corrections in the texts and also serves as the earliest known copy of any complete book
of the Bible. The Isaiah B text, although incomplete, agrees more closely with the Masoretic Text than does Isaiah A.

---

* The Dead Sea documents are identified by a number specifying the cave from which the particular text was discovered.
After the cave number is identified, the letter "Q" is used to describe the location of discovery as "Qumran." The letter
"Q" then is usually followed by an abbreviation of the name of the biblical book itself. In some cases, an additional super-
script letter is added which denotes the order in which the particular manuscript was discovered when more than one
copy of the same book exists. For example, the famous Isaiah Scroll is referred to technically as 1QIs^a, meaning that it was
the first Isaiah scroll discovered in Cave 1 at Qumran, while the Hebrew University Scroll of Isaiah is identified as 1QIs^b.

Not only did the archaeologists search the Qumran hills, but the Bedouin went on to pursue their own searches in other areas and found caves to the southeast of Bethlehem. These caves produced self-dated manuscripts and documents from the Second Jewish War (AD 132–135), which helped to establish the antiquity of the Dead Sea Scrolls. There was also found in these caves an additional scroll of the Minor Prophets, the last half of Joel through Haggai, which closely supports the Masoretic Texts. Also found was the oldest known Semitic papyrus, which had been scraped clean and inscribed for the second time (known as a *palimpsest*) in the ancient Hebrew script that is dated from the seventh to eighth centuries BC. Additional manuscript materials were found at another site known as Khirbet Mird. These items included a parchment fragment from the first century AD of Psalm 15. Furthermore, a portion of Psalm 16 was discovered at Wadi Murabba'at in 1960.

Several of the Dead Sea Scrolls manuscripts were rolled up and placed in unique jars like this one found in cave 1.

From the myriad of manuscripts found in the Qumran caves one can see the different manuscript families represented in the Dead Sea Scrolls. The proto-Masoretic tradition, from which the consonantal Masoretic Text is derived, is recognized from the Qumran documents. In addition to these, the proto-Septuagintal family and the pre-Samaritan textual tradition is found here, forming the foundation that eventually became the *Samaritan Pentateuch*. The discovery of these early textual traditions does not, however, necessarily mean that the Masoretic texts that the present Hebrew Bible is based upon are inferior to these early traditions. Nothing from the Dead Sea Scroll discoveries calls into question the reliability and authority of the Masoretic Text used today as the foundation of the Old Testament Hebrew Bible.

The interior of Qumran cave 4, where thousands of intact manuscripts and fragments have been discovered, including portions of the book of Isaiah. The man-made niches used for storing various scrolls can still be seen in the walls. (Photo by Zev Radovan.)

Deciphering the Qumran Literature

Over the past 60 years, scholars have identified over 800 separate biblical and nonbiblical texts that possess content unique to themselves in complete, partial, or fragment form. Among them is represented every book of the Hebrew Bible except Esther, and in the case of Deuteronomy, Psalms, and Isaiah multiple copies have been identi-fied. Also included are portions of the Septuagint (the Greek translation of the Hebrew Bible) and even some apocryphal texts such as the *Book of Tobit* (Aramaic and Hebrew), *Letter of Jeremiah* (Greek), and the *Book of Ben Sira/Ecclesiasticus* (Hebrew). Of the com-plete biblical collection, however, only the Isaiah scroll has been preserved in its entirety, and it remains the oldest complete manuscript of any book of the Bible, being dated as early as the second century BC.

A Survey of the Caves' Content

According to Qumran specialist Farah Mebarki, a summary of the entire biblical and nonbiblical collection can be organized by type, language, and category. Included among the types of literature are the scrolls, decomposed volumes, phylacteries, and *mezuzot*, consisting of tiny rolls of parchment with passages from the Torah, which are usually placed on the doorpost of a Jewish home or business. By arranging the texts according to language and writing, one can expect to see Hebrew, Aramaic, Greek, Latin in the form of a seal, cryptic writing that contains encoded Hebrew messages, and possi-bly Nabatean, a language indigenous to the area of Petra (southern Jordan). Among the categories are texts from the Hebrew Bible, apocryphal and pseudepigraphal writings of the Protestant Old Testament, and Essene or Qumranite literature. Among these fasci-nating scrolls are distinguishing characteristics that make each text unique and worthy of our consideration. The following list is a description of the more significant biblical and extrabiblical documents discovered at the 11 Qumran caves. [2]

- *Cave 1:* Of the two Isaiah scrolls (A and B) discovered, Isaiah A is the most well-preserved complete copy of any text, containing distinctive scribal notations above the line of text or in the margin. It is currently the oldest complete book of the Bible. The Isaiah B scroll is an incomplete copy of the latter half of the book that more closely resembles the medieval Maso-retic Hebrew text than does Isaiah A. In addition to these major finds, frag-ments of Genesis, Leviticus, Deuteronomy, Judges, Samuel, Isaiah, Ezekiel, Psalms, and a unique section of Daniel 2:4, where the language changes from Hebrew to Aramaic, were collected.

  Among the nonbiblical literature discovered was a commentary on the book of Habakkuk containing the first two chapters of the book and a cor-responding interpretation; the Manual of Discipline, articulating the rules and regulations of the sect; the War Scroll, which gives an account of prep-aration for the end-time war between the Essenes and their enemies; the Thanksgiving Hymns, which contain 30 hymns resembling the Old Testa-ment Psalms; and the Genesis Apocryphon, which preserves the accounts of the Genesis patriarchs in Aramaic.

  What is more, fragments of books such as Enoch, Sayings of Moses, Book of Jubilee, Book of Noah, Testament of Levi, Tobit, and the Wisdom of Solomon were discovered, as well as fragmentary commentaries on Psalms, Micah, and Zephaniah.

- *Cave 2:* Though the second cave was not nearly as productive, by 1952 archaeologists uncovered hundreds of fragments including two of Exodus, one of Leviticus, four of Numbers, two of Deuteronomy, one of Jeremiah, Job, and Psalms, and two of Ruth.

- *Cave 3:* The same year that excavations were occurring in cave 2, researchers discovered a unique text divided into two halves known as the Copper Scroll. According to the pioneering work of de Vaux, the fragile scroll is the only one of its kind discovered at Qumran. It is written on metal and contains unique Mishnaic Hebrew text. Due to its fragile composition, X-ray examinations were done; they revealed that the unique text describes at least 60 locations of various treasures hidden throughout Jericho, Qumran, and Jerusalem areas, none of which have been discovered. Shortly after the X-ray examinations, researchers found it difficult to unroll the crumbling scrolls, opting to cut them from top to bottom into several long strips and display them at the Jordan Archaeological Museum in Amman.

The Copper Scrolls as they were originally discovered in Cave 3. (Photo by Zev Radovan.)

- *Cave 4:* This location is seen by many to be the most productive of the 11 caves since it produced nearly 100 copies of Bible books and at least 15,000 fragments. Included among these discoveries is one of the oldest known texts of biblical Hebrew, a fragment of the book of Samuel that dates to the third century BC. Other texts include commentaries on the Psalms, Isaiah, and Nahum. Interestingly, a fragment of Daniel

The Copper Scroll discovered in cave 3 contains directions to hidden treasure. To date, no treasure described on the scroll has been found. Portions of the scroll are housed at the Citadel Museum in Amman, Jordan. (Photo by Zev Radovan.)

7:28 and 8:1 was discovered showing the transition of the Aramaic language back to the Hebrew.

- *Cave 5:* Though not as productive for archaeologists, this site contained fragments of the apocryphal book Tobit and an assortment of decayed biblical books.

- *Cave 6:* Unlike most of the other locations, cave 6 yielded papyrus fragments of Daniel and 1 and 2 Kings.

- *Caves 7-10:* In 1955, while nearing the end of excavations, archaeologists found a very few items, such as 18 Greek fragments and one ostracon (clay shard with writing), along with materials used for the storing and bundling of scrolls.

- *Cave 11:* Despite being the last excavated, in 1956, this cave produced a partial copy of the Psalms, including the apocryphal Psalm 151. As a result, scholars now possess 36 canonical texts ranging from Psalm 90 through 150, many of which are attributed to King David. Also found was a partial copy of Leviticus, Apocalypse of the New Jerusalem, and an Aramaic paraphrase (known as a *targum*) of Job. Furthermore, two or three nonbiblical Temple Scrolls were discovered, which describe various themes relating to the Temple in Jerusalem and the book of Deuteronomy, such as laws addressing the construction of the Temple, purity rules, and regulations regarding judges, idolatry, slaves taken in war, curses, false prophets, incest, and betrayal. One of these scrolls has also been recognized as the longest of all the Dead Sea Scrolls, measuring almost 28 feet in length.

Scroll of Psalms discovered in cave 11 at Qumran. (Photo by Zev Radovan.)

It is particularly important for Christians to understand and appreciate the enormous testimony of Scripture the Lord has providentially preserved for our benefit, especially as it pertains to the reliability of the Old Testament.

Dating of the Manuscripts

In 1955, Professor Yigael Yadin purchased four of the Dead Sea Scrolls found in cave 1 for approximately $250,000 by answering an ad in the *Wall Street Journal*. (Photo by Zev Radovan.)

Ruins of Khirbet Qumran. The settlement itself housed approximately 200 inhabitants. Numerous inkwells, stone benches, pottery, coins, ritual baths, cisterns, and kilns, as well as a refectory, a scriptorium, and a well-developed irrigation system have been discovered. (Photo by Zev Radovan.)

The Dead Sea Scrolls have been dated in a variety of ways. Radiocarbon (carbon-14) dating of the manuscripts has determined that the fragments are approximately 2000 years old. The paleographical method dated the texts to between 125 and 100 BC. More recent dating by Accelerator Mass Spectrometry (AMS) between 1991 and 1998 placed the date for the Isaiah Scroll between 202 and 93 BC (combining results from Zurich and Tucson laboratories).

The paleographical method operates on the basis of comparison of the structures and shapes of the particular characters of the text with that of the structures and shapes of external sources that have already been dated, such as coins and inscriptions. This method has been improving over the years and has been proven to be a relatively reliable technique of dating the manuscripts.

Dating the texts on the basis of archaeological data is another method of dating, and is often the least valuable of the three mentioned. This method researches only within the confines of the time period of the Qumran community, looking to the upper and lower limits of the period of residence in Khirbet-Qumran, from approximately the middle of the second century BC to about AD 68. The problem with this method is that many of the texts that were discovered in the caves precede the time period of the residence in Qumran. Some scholars believe that the texts were not copied in Qumran, but were brought into the Qumran community from outside areas.

The oldest Qumran texts are fragments from Exodus and Samuel: 4QEx^f is dated c. 250 BC and 4QSam^b comes from c. 225 BC.

The Residents of Qumran

While scholars are reasonably certain of the number of inhabitants (between 150 and 200) who functioned as a monastic community at Qumran (also known as Sokoka), they are not absolutely convinced of their identity. Many believe they were *Essenes,* originally an Aramaic word (*hasayya*) meaning "the pious ones." According to Roman historian Pliny the Elder, the Essenes lived west of the Dead Sea and north of Ein Gedi, [3] which is consistent with the view that identifies the Essenes as the inhabitants of Qumran. The Jewish historian Flavius Josephus fixes their population in Israel at approximately 4,000 [4] and adds that the sect was flourishing in the second century BC during the time of the Maccabees and Pharisees and continued until the destruction of the Jewish temple by the Romans in AD 70. [5]

Others reject this traditional view and see the Qumranites originating either as a reaction to the moral laxity of the priesthood during the Babylonian exile (sixth century BC) or during the second century BC as a group separated from a yet earlier (third- century BC) apocalyptic Essene community. Some speculate this schism was due to doctrinal, moral, interpretive, ritual, and calendrical differences, which may explain the apparent variations of doctrine and practice among those within the movement. Although none of their own texts describe the group as "Essenes," but only as "pious" and "saints," Pliny the Elder, Philo of Alexandria, and Josephus identify them as either "pious," "Essenes," or "Essenians."

Functionally, unlike the Sadducees who held political power and officiated daily in the Jerusalem temple, and the Pharisees who delighted in demonstrating personal virtue through pomp, the Essenes rejected the temple sacrifices and rituals. Instead, as a reaction to the priestly corruption in Jerusalem, they appear to have been preoccupied with ritual cleansing and "separating themselves from the dwellings of the men of iniquity." [6] Their remote location in the arid desert and the presence of at least ten ritual cleansing pools excavated at the site attest to these practices. Theologically, while adopting holy behavior consistent with a mystical interpretation of the Law of Moses, the Essenes viewed life as a moral and spiritual struggle between the "Sons of Light" and the "Sons of Darkness." This struggle would eventually climax in a messianic-led war between good and evil, followed by divine judgment and the new creation. Therefore, in preparation for that great apocalyptic day, prayers, meditation, reflection, praises, work, ritual purification, and the reading or development of new literature were daily activities.

Some believe these ruins at Qumran housed a scriptorium, where scribes could read and copy the Scriptures.

The extent to which the Essenes were involved in the copying of biblical manuscripts and the production of new literature remains a mystery and has been the center of debate for the last 60 years. However, support for Essene participation comes from the discovery of three inkwells found in the scriptorium, where most of their scrolls were stored. In close proximity to the inkwells, large rectangular stone library tables were unearthed, which were most likely used for reading, unfolding, and copying. Furthermore, the discovery of hundreds of small, flat, saucer-bowl-shaped receptacles made of clay lends support. These may have been used for eating, or perhaps used as ink receptacles, which would point to a manuscript-producing environment. Scholars have suggested a range of theories in attempting to explain the origin of the scrolls. Among these are suggestions that the scrolls were part of the Jerusalem temple library or authored by the various sects of Judaism.

This stone bench and table were unearthed in the ruins of Qumran. Some believe these may have been used to read and possibly copy some of the biblical scrolls.

In contrast to the Essene theory, there is a growing minority opinion among some archaeologists. According to Yizhak Magen and Yuval Peleg, who excavated the site from 1993 to 2003, Qumran was used as a pottery factory and was inhabited by only a few dozen workers. Magen sees no connection between the Dead Sea Scrolls and the Essenes or any other inhabitants of Qumran. Rather, the manuscripts were hidden in nearby caves by refugees who fled Jerusalem to escape the Roman invaders during the Jewish revolt in AD 66–70. He supports his theory by describing the evidence discovered at Qumran as being consistent with a pottery-manufacturing environment.

For example, up to seven tons of clay deposits were discovered in many of the community's reservoirs and ritual baths (*mikva'ot*). Also discovered were unusually high amounts of industrial waste, tens of thousands of clay fragments, many pottery kilns along with fully formed vessels, and nearly 1,400 coins, all of which is consistent with a commercial atmosphere.

But why store the scrolls at Qumran? For Magen, it was the logical place since it lies directly on the route refugees would have taken from Jerusalem in order to arrive at the hilltop fortress of Masada. In fact, the clay jars used to store many of the scrolls were probably provided by the pottery factory, since refugees would not have wanted to carry heavy clay storage containers during their hasty and long flight south to safety. According to this theory, it appears unlikely that the Essenes would have hidden the scrolls since many of the documents were haphazardly deposited in caves, without customary reverence. In addition, many of the scrolls were discovered at various locations along the refugee escape route adjacent to the northwest end of the Dead Sea, including Masada. [7]

The Scrolls and Scribal Practice

It is from the Dead Sea Scrolls that scribal practices have been discovered and researched. Manuscripts from the Judean Desert reflect a variety of scribal practices, since many of the documents were copied at other locations in Israel. So the documents as well as the scribal practices found in this territory reflect not only the scribal tradition of those who lived and wrote in that community, but also the tradition and practices of the scribes of Israel as a whole. Scribal practice may be supported by research of the content of the document as well as the physical components that make up the scrolls, such as the parchments, ink, and so on.

Though the majority of Dead Sea Scroll documents from the Judean Desert were written on leather or papyrus (a form of ancient paper created from the flattened, dried papyrus plant found in Egypt), scholars have found that the materials used at the different locations were related to the content of the documents. It seems that leather was used for writing more formal literary content,

Preparing parchment to be used for writing the Scriptures. (Photo by Zev Radovan.)

while papyrus was for more personal usage, such as letters and documentary texts. Papyrus may have also been used for personal copies of formal documents as well.

What can be gathered from the discovery of the Dead Sea Scrolls is the myriad of scribal practices that were widely used throughout Israel from the third century BC to the second century AD. Insight is given into the procedures of transmission and copying of the Hebrew and Aramaic texts, such as the materials used and the techniques implemented.

The Scrolls and Reliable Transmission

Prior to the discovery of the Dead Sea Scrolls, our earliest complete manuscript of the Old Testament was dated to the eleventh century AD (see chapter 1). The more ancient Qumran manuscripts had a great impact on the scholarly world, verifying the validity and reliability of the Masoretic transmission tradition and the Masoretic Text, on which we base our English Old Testament text. Some of the Qumran biblical texts are dated hundreds of years before Christ and closely parallel the corresponding portions of the Masoretic Text, which dates from AD 800 to 1000. The differences found are only minuscule and do not alter the meaning of the text in any way. The Qumran manuscripts give much earlier evidence of the Old Testament text than anything previously known.

The differences that do exist between the Dead Sea Scrolls and the Masoretic Text are largely those of word order and spelling errors, being confined only to individual words and even letters. Overall agreement between the two texts is remarkable. It is amazing to note that though the text underwent hundreds of years of transmission, so little alteration was made to it.

The Example of the Isaiah Scroll

The Isaiah Scroll shows how insignificant the above-mentioned discrepancies really are. Isaiah 40:12 of the Masoretic Text uses the Hebrew word *mayim*, translated "waters," while the Dead Sea text uses the Hebrew word *me yam*, which translates "waters of the sea." When comparing the Isaiah B Scroll, which dates to the first century BC, to the *Codex Leningradensis* (AD 1008), the two texts are almost word-for-word identical to one another. There are a few differences, but they are only very minor deviations that are merely orthographic and linguistic.

The book of Isaiah was one of the more popular books at Qumran, with twenty-one manuscripts being recovered throughout the excavation of the caves. The Great Isaiah Scroll (1QIsa^a) was the only virtually complete scroll found and

Portions of the book of Isaiah were found in caves 1 and 4, including a complete copy known as the Isaiah A, pictured here. It is over 25 feet in length and dates to the second century BC. The scroll, opened to Isaiah 40:3, was stitched together at several points, which are visible on each end of the scroll as well as on the left side of the text above. Scholars have estimated that approximately 95-plus percent of the Isaiah text is identical to the later Masoretic Text, from which the English Old Testament is translated. The remaining 5 percent disagreement is attributed to minor scribal mistakes and differences that affect no major doctrine. (© John C. Trever, PhD; digital image by James E. Trever.)

thought by some to be placed at Qumran for safe preservation but somewhat earlier by more recent AMS scientific dating. This scroll's copy date was determined to be around 125 BC using the paleographical dating method. All sixty-six chapters are preserved within its fifty-four columns, suffering only minor damages in the leather that resulted in small gaps in the scroll. This scroll, although containing many variant readings, is for the most part in agreement with the Masoretic Text. Scholars have taken much interest in these variant readings found in the Great Isaiah Scroll. It appears the Qumranites believed that Isaiah foretold of God's plan of the time period in which the community lived, thus they quoted the book as authoritative Scripture and wrote commentaries on it.

Many of the other manuscripts of the book of Isaiah, such as 1QIsa^b, 4QIsa^a, 4QIsa^b, 4QIsa^d, 4QIsa^e, 4QIsa^f, and 4QIsa^g, follow closely with the Masoretic Text. On the other hand, 1QIsa^a and 4QIsa^c contain many variants from the Hebrew text, providing insight on the book's composition in its later stages and what many consider improved readings of the text.

There are four categories of these variant readings within the Isaiah Scroll, the first of which deals with particular verses that are present in some texts but absent from others. One example comes from the second chapter of Isaiah, where the latter half of verse 9 and all of verse 10 are completely absent from 1QIsa^a.

The second category of variant readings involves scribal errors made in the transmission process. These errors are somewhat more difficult to identify because what scholars may deem an error may, in fact, be an alternative reading or different textual tradition. However, there are many variants in certain texts that cannot be explained in any way besides human error during copying. An example of this kind of error can be found in Isaiah 16:8-9. In this passage, the Masoretic Text and the Septuagint contain a more extended version of the passage than does the 1QIsaᵃ.

The third has to do mainly with grammatical variations. These are merely variations in spelling, forms of names, word order, and the like. There are many of these variants throughout the different texts, but they do not have any effect on the meaning of the texts and, for the purposes of interpretation, are considered meaningless. These variants do, however, give us insight into and evidence of the use of the Hebrew language, the use of spelling systems, and the use of other conventions by the scribes at the time of the late Second Temple period.

The fourth category involves the wider spectrum of variant readings. These include sections of verses whose readings slightly differ in their syntax and sentence structure. An example of this kind of variant can be found in Isaiah 53:11, where the NIV translation is somewhat altered by the addition of the word *light* from the texts of the Dead Sea Scrolls and the Septuagint. Other translations rely on the Masoretic Text, which does not contain the word *light*.

The current textual evidence from the scrolls and the Masoretic Text, however, points to a single main edition of the book of Isaiah that was circulated in Judaism during the late Second Temple period. The textual variants (described above) in the text appear to be classifiable as individual variants, meaning that each instance of a variant seems to be

This tattered Dead Sea Scroll manuscript is known as the Messianic Testimony (4Q175) and was discovered in cave 4 during excavations at Qumran in 1952. The first-century BC document written in Hebrew contains an accurately copied listing of Old Testament passages relating to the coming Messiah. These include describing the Messiah as a prophet from Deuteronomy 5:28-29; 18:18-19; as a priest from Deuteronomy 33:8-11; and as a king from Numbers 24:15-17. Joshua 6:26 is also quoted in connection to a coming disaster brought on by wicked persons. It is interesting to note that document appears to recognize the three-fold office of the coming Messiah as prophet, priest, and king. (Photo by Zev Radovan.)

isolated. The variants are not ones that reflect a general, systematic tendency to purposefully alter or revise the original meaning of the text.

The Scrolls and Their Contribution

In sum, the Dead Sea Scrolls have made an immense contribution to the Masoretic Text in the field of textual criticism. Upon careful study of these manuscripts we can see they have helped confirm that the Hebrew text that we have today is extremely accurate and has maintained essentially the same voice over time. It should be noted that scholars still hold the Masoretic Text as authoritative over the older manuscripts of the Dead Sea Scrolls. According to Ernst Würthwein, in evaluating the significance of any particular surviving manuscript, the age of the manuscript should neither be the sole nor primary criterion of its worth. The Dead Sea Scrolls attest to the reliability and the faithfulness of the Masoretic tradition of the Old Testament. We can rest assured that the current Old Testament is a faithful copy of the original words penned by the original author, handed down for generations. [8]

The Ketef Hinnom Silver Scrolls

Although the Dead Sea Scrolls have offered us a key ancient witness to the integrity of the Hebrew Scriptures, another of the most important biblical discoveries of all time was unearthed in 1979 by a team of archaeologists led by Gabriel Barkay of Bar-Ilan University and his assistant, Gordon Franz. As excavators were concluding their investigations of pre-exilic (seventh-century BC) tombs in southern Jerusalem overlooking the Valley of Hinnom, they unearthed two tiny objects now known as the "Ketef Hinnom Silver Scrolls" or the "Ketef Hinnom Amulets." The Silver Scrolls give us an earlier confirmation of a portion of the book of Numbers. They contain the priestly benediction of Numbers 6:24-26 and phrases from other biblical books, including Exodus 20:6 and Deuteronomy 5:10 and 20:6. Although Judith Hadley is credited with the find, several other student-volunteer excavators assisted in locating the fascinating object.

Setting and Background

The Ketef Hinnom tombs were originally hewn from the living rock prior to Israel's exile into Babylon during the sixth century BC. Most of these family tombs contained stone slabs with carved-out headrests (pillows) for the deceased. Located directly underneath the slab was a repository (pictured here) where the bones of those previously deceased were transferred in order to make room for new burials upon the slabs.

The process of placing the bones of the deceased into the repository led to the development of the familiar biblical

The Ketef Hinnom tombs were a pre-exilic master-planned tomb complex that once contained stone roofs that have been since quarried away. The area inside the open receptacle pictured here is where the two silver scrolls were discovered.

phrase of being "gathered together with/to your fathers." Ancient pre-exilic tombs such as these are rarely found intact, and are usually targeted for the quarrying of stone (as these tombs were) for ancient building projects.

The silver scrolls were found in the repository of chamber 25 of tomb 24, which fortunately had a collapsed roof that sheltered the contents from intruders and preserved the precious artifacts for nearly 2,600 years. Nearing the last day of the excavation, Barkay and his associates unearthed a cache of finds including oil lamps, fine pottery, storage jars, jewelry, ornaments, and more importantly, the incised biblical silver scrolls. When the two scrolls were originally discovered, they were tightly rolled and in the latter stages of disintegration. For the next three years specialists in Germany and England were offered the opportunity to unroll the tiny amulets, but because of their fragility, there were very few who would risk destroying the brittle objects. Ultimately, the Israel Museum carefully unrolled the brittle scrolls with the aid of a special liquid solution that helped maintain the integrity of the fragile metallic documents. After the scrolls were finally unrolled, the first scroll measured 1.0 inches wide and 3.75 inches long. Epigraphers deciphered the inscriptions on the scroll as containing paleo-Hebrew script (rounded Hebrew characters written prior to the Babylonian captivity) and phrases reflected in several passages of the Old Testament.

The 18 lines preserved on the first scroll read as follows:

> YHW...the grea...the covenant and... raciousness towards those who love...and those who keep...the eternal?...blessing more than any...re and more than Evil. For redemption is in him. For YHWH is our restorer... rock. May YHWH bles...you and...keep you...YHWH make...shine....[9]

The second scroll contains 12 lines of paleo-Hebrew script and measures 0.5 inches wide by 1.5 inches long. It reads,

The Hebrew-inscribed silver scrolls are the oldest copy of biblical passages in the world, dating 400 years prior to the Dead Sea Scrolls. (Photo by Zev Radovan.)

> May be blessed...by YHW...the warrior (or helper) and the rebuker of...vil: May bless you, YHWH, keep you. Make shine, YH-H, His face...you and g-rant you p-ce....[10]

Today, the scrolls can be seen on display at the Israel Museum; the tombs, located behind the Menachem Begin Heritage Center (directly below the Scottish Presbyterian Church) in Jerusalem, can also be seen.

The Biblical Significance of the Silver Scrolls

Since the scrolls (dated to the early sixth century BC) predate the famous Dead Sea Scrolls (dated to the 200s BC) by about 400 years, they are currently the oldest copies of biblical passages in the world.* From these scrolls emerge several important details concerning biblical transmission and history.

First, if Numbers and Deuteronomy had already been written by this time, the incisions offer early confirmation of the accuracy and great care of the scribal transmission process when copying the Hebrew Scriptures. Previous to this discovery, the Dead Sea Scrolls discovered at Qumran had confirmed that 95 percent of the scrolls were virtually word-for-word identical to the later Masoretic Text, which was used to construct our English Old Testament. The 5 percent consisted of minor errors of spelling or the like that did not affect the meaning or doctrine of the text. Likewise, the passages written on the silver scrolls are substantially the same as the Dead Sea Scrolls and the Masoretic Text. This provides an unbroken chain of early textual transmission stemming from c. 600 BC to AD 1000.

In addition, some minimalist scholars had argued that the Hebrew Scriptures were written late in the Hellenistic age (fourth to third century BC). However, this position has become harder to sustain in light of the Silver Scrolls, not to mention the previously discovered Dead Sea Scrolls. Though the Silver Scrolls themselves do not conclusively prove the book of Numbers and Deuteronomy had been written prior to 600 BC, they certainly are consistent with arguments supporting the much earlier dates of authorship for both books. Moreover, since the tiny scrolls were used as amulets for protection from evil, it was recognized that the words inscribed held authority and power.† This is consistent with the assertion that those who wore the amulets understood the passages as being the very words of God.

Second, the Silver Scrolls contain the oldest extant biblical passages using the Lord's name (YHWH), demonstrating that YHWH was not a later development as some critical scholars previously believed. Third, the scrolls also reveal that the priestly benediction was in early use, showing that the Hebrew priestly order and ritual was most likely developed not after the Babylonian captivity in the late sixth and fifth century BC, but as a much earlier phenomenon—which is consistent with scriptural descriptions of a thriving priestly order dating to the time of Moses.

---

* In 2004, the Western Semitic Project at the University of Southern California, led by Dr. Bruce Zuckerman, confirmed an early sixth-century BC date through computer-enhanced analysis. See Gabriel Barkay, Marilyn J. Lundberg, Andrew G. Vaughn, Bruce Zuckerman, "The Amulets from Ketef Hinnom: A New Edition and Evaluation," *Bulletin of the American School of Oriental Research* 334 (May 2004), 41-70.

† It is interesting to note that the Ekron inscription discovered in 1996 contains a similar phraseology as the Silver Scrolls, which read, "May Yahweh bless you and keep you." The Ekron inscription calls upon a goddess to bless King Achish: "May she bless him and keep him." The similar phrases may be indicative of the special power believed to be inherent in the priestly benediction of Numbers 6:24-26 and the reason for its use as an amulet to ward off evil.

3

THE TRANSMISSION OF THE OLD TESTAMENT—SUMMARY

The transmission of the Hebrew Bible has been regarded as a holy tradition by Jewish rabbis for hundreds of years. In the rabbinical tradition, two key principles have been conveyed: first, to use the Hebrew Scriptures to their fullest spiritual potential; and second, to faithfully preserve the text. According to one of the world's leading experts on transmission of rabbinic traditions, Birger Gerhardsson, the dominant attitude was the desire to faithfully reproduce the sacred biblical text in its untouched traditional state.

The Process of Textual Preservation

The discovery of the Dead Sea Scrolls has given us much insight into the origins of textual preservation. As already mentioned above, the lines of the pre-Masoretic Text had already existed, meaning that much care has already been given to a system in which the biblical text was well preserved centuries prior to the work of later Masoretes. Rabbinic material has been consulted to resolve the issue of how this textual preservation came about.

Private copying of the Hebrew Scriptures, primitive as it may have been, may have occurred around

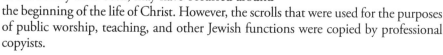

Though not part of the Dead Sea Scroll collection, the Nash Papyrus (dated to c. 150 BC) contains a portion of the Decalogue: Exodus 20; Deuteronomy 5:6-21; and the Shema, Deuteronomy 6:4-9. (Photo by Zev Radovan.)

the beginning of the life of Christ. However, the scrolls that were used for the purposes of public worship, teaching, and other Jewish functions were copied by professional copyists.

The term *sopher* (plural: *sopherim*—see chapter 1), or "Scripture specialist," can connote two main senses: it could refer to one who was a skilled writer or copyist. On the other hand it could refer to someone who "knows the Scriptures" or "one who is schooled in the Scriptures." The meaning of the term had changed somewhat by the time of the exile to Babylon (sixth century BC). It still meant someone who specialized in the writing of the Torah and who taught and worked with the Scriptures.

Those who were responsible for the normal transmission of the sacred documents were ones who knew the Scriptures by heart due to either their education, or the frequency of writing the same book repeatedly. There were some who were capable of writing out the whole of Scripture from memory, which was not an uncommon thing during this ancient time period. Regardless of their ability to memorize the Hebrew texts, rabbinic Judaism unwaveringly employed the rule that the Torah was not be copied from memory. The written Torah was to be transmitted in written form and therefore must be copied down from a written source (known today as a *Vorlage*). This rule was emphatically enforced and was never to be breached. The copyist was not permitted to create a manuscript without a *Vorlage* in front of him. This rule made it possible to avoid any problems that could arise with corruption of the system used to check the reading of a text and the written form of the text (later established as the Kethib-Qere system in the Masoretic tradition, as described in chapter 1).

The Codex Sinaiticus at one time contained the entire Old and New Testament in Greek. Today the codex contains the entire New Testament and most of the Old Testament. The pictured section of the manuscript contains the ending of the book of Jeremiah and the beginning of Lamentations. (Photo by Zev Radovan.)

There was much more involved in the transmission of the biblical texts than merely copying what was seen on a piece of paper. According to rabbinical texts, copyists were required to read the Hebrew texts out loud as they wrote them down. The copyist needed to give attention to how the Scriptures were read because it was also required that the copyist possess sufficient knowledge of both a tradition of *kethib* as well as of *qere*. They were also equipped with the tradition that would enable them to check their works in various areas. This tradition was employed well before the time of Christ, and it grew more precise over the centuries until it was standardized in the Masoretic system.

The preservation of the Hebrew Scriptures involved more than merely supplying the demand for more books in the Jewish religious culture. This preservation tradition springs from a reverence of the Pentateuch and a desire to aid in the effort to supply Israel with copies of these sacred texts.

A word about the oral transmission of the Old Testament should be mentioned. Oral tradition was very important in the Jewish culture and served as one of the main ways to transfer information, among many other things. The Torah, being a central part of Judaism, was transmitted orally as well as in written form. Birger Gerhardsson provides locations of the most important centers for the preservation of this tradition, with texts such as the oral Torah. The home was seen as the foundation where the Torah could be preserved faithfully in deed and in discussion within the family. The children in the home were raised in an environment in which all actions and behavior were affected by the teachings found in the Torah. It was not uncommon to expect Jewish children to memorize vast quantities of Scripture. These kinds of customs continued on in the community from private family devotional life into the public domains. The Scriptures of the Torah were used in public Jewish ceremonies as well, such as during feast days in the Temple. Rituals that were done during these gatherings were aimed at making the people familiar with the text in the Torah. Another area where a young person could be exposed to the oral Torah was in a qualified school. These schools were often held in the synagogue, where scholars could be trained in fields dedicated to the scribal transmission of the text.[1]

Summary and Conclusions

The Old Testament is the most accurately documented book from before the time of Christ. There are literally tens of thousands of manuscripts, and some of the fragments that date as early as 600 BC. The Dead Sea Scrolls provide the best test of how accurately the Old Testament was copied over the centuries since they provide a comparison of what the text was like about a thousand years earlier than the one we had before the scrolls were discovered. Millar Burrows wrote, "It is a matter of wonder that through something like a thousand years the text underwent so little alteration.... Herein lies its chief importance, supporting the fidelity of the Masoretic tradition."[2] F.F. Bruce added, "It may now be more confidently asserted than ever before that the Dead Sea discoveries have enabled us to answer this question [of the reliability of the Old Testament text] in the affirmative with much greater assurance than was possible before 1948."[3] Old Testament expert Gleason Archer concluded that the Isaiah text "proved to be word for word identical with our standard Hebrew Bible in more than 95 percent of the text. The 5 percent of variation consisted chiefly of obvious slips of the pen and variations in spelling."[4] A sample typical of the whole Hebrew text was taken from the famous Isaiah 53 passage. In a thousand years of copying it, there was only one word difference ("light" in v. 11), and it made no difference in the meaning of the text!

Old Testament Manuscripts			
Name	Date Original Was Written	Earliest Copy or Copies	Biblical Books
Dead Sea Scrolls (DSS)	15th or 13th to 4th century BC	250 BC–AD 68	Includes 223-plus biblical manuscripts from every book of the Old Testament except Esther
DSS Isaiah Scroll A	8th century BC	150–100 BC	Complete copy of the book of Isaiah
DSS Habakkuk Commentary	7th century BC	64 BC	Portions of Habakkuk
Rylands Papyrus 458	15th or 13th century BC	150 BC	Contains Greek portions of Deuteronomy 23–28
Nash Papyrus	15th or 13th century BC	150 BC–AD 68	Portion of the Decalogue (Exodus 20); Deuteronomy 5:6-21; Shema (Deuteronomy 6:4-9)
Peshitta	15th or 13th to 4th century BC	AD 100–200	Entire Old Testament in Syriac
Chester Beatty Papyri	15th or 13th to 8th century BC	AD 150	Large portions of Genesis, Numbers, Deuteronomy, Isaiah, Jeremiah, Daniel, Esther, and Ecclesiastes
Targum of Onkelos	15th or 13th century BC	AD 200	Torah
Codex Vaticanus (B)	15th or 13th to 4th century BC	AD 325	Entire Greek Old Testament and Apocrypha in uncials except portions of Genesis, 2 Kings, Psalms, 1 and 2 Maccabees, and the Prayer of Manasseh
Codex Ephraemi Rescriptus	13th–10th centuries BC	AD 345	Contains Job, Proverbs, Ecclesiastes, Song of Solomon
Codex Sinaiticus (aleph)	13th–4th centuries BC	AD 350	Half the Old Testament in Greek uncial
Latin Vulgate	15th or 13th to 4th century BC	AD 390–405	Entire Old Testament in Latin

Name	Date Original Was Written	Earliest Copy or Copies	Biblical Books
Codex Alexandrinus (A)	15th or 13th to 4th century BC	AD 450	Entire Old Testament in Greek uncial
British Museum Oriental 4445	15th or 13th century BC	AD 850	Pentateuch
Codex Cairensis (C)	13th–4th centuries BC	AD 895	Former and Latter Prophets
Aleppo Codex	15th or 13th to 4th century BC	AD 900	Oldest complete Hebrew text of the Old Testament
Babylonian Codex of the Latter Prophets	7th–4th centuries BC	AD 916	Isaiah, Jeremiah, and the 12 Minor Prophets
Codex Leningradensis B19A (L)	15th or 13th to 4th century BC	AD 1008	Complete Hebrew text of the Old Testament
Samaritan Pentateuch (SP)	15th or 13th century BC	10th–11th century AD	Written in Samaritan characters

Chart from H. Wayne House and Joseph M. Holden, *Charts of Apologetics and Christian Evidences* (Grand Rapids, MI: Zondervan, 2006), chart 43. Used by permission of Zondervan.

Note: Whether the books of Moses were composed in the fifteenth or thirteenth century BC depends on how one views the date of the Exodus. Most conservative scholars embrace the earlier date of around 1440 BC for the composition of the Pentateuch, while some conservative scholars and liberal scholars prefer the later date of thirteenth century BC for its composition.

PART TWO

THE RELIABILITY OF OLD TESTAMENT HISTORY

~

In the previous part, we have seen that the texts of the Old Testament provide an accurate and faithful representation of what was originally recorded with little evidence of distortion or alteration within the process of transmission. But what about the content of the Old Testament itself? Even if the manuscript tradition has been proven to be reliable, it is at least possible that the Old Testament is an accurate and faithful copy of something that is false. Throughout church history, the historical reliability of the Old Testament narratives has been debated, including issues of authorship, theological continuity, and historicity. If the text of the Hebrew Old Testament is to be taken seriously it must be established as trustworthy, giving accurate assessments of the historical (as well as spiritual) claims that it makes.

With modern scholarship making more and more advances in the field of Old Testament studies, a wealth of evidence has been discovered that corroborates the historical reliability of the Old Testament at many levels. It must be kept in mind, however, this part of the book is in no way exhaustive. So this part limits itself to a few key case studies in hope of demonstrating that some of the most frequently raised issues, especially with the books of Moses and the Prophets, are not difficulties for the historical reliability of the Old Testament.

Finally, we will briefly consider the canon of the Old Testament, from the divine selection to the human confirmation of the books we currently find within the Old Testament.

4

MOSES, THE PENTATEUCH, AND
THE MAJOR PROPHETS

The first five books of the Old Testament form the most seriously challenged section of the Bible. And the first challenge is to Moses' authorship of the Pentateuch (the five books of the Law) through what has been called the *documentary hypothesis* or *JEDP theory*.

The Reliability of Mosaic Authorship of the Pentateuch

Challenges to Mosaic authorship have been an issue since the seventeenth century AD, when Benedict Spinoza voiced his denial of it in his *Theological-Political Treatise* (1677). Jean Astruc, in 1753—actually, in an attempt to refute Spinoza—was the first to propose a primitive version of the documentary theory.

Soon after, in the nineteenth century, many critical scholars adopted this theory. Astruc limited his analysis to Genesis. Johann Gottfried Eichhorn was the first to apply this theory to the entire Pentateuch, with a series of publications beginning in 1780. Wilhelm M.L. de Wette also made a significant contribution to this discussion in positing that Deuteronomy was its own independently constructed source in his *Dissertation Critico-Exegetica* in 1805; a year later this hypothesis was repeated in his *Beitraege zur Einleitung*. De Wette actually went so far as to say that none of the Pentateuch was composed prior to the time of David! However, it was Julius Wellhausen who popularized (not created—a common misconception) the idea that the Pentateuch was written by various persons whom he called *Jehovist* (J, also known as Yahwist), *Elohist* (E), *Deuteronomist* (D), and *Priestly* (P), each one supposedly distinguished by their literary characteristics. Thus the name *JEDP theory* refers to the various sources hypothesized.

Professor Gleason Archer's Critique of JEDP

Professor Gleason Archer, noted Harvard PhD and Old Testament expert, lists nine difficulties for the JEDP theory. He also argues for the Mosaic authorship of the Pentateuch.[1]

1. The theory employs circular reasoning. It assumes that the Bible is not a supernatural book and then attempts to give a natural explanation for its origin, claiming that in some way this explanation also proves the nonsupernatural character of the Bible.

2. Though documentary theorists base their theory on the textual evidence, when the textual evidence seems to counter their theory it is ignored.

3. Authors have always been capable of using more than one style and more than one name for God.

4. Archaeological evidence that confirms individual historical details that indicate the Pentateuch was written long before the time of David is simply ignored (see part 6 of this book).

5. The theory starts with the assumption that Israel's religion is of human origin like other religions, and as such needs an explanation of its evolution.

6. Supposed "discrepancies" are noted to prove a diversity of sources, even though the passage in question, read in its context, makes plenty of sense.

7. A double standard is applied to the Hebrew Bible. Other Semitic sources describe various entities in differing styles of language, yet their singular authorship, authenticity, or antiquity is not called into question.

8. The theory falsely assumes we have no literature contemporary to the Pentateuch to which we can compare it. The theory also explains away instances that it cannot account for by claiming Masoretic scribal additions or alterations of the text.

9. Scholars who hold the theory assume they, living 3,400 years after the fact, can better understand these texts than can the New Testament authors, whom these scholars judge to live 600 to 1,000 years after the fact (according to their dating of the Pentateuch).

In addition to Archer's responses, the JEDP theory has come under increasing attack by scholars in recent years since no JEDP "documents" have ever been found—no traces can be found in the hundreds of biblical texts found in the Dead Sea Scrolls or anywhere else. Yale scholar William W. Hallo points out:

> The literary-critical study of the Hebrew Bible has had a checkered history. The [JEDP] documentary hypothesis with which it began over two centuries ago remains to this day a hypothesis, the [JEDP] documents which it reconstructed [are] beyond recovery; their precise extent, their absolute and relative dates, and their changes over time [are] all matters of dispute; and the applicability of the hypothesis beyond the Pentateuch [is] severely limited.... Given such disparate and even desperate reactions to two centuries of modern Biblical scholarship, it is perhaps

not surprising that much of the most exciting work…has been…from… epigraphic [archaeological] discoveries. [2]

More Reasons to Affirm Mosaic Authorship

There also exist further independent reasons for affirming Mosaic authorship. First, *Scripture itself attributes authorship of the Pentateuch to Moses.* Within the Pentateuch itself it is repeatedly stated that Moses wrote down the words of the law given directly to him by Yahweh (Exodus 17:14; 24:4,7; 34:27; Numbers 33:1-2; Deuteronomy 31:9,11). Books within the rest of the Old Testament also give witness to this fact. The book of Joshua attests to Mosaic authorship in 1:8 and 8:31-32, identifying them as the "book of the law" or the "book of the law of Moses." The title "law of Moses" is used by David in 1 Kings 2:3 to refer to the first five books written by Moses, while 2 Kings 14:6 gives the same title, quoting from Deuteronomy 24:16. Again, 2 Kings refers to the same title of the Pentateuch.

Other references to the Mosaic authorship are found in Ezra 6:18, Nehemiah 13:1, Daniel 9:11-13, and Malachi 4:4. The authorship of the Torah is always attributed to Moses throughout the Old Testament and even into the New Testament. The Gospels refer to the writings of the Torah as "Moses" in John 5:46-47 and 7:19 and Acts 3:22. Other places in the New Testament refer to Moses as the author of the Torah, such as in Romans 10:5. It is also interesting to note that Mark 12:26 states that God Himself uttered the words written in Exodus 3:6 to the historical Moses.

Second, upon further investigation, *other internal evidences attest to Moses' authorship of the Pentateuch as well.* Independent investigation of the historical events recorded, of the contemporary issues of Moses' day, of the descriptions of the plants and wildlife, and of the conditions of geography and climate has led scholars to believe that the author was originally a resident of Egypt and not of Israel. Investigation also confirms that the author of the Pentateuch was an eyewitness of the Exodus and wilderness wanderings, and one who possessed a very high degree of education, literary skill, and familiarity with Egypt and the Hebrew way of life. Moses is the most reasonable choice as author since he appears to have possessed all the qualities and training necessary to fulfill the role of author.

The many geographic details recorded in passages such as Exodus 15:27 suggest that the author was an actual participant in the events themselves. Genesis and Exodus show the author's familiarity with the land of Egypt and with Egyptian names, expressions, customs, and culture. In addition, the unity of arrangement and harmony that underlies the Torah also points to a single author of the text. And taking into account that the Pentateuch was written over a period of about four decades through progressive revelation given by God, we would expect differing writing styles.

Third, *the late date many critics assigned to Deuteronomy (the seventh century BC) has been thoroughly discredited* by the excellent scholarship of Meredith Kline. In his landmark work *The Treaty of the Great King*[3] he demonstrates that Deuteronomy follows the form of the typical Hittite suzerainty treaty of the second millennium BC. This is the very time during which Moses would have written Deuteronomy.

The Historicity of Adam and Eve

The first chapters of Genesis are generally considered by critical scholars to be myth and not actual historical events. They cite the poetic structure of the text, the parallels with ancient myths, and its contradiction of the theory of evolution as evidence that the accounts are legendary. But Genesis presents Adam and Eve as historical, literal people who began the human race. Indeed, an early archaeological discovery supports a literal Adam and Eve. In 1932 E.A. Speiser of the University Museum of Pennsylvania discovered a seal near the bottom of the Tepe Gawra Mound, 12 miles from Nineveh in Mesopotamia, that he dated about 3500 BC. It shows a naked man and woman both bent over as if they were downcast. Behind them is a serpent. The seal is about one inch in diameter, engraved on stone, and is now in the University Museum in Philadelphia. Professor Speiser noted that the image is strongly suggestive of the Adam and Eve story.

Both the Old and New Testaments continually refer to Adam and Eve as literal persons, recording the most important events in their lives, documenting the events of their descendants, placing Adam at the beginning of human genealogy, and telling of their literal existence as key to an accurate understanding of original sin.

Despite the common assumption by some that Genesis is a form of poetry, the casual reader will immediately recognize that its structure and genre do not necessarily follow the typical pattern of Hebrew poetry. When Genesis is compared with the poetic structure of Psalms and Proverbs, the differences are clearly evident. Genesis predominately contains narrative and tangible real-life descriptions and does not appear to contain significant amounts of poetry, whereas Psalms and Proverbs are poetic and melodic. The creation account of Genesis 2 reads like any other historical narrative found in the Old Testament. This is evidenced by the structure of the text, in that the account is introduced like other historical narratives with the phrase, "This is the account of…." Moreover, Jesus and the apostles viewed the creation account as an actual historical event (see Matthew 19:4; Romans 5:14; 1 Corinthians 15:45; 1 Timothy 2:13-14). In fact, no New Testament passage treats the events recorded in Genesis as poetic or mythological.

Reasons for Accepting Genesis 1–11 as Historical

There are, in fact, many good reasons for accepting the historicity of Adam and Eve and, for that matter, the whole of Genesis 1–11:

1. Genesis 12 begins with what is called a *waw*-consecutive verb ("and he said"), which indicates that what follows is a continuation of chapter 11 and not a break.

2. The structure of Genesis is connected by the phrase "these are the generations (history) of…," which occurs ten times. Each time this phrase occurs it narrows the focus to something that has previously been discussed: the heavens and the earth (2:4), Adam (5:1), Noah (6:9), Noah's sons (10:1),

Shem (11:10), Terah (11:27), Ishmael (25:12), Isaac (25:19), Esau (36:1), and Jacob (37:2).

3. Since six of the phrases mentioned in point 2 occur in Genesis 1–11 and four in Genesis 12–50, it is clear that both sections should be understood in the same way. They form the literary connectives that hold the whole historical record together.

4. There is a connective between both sections in the history of Abraham, Sarah, and Lot, which begins near the end of Genesis 11 (verses 27-32) and continues in chapters 12–25.

5. Genesis 12 makes little sense by itself without the preparatory genealogy given in chapter 11. Only hermeneutical gymnastics could bring one to take Abraham, Isaac, and Jacob as historical, but not Adam, Noah, Shem, Ham, and Japheth.

6. The New Testament cites indiscriminately from both sections as historical. This is demonstrated below by numerous citations that confirm 15 persons or events from Genesis 1–11.

Therefore, Genesis 1–11 is just as historical as Genesis 12–50. Any hermeneutic which undermines the historicity of Genesis 1–11 is thereby undermining the full inerrancy of the Bible. And with it, they are undermining the authority of Christ, the New Testament writers, and many important Christian doctrines based on the historicity of Genesis 1–11. Consider all the New Testament references that support the historicity of the early chapters of Genesis:

1. The creation of the universe (Genesis 1)—Mark 13:19; John 1:3; Colossians 1:16

2. The creation of Adam and Eve (Genesis 1–2)—Mark 10:6; Mark 13:19; 1 Timothy 2:13; 1 Corinthians 11:8-9; 15:45

3. God resting on the seventh day (Genesis 1)—Hebrews 4:3-4

4. The marriage of Adam and Eve (Genesis 2)—Matthew 19:4-6; Mark 10:7-8; Ephesians 5:31; 1 Corinthians 6:16

5. The temptation of Eve (Genesis 3)—1 Timothy 2:14; 2 Corinthians 11:3

6. The disobedience of Adam (Genesis 3)—Romans 5:12,14-19

7. The sacrifices of Abel and Cain (Genesis 4)—Hebrews 11:4

8. The murder of Abel by Cain (Genesis 4)—Matthew 23:35; 1 John 3:12; Jude 11

9. The birth of Seth (Genesis 4)—Luke 3:38

10. The translation of Enoch to heaven (Genesis 5)—Hebrews 11:5

11. Marriage before the Flood (Genesis 6)—Luke 17:27

12. The Flood and the destruction of mankind (Genesis 7)—Matthew 24:39

13. The preservation of Noah and his family (Genesis 8–9)—1 Peter 3:20; 2 Peter 2:5

14. Noah's son Shem and his descendants (Genesis 10)—Luke 3:35-36

15. The birth of Abram (Abraham) (Genesis 11)—Luke 3:34

In view of this, to deny the historicity of these early chapters of Genesis is to deny, first, the inspiration of the New Testament; and second, the authority of Christ, who affirmed six of those chapters Himself (1, 2, 4, 8, 11, and 12). What is more, denying the historicity of Genesis 1–11 undermines crucial New Testament doctrines that are based on them. These include 1) the doctrine of marriage (Matthew 19:4-6); 2) the doctrine of the essential equality of men and women, who are both in "God's image" (Genesis 1:27; 1 Corinthians 11:7-12); 3) the doctrine of the essential unity of the human race (Acts 17:26); 4) the doctrine of the Fall of mankind (Romans 5:12-14); and 5) the doctrine of redemption by the last Adam (1 Corinthians 15:45).

Adam and Eve and Darwin's Theory

Sometimes the historicity of Adam and Eve is dismissed due to its incompatibility with Darwin's theory of evolution. His book *On the Origin of Species* (1859) sought to explain the origins of the biological species by means of natural selection, contradicting the biblical assertion that species reproduce after their own kind. According to current macroevolutionary theory, the process of the development of plants, animals, and humans is governed by the unguided principle of survival of the fittest. Over the process of millions of years, variations in species begin to emerge as they evolve and adapt to their surrounding environment, enabling them to be better equipped to survive and then produce offspring with these same capabilities. Other species that have not developed with such characteristics would lack the capabilities necessary to thrive, which would lead to their eventual extinction.

Darwin's theory of evolution leaves no room for divine intervention in the emergence of life, which poses a direct contradiction to the creation account presented in Genesis, leaving many to doubt the reliability of the text of that book (see Genesis 1:1,3,6,9,21,27). However, there is no reason to accept the conclusions of macroevolutionary theory.

The fossils say no. First, no conclusive fossil evidence exists to support the evolutionary contention that certain kinds can transition into other kinds (for example, reptiles into birds, chimps into humans). All the so-called "missing links" have been either refuted as frauds or closely examined and discovered to be either animal or human, but not both.

Indeed, top evolutionists have acknowledged the lack of fossil evidence to support evolution. Darwin asserted that the lack of transitional fossils in the geological record is "the most obvious and gravest objection which can be urged against my theory." [4] *American Scientist* magazine contains the statement, "As Darwin noted in the *Origin of Species*, the abrupt emergence of arthropods in the fossil record during the Cambrian presents a problem for evolutionary biology."[5] The late Harvard scientist Stephen Gould admitted, "The evolutionary trees that adorn our textbooks have data only at the tips and nodes of their branches." Even in his later attempt to modify this statement he admitted that "transitional forms are generally lacking at the species level."[6] Niles Eldredge said, "Most families, orders, classes, and phyla appear rather suddenly in the fossil record, often without anatomically intermediate forms."[7] W. Ford Doolitle said, "The history of life cannot properly be represented as a tree." Carl Woese noted that "there would never have been a single cell that could be called the last universal common ancestor." Cornell University biology professor William Provine said, "The evidence for the big transformations in evolution are not there in the fossil record."[8]

Additionally, Antonis Rokas declared that "phylogenetic incongruities can be seen everywhere in the universal tree, from its root to the major branching within and among the various taxa to the makeup of the primary groupings themselves."[9] Sir Fred Hoyle used a lively description: "The evolutionary record leaks like a sieve."[10] After science had spent 150 years looking for missing links, Oxford biologist Mark Pagel "saw in the fossil records rapid bursts of change, new species appearing seemingly out of nowhere and then remaining unchanged for millions of years—patterns hauntingly reminiscent of creation."[11]

Observation and experimentation say no. By contrast, science has supported the biblical view of the reproduction of each kind as being after its kind. That is, reptiles do not become birds. Experience and experimentation demonstrate that each kind reproduces after its own kind—no one has shown this to be false. Natural selection or survival of the fittest cannot account for the beginning of new kinds. There has been no experiment in the laboratory or observed experience in nature where natural selection produced a new biological kind.

There is certainly merit to the notion of survival of the fittest as a way to *weed out* weaker and sick animals and kinds, leaving the stronger animals to remain and reproduce. However, at best the principle of natural selection can only lead to the *survival* of kinds, not the *arrival* of kinds. Moreover, it should be noted that there is no fossil evidence that supports the claims that sudden drastic mutations, such as the addition of an organ or appendage, have occurred over a short time, say a thousand-year period. Studies in genetics have showed that the range of variations that are possible within a species are very limited and give no support to the possibility of the development of new kinds.

Biochemistry says no. Darwin described the criterion that would be fatal to the linchpin of his theory of evolution when he said,

> If it could be demonstrated that any complex organ existed, which could not possibly have been formed by numerous, successive, slight modifications, my theory would absolutely break down. But I can find out no such case.[12]

Even the most basic biological forms of life (for example, amoebas) have been scientifically shown to consist of complex information systems and patterns that reflect the involvement of intelligence. In fact, according to the famous evolutionist Richard Dawkins, there is the equivalent of 1,000 sets of encyclopedias of information in a one-celled animal. [13] These patterns and systems often resemble the workings, order, and precision of a factory assembly line (for example, DNA, RNA, replication, transport, coding, assembly, and so on), all of which can only be accounted for by a complex and intelligent cause.

In all cases of human experience there appear to be intelligent causes responsible for the existence of complex information systems. [14] If we are to be consistent in our thinking, this would hold true for all biological information systems, especially since all specified complexity (like information contained in a sentence) implies a designer. Darwin's criterion in the above quotation has been met by biochemist Michael Behe. Behe has demonstrated that the basic components of the cell appear to be irreducibly complex, meaning all of its components must be fully formed and functioning together for the cell to thrive. Thus, the cell could not have developed (evolved) through numerous, successive, and slight modifications. Evolutionary theory cannot account for the origin, development, and sustaining of the cell by slight successive changes over long periods of time. In such a case the cell's complexity would be reduced and could not survive.

As an analogy, the workings of the cell are much like the workings of a car. All the necessary system components (that is, engine, gasoline, spark plugs, transmission, battery, fuel injectors, and so on) must be present, complete, and functional all at once—or the car will not operate. For biological life this is certain death or even extinction. Behe uses the example of a mousetrap. If one of its component parts is broken or missing it will not catch mice. In other words, the mousetrap is irreducibly complex—any reduction in the complex parts will render the trap useless for its purpose of catching mice.

Dating methods are not definitive. The rejection of Adam and Eve's historicity because of an alleged contradiction between early evolutionary dates of man's origin with Genesis's timeline is unfounded for several reasons. First, there are both biblical and scientific arguments that can be used to support a young-earth view—that the creation of mankind occurred 10,000 or fewer years ago.* Fossil dating methods to determine the antiquity of human origin are often inaccurate and not always trustworthy. Moreover, in some cases it is not clear whether the fossil remains analyzed are actually human. The well-known carbon-14 dating method is subject to the objection of whether the fossil

---

* For example, noted physicist Gerald Schroeder argues that the universe is both 15 billion years old (judged from our perspective looking back) but yet only thousands of years old because there were only six literal days (from God's perspective looking forward). Genesis speaks from God's perspective, but since the universe has expanded, looking back from our perspective we judge the passage of time to have been much greater. Time is relative to space, and as space expands, time expands with it. So both the Bible (with its literal days of creation) and modern science could be correct (see Gerald Schroeder, *The Science of God* [New York: Free Press, 2009]). Other young-earth views challenge the constancy of the speed of light, the reliability of scientific dating methods, or both (see Henry M. Morris, *Biblical Cosmology and Modern Science* [Philadelphia: P&R Press, 1970]).

was in a pure state. It is not always easy to discern whether there was a constant and uninterrupted rate of decay or whether the sample was contaminated by outside forces. It is also worthy of note that some dating methods, carbon-14 among them, are only accurate for thousands of years, not for hundreds of thousands or millions of years. Therefore, some dating methods used to analyze fossils are, at best, dependent upon the speculations of the analyzer or are altogether inaccurate. Because the dating methods are based on analysis of bone fragments, scientists' attempts to reconstruct origins are very speculative. Therefore, the foundations of the objections made against the historicity of Adam and Eve are speculative. Second, the objection fails to understand that some Christians hold to an old-earth chronology that leaves room for an earlier date for Adam.

The Reliability of Controversial Mosaic Narratives

The general reliability of the Old Testament narrative has been supported with numerous archaeological finds. As Nelson Glueck has boldly asserted, "As a matter of fact, however, it may be stated categorically that *no archaeological discovery has ever controverted a biblical reference.* Scores of archaeological findings have been made which confirm in clear outline or exact detail historical statements in the Bible." [15]

With the resurgence of Near-Eastern historical research and the successful excavation of Bible lands, Mosaic narratives have been given more ample historical support. The following chart will chronologically outline the general reliability of these key passages (see more detailed discussion in chapter 17, "Exodus and Conquest").

The Historical Reliability of Genesis and Exodus: Summary of Major Points

Scripture	Controversy	Evidence of Reliability
Adam and Eve Genesis 1–3	The literal existence of Adam and Eve is untenable.	• The biblical text refers to Adam and Eve as real historical persons who gave birth to real children (Genesis 4:1,25; 5:1ff.). • The Genesis text refers to its events as historical, using the Hebrew word *toledoth*, which is variously translated "history," "generations," "account," and "records" (Genesis 6:9; 9:12; 10:1; 11:10; 17:7,9); these events include creation (2:4) and lineage of Adam and Eve (Genesis 5:1ff.) • Adam is listed at beginning of the ancestry of Jesus (whose existence has been securely established) (Luke 3:38). • Unless there was a literal first man and woman, the human race of today could not exist.
Date of Adam and Eve Genesis 1–5	A late date for Adam and Eve is not scientific.	• An early date is built on questionable assumptions that there are missing genealogical records (see Genesis 5; 11; 1 Chronicles 1:1-24) and that the creation "days" in Genesis 1 are not 24-hour periods. • The early date is built on the assumption that early fossil dating is accurate, and that these early fossils were human. These "human" fossils have been based on scant remains that have proven to be unreliable and speculative.
Genesis and Myth Genesis 1–9	The early chapters of Genesis (1–2) are poetry and myth similar to Mesopotamian legends.	• Genesis 1 is not written in Hebrew poetical form (couplets and parallelism; for example, see Psalms or Proverbs) despite the presence of what some believe to be parallel ideas in the days of creation (Genesis 1). • According to Dr. Walter Kaiser, the events of Genesis 1–11 are written in regular prose form (not poetic parallelism). Normal "use of the *waw*-consecutive with the verb to describe sequential acts, the frequent use of the direct object sign and the so-called relative pronoun, the stress on definitions, and the spreading out of these events in a sequential order indicates that we are in prose and not in poetry." [16] • Genesis 2–9 is written in plain historical narrative (like other historical narratives found in the Old Testament) without the presence of typical Hebrew poetical form. • The New Testament (Jesus, Matthew, Paul) considered the creation and Flood literal historical events (Matthew 19:4; Romans 5:14; 1 Corinthians 15:45; 1 Timothy 2:13-15). • Near-Eastern scholars such as K.A. Kitchen and others have confirmed that the earlier Mesopotamian myth accounts (of creation and the Flood) should not be viewed as source material for the early chapters of Genesis, which were written later. Kitchen affirms that early legend or myth does not become more historical or simplified over time. [17]

Scripture	Controversy	Evidence of Reliability
Genesis and Science Genesis 1–9	Genesis contradicts the science of modern evolutionary theory.	• The creation account described in Genesis 1 stands in contradiction to macroevolutionary theory. However, it is important to note that the Bible (domain of Christian theology) and nature (domain of scientific inquiry) do not stand in contradiction to each other, since both domains have the same author—God. The interpretations of nature by fallible scientists and the interpretations of the Bible by fallible theologians are what stand in real conflict. • Macroevolutionary theory cannot adequately account for basic philosophical questions such as 1) How can something come from nothing? 2) How do information systems (for example, DNA) come from nonintelligent causes? 3) How does life emerge from nonliving causes? These questions are answered in Genesis. • Information systems such as DNA, the apparent fine-tuning of the universe and the galactic and solar habitable zones, and complex life require an intelligent cause for their existence. Natural, nonintelligent causes cannot explain the origin and sustaining of these conditions. • Biochemist Dr. Michael Behe has demonstrated through the concept of "irreducible complexity" (see *Darwin's Black Box*) that simple cells and simple life forms could not have developed in a slow, incremental Darwinian fashion over long periods of time. Rather, they must have developed fully formed with all biological systems present all at once. In other words, these forms are irreducibly complex. These scientific observations are confirmed by Dr. William Dembski (see *The Design of Life*) and Dr. Stephen Meyer (see *Signature in the Cell*).
Noah and the Flood Genesis 6–9	Noah and the Flood story reflect legend similar to other ancient myths.	• Considering Noah and the Flood to be myth comes from an overemphasis on surface similarities between mythical and biblical accounts and the neglect of identifying the significant differences. These similarities do not demonstrate dependency but rather indicate both accounts share a common historical event. The earlier accounts are written in a highly mythical manner, whereas the later Genesis account is written in a historical, nonmythical style that indicates the later Genesis account is not dependent upon earlier Mesopotamian accounts. Near-Eastern experts have shown that myth never becomes more historical and simpler over time. • The Old Testament considers Noah and the Flood historical, indicated by the use of biblical words such as Noah's "history," "generation," and "genealogy," and even "nations" that came from him (Genesis 6:9; 10:1-11; 1 Chronicles 1:3-4; Isaiah 54:9; Ezekiel 14:14,20). • The New Testament considers both Noah and the Flood historical (Matthew 24:37-38; Hebrews 11:7; 1 Peter 3:20; 2 Peter 2:5; 3:5-15).

Scripture	Controversy	Evidence of Reliability
		• Scientific evidence gained from aquatic and nonpolar life, as well as geological evidence, demonstrates the earth was previously covered with water. [18] • The presence of over two dozen literary works (for example, the Gilgamesh Epic, the Atrahasis Epic, and so on) and archaeological finds (for example, the Sumerian Kings List) mentioning the great Flood, from various people-groups (Chinese, Hindus, Indians, Mexicans, Hebrews, Greeks, Hawaiians, Mesopotamians, and so on) attests to the historicity of the Flood account in Genesis. [19]
Noah's Ark Genesis 6–9	A wooden vessel could not survive catastrophic flood conditions over a long period of time. Besides, Noah's Ark probably did not exist.	• According to one naval architect, the design (long and rectangular) of the Ark was the one best-suited for stability and durability. [20] • The gopher wood materials used to build the Ark have been recognized for their strength and flexibility under pressure. Some have considered the Ark to be more stable than our modern shipping vessels and modern ocean liners. [21] Unlike modern cruise ships, Noah's Ark was built for stability, not for speed (which reduces stability). • Instead of the extreme cargo weight (animals, feed, supplies, and so on) being a liability for the Ark, the weight provided the boat with stability in turbulent waters. • Ancient and medieval writers such as Josephus, [22] Theophilus of Antioch (AD 115–185), [23] Epiphanius of Salamis (AD 315–403), [24] Chrysostom (AD 345–407), [25] Isidore of Seville (AD 560–636), [26] Jehan Haithon (13th century), [27] Sir John Mandeville (d. 1372), [28] and Adam Olearius (AD 1603–1671), [29] acknowledge the existence of Noah's Ark.
Tower of Babel Genesis 11	The confusion of languages at the Tower of Babel is mythological. Originally, no extrabiblical mention of the event existed.	• Recent archaeological excavation in Mesopotamia has unearthed remains of at least 30 enormous stair-stepped pyramid-shaped towers, known today as *ziggurats*. The most ancient of these is located at Eridu and dates from the late fifth to early fourth millennium BC, lending historical credibility to the Genesis account. Among its many functions was to provide a place for a temple, which was located on top and dedicated to a god or gods. • The building materials described in Genesis 11:3 (thoroughly burnt "bricks" and "bitumen for mortar"—ESV) have been confirmed to have been in use in Mesopotamia (at Samarra) by the sixth millennium BC. For example, the Ziggurat of Ur-Nammu at Ur is made from these materials. • Mesopotamian literature reflects the Genesis account of the confusion of languages. For example, the fourth-millennium BC Sumerian legend known as "Enmerkar and the Lord of Aratta" contains allusions to a unified language and a subsequent diversifying of language by the gods (see "The Spell of Nudimmud").

Scripture	Controversy	Evidence of Reliability
Early Writing Genesis 1–11	Written languages did not exist during the period Genesis was supposedly written. Thus, the events Genesis describes could not have been written down.	• The word *Babel*, the term used in association with this event by God (11:9), is still used today to refer to unintelligible speech. Furthermore, the Mesopotamian area of "Babylon" adopted this name from early times, and it is located in the general vicinity of the Land of Shinar, where the events took place. • Of the two major theories of the origin and development of language (*monogenesis* and *candelabra* theories), neither can explain the linguistic phenomena of unity and diversity of current language. However, the confusion of languages at the Tower of Babel adequately explains why diverse languages have similar words and speech, without the need for development over long time periods. • Archaeologists have uncovered evidence of written languages (pictographs) on clay tablets dating to the mid-fourth millennium BC. This is nearly 2,000 years prior to the events of Genesis being written down. • God could have revealed these events to the author of Genesis at a later time. To reject this possibility would require the rejection of miracles. However, a dismissal of miracles would first require evidence that God does not exist. For if God exists, then miracles (which are acts of God) are possible. • The repeated phrase "this is the account of…" (Genesis 2:4; 5:1) implies that Moses had earlier records from which to compile Genesis. Other extrabiblical works are mentioned throughout the Old Testament as sources for biblical authors, such as the Book of Jasher (Joshua 10:13) and The Books of the Wars of the Lord (Numbers 21:14); "The Chronicles of Samuel…Nathan the prophet…and… Gad the seer" may also fit in this category (1 Chronicles 29:29 ESV). • Due to the presence of the repeated phrase "This is the generation of…," Near-Eastern scholar P.J. Wiseman posits that the history of Genesis was originally written on clay tablets that would be continually passed on to succeeding generations. [30] This is consistent with Moses collecting these sources and editing them into their final version, especially since Genesis could not have been written any later than Moses' time period (that is, mid-second millennium BC).
Historical Support Genesis 1–11	Most ancient people considered the Genesis accounts mythical.	• Jesus and the New Testament writers believed the early chapters of Genesis were historical. Examples include 1. creation of the universe (Genesis 1)—Mark 13:19; John 1:3; Colossians 1:16; 2; 2. creation of Adam and Eve (Genesis 1–2)—Mark 10:6; 1 Timothy 2:13; 1 Corinthians 11:8-9; 15:45; 3. God resting on the seventh day (Genesis 1)—Hebrews 4:3-4;

Scripture	Controversy	Evidence of Reliability
		4. the marriage of Adam and Eve (Genesis 2)—Matthew 19:4-6; Mark 10:7-8; Ephesians 5:31; 1 Corinthians 6:16;
		5. the temptation of Eve (Genesis 3)—1 Timothy 2:14; 2 Corinthians 11:3;
		6. the disobedience of Adam (Genesis 3)—Romans 5:12,14-19;
		7. the sacrifices of Abel and Cain (Genesis 4)—Hebrews 11:4;
		8. the murder of Abel by Cain (Genesis 4)—Matthew 23:35; 1 John 3:12; Jude 11;
		9. the birth of Seth (Genesis 4)—Luke 3:38;
		10. the translation of Enoch to heaven (Genesis 5)—Hebrews 11:5;
		11. marriage before the Flood (Genesis 6)—Luke 17:27;
		12. the Flood and the destruction of mankind (Genesis 7)— Matthew 24: 38-39.
Destruction of Sodom and Its Location Genesis 18–19	Sodom is a legendary city from Jewish folktales.	• After W.F. Albright conducted an exploration of the southeastern Dead Sea area in the early twentieth century, Sodom was no longer relegated to the pages of myth. He posited that the location of the city should be at the southeastern shores of the Dead Sea, the area known today as Bab edh-Dhra. Though chronological (too early dates) and geographical challenges still exist for identifying this location as Sodom, Albright forcefully shifted the Sodom story from "myth" to plausibility. • Recent geographical research and archaeological excavation by Dr. Steven Collins at Tall el-Hammam, which is located northeast of the Dead Sea, appear to answer the geographical and chronological challenges still hampering the southern location. After eight seasons of excavation, Collins has unearthed impressive archaeological evidence (to be published soon) to support his identification of Tal el-Hammam as Sodom. Evidences include a massive destruction layer, catastrophic high-heat indicators, 40 geographical markers supporting the biblical descriptions, strata supporting the chronological context of Sodom, absence of Late Bronze Age pottery, and a hiatus in population (even though this was a prime location) of nearly 700 years after its fiery destruction (see full article on Sodom in this book).

Scripture	Controversy	Evidence of Reliability
The Patriarchs Genesis 12–50	The biblical patriarchs in Genesis are legendary figures.	• Near-Eastern scholars such as William F. Albright, Edwin Yamauchi, P.J. Wiseman, K.A. Kitchen, and others are convinced by the archaeological evidence of the historicity of the Genesis patriarchs. The detailed descriptions of geography, customs, cultural characteristics, religion, linguistics, and law codes within the Bible have established the historical nature of the patriarchal narratives when compared to actual geography and archaeological finds. [31] • Archaeological discoveries throughout the Near East have clarified and added to the argument for historicity. For example, the Amarna Tablets, Nuzi Tablets, Mari Letters, and Ras Shamra Tablets have contributed to our understanding of the similar cultural, legal, and religious expressions during the patriarchs' time period and among their contemporaries.
The Historical Nature of Exodus and Deuteronomy	Moses could not have written such a sophisticated law code like the one found in the Pentateuch by the fifteenth century BC, according to the Documentary Hypothesis of Graf and Wellhausen.	• Archaeological discoveries in the twentieth century answered this hypothesis. For example, in 1929, archaeologists (Claude F.A. Schaeffer and George Chenet in northern Syria, working in ancient Ugarit, today known as Minet el-Beida) unearthed a royal palace, scribal school, and a library adjoining a temple that contained a cache of archive documents dating to the late fifteenth century BC. The tablets were written in a variety of languages; however, the most often used was a Canaanite language that is very similar to Hebrew. The tablets were understood to be describing a sophisticated law code very similar in style to the Law of Moses. These texts also describe the dark religious practices of the Canaanite peoples in the land prior to Joshua's conquest. These wicked practices offer confirmation of the Canaanite deities, practices, and religious customs described in the Old Testament, including 1) the suffocation of children, who were buried alive, evidenced by the discovery of thousands of clay jars containing the remains of children who were sacrificed; 2) absence of morality among the gods; 3) orgiastic worship of nature; 4) male and female religious prostitution; 5) malice and jealousy among the gods; 6) other types of child sacrifice; 7) pornographic nudity with serpent symbols; 8) high religious mythology; and 9) sensual idol worship. These finds give new meaning and significance to the divine command given to Joshua and the Israelites to amputate the moral gangrene of the Canaanites and their religion.

Scripture	Controversy	Evidence of Reliability
The Timing of the Exodus Exodus 12	Critical scholars have pushed the time of Israel's migration to the Holy Land forward to the late thirteenth century BC.	• The Ras Shamra texts use a number of terms similar to those associated with religious offerings described by Levitical terminology. These include "whole" (*ishsheh*), "burnt" (*kalil*), "peace" (*shelamin*), and "guilt" (*asham*) offerings. Because of the presence of sophisticated law codes contemporary to Moses' time as evidenced in the Ras Shamra Tablets, it can no longer be asserted that Moses could not have penned the Mosaic law as early as the fifteenth century BC. Moreover, the texts have contributed much to our understanding of the development of the Hebrew script, as well as our understanding of the Old Testament, from about 1500 BC to the modern day. Furthermore, this discovery has dealt a mortal blow to negative higher critics who had asserted that Aramaic words contained in the Old Testament did not develop until after the exile to Babylon (sixth century BC). Several Aramaisms were found in the Ugaritic and Ras Shamra texts contemporary with Moses, which refutes this notion. (See our section on the Exodus in the archaeological portion of this book).
		• The biblical text indicates that the Exodus occurred in the late sixteenth to mid fifteenth century BC, and the text says Israel entered Canaan forty years later (Exodus 12:40; 1 Kings 6:1; Judges 11:26; Acts 13:19-20).
		• The Merneptah Stele (an official Egyptian government inscription) confirms that Israel was already in Canaan by the late thirteenth century BC, which eliminates any possibility of arguing for a late-thirteenth-century date for the Exodus.
		• Other plausible solutions have been proposed that make it no longer necessary to accept a late date for the Exodus. First, Donovan Courville has argued that there are about 600 extra years in the Egyptian chronology due to the listing of "sub-rulers" living simultaneously with Egyptian pharaohs. Previously, these rulers were thought to be successor kings, but now it is possible that they were contemporaneous with other rulers, which would shorten the Egyptian chronology considerably. When these chronological adjustments are made, it appears that Israelite history and the chronology of the Egyptian kings harmonize—including the early Exodus date of the mid-fifteenth century BC. Second, some have suggested (based on recent archaeological excavation) lowering the date of the Middle Bronze Age (MBA) to about 1400 BC (instead of about 1550 BC), which would bring harmony between the fall of the cities of Canaan and Joshua's account of the conquest. Further, the late date for the Exodus could be based on the mistaken notion that the city of "Raamses" (Exodus 1:11) was named after Ramses the Great, and that there was an absence of building projects in the Nile Delta before 1300, both of which would make the biblical account of the condition described in Exodus implausible

Scripture	Controversy	Evidence of Reliability
		prior to 1300.[32] These ideas can be answered by recognizing that 1) the name "Ramses" may be referring to an earlier individual; after all, Ramses the Great is Ramses II (there must have been an earlier individual by this name—that is, Ramses I); 2) Genesis 47:11 describes the Nile Delta region as "Raamses" (the same place Jacob and family settled).[33] • The date adjustments considered above would also fit nicely with certain Egyptian literary finds. For example, there are parallel accounts of the plagues that occurred at the time of the Exodus. The Ipuwer Papyrus (a 13th-century BC manuscript copy, meaning that the original was written earlier) was discovered in Egypt in 1828; it was translated in 1909 by Alan H. Gardner and found to have a direct parallel to the plagues brought on Egypt by God through Moses in Exodus (see chapter 17, "Exodus and Conquest," for more detailed discussion). • Meredith Kline has argued convincingly that the critics' seventh-century BC date for Deuteronomy should be rejected.[34] Rather, Kline argues that the form of Deuteronomy reflects the Hittite suzerainty treaty common in the second millennium BC, the same time period during which Moses is traditionally considered to have authored Deuteronomy.

Chart © Joseph M. Holden, 2013.

A Final Word on the Pentateuch

While literally thousands of finds have validated the persons and events presented in the Old Testament, not a single archaeological find has refuted anything in the Pentateuch. Noted biblical scholar Donald J. Wiseman affirms that "The geography of Bible lands and visible remains of antiquity were gradually recorded until today more than 25,000 sites within this region and dating to Old Testament times, in their broadest sense, have been located." [35]

The Historicity of the Major Prophets (Isaiah and Jeremiah)

The Historicity of Isaiah

During the past two centuries, the book of Isaiah has been subject to endless scrutiny and criticism. In particular, the book's nature and structure have engendered an array of views, ranging from the traditional view that Isaiah is one unitary book to a popular theory that it is a collection of three books (chapters 1–39; 40–55; 56–66) that were written at three distinct time periods.

However, in the discussions and debates concerning the supposed threefold division of the book, there appears no evidence from the text of Isaiah itself. Moreover, evidence from the Isaiah Scroll found at Qumran confirms the view of a single book. The book was found as a single unit, not stitched together, and

Discovered in 1931 on the Mount of Olives by E.L. Sukenik of the Hebrew University in Jerusalem, this first-century AD stone funerary inscription bears the name of king Uzziah (Azariah), who is mentioned in 2 Chronicles 26:21-13 and Isaiah 6:1. Most believe it is a copy of an earlier inscription originally attached to the king's tomb. The inscription reads, "To this place were brought the bones of Uzziah, king of Judah; do not open!" The final phrase of the inscription may reflect Uzziah's leprous condition. (Photo by Zev Radovan.)

The prophet Isaiah rebukes a man named "Shebna" for building a tomb for himself in a very conspicuous place near the Temple (22:15-17). In 1870, Charles Clermont-Ganneau discovered this eighth-century BC Hebrew lintel inscription over a rock-cut tomb in the village of Silwan (Jerusalem). Later it was deciphered by Nahman Avigad and shown to belong to the royal steward of the king. Though only a partial name inscription remains, many believe this was the tomb of Shebna, the royal steward "who is over the house" (NKJV) of King Hezekiah. (Photo by Zev Radovan.)

not separated into three scrolls. In this complete scroll, one can see the text at 33:34, where the scribe intentionally left a blank space that was equal to about three lines, designating a break at the end of the column in order to begin a new column at chapter 34. Chapter 34 is very close to the midpoint of the book, and it would seem that there was reason to divide the book between chapters 33 and 34 as opposed to dividing it into three books between chapters 39 and 40, and 55 and 56 respectively. One theory addresses this twofold division from the standpoint of chronological significance, with chapters 1 through 33 dealing with the time period from Uzziah to Ahaz and chapters 34 through 66 with the time of Hezekiah and later. One can also see that each half corresponds well to the other in terms of the topics covered in seven parts.[36]

One view that favors a three-part structure attempts to offer traces of evidence that reveal its composition occurred at different time periods and different locations. There is little doubt that chapters 1 through 39 belong to the eighth century BC; that section contains geographical and cultural references to that era. Evidence that chapters 40 through 55 are based in Babylon (which this theory proposes) is not strong since these chapters do not convey knowledge of the metropolis of Babylon, but more appropriately belong to Israel and the Levant. For it was in that historical-geographical context that it seemed most appropriate for Isaiah to warn Hezekiah about the dangers of trifling with Babylon. Furthermore, chapters 56 through 66 do not pose any descriptive inconsistencies with composition in seventh-to-sixth-century BC pre-exilic Judah.

What is more, the Gospel of John, chapter 12:38-41 supports the unity of Isaiah. John the Apostle attributes quotations from both the first half and second half of the book to one and the same Isaiah. John writes, "...that the word of Isaiah the prophet might be fulfilled, which he spoke" (verse 38 NKJV), which is followed by a quote of Isaiah 53:1. John continues in the very next verse (verse 39) and says, "Isaiah said again," followed by a quote of Isaiah 6:9-10. The context, quotes, and the presence of the word *again* confirms that there is only one Isaiah responsible for both parts of the book, and therefore the book should be considered a unity. The evidence supports a unitary view of the book of Isaiah, while alternative views of the book are inconsistent with normative prophetic composition, recording, and usage in the biblical world.

The Historicity of Jeremiah

Jeremiah wrote the longest and most complexly formatted book in the Old Testament. The narrative sections contain many allusions to contemporary history as well as to various people who lived during Jeremiah's lifetime.* Any attempt to date parts of Jeremiah

This late seventh-century BC stamp seal impression is written in the Hebrew script and reads, "Belonging to Baruch, son of Neriah, the scribe." Baruch was the scribe of the prophet Jeremiah; he wrote down the book of Jeremiah (Jeremiah 36:1-32). (Photo by Zev Radovan.)

---

* See chapter 20 of this book, which identifies individuals such as Jehucal the son of Shelemiah (Jeremiah 37:3); [Pashhur] the son of Immer (20:1); Sarsekim, who was Nebuchadnezzar's chief officer during the invasion of Jerusalem (39:3); and Baruch, son of Neriah, the scribe of Jeremiah (36:4).

to a later period, such as the fifth to third century BC, appeals for support to the lack of extrabiblical knowledge of pre-exilic history. This however, is an argument from silence. The absence of pre-exilic history does not justify positing a later date for Jeremiah, nor does it undermine its reliability. The absence of historical references by no means indicates a latter or contradictory narrative.

Although the prophetic writings in the Hebrew Old Testament display many differences between each other, they nonetheless possess common characteristics. First of all, every prophetic book explicitly declares the author who wrote it and puts forth the contents as a message given to them by God Himself. What is more, nearly all the books contain a series of messages, oracles, or narratives of varying lengths that support the message. The only books excluded from this pattern are Nahum, Obadiah, and Habakkuk. With the exception of these books and the book of Jonah, the prophetic books were written down on separate occasions. Specific oracles and messages were given to prophets and written down by a scribe or amanuensis and were kept in a scroll as a series, although there are many instances where the prophet did write down his own words. There is a great amount of consistency and unity found within the text itself, which attests to the reliability of the Old Testament writings.

Conclusion

The historicity of the Old Testament is widely supported by archaeological findings (see part 6). Every major aspect from Genesis to the post-captivity period is confirmed as history, not only by the New Testament writers, but by extrabiblical sources as well. The once critical scholar Dr. William F. Albright gradually grew to accept a more conservative view as a result of a lifetime study of the archaeological facts. He wrote,

> Thanks to modern research we now recognize its [the Bible's] substantial historicity. The narratives of the patriarchs, of Moses and the exodus, of the conquest of Canaan, of the judges, the monarchy, exile and restoration, have all been confirmed and illustrated to an extent that I should have thought impossible forty years ago. [37]

More recently, a magazine not known for conservative leanings concluded an article titled "Is the Bible True?" with these words:

> In extraordinary ways, modern archaeology has affirmed the historical core of the Old Testament—corroborating key portions of the stories of Israel's patriarchs, the Exodus, the Davidic monarchy, and the life and times of Jesus. [38]

ALLEGED ERRORS VS.
ARCHAEOLOGICAL DISCOVERIES

C ritics have long insisted that there are errors and contradictions in the Bible. To be sure, there are difficulties to sort through in order to arrive at a plausible explanation of a text in question. Since other works have adequately treated specific contradictions at length, [1] we will simply offer ways of approaching passages that will help guard against reaching unwarranted conclusions. In most cases we have discovered that Bible difficulties may be resolved by correcting the following logical and hermeneutical mistakes.

Mistakes to Avoid in Approaching Biblical Passages

Assuming that extrabiblical literature determines the historicity of a biblical passage. Conservative and liberal Bible scholars often fall prey to this in their effort to identify the genres contained in Scripture with genres of authors from the Greco-Roman or Near-Eastern literature. Once the identification is made, scholars illegitimately transfer the license to fabricate narrative (as was often done by ancient nonbiblical authors—for example, Greco-Roman biographers) to the biblical text, deeming a passage "poetic," a "special effect," "legend,"* or some combination of these. Though extrabiblical literature can be beneficial in clarifying or illuminating a text, the best interpreter of Scripture is Scripture.

Assuming that no additional information will clarify a text. [2] Some are quick to pronounce the text in error simply because it is not fully understood. But this wrongfully

---

* For an example of this mistake as it applies to the New Testament, see Michael Licona, *The Resurrection of Jesus: A New Historiographical Approach* (Downers Grove, IL: InterVarsity Press, 2010), 34, 185-186, 306 fn. 114, 548-553. Also see our discussion of Licona in chapter 12.

assumes that a lack of information or knowledge is equivalent to a contradiction in knowledge or facts. Rather, we should simply acknowledge our lack of information and understanding and wait for more information to surface. There will be some mysteries (for example, Deuteronomy 29:29) that will have to wait for clarification; this is how all other disciplines (for example, science) must operate.

Assuming that the Bible conveys factually incorrect information instead of giving it the benefit of the doubt. Historians have long agreed that ancient documents should be considered innocent until proven guilty. This is how we treat nonbiblical ancient documents, such as the histories of Julius Caesar and Alexander the Great, even though these works have much less documentary support than the Bible. Besides, no one would approach life with a guilty-until-proven innocent assumption, for this would lead to practical absurdities involving, among many things, road signs, shopping, restroom gender identification, and business transactions.

Assuming that our personal interpretations of Scripture are as inerrant as the divinely inspired text. Several alleged errors in the Bible can be traced to this common mistake. We must recognize that many Bible difficulties are due to conflicts between our own *interpretations* of a given text rather than actual contradictions contained in the Scripture itself. In other words, the conflict often exists at the *interpretive* level and not at the textual level. Recognizing that we have a fallible interpretation of the infallible text will go far in protecting us from viewing Scripture as a flawed revelation.

Assuming that words have meaning in themselves instead of discovering the whole context of a biblical passage in order to gain its meaning. On a micro level, some difficulties in Scripture are easily solved when we realize that words have *usage* and sentences have *meaning*. For example, the word *run* can mean a number of different things depending on how it is used (for example, a drip of paint on a wall, a tear in a stocking, a score in a baseball game, to jog or sprint, to operate a machine, and so on) in a sentence. The complete sentence (and often surrounding sentences) will many times provide the reader a clear understanding of how the word is being used.

On the macro level, the context of a statement is essential for understanding what is being said. For example, the Bible says that Adam and Eve would "*not* surely die" (Genesis 3:4 ESV) if they ate of the fruit from the forbidden tree. However, this seems to be a contradiction of God's earlier statement that they would "surely die" if they ate of the fruit (Genesis 2:17 ESV). We solve the apparent contradiction by understanding its context. The former statement (Genesis 3:4) is an inerrant record of Satan's lie, whereas the latter statement (2:17) is an inerrant record of God's statement of truth. The fundamental principle that guides real-estate investments—location, location, location—also holds true in hermeneutics; the meaning of a passage is discovered by understanding the sentence in its context, context, context!

Failing to understand that the Bible is the best commentary on the Bible. Difficult passages can often be understood by appealing to clear passages. This means we can eliminate interpretive options based on what is clearly understood to be true in other passages. For example, the difficult passage of James 2:24 asserts that "a man is justified by works, and not by faith only"(NKJV). It would appear that the verse teaches salvation by faith and works. However, Paul's clear teaching in Romans 4:5 that righteousness comes only through faith and not by works should provide us with the truth of salvation by which we understand James 2:24. We can now understand that James is referring to man's justification in the eyes of other men, since we humans do not know who is of faith except through seeing the actions and works of one another. Conversely, Paul is speaking about righteousness in the eyes of God, who needs no works to see since He already knows our heart.

Forgetting that the Bible had human writers who used human expressions and language. The Bible was written by humans and for humans and therefore utilizes human language for our understanding. This means that at times writers use linguistic expressions that are from an observational or phenomenological perspective; that is to say, the writers often expressed truths based on how things *appeared* to them from their vantage point. For example, Joshua 10:12-13 says the sun stood still. We all know that it is the earth that rotates relative to the sun, not the other way around; nevertheless, Joshua explained the phenomenon as it appeared to him and not necessarily like it actually happened (that is, the earth most likely stopped its rotation as well as the moon). This is a perfectly acceptable means of communicating the truth of what occurred—just as our modern observational expressions of *sunrise* and *sunset* are adequate to communicate truth.

Critics like Bart Ehrman, the renowned New Testament scholar who has argued against the reliability of the New Testament in his recent books, often challenge the Scripture's reliability due to minor scribal transmission mistakes found in the text. These come from human scribal error: minor mistakes such as in spelling, numbers, word and letter reversals, writing something twice that should be written once, skipping over a phrase or verse, and so on. We must remind ourselves that these mistakes are not a result of God's error in revelation; rather, they are results of subsequent human error in transmission. In addition, these cumulative scribal errors affect no doctrine or meaning of the text in question. The passages affected are understood by exercising common sense or inspecting and comparing manuscripts. The original inspired text of the Bible (made up of the *autographs*) is both inerrant in its text and meaning, whereas the transmission copies (*apographs*) with their minor scribal errors in the text nonetheless remain inerrant in representing the voice of God (*ipsissima vox*). It simply does not follow that since the Bible was written by humans it *must* be in error, since humans do not *always* err—only *sometimes*.

Failing to recognize that biblical writers had to carefully select which material to include in their books. As is the case with all writers and historians, decisions must be made concerning what details to include in one's reporting. To include "everything" would be impossible and even unnecessary. It would probably hinder the process of communication rather than enhancing it. The writer writes to an audience (or reader) with a specific theological purpose, so not everything will apply to the writer's issue at hand, but only those things that achieve his purpose. To assume something is false or does not exist because there is nothing written about it is to make a fallacious argument from silence. This charge against Scripture wrongfully attempts to establish truth based on what was not stated rather than on what was expressly stated in writing.

Names and Loan Words

The Old Testament documents are well-grounded in historical reality and give an accurate reflection of historical people, places, and events that took place in the context of everyday life. The renowned Old Testament scholar Robert Wilson has pointed out that there are 26 kings mentioned in the Hebrew Old Testament, and the spelling of the names of all but three are virtually identical to what has been deciphered in inscriptions written by the kings themselves. These names were copied with great accuracy over the centuries. Of the 120 consonant letters present in these names, none are out of their correct order in Scripture. This precise transmission stands in stark contrast to, as an example, a document written by an Egyptian priest named Manetho in approximately 280 BC. He writes 140 names of the kings of Egypt, but only 49 are recognizable when compared to relevant monuments and inscriptions. According to Wilson, over 40 kings of Israel and Judah are mentioned in the prophetic and historical books of the Bible, and all of these have been verified and found to be listed in the correct order when checked against historical records of the surrounding nations.

Another line of evidence supporting the historical reliability of the Old Testament is the usage of foreign words by biblical authors. The use of these words gives proof of the date and order of the documents. For example, early chapters of Genesis use a number of Babylonian words, while Egyptian words are used in the later chapters. Solomon's writings contain Indian and Assyrian words. During the time of the kings of Judah and Israel, one will notice a return to Assyrian and Babylonian terms. In addition, the books of Daniel, Ezra, Nehemiah, Esther, and Chronicles introduce numerous Persian words into the Bible. The use of Aramaic in one verse in Jeremiah and half of Ezra and Daniel reflects the evidence that Aramaic was the common tongue in Western Asia, commonly used in business transactions at the time.

The use of different words and languages in the Old Testament is reflective of the nation that was in power in that day. It would be highly unlikely that the books of the Old Testament were written by authors at a later date than the events they describe, as some critics claim, for such writers would have been required to know the language and customs of that earlier time period. This information would have not been known (or available) to them centuries later, outside of the biblical testimony. [3]

Archaeological Discoveries Supporting the Reliability of Old Testament History

The following chart gives a summary of major discoveries that support or confirm the Old Testament's historical accounts.

Lachish Reliefs	In 1847, Austen Henry Layard discovered Assyrian king Sennacherib's palace wall relief in Nineveh, which depicted his siege of Lachish (Isaiah 36:1-2). This discovery was the first of its kind; it sent shock waves through England since it confirmed an event described in the Bible. Today, in southern Israel at Lachish, Sennacherib's earthen siege ramp is still visible!
Beth Shan	The biblical city of Beth Shan has been excavated since the 1920s and 1930s and has revealed an occupation beginning from approximately 4500 BC and extending to the eleventh century AD. It is the location where the bodies of King Saul and his sons were fastened on the city walls (1 Samuel 31:8-13) after their deaths in battle with the Philistines. The temple unearthed at the site also may be the Temple of Dagon, where Saul and Jonathan's armor and heads were exhibited (1 Chronicles 10:10). In addition, Beth Shan was also known as Scythopolis, one of the ten cities of the Decapolis (*deca* = ten; *polis* = city) in the first century AD. Today, nine of the ten cities of the Decapolis (Matthew 4:25; Mark 5:20; 7:31) have been positively identified. Many of them are in Jordan, including Philadelphia, Scythopolis, Damascus, Hippos, Raphana, Gadara, Pella, Abila, and Gerasa. The identification of the city of Dion (thought to be Tell el-Ashari) remains uncertain.
Kurkh Monolith Inscription	The stele inscription was discovered in the Turkish village of Kurkh. It was erected by the Assyrian king Shalmaneser III to commemorate in part his victory at the battle of Qarqar, which is not mentioned in the Bible. The stele records the ninth-century BC battle in which Israel's king Ahab is mentioned to have contributed "2,000 chariots, 10,000 foot soldiers" to a military alliance.
Winged Bull of Sargon II	The Bible only mentions Sargon one time (Isaiah 20:1), and his name was unmentioned in any source outside the Bible, causing critics to question whether he even existed. However, while excavating what is now known as Sargon's Palace at Khorsabad in 1843, Paul-Emile Botta unearthed a massive 10-ton, 15-foot-high sculpture known as a *lamassu* (winged bull with human head) of Sargon II (722–705 BC). The text within the sculpture chronicles Sargon's capture of Samaria (Isaiah 20:6) and his title, ancestry, and achievements as king. One inscription reads, "I besieged and conquered Samaria.... I led away captive 27,280 people." After deporting the Israelites he imported other peoples into the area along with their religions. Because of this foreign influence in Samaria, by the time Jesus arrived in the first century the Jews and Samaritans were mortal enemies (John 4:9), in part because of the perceived impure genetic mixture and heretical religious beliefs.

Black Obelisk of Shalmaneser III	Discovered by A.H. Layard in the palace of Nimrud, this ninth-century BC obelisk illustrates the military victories of Assyrian king Shalmaneser III (858–824 BC). Worthy of note is that one panel depicts Jehu (or Joram) bowing before Shalmaneser III (not to be confused with Assyrian king Shalmaneser V, mentioned in 2 Kings 17:3-6) while making an alliance or paying tribute (2 Kings 8-10). The inscription reads, "Tribute of Yaua (Jehu or Joram), house of Omri, I received silver, gold, a golden bowl, a golden vase with pointed bottom, golden tumblers, golden buckets, tin, a staff for a king, spears."
Ziggurat at Ur	The remains of a massive ziggurat located at the biblical city of Ur (now Tell al-Muqayyar) were discovered in 1924 by Sir Leonard Woolley. This was a structure Abraham would have been familiar with (Genesis 11:1-9,27-29). Its discovery also supports the plausibility of the Tower of Babel events mentioned in Genesis 11:1-9.
Royal Steward Inscription	In 1870, Charles Clermont-Ganneau located a tomb lintel inscription in Jerusalem, adjacent to the Temple Mount near the Kidron Valley. The partial name inscribed on the lintel appears to be that of an eighth-century BC biblical figure named Shebna. According to the inscription, Shebna was the steward over the household of King Hezekiah. Isaiah mentions this man as living above his means and says he carved out a tomb for himself in a very conspicuous place (Isaiah 22:15-19). The words of the inscription implore passersby to not open the tomb since no silver or gold was contained inside.
Cylinder of Nabonidus	In 1854, as J.E. Taylor inspected the ancient ruins and ziggurat of the biblical city of Ur, he found four clay cuneiform cylinders written by Babylonian king Nabonidus (sixth century BC) that documented the history of the ziggurat and various renovations to buildings. Toward the end of the inscription, Nabonidus offers a prayer for long life for himself and his son Belshazzar! Daniel 5 records that King Belshazzar saw the handwriting on the wall that spelled his doom, and it was only Daniel who could translate the inscription. Prior to this discovery, critics thought the Bible was in error when referring to Belshazzar as "king" (Daniel 5:1), since no extrabiblical sources recorded him on the Babylonian kings list. Now we understand that Belshazzar was Nabonidus's son; he was left in Babylon as a co-regent king since his father was away a great deal of the time. This also explains why Daniel could rise no higher than "third ruler" in the kingdom (Daniel 5:29)—Nabonidus and Belshazzar were king and co-regent respectively.
Prayer of Nabonidus	Interestingly, an Aramaic document was recovered from among the Dead Sea Scrolls (4Q242). It is now known as "The Prayer of Nabonidus." The prayer was most likely copied from an older version of the work sometime during the first century BC. It is written in the first person and tells of Nabonidus's affliction with an ulcer for seven years while he was at Tema.

The prayer mentions that it was an exorcist—a *Jew from among the exiles of Judah*—who ultimately forgave his sins. He begins to recount the story of his approach to the gods and then the rest of the text is missing. At very least, we see here an independent corroboration of the books of Jeremiah (Jeremiah 29:10-12) and Daniel (Daniel 9:2), when they report that the Jews lived in Babylonian captivity during the sixth century BC. The prayer also provides a historical and social background consistent with the books of Esther, Ezra, and Nehemiah.

Royal Bricks

Several biblical kings have engaged in enormous building campaigns (for example, Nebuchadnezzar, as recorded in Daniel 4:30), leaving monuments and inscriptions to their achievements. The clay bricks used to build many of these structures contain either a stamp or handwritten inscription bearing the name of the builder. Archaeologists have located over a half-dozen kinds of these bricks, belonging to biblical kings such as Shalmaneser, Sargon, Esarhaddon, Nebuchadnezzar, Cyrus, and others.

Ekron Inscription

In 1996, Seymour Gitin and Trude Dothan unearthed a seventh-century BC inscription at the Philistine city of Ekron that provided the names of two individuals, Achish and Padi, who served as kings of the city. First Samuel 21:11 and 27:2 tell of David fleeing from Saul and joining Achish, the king of Gath. Though the Achish of the Ekron inscription is not the same person as the Achish who lived earlier, during David's time, it shows a remarkable continuity of names that spans centuries within Philistine culture. The other individual mentioned in the Ekron inscription, Padi, is referred to several times in the Taylor Prism (Sennacherib's annals of his Judean military campaigns against Hezekiah in 701 BC) as the man Sennacherib established as a vassal king over Ekron.

The annals of Sennacherib also record that the inhabitants of Ekron surrendered Padi to Hezekiah since the Philistine remained loyal to the Assyrian vassalage. The annals tells of King Hezekiah placing Padi under arrest for a short time (between 705–701 BC) before he was reappointed as Assyria's vassal king by Sennacherib in Ekron. Though Padi is not mentioned in the Bible, the Ekron and Taylor Prism inscriptions offer us insight into the events behind the scenes during the time when King Hezekiah was confronted by the Assyrian war machine led by Sennacherib (2 Kings 18–19).

Azekah Inscription

Two tablets discovered in Nineveh contain the history of the Assyrian attack (either by Sargon II or Sennacherib) on the biblical city of Azekah (2 Chronicles 32:1-2,21-22). The inscriptions describe in vivid terms the Assyrians' siege of the city and mention by name King Hezekiah as the individual who fortified Azekah. The tablets provide historical attestation to Hezekiah's existence and the Assyrian wars in Judah during the late eighth century BC, as the Bible records in 2 Kings 18-19 and 2 Chronicles 32.

Altar of Jeroboam I	Excavations at Tell Dan (originally known as Laish) have revealed many fascinating features relating to the Old Testament times. These include the Tell Dan Stele, which for the first time in modern history provided an extrabiblical mention of the "house of David"; the oldest intact mud-brick gate structure yet found, which dates to the time of the patriarchs (Middle Bronze Age); and one of two altars established by Jeroboam I in Dan and Bethel. This place of worship, discovered by archaeologist Avraham Biran, included a golden calf. The Bible reports it was instituted by Jeroboam (1 Kings 12:25-31) as a substitute location of worship (instead of Jerusalem) for those living in the northern ten tribes of Israel. Jeroboam's negative religious reforms included acting as high priest himself, allowing unqualified persons to serve as priests, and changing the date of the Feast of Tabernacles (1 Kings 12:31-33).
The Weld-Blundell Prism	In 1922, English archaeologist Herbert Weld-Blundell led an expedition to Larsa (Iraq), where he discovered an ancient clay prism containing a list of Sumerian kings who ruled from 3200 BC to 1800 BC. The text makes reference to the kings who ruled "before the flood" and "after the flood." What is more, the list supports the Genesis account by describing extremely long life spans prior to the Flood (Genesis 5:27) and reduced life spans afterward. The four-sided prism is written in the Old Akkadian cuneiform language and currently resides in the Ashmolean Museum of Art and Archaeology at the University of Oxford. Nearly two dozen other archaeological and literary finds from various ethnic groups also attest to a catastrophic flood that destroyed mankind except for a surviving family or individual. The prism's extraordinary parallel with the Genesis account of Noah and the Flood (Genesis 6–9) adds independent corroboration to the historicity of the event.
Ras Shamra Tablets	In 1928, a farmer (Brahim) in northern Syria accidently discovered a vault in his field. Later this area would be known as Ras Shamra due to the expedition and excavation led by F.A. Schaeffer and George Chenet. Then in 1929, archaeologists unearthed a scribal school and library adjoining a temple. The fifteenth-century BC tablets found at the location contained a script previously unknown to scholars, but it soon would be understood to be Canaanite, a language similar to Hebrew. The tablets describe the dark religious practices of the Canaanite peoples indigenous to the land prior to Joshua's conquest. These wicked practices offer confirmation of the deities, practices, laws, and religious beliefs and customs of the heathen described in the Old Testament, which include 1) the burying alive of children, 2) child sacrifice of other kinds, 3) male and female religious prostitution, 4) the malice and jealousy among the gods, 5) absence of morality among the gods, and 6) idol worship among others. Moreover, these tablets have provided an answer to the critical argument that denied the possibility of Moses writing a sophisticated religious law code as early as 1440 to 1400 BC. In addition, the Ras Shamra tablets have contributed

to our understanding of the development of the Hebrew script from about 1500 BC to the modern day. This discovery has also dealt a blow to negative higher critics who asserted that Aramaic words included in Moses' writings did not develop until after the exile to Babylon (sixth century BC). Several Aramaisms were found in the Ugaritic texts, which are contemporary with Moses, which refutes this notion.

The Madaba Map	Originally obscured in an earthquake in the eighth century AD, a Greek mosaic floor map was accidently rediscovered during the construction of a Greek Orthodox church in 1884. Currently, the map is located on the floor of the St. George Greek Orthodox Church in Madaba, Jordan. It lists the names of important biblical cities and landmarks, including Jerusalem, and their orientation in relation to various geographical features such as the Dead Sea and the Jordan River. Dating to the mid sixth century AD, it remains the oldest surviving map of the Holy Land. Its value has been confirmed by archaeologists, who utilize it to locate places of interest. For example, the central *Cardo* thoroughfare with its pillars and road in Jerusalem, the Damascus Gate, the Nea Church, and the location of Ashkelon were found to be in the exact locations described by the map.
Nuzi Tablets	In the early twentieth century, American archaeologists began excavating Nuzi (in northern Iraq), a developed Hurrian administrative center first settled around 3000 BC. Here, they discovered archives containing thousands of clay cuneiform tablets (dated to 1500 to 1350 BC) that record various social institutions, religious codes, family records, inheritance rights, marriage arrangements, birthrights, and so on. Contradicting critics' claims that Genesis was written at a much later time, the texts describe practices similar to those recorded in Genesis 15–31, including 1) the sale of birthrights (Genesis 25:29-34); 2) the choosing of a surrogate wife by a barren wife (Genesis 16:5); 3) laws of sistership (Genesis 20:12; 26:7); 4) inheritance of personal belongings; 5) adoption of slaves; 6) marriage arrangements; 7) deathbed blessings (Genesis 27; 48); 7) the care for children and surrogate mothers (Genesis 21); and 8) how a family's name is carried on when no genetic heir is found (Genesis 15:2).

The practices described in these tablets may explain why Abraham was reluctant to expel Hagar and Ishmael (Genesis 21:10-11), and why Abraham adopted a slave (Eliezer), relative or freeborn, to care for him in his elderly years, carry on his name, and inherit his possessions (Genesis 15:2-4; 24). The Nuzi texts' close parallel to the cultural practices of the patriarchs confirm that the Genesis narratives are historical because they fit the cultural practices of their time. Furthermore, the archives at Nuzi confirm that written records pertaining to family were faithfully kept through the centuries.

| Ebla Tablets | By the early 1970s, excavations conducted in northern Syria at Tell-Mardikh had yielded more than 15,000 clay tablets that provided scholars with additional knowledge of an otherwise unknown empire called *Ebla*. The Ebla tablets, dating to 2300 BC, provided researchers with early and rare information of the language, religion, geography, culture, and customs of the patriarchal period, roughly spanning the time from 3300 to 1600 BC.

Previous to this discovery, critical scholars argued that many of the words used in the Genesis stories were developed late, long after the stories Genesis describes, and therefore the text could not have been written any earlier than around 700 BC. However, the tablets changed this critical climate when it was recognized that the patriarchal narratives found in Genesis accurately utilized or reflected many of the words, names, customs, and locations found in the earlier Ebla tablets. This eliminates the notion of late word origination and supports Genesis as accurately reflecting the ancient world prior to 700 BC. In addition, personal names, locations, and deities found in the tablets are also mentioned in Genesis and the Old Testament. Names such as Adam, Ishmael, Israel, and Eber, as well as locations such as Megiddo, Hazor, Gaza, Dor, Zared, Nahor, Shechem, and Jerusalem, and deities such as Dagon, El, Baal, Molech, Ya, and others, are consistent with the accounts of Genesis and the Old Testament and buttress their historical reliability. |

Chart © Joseph M. Holden, 2013.

Conclusion

While an exhaustive study of the reliability of the Old Testament is outside the scope of this chapter,* we have considered some of the most salient objections. Still other issues, such as the historicity of Daniel or problems confronting morality, could be considered; but the foregoing examples have served, we believe, as helpful case studies for showing that critical objections usually have some initial appeal, but upon further scrutiny they do not hold up. [4]

---

* For a more exhaustive study and a passage-by-passage assessment of Bible difficulties for both the Old and the New Testaments, we refer the reader to Norman L. Geisler and Thomas A. Howe, *The Big Book of Bible Difficulties* (Grand Rapids, MI: Baker, 1992).

THE CANON OF THE OLD TESTAMENT

Virtually all scholars agree that there is an established canon of books that comprise the Old Testament, though the canon's development and extent are a matter of dispute between Roman Catholics and Protestants. The *canon*, as we shall discuss here, refers to the divinely inspired writings of the 39 books of the Old Testament accepted by Judaism and all sections of Christianity.

As scholars have sought to understand the historical process of Old Testament canonization, they have generally proposed successive criteria that a text had to meet: It must be 1) inspired by God; 2) recognized as inspired by men of God; and 3) collected and preserved by the people of God. [1] In this sense, the books of Scripture that were inspired by God and written through men possess a self-authenticating nature. The books' authoritative nature is not given to them because they were included in the canon; rather, they are recognized by the Israelite nation as possessing divine authority; therefore, they were included in the canon. After the publication of a prophetic message, the work would be recognized as divinely inspired by the people of God and would then be preserved and copied for future generations.

Transmission and Collection of Biblical Materials

The earliest techniques of transmission of biblical materials were oral. In Deuteronomy, Moses commanded the people of Israel to teach their children and future generations the laws and statutes of God. These oral-transmission traditions were later written down for the sake of preserving the sacred message, thus ensuring their accuracy. The biblical text reflects a high reverence given to the Law of Moses. The Old Testament also contains evidence of biblical authors referencing earlier biblical writings (for example, Daniel 9:2), as well as rebukes to Israel for not obeying what was previously written.

Scholars have recognized that after the destruction of the first Temple a renewed emphasis on the collection and study of Scripture emerged. Sanders states that it was this major event that brought about the collections of what we now know as the Law and the Prophets. According to tradition, prophecy ceased in Israel around 400 BC after the death of the last prophets (Haggai, Zechariah, and Malachi). The Holy Spirit ceased to communicate to Israel directly through the prophets. Because of these circumstances, the people relied upon *bath kol* (literally "daughter of a voice"). *Bath kol* was not considered as authoritative as the prophets' teachings, but was "a voice [that] fell from heaven" without the personal or physical manifestation of the messenger (for example, Daniel 5:31; Matthew 3:17). With this Jewish tradition in place, scholars such as R.K. Harrison argue that the canon was probably completed by about 300 BC. No further books were being added as Scripture.

Divisions of the Hebrew Bible

The Hebrew Bible now has three recognized divisions: the Law (Torah), the Prophets (Nevi'im), and the Writings (Ketuvim), forming the consonantal acronym *TaNaK*. Sometime prior to Christ's ministry this threefold designation was in use (Luke 24:27,44). Some scholars believe that the Hebrew Scriptures were canonized in these three stages in accordance to their dates of composition: the Law around 400 BC, the Prophets around 200 BC, and the Writings approximately AD 100. This assumption is, however, unlikely due to the fact that more recent scholarship dates the Old Testament canon as having been finalized between the fourth century and second century BC. What is more, some of the books and passages in the Old Testament were quoted as "Scripture" (Matthew 21:42), "words of the Lord" (Daniel 9:2), or "the Spirit says" (Matthew 22:43-44) prior to the dates proposed above (Ephesians 4:8; see also Psalm 68:18; Acts 13:35; see also Psalm 16:10). Other theories have been put forward, one of which states that the Old Testament canon was not finalized until the Council of Jamnia (Jabneh) around AD 90, which has been refuted by Roger Beckwith. [2]

There is, however, much evidence that supports the claim that the Old Testament was originally canonized in a twofold division between the Law (the first five books) and the Prophets (seventeen books). The way in which the historical books are linked together as one unit supports this claim, as well as the fact that the New Testament most commonly refers to the Old Testament as "the Law and Prophets." This was the standard way to refer to the Old Testament in even Old Testament times (see Zechariah 7:12; see also Daniel 9:2,10-12), during the intertestamental period (2 Maccabees 15:9), in the Qumran community just before the time of Christ (*Manual of Discipline* 9.11), and by Jesus and New Testament writers (see Matthew 5:17; Luke 16:31). Indeed, Luke 24:27 refers to "Law and Prophets" as "all the Scriptures."

While some believe that the third category (the Writings) was created for liturgical reasons to accord with the Jewish festal year, it, this tripartite division of the Old Testament may have resulted from topical arrangement into legal, historical, and nonhistorical books. There are possible allusions to an early threefold division in the prologue to Ecclesiasticus (Ben Sira or Sirach) in the middle of the second century BC, where the writer refers to "the law and the prophets and the other books of our fathers," though this last category is undefined and may not even be a reference to inspired books. The alleged New Testament reference to a threefold division (Luke 24:44) does not refer to a third section called "Writings." Rather, it probably singles out "Psalms" for their messianic significance.

Sequence of Canonical Recognition

The first section of the Hebrew Bible, the Law or Pentateuch, may be the first section of the Bible to be written and recognized as canonical, which would explain why it is referenced numerous times throughout the rest of the Old Testament. There is no doubt that the Pentateuch was recognized as complete and canonical by the time of Ezra and Nehemiah in the fifth century BC. There is also good reason to believe that it had been regarded as such even earlier. With the Hebrew Bible being translated into the Greek language by the mid-second century BC, the Pentateuch became a part of the Septuagint Bible (LXX); the Samaritans deviated from the Jews shortly thereafter with the creation of their revised version of Moses' writings (the *Samaritan Pentateuch*). The evidence of the Pentateuch's inclusion and preservation reveals that the books of the Law were considered a complete canonical unit within the Old Testament canon.

First-century Jewish historian Josephus does have three categories of books, but he does not call them "Writings" but "four books containing hymns to God and precepts for the conduct of human life."[3] However, the later "Writings" section of the Jewish Old Testament had 11 books in it. While Josephus numbers the total Old Testament books as 22 just before AD 100, nevertheless, these are the same as the 39 books of the Protestant Old Testament. They are just numbered differently (the 12 Minor Prophets are counted as one book and all the double books (Samuel, Kings, Chronicles, and Ezra-Nehemiah) are listed as one book each. Also, the 22 books of Josephus are the same as the later 24 books of the Jewish Old Testament, for Ruth was attached to the end of Judges and Lamentations to the end of Jeremiah in order to number the books at 22, the same number of letters as in the Hebrew alphabet. There has been no doubt that these books made up the Hebrew Old Testament canon. Individual attestations provide evidence of their canonicity from the first century AD or earlier. What this implies is that there has been an established canon of the Hebrew Old Testament since before the Christian era.

The final threefold division of the Old Testament—Law (5), Prophets (8), and Writings (11)—did not come until the time of the Mishnah (*Baba Bathra*) in the fifth century AD.

It is also worthy of note that the Old Testament books were most likely immediately adopted as the Word of God by the people of God very soon after they were written. When Moses wrote his book it was preserved inside the Ark of the Covenant in the Tabernacle (Deuteronomy 31:9). Joshua's books were added to it (Joshua 24:26). Later, we see that Daniel had the Law and the Prophets up to his time, including the contemporary prophet Jeremiah (Daniel 9:2,6,10-11). Still later Zechariah spoke of "the law and... the former prophets" (Zechariah 7:12). So, the books of the Old Testament were recognized by the people of God immediately, though the *official* divisions of the Scriptures took over a thousand years to establish.* This immediate acceptance of the Hebrew Scriptures is supported by more than 2600 claims within the text that it is divinely

---

* This was primarily due to God's progressive revelation to Israel, which began with Moses (1400 BC) and culminated with Malachi (400 BC).

inspired.* This, along with appropriate content, would be enough to immediately bring the acceptance of the Scriptures in the eyes of the Jews.

The Intertestamental Period and the Apocrypha

There has been much dispute throughout church history about the validity and inspiration of the texts written during the intertestamental period (the 400-year period of time between the end of the Old Testament and the beginning of the New Testament).

The Pseudepigrapha

One group of writings that has been universally rejected by all in the church is the *Pseudepigrapha*. These books are seen as unauthentic in regard to the overall content and authorship. The pseudepigraphal works claim to be written by biblical authors and to be authoritative, but their contents reveal nothing of the sort. These books were written as early as 200 BC to as late as AD 200. These writings are known in Roman Catholic circles as the Apocrypha—which is not to be confused with the same term used by the Protestant church to identify a completely different group of books (see below). The pseudepigraphal books are comprised of visions, dreams, and revelations in the style of apocalyptic literature found in Ezekiel, Daniel, and Zechariah.

The Apocrypha

A similar group of books, known to Protestants as the *Apocrypha* (meaning "hidden" or "doubtful"), have been accepted by some in the church, though others view them as extrabiblical. These books were translated into the Greek language and added to the Septuagint in the third century BC along with the rest of the Hebrew Bible. The close pairing with the Septuagint led some early church leaders to regard the writings found in the Apocrypha as nearly or just as authoritative as the rest of the Old Testament Scriptures. Eleven of the fourteen Apocryphal books were instituted as inspired canonical texts (called *deuterocanonical*, meaning "second canon") by the Roman Catholic Church in 1546 at the Council of Trent during the Counter-Reformation period. This may have been due to pressures resulting from the Protestant Reformation; the Church hoped to present scriptural support for purgatory, prayer for the dead, and justification by works.

The discovery of the Dead Sea Scrolls at Qumran has given insight into the historical view of the Apocryphal books. Interestingly, there were no commentaries found in the caves at Qumran on any book within the Apocrypha. Only the canonical biblical books were found, written on special parchment in the sacred script. Based on the findings at Qumran, the Apocrypha was not viewed as canonical by the Qumran community. It was only during and after the time of Augustine (AD 354–430), when he, along with the local councils he influenced, declared the books of the Apocrypha inspired, that they gained wider usage and, eventually, inclusion in the Roman Catholic Church's canon as infallible. Even here, Augustine's reasons for inclusion in the canon appear to be sentimental and not theological; he declared the books to be canonical because of the glorious martyrs included in the texts. By contrast, the books of the Hebrew Bible

---

* Of the 2,600-plus claims of divine inspiration, 680 are found in the Pentateuch, 418 in the historical books, 195 in poetical books, and 1,307 in the prophetic literature.

were received into the canon, quoted often, and had long been generally recognized as inspired and authoritative texts.[4]

It is also interesting to note that Jesus and the apostles never directly quote from the books of the Apocrypha, even though it is likely that they were included in the Septuagint Bibles Jesus and the apostles used. This was because they knew the Apocrypha was not inspired and there had been no prophet to speak to the people, by the text's own admission (1 Maccabees 9:27; 14:41).

Negatives and Positives of the Apocrypha

There are also instances of historical and doctrinal errors found in the Apocrypha. For example, there are references to Nebuchadnezzar as the king of Assyria, reigning at Nineveh, rather than as king of Babylon and reigning from that city (Judith 1:15). Further, the Jews were said to be in Babylon for "seven generations" (Baruch 6:2), rather than 70 years as stated in Jeremiah 25:11. The use of superstition and magic is condoned when it is said that the smoke from a fish's heart will drive away evil spirits (Tobit 6:5-7). Moreover, salvation by works (for example, giving of alms) is put forth as a legitimate method of deliverance from sin and gaining right standing before God (Tobit 4:11; 12:9). What is more, money (silver) is given as a sacrifice for the sins of the dead (2 Maccabees 12:43). Other passages contradict the teachings that are found in the rest of the Old Testament, such as those Apocryphal verses that mention purgatory and prayer for the dead, which are nowhere else mentioned.

It seems apparent as well that none of the books of the Apocrypha ever claim to be divinely inspired. Phrases such as "Hear the word of the LORD" are never found in the Apocrypha, whereas this phrase is common in the rest of the Old Testament Scriptures. Based on evidence like this, one can conclude that the writers were being careful to avoid having their writings viewed as inspired Scripture.

The Apocryphal books do contain a good amount of historical information pertaining to the nation of Israel during the intertestamental period, and some people have valued them for their homiletic and historical qualities. These books do give good insight on the history of the Jews during the silent period (400 BC to the time of Christ) and are a valid witness to Second Temple Judaism. They are also regarded by some as an essential resource in appreciating the Jewishness of Jesus and of the early Christian movement that began in His name.

Acceptance or Rejection of the Apocrypha

The books do deserve to be read and studied for their own merits—not as inspired Scripture, but as we would study any other ancient written historical account. This approach is evident among the early Church Fathers. Even though Augustine accepted the Apocrypha, Jerome, who knew the languages of Scripture and was the translator of the Latin Vulgate Bible (AD 405) rejected them; he reluctantly made a translation of part of the Apocrypha to be added to the Vulgate. The vast majority of Church Fathers (from AD 100 to AD 400) rejected the canonicity of the books, including Origen, Cyril, and Athanasius.

Based on, as mentioned, Augustine's acceptance of the Apocryphal books (c. AD 400) and those he influenced after that time, the Roman Catholic Church has accepted 11 of the 14 Apocryphal books into the Old Testament:

1. The Wisdom of Solomon (c. 30 BC)

2. Ecclesiasticus (Sirach) (c. 132 BC)

3. Tobit (c. 200 BC)

4. Judith (c. 150 BC)

5. 1 Maccabees (c. 110 BC)

6. 2 Maccabees (c. 110–70 BC)

7. Baruch (c. 150–50 BC)

8. Addition to Esther (140–130 BC)

9. Prayer of Azariah (second or first century BC) (included in Roman Catholic Bibles as Daniel 3:24-90)

10. Susanna (second or first century BC) (included in Roman Catholic Bibles as Daniel 13)

11. Bel and the Dragon (c. 100 BC) (included in Roman Catholic Bibles as Daniel 14)

The other three Apocryphal books are

1. The Prayer of Manasses

2. 1 Esdras

3. 2 Esdras

Jews and Protestants, however, have rejected the Apocrypha because 1) It does not claim to be inspired by God; 2) it was not written by prophets of God (1 Maccabees 9:27); 3) it was not confirmed by supernatural acts of God (Hebrews 2:3-4); 4) it does not always tell the truth of God—for example, it supports praying for the dead (2 Maccabees 12:46) and working for salvation (Tobit 12:9); 5) it was not accepted by the people of God (Judaism); 6) it was not accepted by Jesus, the Son of God (Matthew 5:17-18; Luke 24:27), who never once cited it; 7) it was not accepted by the apostles of God (who did not ever quote it); 8) it was not accepted by the early church of God;* 9) it was rejected by the great Catholic translator of the Word of God (Jerome); 10) it was not

---

* Most early Church Fathers rejected the Apocrypha. Of the few who cited it, Roger Beckwith, authority on the Old Testament canon, noted that "when one examines the passages in the early Fathers which are supposed to establish the canonicity of the Apocrypha, one finds that some of them are taken from the alternative Greek text of Ezra (1 Esdras) or from additions or appendices to Daniel, Jeremiah or some other canonical book, which…are not really relevant; that others of them are not quotations from the Apocrypha at all; and that, of those which are, many do not give any indication that the book is regarded as Scripture" (Roger Beckwith, *The Old Testament Canon of the New Testament Church* [Eugene, OR: Wipf & Stock Publishers, 2008], 387).

written during the period of the Old Testament prophets of God. According to Jewish teaching, the line of Jewish Old Testament prophets ended by 400 BC; the Apocrypha was written starting in 200 BC. Josephus declared, "From Artaxerxes [fourth century BC] until our time everything has been recorded, but has not been deemed worthy of like credit with what preceded, because the exact succession of the prophets ceased."[5] The Jewish Talmud adds, "With the death of Haggai, Zechariah and Malachi the latter prophets, the Holy Spirit ceased out of Israel."[6]

In spite of all this evidence, the Roman Catholic Church officially and infallibly added these books to their Old Testament in AD 1546. But Protestants point out that this canonization was unfounded because it was done 1) by the wrong group (Christians, not Jews); 2) at the wrong time (about 1,700 years late!); 3) on the wrong basis (on the authority of the *Church*, not on the authority of *God* (for example, through a prophet of God); and 4) for the wrong reason: to help the Roman Church defend its dogma (such as prayers for the dead) against Protestants. For example, the Church accepted 2 Maccabees, which supports praying for the dead: "It is therefore a holy and wholesome thought to pray for the dead that they may be loosed from their sins" (2 Maccabees 12:45[46]). But it rejected 2[4] Esdras, which was against it: "Just as a father does not send his son...to be ill or sleep or eat or be healed in his stead, so no one shall ever pray for another on that day ["when they shall be separated from their mortal body"—verse 88]" (2[4] Esdras 7:105).

The New Testament Authors' Reverence for the Old Testament Canon

The inspiration of the Old Testament as a whole is evidenced by the way the New Testament authors used the Old Testament Scriptures. Scholars have noted that the amount of Old Testament quotations found making up the New Testament is from about 4 percent to 10 percent. The percentage depends on whether one includes allusions and parallel references to the Hebrew texts as well as direct, word-for-word quotations. It is without doubt that the New Testament authors viewed the Hebrew Scriptures as authoritative and divinely inspired. The writings of these authors are never in conflict with what the Old Testament says; rather, they complement and reveal the fulfillment of the Hebrew text by clarifying to us its application and original intent. Jesus displays a great example of this in His Sermon on the Mount (Matthew 5:21-43). Here He explicitly tells His disciples that He has come not to abolish the law, but to fulfill it; He applies the Hebrew Scriptures in a deeper and broader way than had been done previously.

The New Testament authors held the Hebrew Bible in very high reverence down to the letter, basing whole arguments on a single word*—and in some cases the grammatical form of a single word, as in Galatians 3:16. Even the formulas used by the authors when introducing direct quotes from the Old Testament give insight into their view of the Scriptures. These formulas reflect a strong belief in the canonicity and binding nature of the words uttered in the Old Testament. Statements such as "It is written..."

---

* See Matthew 2:15; 4:10; 13:35; 22:44; Mark 12:36; Luke 4:8; 20:42-43; John 8:17; 10:34; 19:37; Acts 23:5; Romans 4:3,9,23; 15:9-12; 1 Corinthians 6:16; Galatians 3:8,10,13; Hebrews 1:7; 2:12; 3:13; 4:7; 12:26.

assume the authority, finality, binding nature, and eternity of the Scriptures.* This phrase is used more than 90 times in the New Testament and is often placed by the author in the Greek perfect tense (which indicates a completed *past* action with abiding results in the *present*), meaning the Scripture was completely written in the *past* and continues in the *present* to be the binding, written Word of God, thus referring to its eternal nature. In other words, there will never be a time when the Scriptures will not be the Word of God.

To reinforce this point, the formulas used in the New Testament also convey the conviction of the writers that the Hebrew Scriptures were indeed applicable to their contemporary audiences. That is to say, the Scriptures of the Old Testament possessed eternal contemporaneity. In regard to quotations or references, the New Testament uses present-tense verbs such as "He says" as opposed to "He said"; it directs the force of these passages squarely upon the readers by using pronouns such as "we" and "you," as opposed to other pronouns such as "them."† The apostle Paul echoes this view in Romans 15:4, when he states that what was written in the Old Testament Scriptures was written for our learning and example (see also 1 Corinthians 10:6).

The Stamp of Authority

The New Testament authors also show reverence for the Old Testament Scriptures by using interchangeable language describing what the Scripture says and what God says. Their formulas usually are seen in phrases such as "the Scripture says…" or "God [or "the Spirit"] says…." For example, God instructs Moses to speak to Pharaoh, "Thus says the LORD the God of the Hebrews…" (Exodus 9:13,16 NKJV), but in Romans 9:17 Paul writes of the same passage and says, "The Scripture says to Pharaoh…." Other examples of such interchangeable language are found in Genesis 2:24 and Matthew 19:4-5; Psalm 2:1 and Acts 4:24-25; and Isaiah 55:3 and Acts 13:34). The equating of Scripture's speaking with God's speaking shows the utmost regard for the Scriptures as being God-breathed, thus revealing the very mind of God Himself. With this said, it is important to note that Jews would make an ontological distinction between God and His Word. Jews would find it highly inappropriate to worship the Scripture as God since they are not equals, and this would certainly be considered a form of idolatry known as "bibliolatry." The Scriptures, though inerrant, infallible, and authoritative, are an expression of God's voice to reveal Himself (John 5:39), give us examples (1 Corinthians 10:6), sanctify His church (John 17:17), and to thoroughly equip and instruct the people of God (2 Timothy 3:16-17).

Their prolific use of the Old Testament demonstrates that the New Testament authors revered the Scriptures as the highest written authority among mankind. These writers employed the Old Testament texts in a variety of different ways, using them in their sermons, prayers, and historical accounts; when addressing Jews and Gentiles; in churches for exhortation as well as rebuke.

---

* See John 7:38,42; 15:25; 19:37; Romans 4:3; 7:7; 9:17; 10:11; 11:2; 1 Corinthians 14:24; 2 Corinthians 6:2; Galatians 3:8; 4:30; 1 Timothy 5:18; James 2:23; 4:5.

† See Matthew 15:7; 22:31; Mark 7:6; 12:19; Acts 4:11; 13:47; Hebrews 10:15; 12:5.

We can conclude with no more significant example than Jesus Himself. When Satan tempted Him in the wilderness, He appealed to the authority of the Old Testament Scriptures to rebuke the tempter (Matthew 4:4,7,10). Jesus regularly referred to them in His ministry: when speaking to His opponents (John 5:39); quoting it in prayers; during His most intense times of suffering on the cross (Matthew 27:46); as well as in His resurrected glory (Luke 24:45-46). Down to the words (Matthew 22:43, see also 1 Corinthians 2:13), the tenses of the verbs (Matthew 22:32, see also Galatians 3:16), and the smallest parts of the words (Matthew 5:17-18), He unabashedly endorsed the divine authority of the Hebrew Old Testament Bible.

PART THREE

THE RELIABILITY OF NEW TESTAMENT MANUSCRIPTS

In this part, we will survey the manuscripts of the New Testament: both their transmission process and the individual manuscripts produced by that process. We will also consider objections to the reliability of the New Testament. Special attention will be given to this point because of recent publications that advocate the view that there are errors in the New Testament, especially those books put forth by New Testament scholar Bart Ehrman. We will begin with a look at the transmission process, since it has come under recent attack.

THE TRANSMISSION OF THE NEW TESTAMENT

In the age of classical antiquity, scribes served a crucial function in the production of literary and nonliterary works. They were employed within Mesopotamia, Egypt, Israel, and the Greco-Roman Empire. Professional scribes, who were trained craftsman, were commonly employed in the commercial book trade or for a library or government post. Many of these professional copyists had expertise in fine bookhand or calligraphy. Still other scribes were amateur copyists or even educated slaves. Customarily, scribes were paid not only by the length of the text, but also by the type of hand used, which affected the quality of the product. Thus, the work of professional scribes commanded higher pay but also produced higher-quality work, which became very important in the explicability of historical texts.

Scribes were responsible for copying such items as books, petitions, receipts, letters, and deeds. Nevertheless their greatest achievement of the last 2,000 years is seen in the craftsmanship of the reproduction of the New Testament manuscripts.

Scribal Function and Practices

A scribe was a skilled copyist. Scribes were responsible for hand-writing both a new copy or first draft of a manuscript, and also a *fair copy*. A new copy was produced from direct oral dictation by an author or lector. As the lector spoke clearly and at a moderate pace, the scribe, sometimes called a secretary, would copy every word until the piece was completed. After that point, communication between the author and the scribe was critical. The author would examine the text and make revisions as needed, and then the scribe would create a new copy called a fair copy, or final draft. In the case of a New Testament manuscript, a fair copy would be made for the author, such as Paul, and also for the congregation to which the letter or book would be read aloud. Finally, a copy would be made available for others to copy; in this way the manuscript was published. The work of scribes would continue as additional copies would be made by various copyists. Since there was no notion of copyright in the ancient world, scribes could even make a copy for themselves.

The practice of the scribe was to sit on the ground or upon a small bench or stool with legs crossed, with the bottom of his tunic extended across his knees. This provided a flat surface on which to lay his scroll, which was held in position with his left hand. These scrolls were most commonly made of papyrus, which was utilized from about 2100 BC, or parchment made from animal skin, which began to be used later in the fourth century AD. Parchment was popular for the creation of codices (ancient books, as opposed to scrolls) and is referenced in Revelation 5:1, 2 John 12, and 2 Timothy 4:13.

After taking up position, the scribe would then take a pen and penknife (3 John 13), dip the pen in ink contained in an inkhorn, and commence writing. The ink used for papyrus was black, carbon-based, and made from soot, water, and gum. The ink used for parchment could be made from nut galls, water, iron, and gum arabic. As the ink on the text aged, it became a brownish-rust color. At the ending of the fourth century AD this kind of ink was also used on papyrus. Other materials employed by scribes included a ruler, a straight edge, a thin lead disk, compasses, a sponge, and a piece of pumice stone. With pen and scroll in hand, the scribe would sit ready under the guiding voice of the lector.

Papyrus stalks are a familiar sight to Egyptians on the Nile River. Manuscripts written on papyrus are rare. (Photo by Zev Radovan.)

The papyrus would be lined (much like our standard notebook paper) by using the horizontal fibers of the sheet as a guide. On parchment, scribes would mark the sheet and then draw both horizontal and two or more vertical lines to signify the margins. One of two types of handwriting, bookhand and ruling hand, was employed. These and many other styles of handwriting can factor in significantly to the dating of a document (see below). Bookhand was a more reformed style, consisting of carefully written upright letters separate from each other, penned in a more fastidious fashion. Ruling hand, or "documentary hand," was executed more quickly and less conscientiously. It was a cursive script and a type of shorthand used mainly for everyday purposes. In this form the use of *ligatures* (joins between letters) was possible, which enabled the scribe to keep his pen to the scroll between letters. Even with ruling hand, the careful penmanship of the scribe allowed for the greater preservation of the text.

In order for a document to be committed to print adequately, the process of dictation to pen had to be done purposefully and slowly. A literary work might have taken a number of days to dictate and then weeks to complete. The time actually used in copying the script might have been between five to six hours a day. In addition to the time spent writing the script, more time was needed to mix the ink, make ready the papyrus, rest the hand, and sharpen the pen nib from time to time. Then editing and writing of the fair copy (or copies) completed the laborious task. The careful writing of Paul's letter to the Roman church by Tertius (Romans 16:22) may have taken two or three weeks or more from the time of dictation to the completion of the final draft (fair copy).

Practical Adjustments

New Testament manuscripts were mostly transcribed by Christians themselves. Due to the value they themselves placed upon the Scriptures they were committed to this craft and became faithful stewards of furthering the gospel to the "ends of the earth." In early times, these manuscripts were not commercially produced but rather copied and shared among small Christian communities and congregations. It is conjectured that many of these scribes actually were not professionals because clear bookhand is found infrequently in documents prior to AD 400; small churches may have not had the means to afford professionals.

Although fine bookhand is not evidenced in early Christian texts, Christians were still found to be fastidious in hand. Warnings from the authors, such as Paul himself, encouraged the faithful and accurate hand of the scribe. Galatians 1:6-9 is only one of the examples of such a warning. Here Paul declares accursed by God anyone who would alter his gospel. In fact Christian scribes made their mark upon paleographic history by developing what has been called a type of "reformed documentary" hand of writing. It was a more reformed ruling hand script because it used fewer ligatures and more precise letter formation than a regular documentary hand.

Christian manuscripts were written primarily for practical use and less for aesthetic purposes. They were orally shared and circulated among Christian congregations, in which a limited number of people enjoyed literacy. In fact, to facilitate public reading, copyists of Christian manuscripts would write fewer lines and letters to the line than was normal in practice.

Another practice distinct to Christian scribes was the scribal convention of the *nomina sacra*. The *nomina sacra* convention created a form of contraction out of a religious word. It abated the written form of these words by contracting the letters or syllables found in the middle of the word and connecting the first and last letters or syllables with a line. It is evident that the mostly illiterate audience to which these Christian manuscripts were addressed was considered by the scribes. One common *nomina sacra* was to use the Greek *chi* (which looks like our English *X*), the first letter of the name *Christ* in Greek, with one of the following letters (for example, the Greek letter for *s* or *r*) and placing a line over the top. For example, "X-mas" means *Christmas*, and this form is most likely how the earliest Christians would have written it! They liked to abbreviate, which saved space and costly writing materials.

The Scriptorium and Other Later Developments

As the church attained sanction from the state in the fourth century AD, the use of the scriptorium became more frequent. The scriptorium was a place used for the production of documents. Rather than dictating a literary work to one scribe, in a scriptorium a lector could dictate the work from the exemplar text to several scribes simultaneously, thus producing many copies. Scribes would sit around the lector, and each would copy the same text as the author read aloud.

Although the scriptorium satisfied the desire for multiple copies in a short amount of time, it also opened the door to more distractions, which sometimes resulted in technical mistakes. A simple cough or sneeze by one of the scribes could interfere with the dictation of the script. Thus, the *corrector* held the invaluable position of examining the scripts for error. After the work was copied, the corrector of the scriptorium would inspect the finished work. The corrector would then correct these mistakes with different ink or secondary placing as needed. Also, during this time (fourth century) commercial book manufacturers were more commonly used to copy New Testament scripts and would use scriptoria to do so. In the scriptorium, scribes were paid by the number of lines written. In AD 301, scribes could receive between 20 and 25 denarii per 100 lines, depending upon the speed and quality of their handiwork.

The dawning of the Byzantine period brought even greater development in the transcribing of the New Testament manuscripts. It was in this time period that monks became beneficiaries of the scribal practice. Unlike copyists of the earlier days of classical antiquity, these scribes did not need the role of the lector in transcribing documents. Although the scriptoria were still in existence, many monks preferred to work privately in their own cells using the exemplar text as their master copy and archetype. Monks closely adhered to the ideology of Jewish scribes found in Deuteronomy 12:32; they were purposefully diligent not to "add" or "take away" from the text.

Scribal practices among monks included several tasks. They would engage in reading, memorizing, and repeating small portions of the text before actually committing the words to its written form. Colophons were notes written by scribes and found at the end of books, which expressed among other things relief from the laborious task. Sometimes colophons would even attest to the physical discomfort of hand or body experienced by the scribe himself.

Although monks primarily copied only for themselves or a benefactor to the monastery, pressure for quality was not only inward—from the importance they themselves bestowed upon the texts—but also from the outside, with rules and punishments enforced within the monastery. Monks were chastised with various penances for making mistakes in the text or showing even simple signs of negligence, such as not handling writing tools responsibly. Although the task of transcribing could prove to be a laborious one, the work of scribes has proved to be invaluable in the preserving of the New Testament manuscripts.

Dating Scribal Handwriting

The dating of New Testament manuscripts has yielded astonishing results due to the collection of paleographic evidence. Although no original manuscripts (*autographa*) have been preserved, New Testament texts have been dated to within 30 to 300 hundred years of the time the autographs were written. Paleographers are specialized historians who study ancient texts, including the over 5,800 manuscripts that make up the New Testament. According to these historians, surviving manuscripts of the New Testament date between the early second and the fifteenth centuries AD. This is remarkably close in time to the autographs, considering that the original documents of the New Testament were most likely written between about 50 AD and 95 AD. Some whole Gospels and epistles are preserved in manuscripts that were written within 100 to 150 years from the time of their composition. And the vast majority of the New Testament text was preserved within documents dating less than 200 years from the original.

This find is remarkable when compared to the situation of most other ancient books, which date to from 500 to 1500 years after the autograph (for example, the copies of Homer, Plato, Aristotle, or Livy). Only a very limited number of manuscripts of these secular works actually exist, and only a few date from the second century AD. In a word, the New Testament manuscripts are the most well-attested and well-supported texts from the ancient world, based on their quantity, quality, and early dates.

How have these documents been dated? A closer look at dating methods leads us to a further understanding not only of the reliability of the New Testament documents, but also of the methods themselves.

Several methods are employed by historians to date the handwriting of a script. They include comparing the handwriting in a text with the handwriting in scripts that are already dated. In fact, within the lamentations of various scribes within their colophons at the end of texts, we find actual dates noting the completion of the transcription. Various archaeological finds of both religious and nonreligious works may also include dating that can be used as a reference point for paleographers.

But for many scholars, the examination of the development of script hands is used to clearly distinguish dating. Since scribes for the most part were consistent in their writing style while alive, we can assume that a script in their hand would date to within their working life period of approximately fifty years. As paleographers examine the development of hands, they compare the handwriting style in the text, including how the letters are formed and the angle of the writing. They also analyze the nuances in the handwriting of the edits found abutting the text and their correlations to each other. Organizing the information gained from these observations can denote the handiwork of scribes and allow for a simple chronology.

One can even learn the specificities of individual scribes and their work. This information becomes invaluable; scholars have used the handwriting, theology, and vocabulary of scribes to discern variants in texts. Thus, the dating of the hands of the scribe can prove to be very useful in laying a foundation for the sequencing of scribal trademarks. Historians can attribute common practices of the hands to distinct time periods and places of origin. Perhaps one of the greatest areas of study in early manuscripts exists within the handiwork of the Alexandrian scribes. Alexandrian scriptoral training marks the diligent hand of a scribe who was careful to copy word by word accurately, holding to his belief in the holy inspiration of the text.

The progression of handwriting practices and styles has over time become its own subject of study. Distinguishing time period, skill, and author, it has proved to be a fundamental tool for dating literary compositions. Since different periods of history bore their own chirographic (handwriting) trademarks, examination of these trademarks within the manuscript assists in determining its chronology. Evolution of handwriting can prove to be gradual in nature, but significant changes within the shapes of letters and the script as a whole are found within general ranges of time. An examination of these changes within their posited periods aids paleographers in matching the handwriting on the manuscript to the appropriate time period.

Progression of Styles

Among the earliest manuscripts are the ancient texts dated within the first and second century AD. These writings show evidence of a style of handwriting used within the second and first centuries BC to the third century AD. This was a decorated style using a book-hand script. In particular, it commanded the use of small details on the ends of lettering, known as serifs. The style of writing in the early centuries of the church was somewhat cumbersome.

Then, extending as far as the fifth century AD, we find a particular style of handwriting known for its emphatic form. This form is referred to as the *biblical majuscule* (or *biblical uncial*) style. It employed the use of elongated letters that were written separate from each other and in capitalized form. Additionally, the horizontal sloping strokes of letters were periodically accompanied by thick dots or completed with serifs. Scribes also employed the use of *scriptio continua*. This script was a connected form that did not provide spaces between words or sentences. Although the name can be deceiving, the biblical uncial style of writing is prevalent in both religious and nonreligious literature.

As the uncial bookhand thrived, an introduction of larger and annular ("forming a ring") letters is found in the sixth and seventh centuries. It is in this time period that one can see the lengthening of the central shaft in the Greek letter *omega* as well. As time went on, circular letters changed to become more oval and narrow, setting the stage for the next succession of forms.

In the ninth century a significant change marked paleographic history. Scribal work acquired a drastically new form and changed over its hand from the *majuscule* (uncial) to the cursive *minuscule* script. Its special form of cursive, as seen in its name, was smaller and more compact. It was a style of book hand that allowed scribes to transcribe more speedily while using letters that were well-formed. There was a brief overlapping of majuscule and minuscule writing. Majuscule writing continued on into the tenth and eleventh centuries AD but was primarily used for liturgical books. Minuscule handwriting was so useful that it continued well into the fifteenth century, until it was eventually replaced in the Reformation age by the introduction of the movable-type printing press.

It was also during this time period (900 to 1300) that a greater number and variety of ligatures were employed. (As mentioned, ligatures allowed the scribe to connect letters without lifting the pen, by a simple stroke.) Other noteworthy considerations include the differences in *breathing marks* (dashes used to aid in reading and pronunciation) according to time periods. For example, the breathing marks used prior to the eleventh century are squarer than the annular breathing marks applied after the four-teenth century AD.

Paleographic Categorization of Manuscripts

A broader and more general categorization of manuscripts according to chronology is made by paleographers as follows:

1. papyri (documents written on material made from papyrus plant)
2. uncial (majuscule) script
3. minuscule script
4. lectionaries

Note that within these broadly accepted time frames, two of the four categories are distinguished entirely by the style of handwriting found in texts. The diligent crafts-manship of the copyists has certainly made its mark in the history of New Testament manuscripts.[1]

New Testament Manuscript Distribution by Century and Manuscript Type																			
Cent.	2	3	4	5	6	7	8	9	10	11	12	13	14	15	16	17	18	19	Totals
Papyri	1	31	20	5	9	13	3												85
Uncial		3	16	44	60	29	27	47	18	1									245
Min.			1	1	3	4	22	13	125	436	586	569	535	248	138	44	16	4	2745
Lect.								116	143	241	490	298	313	168	194	73	11		2147

Chart from Norman L. Geisler and William E. Nix, *A General Introduction to the Bible*, rev. ed. (Chicago: Moody Press, 1968, 1986). Used by permission of Moody Press. This arrangement is an adaptation by Darrell L. Bock of material from Kurt and Barbara Aland, *Der Text des Neuen Testaments: Einführung in die wissenschaftlichen Ausgaben sowie in Theorie und Praxis der modernen Textcritik* (Deutsche Bibelgesellschaft, 1982), 90.*

Evaluating Variations in Greek Manuscripts

The gathering of New Testament manuscripts has resulted in a quantity of over 5,800 Greek manuscripts that contain part or all of the New Testament. By their numbers alone, copies of the New Testament stand apart from other ancient writings by a

---

* There is an apparent contradiction in the totals summarized in the Aland list (5,222 items) and the evidence presented by Bruce Metzger (5,366 items). Aland and Aland seem to have excluded from their list manuscripts whose century is uncertain, whereas Metzger, UBS, and Nestle (26th ed.) include all catalogued papyri and uncials but incorporate selected minuscule and lectionary evidence into their lists. More recently, Dr. Daniel Wallace, head of the Center for the Study of New Testament Manuscripts (CSNTM), who is the leading evangelical scholar on the topic, has discovered a number of new manuscripts. According to Dr. Wallace, the total Greek New Testament manuscript count is approximately 5,805; of these about 5,600 can be located and identified.

significant proportion. If it weren't for the rapid multiplication of the New Testament writings within the first century AD, it is highly unlikely that we would have our New Testament today. As discussed, many of these scribes were not only manual laborers but Christians devoted to the proclamation of the gospel message. Though these scribes seem to have been quite devoted to their craft, it is no surprise that mistakes were sometimes made, producing *variants*, or deviations, from the original or accepted text in the manuscripts themselves. Consequently, the more scribes committed themselves to the task of copying the New Testament, the more variants crept into the texts.

New Testament critic Bart Ehrman says,

> Scholars differ significantly in their estimates—some say there are 200,000 variants known, some say 300,000, some say 400,000 or more! We do not know for sure because, despite impressive developments in computer technology, no one has yet been able to count them all.... There are more variations among our manuscripts than there are words in the New Testament. [2]

But even Ehrman admits that "far and away the most changes are results of mistakes, pure and simple—slips of the pen, accidental omissions, inadvertent additions, misspelled words, blunders of one sort or another." [3]

Unintentional Errors

Variants are typically categorized into two groups: intentional and unintentional errors. Textual critics (those who analyze the text in a scholarly manner) argue that most variants found in the New Testament manuscripts are the result of the latter. We will review these kinds of variants first but only in accordance with the contextual manner to which they were made.

Errors of the ear. Historians are careful to recognize that in the early church era, the scribe or scribes would sit, or sometimes stand, at the feet of the lector and copy down word-by-word or phrase-by-phrase an orally delivered message. Obviously, in this process, simple *errors of the ear* will inevitably result. These simple and unintentional errors can be seen in passages like Matthew 19:24 where some manuscripts read *kamilos*—"a rope"—rather than the logical meaning found in other manuscripts: *kamelos*—"a camel."

Much of the confusion is inherent in the similarities in Greek vowels. For example the Greek vowels iota, eta, and epsilon sounded the same or similar when pronounced, as did the vowels omicron and omega. Over time, confusion arose between the long vowel omega and the short vowel omicron, leading to such variants as *echomen* and *echōmen*. A similar mistake in English can be seen in the accidental interchanging of "their" for "there" and "here" for "hear." Many of these errors could have been easily overlooked by a simple scanning of the Greek text, but they become obvious with a closer reading of the script.

Scribal fatigue. As mentioned earlier, the ancient scribe worked rather uneasily, hunched over with scroll stretched out between his knees, one hand holding the script in place and the other used for the various tools surrounding him (pen, inkhorn, sponge, and so on). The laborious process combined with the demanding body posture allowed for mental and physical fatigue that could eventually affect the craftsmanship of the copyist. Due to such conditions, *errors of eye, writing, memory,* and *judgment* were introduced into the text.

Errors of the eye. Variants betraying *errors of the eye* can be seen in the omission of text, repetition of text, transposition (reversing the order of words or letters), and simple misspelling. Sometimes the astigmatic eye would lose its bearings in the text and mistake one group of letters or words for another. This error of the eye would then cause the scribe to skip over the reading and then the writing of text on the manuscript. This mistake is known as *homoeoteleuton.* The repeating of the same word or letter was also a common error of the eye, known as *dittography.* An example of this can be seen in some minuscule scripts that say, "Whom do you want me to release for you, Jesus, Barabbas or Jesus?" In this passage, the word *Jesus* is repeated twice. The technical term for this is *metathesis.* In addition, there are mistakes of transposition. For example, some occurrences within a manuscript will read "Jesus" and others read "Jeuss." Understanding the context of the passages easily solves this problem. Lastly, simple misspellings, abbreviations, or scribal insertions also make up errors of the eye. Such a mistake is seen when the scribe joins words together that should be separated. For example, in English the phrase "Jesus is now here" can easily be written as "Jesus is nowhere."

Errors of writing. When the Christian church was being persecuted, attempts may have been made to duplicate the Scriptures more speedily. Simple *errors of writing* occurred as hasty and unintelligible handwriting met the scroll. If a copyist wrote imprecisely, he would lay the foundation for future error of sight or judgment when a future scribe discerned the text. Then, as exhaustion set in upon the mind, *errors of memory* would most often arise. When considering the multistep process of scribal monks, it is surprising that these errors are not more numerous. Occasionally a copyist might forget the exact word in a passage and substitute a synonym. This is exemplified in passages like Ephesians 5:9. Here the Byzantine manuscripts read "the fruit of the Spirit," but P[46] (from the Chester Beatty papyri) reads "fruit of light."

Errors of judgment make up the remainder of the unintentional causes of the variants found in New Testament manuscripts. Marginal notes sometimes made their way into the scriptural text as the scribe misjudged them to be part of the text itself. This could very well have been the case in Romans 8:1 where manuscripts vary in adding or omitting the last part of the verse. Critics conjecture as to whether this ending was actually a marginal annotation. Most of the errors of judgment can be attributed simply to poor eyesight or dim lighting—body posture obstructing the light and weakened vision of the fatigued eye. Note that such unintentional errors are not necessarily the result of a scribe's lackadaisical approach to his work, but rather stem from the physical and mental frailties of the human faculties. Such errors are common to man, but are especially obvious within their contextual frame. To the textual critic, these simple errors may easily "pop off the page" and take little effort to correct.

Intentional Errors

Finally, we come to the second category of variants: errors committed intentionally or knowingly by the scribe. Intentional errors demand greater effort upon the part of the textual critic. These errors make up the minority of the variant readings. Although natural to do so, it is wrong to assume such errors are the product of bad intentions. Taking into account that most of the New Testament scribes were Christians who valued the Scriptures as of supreme importance, it is more likely to assume that many intentional variants are the result of a scribe trying to emphasize the meaning of a word or words rather than its syntax (grammatical structure). The intentional changes can be categorized into 1) harmonizational, 2) historical or factual, 3) grammatical or linguistical, 4) doctrinal, 5) conflational, and 6) liturgical.

Harmonizational changes were made by scribes who sought to bring "harmony" to various scriptures by "correcting" them to match each other. It is possible that such harmonization could often be a result of the scribe mistakenly assuming the text to be in error when actually it was not. Many of the harmonizational changes made can be observed in the synoptic Gospels, as scribes attempted to harmonize accounts that were portrayed differently by each author. For example, the Luke 11:2-4 version of the Lord's Prayer was transcribed to the more accepted version found in Matthew 6:9-13.

Historical or factual changes also make up some of the intentional changes. Scribes thought they were actually correcting the mistake of a previous copyist. It is obvious that this is the case in Revelation 1:5, where a copyist changed *lusanti* to *lousanti*, thus changing the word from "loosed" to "washed" in regards to our sins. Other scribes may have attempted to change a word to update a name of a city in order to eliminate confusion of history or geography. For example, variants of the geographical terms *Gergesenes, Gadarenes, Gerasenes* are found in three of the Gospels (Luke 8:26; Matthew 8:28; Mark 5:1) describing the place where Jesus healed the demoniac. These were altered to read "near the Sea of Galilee with tombs and a steep bank nearby" for fear of writing a wrong location.

Grammatical or linguistic changes. As time and tradition impeded upon the linguistic nuances or stylistic idiosyncrasies of the scribe or his culture, again, modifications were made. These grammatical and linguistic changes included the spelling of proper names, verb forms, and other syntactical "corrections." Similar examples can be seen in "old" English literature, where modern versions may replace "shall" with "will" or "which" with "whom."

Doctrinal changes. The most intentional of all changes have been the result of the scribes' pursuit of orthodoxy, which resulted in doctrinal changes. The interchanging of "son" and "God" in the variant readings of John 1:18 is an example of such. Here, there is "only begotten son" rather than "only begotten God." Mark 9:29 is an example of such a doctrinal change as well. The addition of "fasting" to "prayer" reflects a change on the part of the scribe that may not have been so intentionally influenced by orthodoxy. It must be emphasized here, though, that making doctrinal changes was a very rare practice by a small group of scribes and was no way mainstream. In discerning the motivation or cause of a change, *intentional* doctrinal alterations of the text should only be considered when nothing else makes sense.

Conflational changes. Christian scribes devoted to the task of copying the Scriptures in their entirety may have sometimes been too fastidious in their inclusion of material. Critics point out that, for fear of omission, sometimes they included too much. Conflational changes may be among the prime examples of this overzealousness. Conflation occurs when two or more variants are joined into one reading. A good example is seen in Mark 9:49, where some texts include "And every sacrifice will be salted with salt." It is quite probable that the words "salted with salt" are the result of a conflational error, but they do not actually change the meaning of the text.

Liturgical changes make up the last group of intentional changes. These include minor changes that were made to follow ecclesiastical usage. An example may be seen in the doxology of the Lord's Prayer, found in Matthew 6:13. Liturgical changes are widely exemplified in the lectionaries. Such changes occurred in places like Luke 2:41, where the names "Joseph and Mary" were likely inserted in place of "his parents." These minor changes were made in order to establish or summarize the earlier context.

Considering the vast collection of New Testament manuscripts, one is overcome by the lofty credibility this mass of evidence demonstrates. The preservation of so great a mass of bibliographical material has ensured that even the book of Revelation is supported by over 300 Greek manuscripts. The greater the amount of documentation, the greater degree to which variants are exposed and errors expunged. Though most of the variants found within the New Testament documents comprise insignificant grammatical errors, textual critics have worked relentlessly over the centuries to correct all error and have successfully provided us with the Bible we possess today.

8

The Manuscripts of the New Testament

Like the Old Testament, the New Testament represented in our English translations is the result of examination of thousands of biblical manuscripts by translators. The process of decision-making resulted in what translators thought most likely represented the original documents. That is, by studying the multitude of Greek manuscripts of the New Testament, textual critics are able to arrive at these original autographs with a high degree of certainty.

Witnesses to the New Testament text may also be contained in ancient translations of the New Testament, called "versions." The Church Fathers also include portions of the Greek New Testament in their numerous quotations in various documents.

Typically, textual critics of the New Testament distinguish manuscripts on the basis of the material out of which they are made. The two most common materials are papyrus, an ancient form of paper made from the papyrus plant; and vellum, a material prepared from cowhide, lambskin, or goatskin, which was usually used for the first codices—ancient books.

When approaching the New Testament documents, it is important to remember that textual critics group these various manuscripts into different types or families (a grouping of manuscripts based on geographical location and similar textual characteristics, such as having the same readings of particular verses in a given family). Most believe the *Alexandrian text-type* (associated with Alexandria, Egypt) to be the oldest and closest to the original autographs. But distinct textual families also emerged in Caesarea in Israel (the *Caesarean* text-type), Rome (the *Western* text-type), and Syria (the *Syrian* text-type, also known as the *Byzantine* text-type, the *Koine* text-type, or the *majority text*).

In the descriptions below, we mention in which family each papyrus or codex is categorized. Such an assessment actually helps to demonstrate the reliability of the New Testament because it shows that we have representations of the text of the New Testament that are geographically diverse at an early date in the history of the church. In other words, the manuscripts spread across the world so quickly that it is almost impossible that some kind of conspiracy to change the text occurred.

New Testament Papyri

The papyri are widely considered to be the earliest and by some the most significant of the documents of the Greek New Testament. This does not have to do as much with their being written on papyrus as it does their early date. Since papyrus is the earliest form of writing material on which we find the New Testament, scholars typically assume that if the text is written on papyrus it is an earlier text. While this is true the vast majority of the time, we do have New Testament documents written on papyrus as late as the seventh century AD.

The chart on pages 118–122 gives a list of significant New Testament papyri manuscripts and catalog designations, arranged by date. In addition, appendix A provides analysis and description of more than 60 of these manuscripts. Of special note in proving biblical reliability are the two famous papyri discussed below: the John Rylands Fragment and the Chester Beatty II papyri.

The John Rylands Fragment is the oldest New Testament manuscript in the world, dating between AD 117 and 138. The early date of this manuscript confirms that all the original Gospels were written in the first century AD, well within the life spans of eyewitnesses to the events they record. (Photo by Zev Radovan.)

The John Rylands Fragment

The Rylands fragment (P^{52}, Gr.P.457) has the distinct honor of being the oldest copy of any piece of the New Testament. The Alexandrian fragment is of John's Gospel, containing part of the five verses from John 18:31-33,37-38. It was discovered in Egypt among the Oxyrhynchus collection and dates back to the early days of the second century AD, most likely between 117 and 138 or even earlier. It is composed on papyrus and its origin is clearly from a codex, thus indicating to many paleographers that New Testament codices did indeed exist in the first century AD.

The uncovering of this fragment has been significant in supporting the earlier dating of the Gospel of John to within the first century AD. For centuries, the historical antiquity of John was questioned. After Bruno Bauer's influential scholarship on the Gospel of John in the eighteenth century, many (for example, C.K. Barrett and Rudolf Bultmann) located the origin of the Gospel in the second century AD, long after the apostle John had died. With the discovery of the John Rylands fragment, that position is no longer tenable and has been widely rejected.

This is a great example of how the discovery of a manuscript can influence critical views of the actual textual content and background of the documents of the New Testament themselves. There is actually a great deal of irony related to this discovery. A papyrus piece of the book of the New Testament said to have been written latest in history—John—is now the earliest fragment of the New

Testament we possess. This small piece of the Gospel of John is no insignificant fragment; it contains Jesus' discussion with Pilate on the nature of truth. It contains parts of both Pilate's question, "What is truth?" and Jesus' remark, "The truth shall set you free." It's almost as if this discovery is a partial answer to that question—at least in response to what used to be a prevailing critical view regarding John's Gospel.

The Chester Beatty II Papyri

The Chester Beatty II Papyri (P^{46}/P.Mich.Inv.6238) are dated to approximately AD 250. This is an excellent papyrus codex, demonstrating the duplication of an early-dated exemplar text. Although portions of this book have been lost (2 Thessalonians and parts of Romans and 1 Thessalonians), it still boasts Hebrews and the Pauline epistles of Romans, 1 Corinthians, 2 Corinthians, Ephesians, Galatians, Philippians, and Colossians. All of these books are embraced within the surviving 86 leaves of 11 by 6.5 inches, which are gathered in a single quire (collection of leaves, or *signature* in modern terminology). The text is large, with some scribal nuances of style. The original, without its lost pieces, was 104 pages of mostly Alexandrian and some Western text-type. There are 71 agreements and in contrast only 17 disagreements that make up the 88 units of variation in the text. Overall the textual fidelity of the scribal hand is admirable.

This folio from the Chester Beatty Papyri (P^{46}) contains 2 Corinthians 11:33–12:9. (Photo PD-Art.)

This document is extremely important to proving biblical reliability because it provides us not only with one of the earliest copies of the Pauline letters, but also with evidence of a mini-canon of Paul's literature. This indicates that Paul's letters were extant and circulating from an early date, and also that they were being put together very early into a single collection.

As mentioned earlier, more than 60 New Testament papyri manuscripts are described and analyzed in appendix A.

New Testament Codices

Despite the literary culture of their time, early Christians preferred the codex form over the scroll. In fact, it was a preference particular to Christian Scriptures and books. Almost the entire collection of Christian texts from the third and fourth century AD are in the codex form: parchment or vellum bound into a book or pamphlet form rather than a scroll. The codex, likely less expensive than the scroll, allowed for more text, easier reference and transport, and greater accessibility. It is no wonder that it became the preferred choice for the New Testament manuscripts. The codices certainly provide us with the most comprehensive collections of New Testament manuscripts.

New Testament Manuscript Codices

I (01). Codex Sinaiticus (aleph), discovered in the St. Catherine Monastery of Mount Sinai, is debatably the most critical and valuable manuscript of the New Testament. Dating to the middle of the fourth century AD, this vellum codex embodies all of the New Testament with the exception of a few verses (Mark 16:9-20 and John 7:53–8:11) and the greater half of the Old Testament, as well as parts of the Apocrypha. The Alexandrian text is remarkably accurate, with limited misspellings and omissions. Large, dignified uncials take up 364½ double-sided pages, mostly in a four-column format. The story of its discovery is most captivating. It is said that 43 of its vellum leaves were rescued from the flames when they were recognized by scholar Constantin von Tischendorf among the waste for kindling the fire lying in a basket. It beautifully displays the hands of three scribes trained in the biblical uncial style.

Codex Sinaiticus is the oldest surviving Greek manuscript of the entire Bible. It is one of the most important texts used to study the Septuagint and the New Testament along with two other early Christian documents it contains, the Epistle of Barnabas and the Shepherd of Hermas. The highly revered artifact was produced in the southeastern Mediterranean region. Written on parchment, it originally contained 743 leaves, or 1,486 pages. It is the oldest surviving complete New Testament and is one of the two oldest manuscripts of the entire Bible.

The Codex Sinaiticus is the oldest complete New Testament written in Greek and dating to approximately AD 350. (Photo by Zev Radovan.)

The codex was written on animal skin in black and red metallic-based ink. Its text is Greek; several Arabic marginal notes were added later. Of its 1,486 original pages, only approximately 822 remain. As for the structure of the text, there are, as mentioned, four columns per page, though only two columns in the poetic and wisdom literature.

Codex Sinaiticus is currently located in four different locations, with the majority of the text in London's British Library. The complete New Testament and portions of the Old Testament manuscripts are dispersed among Leipzig University Library, St. Petersburg National Library of Russia, and Sinai Monastery of St. Catherine. The fourth century AD was an important time period for Christianity in terms of its development, the preservation of the Scriptures, and the development of this codex, which serves as a witness to this period in Christianity's history.

The codex was copied, then revised and corrected, by a team of scribes who were very skilled. It is not exactly clear where it was written, but scholars believe it was most likely either Caesarea or Egypt. The Old Testament portion contains the 48 books of the Greek canon of the Septuagint. The New Testament contains the complete 27 books of the canon with the addition of the early Christian writings of the Epistle of Barnabas and the Shepherd of Hermas. The size of the pages of the codex is the largest of any surviving Greek biblical manuscript, and they employ some of the thinnest parchment that was used.

The text of the Sinaiticus is unique in terms of the variations that are found in it, just as in any other manuscript. The changes found in the text are mostly accidentals, although a very few of them are intentional on the part of the scribes. Study of the manuscript has been very important for the field of textual criticism. Knowledge of the ancient traditions of scribal copying and transmission of ancient texts can be gained through thorough study of it. One can also examine this text in an effort to identify the oldest recoverable wording and gain understanding of how early Christians viewed and interpreted the Scriptures.

The codex underwent rigorous corrections for many years, until about AD 600. About 23,000 revisions were made, with the majority made by six correctors, who corrected things like faded letters, spelling, and inserting omitted texts and deleting texts, in addition to making modifications in how the text was broken across lines.

At the time Constantin von Tischendorf discovered the Codex Sinaiticus in the mid nineteenth century it was located at St. Catherine's Monastery at the base of Mount Sinai, Egypt. The codex is the oldest surviving Greek manuscript of the entire Bible dating to AD 350.

There is a gap in information about the history of Codex Sinaiticus down to the eighteenth century AD. It is not for certain exactly how much the manuscript was used and in what capacity. There is evidence, however, that in the late eighteenth and early nineteenth century its pages were used for bookbinding.

German scholar Constantin von Tischendorf took portions of the Old Testament home with him and used them for bookbinding in 1844. He eventually went on to publish a complete copy of the codex after obtaining the rest of the surviving manuscript.

One of the editions he published was an imitation of the page layout of the original, reproducing the appearance of the characters around 1844. Shortly after 1859, Tischendorf made a similar edition of the codex, which he presented in 1862 to Tsar Nicholas II and Tsarina Alexandra of Russia. In both of these editions notes are included on each of the corrections made, giving information on what was inserted, omitted, or replaced, and who corrected it. A photographic facsimile was produced years afterward and is considered a significant improvement. The New Testament portion of the codex was published in 1911, and the Old Testament was published shortly thereafter, in 1922.

B (03). The Codex Vaticanus is distinct in both its antiquity and composition. Dated between AD 325 and AD 350, this uncial codex contains books of the Old and New Testaments, as well as parts of the Apocrypha. In fact, this parchment/vellum contains all of the New Testament with the exception of the general epistles, Mark 16:9-20, John 7:53–8:11, 1 Timothy through Philemon, and Hebrews 9:14 through the end of Revelation. The 759-leaf codex was catalogued in the Vatican Library in 1475, where it is housed today. It is recognized as one of the greatest collections supporting the reliability of the New Testament.

This portion of Codex Vaticanus B contains the ending of 2 Thessalonians and the beginning of Hebrews. (Photo by Zev Radovan.)

A (02). The Codex Alexandrinus contains virtually the entire Old Testament and most of the New Testament with few exceptions. From the original codex of about 820 leaves, 773 are still intact. The scribal work employed the use of two columns with large uncials on thin vellum. This manuscript is surprisingly well preserved in spite of its early date and multiple locations since it was first bestowed upon the Patriarch of Alexandria. It is dated to the mid fifth century AD, clearly revealing the handiwork of the Alexandrian scribes of Egypt. The number of scribes employed for its composition is arguable, as the text displays varying quality in handiwork, independent textual nuances, and multiple exemplars. It has the distinction of being the foremost validation to the original text of Revelation.

C (04). The Ephraemi Rescriptus has a most distinguished history, attesting to the great achievements made in recovering ancient text invisible to the human eye. Text of both the Old and New Testaments was discovered underneath the text of the sermons of Ephraem contained in this *palimpsest rescriptus* (that is, used, erased, and rewritten manuscript). Chemical reactivation revealed portions from every New Testament book except 2 Thessalonians and 2 John, along with parts of the Old Testament. This text dates back to the fifth century AD and was most likely copied in Alexandria.

D (05). The Codex Bezae Cantabrigiensis was discovered in 1562 by the French theologian Theodore de Beze. Most exceptional in its composition is the inclusion of both Greek and Latin texts, making it the oldest discovered bilingual manuscript of the New Testament. The 406 leaves contain the four Gospels, Acts, and 3 John 11-15, transcribed in Western and various other text-types, with Greek on the left page and Latin on the right. To attempt to date this codex is somewhat difficult, as D.C. Parker declares. He argues that way since this kind of text, because of its contextual setting in the oral period, has no fixed form; texts were constantly being reshaped within the churches' context. [1]

W (032). The Codex Washingtonianus is an uncial manuscript containing most of the Gospels (missing are 25 verses in Mark and, from John, a part of chapters 14 and 16 and all of 15) and portions of the epistles of Paul. It represents both Byzantine and Alexandrian text-types and is dated to the early fifth century AD or late fourth century AD. This clearly written codex is transcribed on 187 sheets of vellum and is formatted in one column.

D (06). The Codex Claromontanus was discovered in France and dated to the middle of the sixth century AD. In many ways it completes the New Testament work of Codex Bezae by embodying many of its missing texts. A Western work, it was transcribed on 533 pages of thin vellum. The bilingual manuscript includes Hebrews as well as the entire collection of Pauline epistles in either or both Greek and Latin. The single-column codex reveals an artistic hand; it resides at the Bibliotheque Nationale in Paris.

The Codex Washingtonianus is an important majuscule manuscript from the fourth or fifth century AD. This image is of the black-and-white facsimile of the manuscript produced in 1912 by Henry A. Sanders and the University of Michigan. Currently, the manuscript is located at Freer Gallery, Sackler Museum, Smithsonian Institution, Washington DC. (The Center for the Study of New Testament Manuscripts [www.csntm.org] has granted permission for this image to be used.)

L (019). The Codex Regius, although poorly written, is significant in its overall agreement with the Vaticanus. It is composed of the Gospels, with a rather unusual addition making up two endings to Mark's Gospel. It is dated to the eighth century AD.

(044). The Codex Athous Laurae contains the Gospels of Luke, John, and part of Mark; as well as Acts, Hebrews, the Pauline epistles, and general epistles. Overall it exemplifies a Byzantine text, but does include parts that are Alexandrian and Western. It dates to the eighth or ninth century AD.

F (010). The Codex Augiensis is a bilingual manuscript encompassing parts of the epistles of Paul and Hebrews. Written in a Western text-type, this ninth-century AD text includes both Greek and Latin.

G (012). The Codex Boernerianus, embodying Paul's epistles, may uniquely be of Irish origin. This ninth-century AD codex is bilingual, written in Greek with an interlinear addition of Latin. It is noted for its close affinity to F2, Codex Augiensis.

(038). The Codex Koridethi is a manuscript of the Gospels dating to the ninth century AD. Mark resembles the earlier text (third or fourth century AD) employed by Eusebius and Origen, whereas Matthew, Luke, and John clearly resemble the Byzantine text.

Papyrus and Codex Manuscripts of the New Testament: Summary Listing of Key Early Witnesses to the New Testament's Reliability			
Name	Date of copy	Date of original	Biblical book(s)
John Rylands fragment (P^{52})	AD 117-138	1st century AD	John 18:31-33,37-38; considered the oldest New Testament fragment known
Chester Beatty II/ P.Mich.Inv.6238 (P^{46})	2nd century AD	1st century AD	Hebrews and all of the Pauline epistles, except for the pastorals
P.Bodmer II/ Inv. Nr. 4274/ 4298 (P^{66})	2nd century AD	1st century AD	Most of John
Inv. Nr. 12 (P^{87})	2nd century AD	1st century AD	Philemon 13-15,24-25
Chester Beatty II (P^4; P^{64}/P^{67})	2nd century AD	1st century AD	Portions of Luke 1–6 (P^4) and Matthew 3, 5, and 26 (P^{64}/P^{67})
P.IFAO Inv. 237[+a] (P^{98})	2nd century AD	1st century AD	Revelation 1:13–2:1
P.Oxy. 3523 (P^{90})	2nd century AD	1st century AD	John 18:36–19:37
P.Oxy. 2683 + 4405 (P^{77})	2nd century AD	1st century AD	Matthew 23:30-39
P.Oxy. 4403 (P^{103})	2nd century AD	1st century AD	Matthew 13:55-57; 14:3-5
P.Rylands 5 (P^{32})	2nd century AD	1st century AD	Titus 1:11-15; 2:3-8

Name	Date of copy	Date of original	Biblical book(s)
P.Oxy. 4448 (P[109])	2nd century AD	1st century AD	John 21:18-20,23-25
P.Oxy. 4447 (P[108])	2nd century AD	1st century AD	John 17:23-24; 18:1-5
P.Oxy. 2 (P[1])	3rd century AD	1st century AD	Matthew 1:1-9,12,14-20
P.Oxy. 208+1781 (P[5])	3rd century AD	1st century AD	Portions of John 1, 16, and 20
P.Oxy. 657 + PSI 1292 (P[13])	3rd century AD	1st century AD	Portions of Hebrews 2–5 and 10–12
P.Oxy. 1229 (P[23])	3rd century AD	1st century AD	James 1:10-12,15-18
P.Oxy. 1228 (P[22])	3rd century AD	1st century AD	John 15:25–16:2,21-32
P.Oxy. 1598 (P[30])	3rd century AD	1st century AD	Portions of 1 Thessalonians 4–5 and 2 Thessalonians 1–2
P.Mich.Inv. 1571 (P[38])	3rd century AD	1st century AD	Acts 18:27–19:6,12-16
P.Chester Beatty 1 (P[45])	3rd century AD	1st century AD	Large portions of all four Gospels and Acts
P.Oxy. 4445 (P[106])	3rd century AD	1st century AD	John 1:29-35,40-46
P.Oxy. 4446 (P[107])	3rd century AD	1st century AD	John 17:1-2,11
P.Oxy. 1780 (P[39])	3rd century AD	1st century AD	John 8:14-22
P.Oxy. 1597 (P[29])	3rd century AD	1st century AD	Acts 26:7-8,20
P.Oxy. 4495 (P[111])	3rd century AD	1st century AD	Luke 17:11-13,22-23
P.Mich.Inv. 1570 (P[37])	3rd century AD	1st century AD	Matthew 26:19-52
P.Yale 415 + 531 (P[49])	3rd century AD	1st century AD	Ephesians 4:16-29; 4:31–5:13
PSI XIV 1373 (P[65])	3rd century AD	1st century AD	1 Thessalonians 1:3–2:1,6-13
P.Mich.Inv. 6652 (P[53])	3rd century AD	1st century AD	Matthew 26:29-40; Acts 9:33–10:1
P.Oxy. 2383 (P[69])	3rd century AD	1st century AD	Luke 22:40,45-48,58-61
P.Barcelona 83 (P[80])	3rd century AD	1st century AD	John 3:34

Name	Date of copy	Date of original	Biblical book(s)
P.Mil. Vogl. Inv. 1224 + P.Macquarie Inv. 360 (P[91])	3rd century AD	1st century AD	Acts 2:30-37; 2:46–3:2
P.Oxy. 402 (P[9])	3rd century AD	1st century AD	1 John 4:11-12,14-17
P.Oxy. 1171 (P[20])	3rd century AD	1st century AD	James 2:19–3:9
P.Oxy. 1355 (P[24])	3rd century AD	1st century AD	Portions of Romans 8–9
PSI 1 (P[35])	3rd century AD	1st century AD	Matthew 25:12-15,20-23
P.Heidelberg G. 645 (P[40])	3rd century AD	1st century AD	Portions of Romans 1–4, 6, and 9
P.Oxy. 402 (P[9])	3rd century AD	1st century AD	1 John 4:11-12,14-17
PSI 1165 (P[48])	3rd century AD	1st century AD	Acts 23:11-17,25-29
PL II/31 (P[95])	3rd century AD	1st century AD	John 5:26-29,36-38
P.Oxy. 4401 (P[101])	3rd century AD	1st century AD	Matthew 3:10-12; 3:16–4:3
P.Oxy. 4497 (P[113])	3rd century AD	1st century AD	Romans 2:12-13,19
P.Oxy. 4498 (P[114])	3rd century AD	1st century AD	Hebrews 1:7-12
P. Antinoopolis 2.54	3rd century AD	1st century AD	Matthew 6:10-12
P.Oxy. 1079 (P[18])	3rd century AD	1st century AD	Revelation 1:4-7
P. Chester Beatty III (P[47])	3rd century AD	1st century AD	Portions of Revelation 9–17
P.Oxy. 4499 (P[115])	3rd century AD	1st century AD	Large portions of Revelation
P.Oxy. 108 +109 (P[15]/P[16])	3rd century AD	1st century AD	1 Corinthians 7:18–8:4 and Philippians 3:10-17; 4:2-8
P.Oxy. 1078 (P[17])	3rd century AD	1st century AD	Hebrews 9:12-19
P.Oxy. 1230 (P[24])	3rd century AD	1st century AD	Revelation 5:5-8; 6:5-8
P.Oxy. 1596 (P[28])	3rd century AD	1st century AD	John 6:8-12,17-22
P.Yale 1543 (P[50])	3rd century AD	1st century AD	Acts 8:26-32; 10:26-31
P.Oxy. 2384 + PSI Inv. CNR 419, 420 (P[70])	3rd century AD	1st century AD	Luke 22:40,45-48,58-61
P.Oxy. 4494 (P[110])	3rd century AD	1st century AD	Matthew 10:13-15,25-27

Name	Date of copy	Date of original	Biblical book(s)
MS 113 (0220)	3rd century AD	1st century AD	Romans 4:23–5:3,8-13
P.Bodmer VII and VIII (P 72)	3rd-4th century AD	1st century AD	1 and 2 Peter and Jude
P.Oxy. 2684 (P 78)	3rd-4th century AD	1st century AD	Jude 4-5,7-8
P.Narmuthis 69.39a + 69.229a (P 92)	3rd-4th century AD	1st century AD	Ephesians 1:11-13,19-21; 2 Thessalonians 1:4-5,11-12
P.Oxy. 4449 (P 100)	3rd-4th century AD	1st century AD	Portions of James 3–5
P.Oxy. 4402 (P 102)	3rd-4th century AD	1st century AD	Matthew 4:11-12,22-23
P.Oxy. 847 (0162)	3rd-4th century AD	1st century AD	John 2:11-22
PSI 2.124 (0171)	3rd-4th century AD	1st century AD	Portions of Matthew 10 and Luke 22
P.Amherst 3b (P 12)	285-300 AD	1st century AD	Hebrews 1:1
Inv. Nr. 5516 (P 86)	300 AD	1st century AD	Matthew 5:13-16,22-25
Codex Sinaiticus (aleph)	4th century AD	1st century AD	The entire New Testament
Codex Vaticanus B (03)	4th century AD	1st century AD	Most of the New Testament except Hebrews 9:14ff, the pastoral epistles, Philemon, Revelation
Codex Alexandrinus A (02)	5th century AD	1st century AD	Most of the New Testament
Ephraemi Rescriptus C (04)	5th century AD	1st century AD	Portions of every book except 2 Thessalonians and 2 John
Bezae Cantabrigiensis D (05)	5th century AD	1st century AD	The Gospels and Acts
Washingtonianus W (032)	5th century AD	1st century AD	The Gospels
Claromontanus D (06)	6th century AD	1st century AD	The Pauline epistles and Hebrews

Name	Date of copy	Date of original	Biblical book(s)
Regius L (019)	8th century AD	1st century AD	The Gospels
Athous Laurae PSI (044)	8th/ 9th century AD	1st century AD	The Gospels; Acts; Paul's epistles; general epistles
Augiensis F (010)	9th century AD	1st century AD	Pauline epistles
Boernerianus G (012)	9th century AD	1st century AD	Pauline epistles
Koridethi—THETA (038)	9th century AD	1st century AD	The Gospels

Chart © Joseph M. Holden, 2013.

Early New Testament Translations in Various Languages

In addition to the nearly 6,000 Greek manuscripts, there are over 19,000 manuscripts of early translations of the Bible into languages like Syriac, Latin, Coptic, Armenian, Georgian, Ethiopic, Arabic, Slavonic, Nestorian, and Gothic. That makes a total of some 25,000 manuscripts. Nothing like this exists for any other book in the ancient world.

One of the greatest authentications attesting to the trustworthiness of the New Testament manuscripts lies in the preservation of the scriptural translations of the early church. To produce a version, one must translate from an original language to another (for example, Greek to English or Hebrew to German). To accomplish such a task, one must not only have a clear knowledge of the languages addressed, but also an understanding of how to preserve both the form and the meaning of the texts. In response to the exhortation to preach the gospel to the ends of the earth, the early church began translation of the Scriptures of the New Testament. Although Greek was a significant language of the day, it was not sufficient for the church's evangelistic calling.

Syriac versions. The bishop of Edessa, Rabbula, is undoubtedly noteworthy for his contribution to the standard Syriac edition of the New Testament we possess today. In the fifth century AD, he worked to revise previously rewritten Syriac versions according to the Byzantine textual character. His revision was dispersed throughout the churches in his diocese. This revised version of the New Testament and a Syriac version of the Old Testament was called the *Peshitta*. Other noteworthy versions come from the works of early Church Fathers such as Origen and Tatian. The Syro-Hexaplaric version is a Syriac rendering that makes up the fifth column of the six-language Hexapla of Origen. Perhaps unduly literal in its translation, it lacks adequate meaning for the language and thus was never fully accepted by Syrian churches. Also, Tatian's compilation of the Gospels into one literary work, the *Diatessaron*, was widely noticed among Syrians.

Latin versions. Remarkably, the Latin versions of the New Testament date back to the third century AD and quite possibly earlier. Within the Roman world, Latin found its place in the military vernacular and as the language of the people, specifically in the West. It was in the third century AD that this common language took its place among local Christians in North Africa and Europe, finding its way into local churches. Perhaps most significant to the history of the Latin version is its later revision, the Latin Vulgate. The Vulgate (meaning "common") is a Latin revision penned by Jerome, which took a seat of prominence for nearly a millennium, into the sixteenth century AD. In fact, there are more manuscripts of the Latin Vulgate than any other version. The Vulgate still proves its significance today, as many of the modern Bible translations are founded upon this distinct version.

Coptic versions. As the church carried the Scriptures into Egypt, the Coptic versions were birthed. Within this later form of Egyptian writing, several dialects were present, including Sahidic, Bohairic, and Middle Egyptian dialects. The Sahidic (Thebaic) dialect was found in Upper (southern) Egypt, and by the fourth century AD the spread of the Scriptures in Egypt began when the New Testament was translated into it. The Sahidic version greatly represents the Alexandrian text-type but also the Western type. The Bohairic or Memphic dialect was spoken in northern, or Lower Egypt. So widespread was this dialect that it became the common dialect of the Egyptian church at large. Fayumic, Akhmimic, and sub-Akhmimic represent the dialects of Middle Egypt; unfortunately, no book of the New Testament has been entirely preserved in any of these Middle Egyptian dialects.

Armenian versions. Although Armenia was the first kingdom to embrace Christianity, its scriptural translation is less assertive. It is argued that the Armenian version is foremost a secondary translation, meaning that the original text was itself a translation rather than the original Greek. The debatable language of origin is Syriac. Although the early Armenian versions stem from within the first half of the fifth century AD, later, more significant revisions of this text came around the time of the eighth century AD. In fact, it is a revised text from this time that has been preserved and accepted up until the present.

Georgian versions. Georgia had its first translation of the Bible by approximately the middle of the fifth century AD. Proceeding from Armenia, its southern neighbor, the gospel in the form of Scripture quickly took root. The Georgian version takes its basis from the Armenian translation, thus making it a secondary translation.

Ethiopian versions. Despite the hypothesis of earlier evangelism into Ethiopia, it is clear that the good news was brought to Ethiopia in the first half of the fourth century AD during the evangelization under Constantine the Great (AD 330). Nevertheless, it was not until the seventh century AD that both the Old Testament was finished and the New Testament was in process. It is likely that Syrian monks residing in Ethiopia are responsible for the full and complete translation from Syriac during the time of the Monophysite Controversy (fifth century AD). Later, the Arabic and Coptic versions colored the Ethiopian version as well.

Arabic versions. The Arabic version is a secondary translation from a combination of Greek, Syriac, Coptic, and Latin versions. The most ancient translation into Arabic likely originates from a Syriac translation made at the time of Islam's appearance. Unfortunately the author of the first Arabic version is unknown.

Slavonic versions. In the ninth century AD the monks and brothers Methodius and Constantine (Cyril) traveled to east-central Europe at the commission of Emperor Michael III in response to the Slavic leader Rostislav to translate the Scriptures and liturgy into the language of the people. They are respected for their development of the Cyrillic alphabet as a tool for their translation. This alphabet is used today in the Bulgarian, Ukrainian, Serbo-Croatian, and Russian languages. Starting in the mid ninth century AD, the Gospels were translated into the Old Church Slavonic version.

Nestorian versions. The Nestorian versions stem from traveling Persian Nestorians of the fifth century AD. Journeying into central and east Asia, they translated the Scriptures into various languages as they went along. These were all secondary translations, as they were based on the Syriac. The earliest preserved copies of the Nestorian versions date hundreds of years later, to the ninth and tenth centuries AD.

Gothic versions. The Gothic version dates back to the fourth century AD. This New Testament version was translated by archbishop and missionary Wulfila. Unfortunately only part of the version has been preserved.

The versions continue to witness to the Greek New Testament manuscripts in a significant and distinct fashion. Importantly, the versions themselves attest to the canonization of Scripture, as only the accepted books formed the basis for the work of translation.

New Testament Citations in the Early Church

In addition to the 25,000 manuscripts of the New Testament, the works of the early Church Fathers validate the dates, locations, and text-types used in the New Testament manuscripts. More importantly, these works provided quotations of the Scriptures themselves. In fact, one could reconstruct the entire New Testament based solely on the more than 36,200 Scripture quotations of the Fathers—with the exception of a few dozen verses!

The Fathers would openly compare the texts of early codices by quoting them. In addition, they would preface their quotations of Scripture with remarks such as "my codex here says," thus opening the door to the text of some of the earliest codices of the New Testament. All 27 books of the New Testament are addressed and validated by the writings of the early Fathers. Almost 36,000 quotations alone come from just five of the Fathers (see chart above). In fact, by AD 110 all the New Testament books, except for 2 John and

Jude, had been cited by either Ignatius, Clement of Rome, Polycarp, or more than one of them. There is no other book, religious or secular, that is validated by such a vast number of individual and selected quotations as the New Testament.

Early Citations of the New Testament						
Writer	Gospels	Acts	Pauline epistles	General epistles	Revelation	Totals
Justin Martyr	268	10	43	6	3 (266 allusions)	330
Irenaeus	1,038	194	499	23	65	1,819
Clement of Alexandria	1,017	44	1,127	207	11	2,406
Origen	9,231	349	7,778	399	165	17,922
Tertullian	3,822	502	2,609	120	205	7,258
Hippolytus	734	42	387	27	188	1,378
Eusebius	3,258	211	1,592	88	27	5,176
Grand totals	19,368	1,352	14,035	870	664	36,289

Chart from Norman L. Geisler and William E. Nix, *A General Introduction to the Bible*, rev. ed. (Chicago: Moody Press, 1968, 1986). Used by permission of Moody Press.

Notable Early Quotations

A direct link to the apostles themselves can be seen in the work of *Polycarp* from the early second century AD. Polycarp was actually a disciple of the apostle John. Significantly, he wrote his own "Epistle to the Philippians," where he referenced and quoted the Scriptures of the Old and New Testament. His work frequently quoted Romans, Galatians, and Philippians and often referred to the books of 2 Corinthians, Ephesians, Colossians, 2 Thessalonians, 1 Timothy, and 2 John.

The early Father *Ignatius of Antioch* loosely quoted the Scriptures on numerous occasions in his seven epistles. His place in early church history is established by his textual validation of the Scriptures and also his martyrdom in Rome. Among his works are citations from Ephesians, Philippians, Colossians, and 2 Thessalonians.

Clement of Rome is recognized for his early place in history and patristic work. He actually lived contemporaneously with the apostles and was influenced by Paul in his own epistle to the Corinthians, written in the late first century before his death in AD 101. In it he quotes not only the Gospels but also Romans. In addition, among other books he cited in his works were Ephesians, 1 Timothy, Titus, Hebrews, James, and 2 Peter.

One of the earliest significant works of the Church Fathers is the *Teaching of the Twelve*, or *Didache*. Dated between AD 100 and 120, this early work contains loose quotations of the New Testament Scriptures. In particular, 1 Corinthians is cited, as are 1 Thessalonians and Revelation.

One of the most powerful early-church witnesses to the New Testament is *Irenaeus*. He is recognized as the first Father who quoted almost every book of the New Testament. The only two books not found in his citations are the tiny one-chapter books of Philemon and 3 John, which he probably had no occasion to quote. He is recognized for his vast quotation of Scripture and has a prominent place in early church history (170 AD) as one who defended the Christian faith against Gnosticism with his work *Against Heresies*.

Clement of Alexandria, active at the beginning of the third century AD, is appreciated for his significant quoting of almost every book of the New Testament. As well as the two omitted by Irenaeus, Clement also omits 2 Timothy and 2 John.

One of the most notable works of the early Father *Tatian* exists only in the form of the words of secondhand witnesses. Tatian's *Diatessaron* was a favorite among early Christians, in particular Syrians; it weaved the four Gospels harmoniously into one single work. Unfortunately this work of the second century AD is completely lost, with no remaining copy. Nevertheless, because of its significance in the early church, several witnesses have preserved it in part by their own commentaries on it. These works include *The Commentary on the Diatessaron* by Ephraem and the Latin *Codex Fuldensis*.

Conclusion

The next closest book to the New Testament in terms of manuscript support is the *Iliad* of Homer, which is attested to by 643 manuscripts, the oldest of these made 500 years after the original. Other works fare even more poorly (see chart at the end of the next chapter). Clearly the New Testament is the most well-attested book from all of ancient history. If one denies the reliability of the New Testament based upon the number of manuscripts and the interval of time between its original composition and the nearest copy, then one also discredits the reliability of every work from ancient history!

THE ACCURACY OF THE NEW TESTAMENT MANUSCRIPTS

The New Testament is more accurately copied than any other book from ancient history. Professor Bruce Metzger of Princeton conducted a research project comparing the accuracy of the copies of the New Testament to other ancient works. He concluded that the Hindu *Mahabharata* "was copied with about 90 percent accuracy and Homer's *Iliad* with 95 percent accuracy."[1] This is a more than sufficient degree of accuracy to convey the essential teaching of the originals.

By contrast, scholars have estimated that the New Testament was copied with up to 99 percent, or even greater, accuracy. Nineteenth-century British manuscript experts Westcott and Hort estimated that only about one-sixteenth of the variants rise above "trivialities," which would make copies 98.33 per cent accurate.[2] Ezra Abbot's figures yield an estimate that the text is 99.75 percent pure.[3] The great New Testament Greek scholar A.T. Robertson declared that "the real concern is with a 'thousandth part of the entire text.'" That statement would translate to 99.9 percent accuracy on anything of real concern.[4]

What is more, even Bart Ehrman, the renowned New Testament scholar who argues against the reliability of the New Testament, admits that the manuscript variants do not affect the central message of the New Testament:

> It would be a mistake…to assume that the only changes being made were by copyist with a personal stake in the wording of the text. In fact, *most of the changes found in our early Christian manuscripts have nothing to do with theology or ideology.*[5]

Misleading Statistics

In view of the foregoing evidence, particularly that in the previous chapter, one can see how misleading statistics from critics such as Bart Ehrman really are. To speak of 200,000 to 400,000 errors in the Bible is completely misleading. First of all, most of the differences are not errors, but simply variant readings. Second, these variants do not represent 200,000-plus places in the Bible. Rather, if one word is misspelled in 3,000 manuscripts, this is counted as 3,000 errors. By this same type of calculation, it has been shown that Ehrman has 1.6 million errors in the first edition of his own book. Mariano Grinbank discovered 16 errors in Ehrman's book *Misquoting Jesus*. [6] Since the first edition is reported to have sold 100,000 copies in its first three months, this would mean (the way Ehrman counts errors in the Bible manuscripts) that there are 1.6 million errors in Ehrman's book! Yet no reasonable person would argue that because of this we cannot trust the copies to convey Ehrman's original thoughts on the matter.

Actually, the more so-called errors (really, variants) there are, the more certain we are of the original. For example, if one received a message like this, one would have no problem collecting the money:

Y#U HAVE WON 10 MILLION DOLLARS

Why? Because, even with the error, 100 percent of the message comes through. And if one received a message like this it would remove all doubt:

Y#U HAVE WON 10 MILLION DOLLARS

YO# HAVE WON 10 MILLION DOLLARS

And the more lines we have (with errors in a different spot), the more we would be sure of the message.

Ehrman also makes an issue over the so-called biases of the manuscript copiers. Yet, as it turns out, their bias does not affect the basic message of the Bible. Consider the following illustration:

1. YOU HAVE WON TEN MILLION DOLLARS

2. THOU **HAST WON** TEN MILLION DOLLARS
[Notice the King James bias here]

3. Y'ALL **HAVE WON** $10,000,000
[Notice the Southern bias here]

Observe that of the 28 letters in line 2, only 5 of them [in bold] are the same in line 3. That is, about 19 percent of the letters are the same. Yet, despite the bias, the message is 100 percent identical! The lines are different in form but not in content. Likewise, even with the many differences in the New Testament variants, *100 percent of the message comes through.*

In the light of all the above evidence, it is fair to say that the New Testament is the most accurately copied book from the ancient world. For it survives in more copies, earlier copies, and more reliable copies than any other work from antiquity by comparison with other classic works from the ancient world, most of which survive on only 10 to 20 manuscripts. Compare the evidence in the following chart:

New Testament Manuscripts Compared to Other Ancient Sources					
Author	Ancient title	Date of original	Date of earliest manuscript	Time gap from original	Manuscript copies extant
Plato	Dialogues	4th century BC	AD 900	c. 1,250 years	20
Homer	Iliad	9th century BC	400 BC	c. 500 years	643
Herodotus	The Histories	484 to 425 BC	AD 900	c. 1,350 years	8
Aristotle	Assorted works	4th century BC	AD 1100	c. 1,400 years	5
Thucydides	History of the Peloponnesian Wars	460 to 400 BC	AD 900	c. 1,300 years	8
Aristophanes	Assorted works	448 to 385 BC	AD 900	c. 1,300 years	10
Sophocles	Assorted works	496 to 406? BC	AD 1000	c. 1,400 years	193
Julius Caesar	The Gallic Wars	58 to 44 BC	AD 900	c. 950 years	10
Tacitus	Annals of Imperial Rome	AD 58 to 120	AD 1100	c. 1,000 years	20
Pliny the Younger	History of Rome	AD 62 to 113	AD 850	c. 750 years	7
Suetonius	The Twelve Caesars	AD 70 to 140?	AD 950	c. 900 years	8
Total manuscripts for ancient sources					932
Greek New Testament manuscripts		AD 45 to 100	AD 117 to 325	30 to 300 years	5,800-plus
Non-Greek New Testament manuscripts					19,200-plus
Total New Testament manuscripts					25,000-plus

Chart adapted from Norman Geisler, *General Introduction to the Bible* (Chicago: Moody Press, 1986), 408, by H. Wayne House and Joseph M. Holden, *Charts of Apologetics and Christian Evidences* (Grand Rapids, MI: Zondervan Publishing, 2006), chart 43. Used by permission of Zondervan.

Conclusion

In the light of all the available evidence, we can agree with the great Greek manuscript expert Sir Frederic Kenyon, who declared,

> The interval then between the dates of original composition and the earliest extant evidence becomes so small as to be in fact negligible, and the last foundation for any doubt that the Scriptures have come down to us substantially as they were written has now been removed. [Thus] both the *authenticity* and the general *integrity* of the books of the New Testament may be regarded as finally established. [7]

In short, we can trust the Bible in our hands as an accurate copy of the original in all essentials. As the famous scholar Philip Schaff noted of the variant readings known in his day, only 50 were of real significance, and *there is no "article of faith or a precept of duty which is not abundantly sustained by other and undoubted passages, or by the whole tenor of Scripture teaching."*[8]

PART FOUR

THE RELIABILITY OF NEW TESTAMENT HISTORY

The reliability of New Testament history is overwhelming when compared to that of any other book from the ancient world. In support of it, we will first review the multiplicity of evidence,* and then we will respond to major objections of the critics. In the following chapters we will consider the cumulative weight of the arguments in favor of the New Testament's historical reliability.

---

* For an expanded view of the evidence, see Norman Geisler and Bill Roach, *Defending Inerrancy* (Grand Rapids, MI: Baker Books, 2012), chap. 5.

HISTORICITY OF THE NEW TESTAMENT

The Existence of Multiple Accounts About Jesus in the New Testament

It is a well-established rule of law that "on the evidence of two or three witnesses a matter shall be confirmed" (Deuteronomy 19:15). But in the case of the New Testament there are eight or nine writers (depending on whether Paul wrote Hebrews) who contribute to the confirmation of the events of Jesus' life: Matthew, Mark, Luke, John, Paul, Peter, James, Jude, and the writer of Hebrews. Even if all the traditional authors are not the actual authors (and even the critics admit that some were), nonetheless, by the critics' own late dates for the New Testament (namely, 70 to 100 AD), they were still written during the time of contemporaries and eyewitnesses of the events. To have 27 pieces of literature written by eight or nine authors contemporary to the events, all of whom were giving the same basic message—about Christ—is unprecedented. Nothing like it exists for any other book from antiquity. This alone should be sufficient evidence for the reliability of the New Testament documents.

This bust of Alexander the Great (356–323 BC) as a youth was probably sculpted by Leochares around 336 BC.

By contrast, the life of Alexander the Great, the basics of which are widely accepted as true, is based on no contemporary writers and only several histories from some 300 to 500 years later. A fortiori (with the greater force), considering that we have 27 documents from contemporaries of the events, we should have no hesitation accepting their general reliability, particularly in regard to the core events on which their testimony overlaps.

The Eyewitness Nature of the New Testament

Not only are there earlier, more multiple, more accurate, and more numerous contemporary documents for the basic New Testament events than for any other ancient history, but these documents were based on eyewitness testimony. This is indeed what the Gospel of Luke claims: "Many have undertaken to draw up an account of the things that have been fulfilled among us, just as they were *handed down to us by those who from the first were eyewitnesses* and servants of the word" (Luke 1:1-3). And Doctor Luke was not only an educated eyewitness, but his writing has been confirmed in numerous details by archaeological and literary sources (see below in this chapter).

Consider the emphasized phrases in the following New Testament references (NIV):

- "*The man who saw it [the crucifixion] has given testimony,* and his testimony is true" (John 19:35).

- "*This is the disciple who testifies to these things and who wrote them down.* We know that his testimony is true" (John 21:24).

- "That which was from the beginning, which *we have heard, which we have seen with our eyes, which we have looked at and our hands have touched*—this we proclaim concerning the Word of life" (1 John 1:1).

- "God has raised this Jesus to life, and *we are all witnesses of the fact*" (Acts 2:32).

- "Peter and John replied…'For we cannot help speaking *about what we have seen and heard*'" (Acts 4:19-20).

- "*We are witnesses of everything he did* in the country of the Jews and in Jerusalem. They killed him by hanging him on a tree, but God raised him from the dead on the third day *and caused him to be seen*" (Acts 10:39-40).

- "…He [Jesus] was buried, that he was raised on the third day according to the Scriptures, and *that he appeared to Peter, and then to the Twelve. After that, he appeared to more than five hundred of the brothers at the same time, most of whom are still living,* though some have fallen asleep. Then *he appeared to James, then to all the apostles, and last of all he appeared to me also*" (1 Corinthians 15:3-8).

- "How shall we escape if we ignore such a great salvation? This salvation, which was first announced by the Lord, *was confirmed to us by those who heard him.* God also testified to it by signs, wonders and various miracles, and gifts of the Holy Spirit distributed according to his will" (Hebrews 2:3-4).

- "We did not follow cleverly invented stories [myths] when we told you about the power and coming of our Lord Jesus Christ, but *we were eyewitnesses of his majesty*" (2 Peter 1:16).

• "To the elders among you, I appeal as a fellow elder, *a witness of Christ's suffer-ings* who also will share in the glory to be revealed" (1 Peter 5:1).

A recent book by Richard Bauckham, *Jesus and the Eyewitnesses,* argues convincingly that the New Testament is based in eyewitness testimony. He concludes that

> reading the Gospels as eyewitness testimony...honors the form of his-toriography they are. From its historical perspective, radical suspicion of testimony is a kind of epistemological suicide. It is no more practical in history than it is in ordinary life.[1]

Bauckham is not alone in his conclusion. Numerous scholars have come to the same conclusion.* In fact, there are around 2,000 biblical scholars in the Evangelical Theo-logical Society, virtually all of whom accept the reliability of the New Testament docu-ments as based in eyewitness testimony!

Given that there are multiple documents based on numerous eyewitness testimo-nies of honest men, the burden of proof falls on the skeptic and critic, not on those who accept the reliability of the New Testament. Critics are swimming upstream, drowning in waves of evidence against their view.

The Confirmation of the Historical Accuracy of Luke's Writings

One of the Gospel writers, Dr. Luke, is known to have been the writer of a highly accurate New Testament document, the book of Acts. The earlier work of Sir William Ramsay (*St. Paul the Traveler and the Roman Citizen*) and the more recent work of the noted Roman historian Colin Hemer (*The Book of Acts in the Setting of Hellenistic His-tory*) have demonstrated the minute historical accuracy of the book of Acts.

Four points are important in this confirmation of the Gospel record: 1) The author of the book of Acts, known as Luke the physician (Colossians 4:14), the companion of the apostle Paul (2 Timothy 4:11), was an accurate historian. 2) He was also the writer of the Gospel of Luke. 3) He wrote Acts before AD 62 (only three decades after Jesus died) while numerous eyewitnesses were still alive. 4) He wrote the Gospel of Luke before he wrote Acts. Hence, the Gospel of Luke was written by an accurate historian by about AD 60 or 61, during the lifetime of numerous eyewitnesses (Luke 1:1-4).

The first point is demonstrated by Hemer, who shows that the writer of Acts has detailed, specific, and firsthand knowledge of numerous things about which he wrote. These include the following:

---

* These include Craig Blomberg (*The Historical Reliability of the Gospels* and *The Historical Reliability of John's Gospel*); F.F. Bruce (*The New Testament Documents: Are They Reliable?* and *Jesus and Christian Origins Outside the New Testament*); D.A. Carson and Douglas Moo (*New Testament Introduction*); William Lane Craig (*Knowing the Truth About the Resurrection*); C.H. Dodd (*History and the Gospels*); Donald Guthrie (*New Testament Introduction*); Gary Habermas (*The Historical Jesus*); Colin Hemer (*The Book of Acts in the Setting of Hellenistic History*); John Warwick Montgomery (*Christianity and History*); Eta Linnemann (*Is There a Synoptic Problem?*); Bruce Metzger (*The Text of the New Testament*); and N.T. Wright (*Can We Trust the Gospels?*), among others.

- a natural crossing between correctly named ports (Acts 13:4-5);
- the proper river port, Perga, for a ship passing from Cyprus (13:13);
- the proper location of Lycaonia (14:6);
- the unusual but correct declension of the name Lystra, the correct language spoken there, and two gods associated with the city, namely Zeus and Hermes (14:12);
- a conspicuous sailors' landmark at Samothrace (16:11);
- the association of Thyatira with cloth dyeing (16:14);
- the proper locations where travelers would spend the nights on the journey being described (17:1);
- the correct designation of Gallio as proconsul (18:12);
- the name Tyrannus, which is attested on a first-century AD inscription (19:9);
- the appropriate route for passing across the open sea from Cyprus when favored by persistent northwest winds (21:3);
- the correct identification of Ananias as high priest (23:2) and Felix as governor (23:24);
- agreement with Josephus on the name *Porcius Festus* (24:27);
- the proper description *gregale* for a south wind that suddenly became a violent nor'easter (27:13);
- correct identifications for stopping places along the Appian Way (28:15).

In over 80 such things the author of Acts did not make a single mistake! He is recognized as a first-rate first-century historian.

Further, the same author also wrote the Gospel of Luke, to which he refers in Acts 1:1 as "the first book" (ESV) or "former book" (NIV) of "all that Jesus began to do and teach until the day when He was taken" (1:2). Not only did Luke refer to the Gospel bearing his name, but both books were written to the same person, "Theophilus" (Luke 1:3 and Acts 1:1), and in the same style of an educated Greek.

This rocky outcropping beneath the Acropolis in Athens is the location where the apostle Paul gave his famous message to the Areopagites about the "Unknown God" described in Acts 17:16-34.

This is supported by other lines of internal and external evidence,[2] including his medical interest, traveling companions, and the testimony of early Church Fathers such as Irenaeus, Tertullian, Clement, Origen, and Jerome.

What is more, Hemer lists 15 lines of evidence supporting a date prior to AD 62 for the book of Acts. Just a few are sufficient to make the point: 1) There is no mention of the destruction of Jerusalem in AD 70. For a historical record of this time and place not to mention this most crucial historical event in the life of first-century AD Jews (if it had already occurred) is akin to writing the life of President John F. Kennedy after his death without mentioning his assassination. 2) Likewise, there is no mention of the Jewish Wars that broke out in AD 64. 3) The apostle Paul is still alive (Acts 28), so the timing of the book must have been before his death in about AD 65. 4) There is no hint of the death of James at the hands of the Sanhedrin, which Josephus says occurred in AD 62.[3] These and almost a dozen more points support a date for Acts before AD 62.[4]

Therefore, we have good evidence to conclude that the Gospel of Luke was written by an accurate first-century AD historian within three decades of the death of Christ while numerous eyewitnesses were still alive to confirm it. Indeed, this is exactly what Luke says in his prologue:

> Just as those who from the beginning were eyewitnesses and ministers of the word have delivered them to us, it seemed good to me also, having followed all things closely for some time past, to write an orderly account for you, most excellent Theophilus, that you may have certainty concerning the things you have been taught (Luke 1:2-4 ESV).

The Confirmation of the Gospels by the Accepted Epistles of Paul

An often overlooked but powerful argument for the basic reliability of the Gospel record about Jesus' life and teaching is found in the accepted epistles of the apostle Paul.[5] Placing late dates on the Gospels and attempting to cast doubt on their reports fails to undermine their historical reliability for many reasons. One is that it is widely accepted by critics that Romans, 1 and 2 Corinthians, and Galatians are genuine epistles of the apostle Paul and that they were written between AD 55 and 57. But these four epistles confirm the basic historicity of the Gospels on the life, teachings, death, and resurrection of Christ.

In fact there are 27 such facts about Jesus in these accepted epistles of Paul, including

- the Jewish ancestry of Jesus (Galatians 3:16);
- His Davidic descent (Romans 1:3);
- His virgin birth (Galatians 4:4);
- His life under Jewish law (Galatians 4:4);
- the existence of His brothers (1 Corinthians 9:5);
- the existence of His twelve disciples (1 Corinthians 15:7);
- one of the disciples was named James (1 Corinthians 15:7);
- some of the disciples had wives (1 Corinthians 9:5);

- Paul knew Peter and James (Galatians 1:18–2:16);
- Jesus' poverty (2 Corinthians 8:9);
- His meekness and gentleness (2 Corinthians 10:1);
- His abuse by others (Romans 15:3);
- His teachings on divorce and remarriage (1 Corinthians 7:10-11);
- His view on paying wages of ministers (1 Corinthians 9:14);
- His view on paying taxes (Romans 13:67);
- His command to love one's neighbors (Romans 13:9);
- His views on Jewish ceremonial uncleanness (Romans 14:14);
- His titles of deity (Romans 1:3-4; 10:9);
- His institution of the Lord's Supper (1 Corinthians 11:23-25);
- His sinless life (2 Corinthians 5:21);
- His death on the cross (Romans 4:25; 5:8; Galatians 3:13);
- His death paid for our sins (1 Corinthians 15:3; 2 Corinthians 5:21, see also Mark 10:45);
- His burial (1 Corinthians 15:4);
- His resurrection on the "third day" (1 Corinthians 15:4);
- His postresurrection appearance to the apostles (1 Corinthians 15:5-8);
- His postresurrection appearances to others, including 500 people, most of whom were still alive when Paul wrote 1 Corinthians (1 Corinthians 15:6), and
- Jesus' present position at God's right hand (Romans 8:34).

These facts not only confirm the general reliability of the Gospels; even apart from the Gospels they provide the essential core of teachings about Christ on which Christianity is based. To put it another way, were there no Gospels such as we have, Christianity would not crumble.

Legal Testimony Supporting the Gospel Witnesses

Simon Greenleaf was a professor of law at Harvard University when he was challenged to apply the rules of legal evidence from the book he authored (*A Treatise on the Law of Evidences*, 1853) to the New Testament witnesses and documents. His conclusions are found in his book *The Testimony of the Evangelists* (1874). He wrote,

> The narratives of the evangelists are now submitted to the reader's perusal and examination, upon the principles and by the rules already stated.... If they had thus testified on oath, in a court of justice, they would be

entitled to credit; and whether their narratives, as we now have them, would be received as ancient documents, coming from the proper custody. If so, then it is believed that every honest and impartial man will act consistently with that result, by receiving their testimony in all the extent of its import.[6]

Greenleaf added, "All that Christianity asks of men on this subject, is, that they would be consistent with themselves....The result, it is confidently believed, will be an undoubting conviction of [the Gospels'] integrity, ability, and truth."[7] Other attorneys have come to the same conclusion. Thomas Sherlock was the first to use the legal approach in his book *The Tryal of the Witnesses of the Resurrection* (1729). Converted skeptical journalist Frank Morison wrote *Who Moved the Stone?* (1930). Attorney and theologian John Montgomery wrote *Christianity and History* (1964). And more recently, Lee Strobel penned *The Case for Christ* (1998). All agree that from a legal standpoint, using the normal rules of legal evidence, the New Testament witnesses would have stood up in a court of law.

Archaeological Confirmation of the New Testament

No book from ancient times has more archaeological confirmation than the Bible. Noted biblical scholar Nelson Glueck declared, "As a matter of fact...it may be stated categorically that no archaeological discovery has ever controverted a biblical reference. Scores of archaeological findings have been made which confirm in clear outline or exact detail historical statements in the Bible."[8]

After surveying the evidence, even the secular magazine *US News & World Report* concluded that: "In extraordinary ways, modern archaeology has affirmed the historical core of the Old and New Testaments—corroborating key portions of the stories of Israel's patriarchs, the Exodus, the Davidic monarchy, and the life and times of Jesus."[9] One-time critical biblical scholar W.F. Albright, known as the "Dean of Archaeologists," not only came to accept the general historical reliability of the Bible, but concluded of the New Testament in particular that "in my opinion, every book of the New Testament was written by a baptized Jew between the forties and the eighties of the first century A.D. (very probably sometime between about 50 and 75 A.D.)."[10]

Many minimalist archaeologists (those holding the view that archaeology offers minimal or no support to biblical history) today are not comfortable with using the Bible as a source for locating biblical cities and unearthing artifacts because it contains religious material and biased recording of history. According to them, to take the Bible as a serious and legitimate source to aid archaeologists is "irresponsible." However, this objection forgets that the Bible itself is an archaeological source from the ancient world that offers details on people, places, and events—and in some cases this information is not found in any other source (for example, Belshazzar's name in Daniel 5, prior to the discovery of the Nabonidus Cylinder).

In addition, nearly all sources from the ancient world contain religious information and were written by people who had religious views. But these sources are taken as reliable and deemed important to our understanding of ancient history. What is more, some of the most beneficial historical sources were written by those intimately involved in the events they record (for example, Jewish Holocaust survivors writing about the concentration camps). So, contrary to the minimalist notion of excluding the Bible from archaeological research, it would be "irresponsible" to omit such a valuable and reliable ancient source as the New Testament when informing ourselves of ancient history.

The last half of this book is filled with these kinds of archaeological facts—those that confirm the historical reliability of both Old and New Testaments. So we will not enumerate them here.

Non-Christian Sources Confirm Basics of the Gospel Record

Noted New Testament scholar F.F. Bruce wrote the major work *Jesus and Christian Origins Outside the New Testament*. Summarizing the evidence on this topic, Dr. Gary Habermas shows that these extrabiblical sources contain the basic outline of the Gospel record about the life and teachings of Jesus.[11] Sources include Tacitus, Suetonius, Thallus, the Jewish Talmud, and Josephus (see more below). From his work Habermas ascertained 12 facts acknowledged by extrabiblical sources within 20 to 150 years after the death of Jesus. He showed that early Jewish and Roman sources confirm the following beliefs about the life and teaching of Jesus and His followers: 1) He was from Nazareth; 2) He lived a virtuous life; 3) He performed unusual feats; 4) He introduced new teaching contrary to Judaism; 5) He was crucified under Pontius Pilate; 6) His early disciples believed He rose from the dead; 7) His disciples denied polytheism; 8) His disciples worshipped Him; 9) His teachings and disciples spread rapidly; 10) His followers believed they were immortal; 11) His followers had contempt for death; 12) His followers renounced material goods. Consider the following historical source chart:

Source	Source date	Jesus existed	Virtuous	Worship	Disciples	Teacher	Crucified	Empty tomb	Disciples' belief in resurrection	Spread	Persecution
									Non-Christian Sources Within 150 Years of Jesus		
Tacitus	115	X			X		X	X*		X	X
Suetonius	117-138	X		X	X			X*		X	X
Josephus	90-95	X	X	X	X	X	X	X	X	X	
Thallus	52	X					X*				
Pliny	112	X		X	X	X		X*		X	X
Trajan	112?	X*		X	X					X	X
Hadrian	117-138	X*			X					X	X
Talmud	70-200	X					X				X
Toledoth Jesu	Fifth century	X						X			
Lucian	Second century	X		X	X	X	X				X
Mara Bar-Serapion	First to third century	X	X	X		X	X	X*			
Phlegon	80?	X					X	X	X		

Chart from Norman L. Geisler and William E. Nix, *A General Introduction to the Bible*, rev. ed. (Chicago: Moody Press, 1968, 1986). Used by permission of Moody Press.

*implied

Considering that these were all, as it were, "adversarial witnesses" and that they nonetheless confirmed these major points about Jesus and His early followers, this is good supplementary substantiation of the basic truths of the Gospel record. (For more detail on this subject, see chapter 22).

The Internal Evidence for the Historicity of the New Testament

In addition to the strong external evidence for the reliability of the Gospels, there is also very good internal evidence. In fact, if one knew nothing about the Bible or Christianity but discovered a New Testament in an antique book sale, he could get a strong sense of its credibility just by reading it. Here are several reasons why:

1. The writers did not try to harmonize their accounts, which shows they were not in collusion but were independent witnesses (see the next chapter, "Responding to Recent Criticisms of the Gospels").

2. The New Testament retained texts that placed Jesus in a bad light. Someone trying to prove that Jesus was God would not have done this.

3. The writers also included difficult passages in the text (which a fraudulent author would not have done).

4. They wrote self-incriminating stories (fraudulent authors do not invent bad stories about themselves).

5. They distinguished Jesus' words from their own (showing they were reporting, not creating, His words).

6. They did not deny their testimony under persecution or the threat of death (which weeds out the insincere).

The cumulative weight of the multiple and independent lines of testimony is overwhelming support for the historicity of the New Testament. No other book in the world has anything close to this much evidence for its authenticity.

RESPONDING TO RECENT
CRITICISMS OF THE GOSPELS

The most current attacks on the reliability of the New Testament have come almost
entirely from one person, renowned New Testament scholar Bart Ehrman. Ehrman
has argued against the reliability of the New Testament from just about every angle in a
series of recent books. The next two chapters will be devoted to engaging his most significant claims.

Contradictions in the Gospels?

Numerous liberal scholars throughout the history of biblical interpretation have
sought to identify contradictions within the Bible. Many of these attempts can be
regarded as popular-level propaganda pumped out by atheist and skeptic organizations,
and most of them do not deserve serious consideration.

Recently, however, Bart Ehrman has been responsible for several New York Times
bestsellers and so is worthy of a lengthy response here. Unlike many critics who find con-
spiracies involving the Bible and who do not warrant much attention due to their lack
of credentials and poor research (such as Dan Brown), Bart Ehrman is a fine historian
who is widely respected within his field of biblical scholarship. While other interpreters may propose similar kinds of things, Ehrman has been the most influential, consistent, and thorough in these allegations so we will engage the form of the arguments
found in his works.

In one of his most recent books, *Jesus, Interrupted* (2009), Ehrman insists that contradictions and discrepancies fill the New Testament, appearing in virtually all of the
parallel stories and teachings of Jesus recorded in the Gospels. In this chapter, we will
address several of these alleged tensions. Ehrman delineates these examples in the second and third chapters from *Jesus Interrupted*: "A World of Contradictions" and "A Mass
of Variant Views." In assessing the instances of discrepancies that Ehrman provides, it
will be helpful to address them within the following categories: 1) *additional details*;
2) *differing accounts*; 3) *contradicting accounts*; and 4) *historically inaccurate accounts*.

Under point 1, we consider various additions of details that occur in one Gospel but not another. Point 2 involves those instances which seem to not involve additional material, but material that seems mildly in conflict, according to Ehrman—we might refer to these as proposed discrepancies, but not direct contradictions. Point 3 involves pieces of data shared between the Gospels, which are, according to Ehrman, in direct conflict with one another. Finally, point 4 posits contradictions, not between the Gospels themselves, but between the Gospels and secular history.

These classifications remain very important in weaving through the maze of supposed inconsistencies that Ehrman attempts to present to his readers. Each of these discrepancy types necessitates a different kind of response—and really, only categories 3 and 4 should raise much concern. This will become clearer as we proceed, as will especially the weakness of Ehrman's cumulative case, which remains built mainly upon categories 1 and 2. But for now, we may note that the force of this point—that really only categories 3 and 4 are at all worrisome for the reliability of the New Testament—rests on what biblical scholars often refer to as literary criticism, a field with which Ehrman is well familiar. Most of his readers, however, are not.

This is important because Ehrman knows good and well that scholars commonly acknowledge differing literary agendas among the Gospel writers; these agendas constrain their choices of certain data over others. For example, Ehrman makes a big deal out of Luke's mentioning Caesar in his birth account while Matthew focuses on Herod, excluding any reference to Caesar. Such an issue is easily resolved when an interpreter takes into consideration the narrative purposes of the Gospel authors. Luke writes to a Roman official, Theophilus, quite probably to help acquit Paul as he stood on trial in Rome. Matthew apparently wrote with a more Jewish audience in view and naturally takes more interest in Herod.

Ehrman's insistence that such differences create a serious obstacle to the credibility of the Gospels remains shocking. The above examples should provide the reader a certain grasp of these categories by illustrating their importance as we move forward in our assessment. Note also that not all of these four discrepancy types will occur in every example.

1. Additional Details

Missing Birth Accounts

Ehrman begins by noting that only Matthew and Luke contain birth narratives. He is right about this. However, the force of this point weakens drastically when we consider the respective authors' literary purposes. Mark's style is one of immediacy. His account is intentionally condensed, and the narrative has a rapid pace. What's more, if the second-century AD historian Papias is correct and Mark's Gospel is really only a narrative collection of Peter's sermons in Rome, then perhaps Mark's source (Peter's sermons) simply did not include the birth story. Maybe this just was not a topic Peter preached on with any frequency. If we expect Mark to be faithful to his source, we should not expect him to include such details. John intentionally focuses on the deity of Jesus, excluding elements that do not serve this theological purpose directly. Therefore, he moves directly from the incarnation (God becoming flesh in Jesus) to Jesus' divine calling and baptism.

The fact that these Gospels exclude mention of Jesus' birth, therefore, hardly causes significant trouble for the veracity of the birth accounts of Jesus. Matthew and Luke include it because it fits their historical purposes. Mark and John fail to mention the birth because it does not serve their broader aims in writing. The same point answers Ehrman's objection that none of the other New Testament writers mention the birth either. Most of these documents are letters, addressed to specific issues in churches. Why should we require that they include a discourse on Jesus' birth in response to questions on spiritual gifts (1 Corinthians) or eschatology (2 Thessalonians)? We shouldn't.

Ehrman's complaint is found wanting at this juncture. Moreover, logic informs us that contradictions are present only when two statements are pitted against each other as mutually exclusive. In this case, the absence of a birth narrative in Mark and John is not a statement at all, and therefore, cannot be said to contradict Matthew and Luke. This is a fallacious argument from silence.

Mark Lacks the Genealogy

Although John does not have the genealogy in the same sense as Matthew and Luke, he does trace Jesus' origins—they go back to the pre-existent Father Himself (John 1:1). What about Mark? What must be kept in mind specifically is that Mark presents Jesus as a servant (Mark 10:45); it was not typical in the ancient world to provide genealogies for servants. Mark wrote his Gospel for the Romans. They had no interest in where this servant came from, but in what this servant could accomplish on their behalf (for example, notice the repeated phrase "immediately" throughout the Gospel).

In contrast, Matthew's Jewish audience looked for the Messiah, the King, unlike Mark's Roman audience, which appears to have had different literary expectations based on the servant characterization of Jesus by Mark. Accordingly, Matthew follows Jesus back to His Jewish roots as Davidic King in the line of Israel's royal ancestry (Matthew 1:1). And Luke presents Christ as a man, Jesus of Nazareth, full of the Holy Spirit. Hence, in Luke Christ's ancestry is traced back to the first man, Adam (Luke 3:38). And again, since John portrays Christ as the Son of God, he traces Christ back to His eternal source and glory (John 17:1-5) with the Father.

Where Was Jesus the Day After His Baptism?

Ehrman notes that the Gospels display differences regarding where Jesus was after His baptism. Mark says He went immediately into the wilderness to be tempted, whereas John does not mention the temptation but has Jesus encountering John the Baptist again the next day; John declares Jesus to be the Lamb of God.

The problem here is clearly not very acute. John's Gospel was the last of the New Testament Gospels to be written, and John seems to document things about Jesus' life that had not been said in previous accounts. So it is no surprise that he leaves out an event included in all three of the synoptics (Matthew, Mark, Luke). John simply does not document the event so there is no way to show a conflict between John and Mark's chronology.

Ehrman's reasoning here also misunderstands Mark's use of "immediately." He clearly does not literally mean the very next moment in Jesus' life since Matthew and

Luke include much in the gaps between the various stories about Jesus that Mark chronicles. Instead, it is a narrative device indicating the urgency of Jesus' message and ministry. This again shows why additional details between narratives really cannot be posed as significant contradictions.

Jesus' Conversation with Pilate

Ehrman mentions several differences between Mark's and John's account of Jesus' dialogue with Pilate. He claims that while there are several differences, he desires to only focus upon three. The first he mentions is simply that Jesus' conversation with Pilate in John is much longer. But the way historians recorded speeches in the ancient world allowed for summarization, condensation, and shortening to fit their narrative purposes; thus, additional material in John hardly counts as a discrepancy.

Second, Ehrman calls attention to the apparent difference between John and the synoptics (Matthew, Mark, Luke) involving the time of Christ's flogging. John seems to place it during the proceedings, whereas the synoptics seem to place it after. Again, Ehrman shows no cognizance of well-reasoned solutions to this so-called discrepancy. The Oxford historian A.N. Sherwin-White suggested the likely possibility here that there were two beatings.[1] The first was a mild beating called a *fustigatio,* intended to warn Jesus, commonly used in such proceedings for this purpose. This warning is the one that Luke records Pilate threatening Jesus with, and John records Pilate making good on that threat. Pilate clearly hoped that this would change Jesus' mind. Unfortunately, from Pilate's perspective, it did not. This resulted in Jesus receiving a second beating after the sentence was issued, the far more severe *verberatio,* from which many did not escape with their life. The account is not contradictory. Two different scourgings with two different purposes are in view.

Third, Ehrman insists that John's thrice-mentioned declaration by Pilate of Jesus' innocence creates problems for creating a unified history with Mark's account, which never has Pilate admitting Jesus' innocence. So what? Again, this entails no direct or even indirect contradiction. It was completely within the ancient historian's rights to choose which details to include and leave out. Clearly, in this case, Mark and John made different choices.

Two Accounts of Judas's Death

Another point of discrepancy that Ehrman insists upon involves what seems to us to be complementary rather than contradictory accounts. In Matthew (27:5), Judas hangs himself. In Acts (1:18), his body falls and his intestines gush out. There is no reason these accounts cannot reinforce one another. The account in Acts merely adds an additional detail regarding what happened after Judas died. In fact, it makes perfect sense since he hung himself from a tree over a cliff and seems to have fallen (either by being cut down or from the sheer weight on the rope or tree) on sharp rocks below, causing his disembowelment.

2. Differing Accounts

Differing Formulas

Other details Ehrman points to are simply incidental, such as the use of differing citation formulas. For example, he faults the Gospel tradition by noting that only Matthew has the phrase "to fulfill what was spoken by the Lord through the prophet" (Matthew 1:22; 2:5,17,23). Luke, according to Ehrman, lacks a prophetic focus and instead prefers to talk about "the Law of the Lord," especially in his nativity scene.

On these observations, it seems highly arbitrary to require authors to use the same phraseology in describing the theological significance of the events they record. One has to allow for stylistic latitude. It seems absurd to require the use of the exact same wording on such occasions since it would obfuscate the very stylistic identity of the authors themselves. This does not seem to be a very thoughtful criticism on the part of Ehrman. Of course the Gospel authors must be allowed to shape their narratives in language that frames their stories of Jesus in ways appropriate to their own literary style. Just the opposite of Ehrman's position could be argued—namely, the fact the authors are divergent in their choice of words is a mark of historicity and not collusion or plagiarism.

Details Lacking in Luke and Matthew

Ehrman sees it as problematic that Matthew includes the following details that Luke does not: 1) Joseph's dreams, 2) wise men, 3) the slaughter of children by Herod, 4) the flight to Egypt, and 5) the holy family bypassing Judah. What are we to make of these missing details? It seems odd on the face of it to make much of them at all, as Ehrman clearly does. Luke also includes material that Matthew does not: 1) John the Baptist's birth, 2) Caesar's census, 3) the Bethlehem trip, 4) the inn and the manger, 5) the shepherds, 6) Jesus' circumcision, and 7) the presentation of Jesus within the temple.

These differences in details have long been explained by interpreters as reflecting a difference in sources and purposes. According to the traditional view of the early church, Matthew was an eyewitness to the events he describes (an assumption Ehrman will not grant, but which has good historical grounds). Luke was not an eyewitness. He likely had to piece together his account through various interviews with eyewitnesses. Thus the traditions handed down to Luke on the one hand and the ones Matthew draws from his eyewitness account seem simply to reflect differing dimensions of the Jesus story.

This should not come as a surprise given different approaches taken by the authors in gathering material for their Gospels. Luke may not have had access to the pieces of tradition Matthew chooses to emphasize, and clearly Luke did not use Matthew in this case, so it seems strange to require Luke to match Matthew's account of Jesus' birth. And even if Luke did have some of these same traditions available to him, again, they may not always have suited his literary goals in writing and so he chose not to include them. Authors must be given the discretion to adopt only the material most relevant to their purposes in writing. The fundamentals of basic literary composition demand this much.

Jesus' Baptism by John

The first recorded event in Jesus' adult life was His baptism by John, accompanied by the testimony of His Father and the Spirit. Ehrman claims that the reporting of the history remains riddled with difficulty due to conflicting accounts. By this, he means variations in the wording that the Father utters in response to Jesus' baptism. For example, Matthew's account has "This is My beloved Son, in whom I am well pleased" (3:17 NKJV), whereas Luke's account probably (depending on the manuscript decision one makes) cites Psalm 2:7: "You are My Son, today I have begotten You" (NKJV).

A problem surfaces here in Ehrman's analysis that we find especially acute elsewhere as well. To begin with, it reveals lack of knowledge of the common practice in ancient history of just offering a paraphrase of what was said. Thucydides, Herodotus, Josephus, Xenophon, and the writer of 1 Maccabees all did this, and apparently so did the Gospel writers. We do not suppose Ehrman would want to say that the history these authors record—even when in parallel material there remain slight differences, such as in the comparisons of Josephus and 1 Maccabees—is to be dismissed because of such subtle differences. This kind of approach would result in a type of agnosticism toward ancient history, as we have emphasized before.

It also confuses the issue to enforce the kind of modernistic standard upon the Gospels that Ehrman does, claiming that the accounts must have the exact words that were spoken. This cannot be true at a theoretical level since most of these dialogues likely took place in Aramaic, and so the Gospel authors would have had to translate them into Greek. Further, practices of *mimesis* (imitation of others on the same historical topic) in many contexts demanded unique transmission of historical material—so a different translation from the Aramaic or (perhaps in Luke's case) a transmission of a different piece of oral tradition would have been preferred.

Ehrman also requires too much of the text. He assumes without argument that unless the text is what scholars call *ipsissima verba* (in the exact words of Jesus), then it can be neither without error nor historical. However, many scholars, both liberal and conservative, hold to the idea that the Gospels merely convey *ipsissima vox* (with the same meaning or voice) of Jesus or, in this case, the voice from heaven. The text can inerrantly communicate the *voice* (that is, the basic meaning) of the Father's statement without being forced to give the exact wording of the statement in all four accounts. Inerrancy requires only the former, not the latter. Ehrman knows that this is a reasonable explanation offered by scholars for assessing these problems, but he writes as though no solution has ever been proposed. This is problematic, and it leaves readers with the impression that inerrancy or even accuracy requires the unduly stringent *ipsissima verba* interpretation of the Scriptures. This—to say the least—severely misrepresents the discussion.

The Length of Jesus' Ministry

Another discrepancy that Ehrman mentions from the life of Jesus, even Ehrman himself acknowledges should not be considered a discrepancy.[2] He focuses here on Mark's use of immediacy language and then compares this to the chronology that we find in John. Based on the occurrence of Passover celebrations, this chronology has led most scholars to conclude a two-to-three-year time length for Jesus' public ministry. But we must agree with Ehrman when he acknowledges that this does not count as a discrepancy since his point is based on a highly tenuous interpretation of the immediacy language in John's Gospel. Mark's immediacy language, as widely acknowledged within scholarship, functions as a literary device and is not intended to specify short time frames. Ehrman knows this, but most of his readers do not.

3. Contradicting Accounts

The Hometown of Jesus

Was it Bethlehem or Nazareth? Matthew emphasizes Bethlehem, while Luke focuses upon Nazareth. Matthew highlights Jesus' birthplace; Luke, his hometown. To create a conflict between the accounts, Ehrman relies on some fairly serious conjecture, meaning that the differences he insists on can hardly be considered irreconcilable. He posits the following: Since Herod decreed that the soldiers must kill all children two years and younger, Jesus and his family *must have stayed* in Bethlehem longer than a month. This would create some tension with Luke's account, which has them returning after about a month.

However, Ehrman's insistence that the stories require this timeline remains highly speculative. Matthew's account does not explicitly state how long Jesus' family remained in Bethlehem, making the proposed contradictions highly tentative or even impossible to prove from the text.

Egypt or Nazareth?

In response to Herod's decree, Matthew has Jesus' family flee to Egypt. Luke informs us that they returned to Nazareth from Bethlehem. Again, it seems hard to understand the force of Ehrman's dilemma here. Although Luke has Joseph and Mary eventually arriving back in Nazareth, there appears no reason why they could not have had a tenure in Egypt prior to this, as Matthew emphasizes. Since Luke does not focus on the decree from Herod, he does not have the same narrative pressure to indicate how they escaped from Herod. Luke chose not to (or did not have materials to) move his story in that direction.

Ehrman overlooks here what biblical scholars have sometimes referred to as "narrative compression." Often, ancient historians compressed the events of the story that they recorded so as to provide just the basic timeline necessary for an intelligible account. This seems to have happened here. Although it is possible, there is no reason to assume that Luke did not have access to the traditions that Matthew discusses. Instead, he simply compresses the timeline of events to fit with the way that he hoped to tell the story. The result is a more concise and relevant narrative. Ehrman places undue pressure on these authors to be comprehensive—as though the Gospels are a type of collective history, written as a collaboration of sorts. But why should we require such a totalistic approach? As mentioned, part of the task of the historian involves choosing what details to include and what not to include. It should not surprise modern critics that the Gospels reflect precisely such a process.

The Resurrection of Jairus's Daughter

Ehrman claims there is a direct discrepancy between the accounts found in Mark 5:21-34 and Matthew 9:18-26. In Mark it says that the girl Jesus healed was almost dead, whereas in Matthew, the girl was dead. Now Ehrman assumes without argument that this is the same event. But only Mark's account specifies the name of the ruler whose daughter Jesus helped—it was Jairus's daughter. Matthew does not say this. In Mark, the event happens right after the sending of the demons into the swine. In Matthew, the event still takes place after the demonized swine event, but there is intervening narrative and teaching. So two different events could be in view—one where a leader's daughter is healed (Mark) and one involving the resurrection of a leader's daughter (Matthew).

But even if we grant that Matthew and Mark document the same event, in Matthew the Greek language actually allows for the meaning that the daughter is "dying now." We find there an aorist (a Greek tense) that, according to recent research on the Greek verb by scholars like Stanley Porter and Rodney Decker, can have a past or present time reference based on the context. The aorist, in fact, makes no comment on the time reference. It just states that the kind of action happened without making any further comment about the details of the action. It is a simple statement of the process; in this case, dying.

In Matthew's account also appears the temporal adverb *arti*, which is glossed in the authoritative Bauer-Danker-Arndt-Gingrich Greek lexicon of the New Testament as indicating something *of the immediate moment*,[3] and in many settings this adverb is translated with a present time reference. For example, in John 13:37, an aorist verb (like we have here) is used with *arti* and should be translated "now" ("Lord, why can I not follow [aorist] you right now [*arti*]"). We see then the flexibility of the language here. So a valid translation of Matthew 9:18 could be "my daughter is now dying," showing that the account is in no necessary conflict with Mark's. Leon Morris opines further the possibility that the language could indicate that the daughter is "as good as dead," or that Matthew is perhaps abbreviating his narrative (a common tactic in chronicles of the ancient world) by combining the opening of the story and the sending of the messengers, as he did in 8:5-13 in the story of the centurion's servant.[4] Yet again, Ehrman, who knows the Greek language, acts as if these incidents are in direct conflict with no possibility of resolution.

Who Is For or Against Jesus?

Ehrman also points to Matthew 12:30 and Mark 9:40, which he claims contain contrary ideas. Matthew's account has Jesus saying, "Whoever is not with me is against me" (NIV). Mark says, "Whoever is not against us is for us" (NIV). This supposed contradiction is really just a result of bad exegesis. In this case, Ehrman fails to take the meaning of these statements in context.

In Matthew, Ehrman fails to cite the remainder of the verse, which states, "and whoever does not gather with me scatters" (NIV). So in this context, clearly Jesus has in mind followers who would scatter because they were not "with Him." When we turn to Mark's account, we find in the following verse that Jesus' explanation of His statement clarifies exactly what He means: "For truly, I say to you, whoever gives you a cup of water to drink because you belong to Christ will by no means lose His reward" (9:41

esv). The conjunction "for" indicates a direct explanatory connection between the statement here in 9:41 and the one in 9:40 that Ehrman cites. So what Jesus says in Mark is in no way inconsistent with Matthew's Gospel when both are considered in context.

The Time of Jesus' Death

Ehrman draws attention to John's remark in his Gospel (19:14) that Jesus was still on trial around the sixth hour (12 noon Jewish time). According to Mark's Gospel (15:25), Jesus eats the Passover and is crucified the next morning, at the third hour (9 a.m. Jewish time). Ehrman notices that this would make His crucifixion much earlier than indicated by John.

As we have seen earlier, what remains most shocking is Ehrman's failure to engage with the often repeated response by conservative scholars to this kind of objection. They typically note the differing time systems employed by John and Mark. John uses Roman time to describe the events in his Gospel, while Mark utilizes the Jewish system. The Jewish day started in the evening at 6 p.m. and the morning of that day began at 6 a.m. In Roman time, midnight to midnight marked a day. (Today's 24-hour day is obviously based on the Roman system.) So when Mark says that Christ was crucified at the third hour, he means around 9 a.m. John stated that Christ's trial was about the sixth hour. This would place the trial *before* the crucifixion at around 6 a.m., and therefore, would not negate any testimony of the Gospel writers. This fits with John's other references to time (for example, John 1:39).

That solves the time issue, but Ehrman also insists that the days are different. According to John, Jesus was crucified on the day before the Passover, while the lambs were being slaughtered (symbolically); whereas Mark and the other synoptics (Matthew, Luke) have Him eat the Passover meal (Thursday night), and they then narrate His crucifixion the next morning. John says Jesus was crucified on the day of "preparation" for the Passover rather than on the day of preparation for the Sabbath, as in the synoptic Gospels.

Ehrman makes passing reference to the possible response that a different sectarian calendar might have been used by John, but this is by no means the strongest or most frequent response to this alleged discrepancy. A much better resolution, discussed by D.A. Carson for example,[5] involves a more careful consideration of John's language. It must be recognized that παρασκευή (*paraskeuē*—"preparation") frequently has reference to Friday—and in this case, Preparation of the Sabbath is Friday (see John 19:31,42; Matthew 27:62; Mark 15:42; Luke 23:54). Barrett famously asserted that this text must refer to the preparation for (that is, before) the Passover, yet could not furnish one reference where παρασκευή (*paraskeuē*) was used for a day before a feast day other than the Sabbath (Saturday), which would fall on Friday.[6] If Carson is correct, then John has Friday in mind with his phrase "Preparation" (*paraskeuē*) Day of the Passover,[7] and *paraskeuē* can refer to the Passover feast or even the entire Passover week. This use of the Greek word in the meaning of Passover is not infrequent at all (for example, see Luke 22:1).

So what John seems to have meant was "the Friday of Passover week," which is perfectly consistent with the Gospels' usage of the day of Preparation of the Sabbath. Therefore, we may conclude as Carson does "that the last supper was eaten on Thursday evening [after 6:00 p.m.] (that is, the onset of Friday by Jewish reckoning), and was a Passover meal," and that Jesus was crucified on Friday as John and the Synoptic Gospels agree. In addition, taking this phrase in John 19:14 to mean the Friday before Passover is supported by the fact that both the Western and Eastern Church adopted this phrase as a synonym for Friday, as is recognized in Greece today.[8]

4. Historically Inaccurate Accounts

A Star in the East

Ehrman is critical, from a historical vantage point, of the whole notion in Matthew's nativity account that a star could have guided the wise men. Matthew portrays the star as a form of divine guidance that was used to lead the wise men to Jesus (Matthew 2:9). We find much of this kind of supernatural activity in many of the secular histories, such as Josephus and Herodotus, which Ehrman depends upon in other instances to indicate problems with the biblical record.

To reject something as nonhistorical precisely because one cannot understand the theological, physical, or supernatural mechanisms used to bring about the event moves the discussion away from history toward philosophy. This leaves great difficulty for Ehrman to object to this event on strictly historical grounds—without importing a number of metaphysical assumptions he would need to defend. After all, if God truly exists, then acts of God (miracles) are possible. The only way for Ehrman to dismiss the miraculous is to demonstrate God does not exist, something that he has not yet accomplished.

Herod's Massacre

Ehrman also objects to Matthew's mention of Herod's decree to slaughter children under two. He claims that such an event cannot be historical since we have no record of it outside of the New Testament. However, this reasoning fails to convince. To begin with, the vast majority of what we know about Herod is found in only one other source, Josephus. So it is not as though we have abundant documentation of the activities of Herod's reign.

One should note the distinctively apologetic nature of Josephus's work. Being officially commissioned by the Roman Empire as he was, Josephus may have trod carefully on certain politically sensitive issues, of which this may have been one. This act seems pretty brutal even for the Romans and their local client rulers (such as Herod).

And there are many details about Herod in Josephus's account that find no testimony elsewhere, but few of them are often called into question. One of Ehrman's strategies involves pitting the New Testament against Josephus in cases where only a New Testament author and Josephus record an event. This procedure endorses a method that Ehrman tacitly denies here. It's simply special pleading.

Moreover, our knowledge of the ancient world remains highly fragmentary and so it just won't do to dismiss data simply because it is not corroborated by ancient extra-biblical sources. Of course, we can have greater certainty about events that do bear multiple attestation. But the reverse principle—that events without multiple attestation are historically unlikely—hardly holds water when dealing with ancient history more broadly. This raises the question of why Ehrman believes an extrabiblical source has superior confirming power over the New Testament—which is itself an archaeological ancient source, with the highest bibliographical support of any work from the ancient world.

Caesar's Census

Likewise, Ehrman complains about the lack of external attestation for the census by Augustus Caesar that Luke records. Our historical sources for Caesar are quite a bit better than the ones we have for Herod. Still, we may return to the principle that events found in only a single source cannot be dismissed prima facie on this criterion alone. And while a number of interpreters used to side with Ehrman in making this point about the census, several scholars now widely accept that there was in fact an earlier registration, as Luke records. Ehrman knows this—or at least he should, given his background. Several factors have led to this shift in consensus, which Ehrman fails to acknowledge.

To begin with, when the people of a subordinate land were asked to take an oath of allegiance to the emperor, it was not unusual to require an imperial census as an expression of this allegiance and as a means of enlisting men for military service; or, as was probably true in this case, in preparation to levy taxes. Due to the tensions between Herod and Augustus, which we know about from Josephus, it does not seem at all far-fetched that Augustus would begin to treat Herod's domain as a subject land, which would require him to order a census so that he could continue to control Herod and his people.

Additionally, a census was a sizable project that likely took several years to complete. In Gaul, for example, a census for the purpose of taxation was begun in 10 or 9 BC and took 40 years to complete. It seems probable that the decree to begin the census in the Judean region was issued in 8 or 7 BC, and thus may not have actually begun until sometime later. Difficulties with organizing and preparing the census may have also led to delaying the execution of the census till 5 BC or even later.

Another consideration is the fact that there were periodic registrations of this sort every 14 years. Some of the documents that report such censuses indicate that one was in fact taken around 8 or 7 BC. Because of this regular pattern of census-taking, any such action would naturally be regarded as a result of the general policy of Augustus, even though a local census might have been initiated by a local governor. This is likely why Luke recognizes the census as stemming from the decree of Augustus.

Finally, we must remember that it was a common practice for a census to require people to return to the place of their origin, or to the place where they owned land. For example, one of Caius Vibius Maximus's decrees (AD 104) ordered all who resided in lands outside of their hometowns to return to their hometowns so an accurate census could be undertaken. Moreover, given the Jews' annual pilgrimage to Jerusalem, it would in no way be uncommon for them to be involved in this kind of travel. These considerations have left little room for skepticism regarding the census at the time of Jesus' birth in much modern scholarship.

Ehrman knows that things are a lot more complex than the picture he portrays and so his assertions on this score can be misleading at best. Luke's account fits nicely with the regular pattern of census-taking in the ancient world, and its date is hardly unreasonable as Ehrman contends. The possibility that this may have simply been a local census, taken as a result of the general policy of Augustus, cannot be excluded. So when Ehrman mocks the very logistics of such an event—Luke's report of travelers returning to their hometown—he reveals even more his own lack of awareness regarding practices in the first century AD. The census could have and did happen. Luke simply provides us with a reliable historical record of an event that was, although not uncommon, not otherwise recorded. So while this event does not find external corroboration outside of the New Testament, methodologically, this in itself does not militate against the authenticity and historical reliability of the Gospels.

Quirinius's Reign

Ehrman also draws attention to the fact that Luke records that Jesus' birth occurred during Quirinius's reign over Syria, while Matthew documents it as occurring during Herod's reign. However, Tacitus and Josephus have Quirinius beginning his reign in Syria in 6 AD, ten years after Herod's death. A number of considerations should be weighed in response to Ehrman on this point.

As an initial consideration, the governor of Syria from about 7 BC to about 4 BC was Quintilius Varus. Varus turned out not to be the most reliable leader, something that later became abundantly apparent in AD 9 when he suffered the loss of several thousand soldiers in Germany at the battle of the Teutoburger Forest. By contrast, Quirinius was a superb military leader, who was able to settle the rebellion of the Homonadensians in Asia Minor. Augustus entrusted Quirinius with the delicate political situation in Israel, a highly volatile region, effectively superseding the authority and governorship of Varus by appointing Quirinius to a place of special authority in this matter when it came time to begin the census, in about 8 or 7 BC.

A number of further considerations should be weighed as well. First, a not unlikely translation of Luke 2:2 could read, "This census took place before Quirinius was governing Syria." In this understanding of the Greek word translated "first" (*prōtos*), it is translated as a comparative, "before." Because of the awkward construction of the sentence, this is not an unlikely reading. The probability that Quirinius was governor of Syria on two different occasions also cannot be ignored—once while prosecuting the military action against the Homonadensians between 12 and 2 BC, and then a second time beginning about AD 6. This proposal is actually corroborated by a Latin inscription discovered in 1764 that has been interpreted to refer to Quirinius as having served as governor of Syria on two occasions. Regardless of the solution one accepts, Ehrman's insistence that Luke must be in error here is hardly necessary as he argues.

Matthew's and Luke's Genealogies Contradict Each Other

Ehrman also insists that the genealogies contained in Matthew and Luke are outright contradictory. However, there is good reason to believe the genealogies are different and complementary, not contradictory. They detail two different types of ancestral lines. Luke gives an *official genealogy*, whereas Matthew provides the *official line*, since he addresses Jewish concerns for the Jewish Messiah's credentials, which required that the Messiah come from the seed of Abraham and the line of David (see Matthew 1:1). Luke, with a broader Greek audience in view, addresses himself to their interest in Jesus as the Perfect Man (which was the quest of Greek thought). Thus, he traces Jesus back to the first man, Adam (Luke 3:38).

While, on the one hand, Matthew provides the genealogy of Jesus in terms of His father Joseph's line, Luke focuses more upon the maternal (Mary's) genealogy. A number of considerations demonstrate the legitimacy of this basic comparison. To begin with, although each genealogy delineates the line of descent from Christ to David, they do so through a different son of David. Matthew traces the line of Joseph (Jesus' legal father) back to Solomon, David's son, the one by whom it is shown that Jesus is a rightful heir to David's throne (see 2 Samuel 7:12ff).

Luke's intention, by contrast, is to demonstrate the humanity of Christ. He can be traced back to a lesser known son of David, Nathan. How? Through His mother Mary. So he traces Christ to David's son, Nathan, through His actual mother, Mary. Yes, this means Mary is also a descendant of David, thus providing the genetic pedigree that was necessary for Christ to sit on the throne of David. The curse placed upon King Jeconiah's seed prohibited any of his descendants (which included Joseph) from occupying the throne. Meaning that, though Joseph provided the *legal* right for Jesus to sit on the throne of David (the king had to descend from Solomon's line), Mary provides Jesus the *genetic* right to the throne. This fits well within Luke's overall portrait of Jesus of Nazareth as a human prophet who came to redeem humanity. Luke writes to a Gentile audience, and so it is important to his narrative to connect Jesus to humanity more broadly, rather than portraying Him as the heir to the Jewish king's throne, which fits with Matthew's narrower narrative strategy.

As a further consideration, it is an unfair assumption that simply because the two genealogies have some names in common (such as Shealtiel and Zerubbabel; see Matthew 1:12 and Luke 3:27), they are, therefore, the same genealogy. For starters, these were very common names in the ancient world; by comparison, even within the same genealogy (Luke's) we find a repetition of the names Joseph and Judah (3:26,30).

Ehrman misses this point. He considers the possibility of explaining divergent accounts on the basis that Luke provides his genealogy through Mary, but dismisses this option as unattractive due to his exegesis of Luke 3:23. He takes this verse as an aligning of the genealogy with Joseph's rather than Mary's line. The reader must keep a few things in mind here, however. First, Luke does not indicate that he makes Joseph the base point for his genealogy of Jesus. A more careful reading of the pericope (section) and the wider context reveals, even in Luke's own words, that Jesus was "as was supposed" (Luke 3:23) the son of Joseph, when in reality he was the son of Mary as a wider reading of the narrative shows. The Greek here for "as was supposed" (ἐνομίζετο, *enomizeto*) indicates that it was a thought, a belief at that time, but not entirely true. It was true in the sense that Mary was Jesus' biological mother, according to Luke's narrative, but Joseph was not His biological father. This provides immediate justification for Luke's tracing His genealogy through Mary rather than Joseph—so this statement should be read not as an acknowledgment of Luke's using Joseph as the base point of his genealogy, but probably a hint that he did precisely the opposite.

And this fits perfectly with what we know elsewhere about Luke—that he was a doctor, and in the ancient world doctors show interest in mothers and birth. In fact, due to Luke's emphasis on women within his narrative, Luke's Gospel has often been called "the Gospel for Women." Coupled with the fact that he never claims to chronicle Jesus' lineage from the perspective of Joseph, these lines of evidence seem to point overwhelmingly toward the genealogy being traced through Mary rather than Joseph. And once it is seen that the genealogy could have been written from this perspective, Ehrman's so-called irreconcilable difficulties evaporate.

If it is granted that it is at least possible that Luke documented the genealogy from the maternal standpoint, Ehrman's case becomes substantially weakened. He presents only a possibility that the two accounts contradict, and—all things being equal—we should give these ancient historical records the benefit of the doubt (as we do with other accounts from the ancient world). Historians tend to operate with the innocent-until-proven-guilty principle in dealing with nonbiblical data from the ancient world, and so should those approaching the history of the earliest Christians and their leader, Jesus.

When viewing Luke then from the maternal perspective and Matthew from the paternal line, the two genealogies can be summarized as follows:

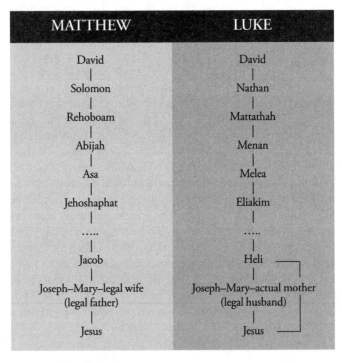

MATTHEW	LUKE
David	David
Solomon	Nathan
Rehoboam	Mattathah
Abijah	Menan
Asa	Melea
Jehoshaphat	Eliakim
.....	.....
Jacob	Heli
Joseph–Mary–legal wife (legal father)	Joseph–Mary–actual mother (legal husband)
Jesus	Jesus

Chart from Norman L. Geisler and William E. Nix, *A General Introduction to the Bible*, rev. ed. (Chicago: Moody Press, 1968, 1986). Used by permission of Moody Press.

As readers can see from the above chart, the addition and omission of names can be easily reconciled when considering what the text already seems to imply—that Luke traces Mary's line rather than Joseph's.

Matthew's Genealogy Contradicts the Old Testament

Ehrman also raises the problem with names that are present in Matthew's Gospel, but are missing in the Chronicles genealogy, which is assumed to be Matthew's source. He presents these problems to his audience as though no one has ever worked through or dealt with the issues before. In particular, he draws attention to the "missing" generations in Matthew's genealogy from Joram and Uzziah:

Matthew 1:8	1 Chronicles 3:11-12
Jehoram	Jehoram
_____	Ahaziah
_____	Joash
_____	Amaziah
Uzziah	Azariah (more commonly Uzziah)

Chart from Norman L. Geisler and William E. Nix, *A General Introduction to the Bible*, rev. ed. (Chicago: Moody Press, 1968, 1986). Used by permission of Moody Press.

Ehrman objects that Jehoram is not in fact Uzziah's father, but rather his grandfather. Ehrman claims that Matthew has twisted the facts in order to keep his numerology tidy and secure (there is an emphasis on 14 generations within the lineage, Matthew 1:17). However, this contention misunderstands the Greek in this instance. To begin with, the Greek in Matthew at many places in the genealogy does not use the word *father* but a prepositional phrase meaning "out of," an idiom for conveying family relationships in such contexts.

In the place of contention—Matthew 1:8—the Greek word γεννάω (*gennaō*, "to bear," "to father") is used, but it entirely misunderstands the Greek idiom to force this word to refer only to a direct biological father. Jesus, for example, is called the "son of David," but there are 31 generations intervening between them. When the text says the "father of," in Jewish idiom this means an "ancestor of." The same kind of idiom is employed here in Matthew 1:8. Ehrman knows better. It is on the verge of downright misleading to say that the text says "father" but that this is an error because a grandfather is in view—these were one and the same in the ancient world. It actually, we believe, shows the strength of the reliability of the New Testament—if Ehrman has to resort to these kinds of details to find errors, the problems must not be as glaring as he insists. So he here is either sloppy in his research or simply smuggling in ideas he knows do not hold the weight demanded of them, but which will nonetheless stir up controversy and sell books.

Ehrman's objection on this point also assumes without argument that genealogies in the ancient world and in the Bible were "closed" genealogies (no gaps). In fact, the evidence supports the existence of "open" genealogies (where generations are skipped), of which Matthew would clearly be one. These open genealogies allowed authors the freedom to highlight the points in the genealogy significant to their narrative purposes without the constraint of having to delineate every person in a family over several thousand years of history. In Matthew's case, yes, it allows the freedom to pursue a numerological pattern, but when one understands the way Jewish genealogies worked in the ancient world, this in no way compromises the integrity of Matthew's. Similar gaps occur in other genealogies, demonstrating a wider biblical pattern with which Matthew aligns. For example, the genealogies in 1 Chronicles 6:6-14 and Ezra 7:3-4, when a comparison is made, show that Ezra omits six generations between Zerahiah and Azariah that the 1 Chronicles account includes:

1 Chronicles 6:6-14	Ezra 7:3-4
Zerahiah	Zerahiah
Meraioth	Meraioth
Amariah	———
Ahitub	———
Zadok	———
Ahimaaz	———
Azariah	———
Johanan	———
Azariah	Azariah
Amariah	Amariah

Chart from Norman L. Geisler and William E. Nix, *A General Introduction to the Bible*, rev. ed. (Chicago: Moody Press, 1968, 1986). Used by permission of Moody Press.

Does this indicate that there is error in the text? No. It just shows a literary pattern in which it was acceptable to record a family's lineage without having to show every single link in the line of descent.

CRITICISMS OF THE RESURRECTION ACCOUNTS AND THE EPISTLES

In the section on the resurrection texts within his recent book, *Jesus, Interrupted*, Bart Ehrman raises a litany of questions concerning consistency of the accounts. For example, he draws attention to the number of women who came to the tomb after the resurrection. He says that John writes that Mary came "alone."[1] However, John 20:1 does not say whether Mary was alone or not. It simply says she came to the tomb. Other accounts mention other women who were present. It simply depends on what the author wants to focus on in his context. John, for example, wants to single out Mary's experience among the group. Others focus on the group.

Sequence of the Events of Jesus' Resurrection

The discussion below irons out all the major difficulties in the order of appearances. In the discussion that follows this one, overwhelming historical evidences for the physical resurrection of Christ are given:

Order of Resurrection Events	Evidence They Provide
1. Mary Magdalene and other women	Empty tomb
(Matthew 28:1; Mark 16:1-3; Luke 24:1-10; John 20:1)	
2. The other women	Empty tomb, angel(s)
(Matthew 28:5-8; Mark 16:6-9; Luke 24:4-9)	
3. Peter and John	Empty tomb, grave clothes
(John 20:3-10)	
4. Mary Magdalene (#1)	Angels, heard, saw, touched
(Mark 16:9-10; John 20:11-18)	

Order of Resurrection Events	Evidence They Provide
5. Other women (#2) (Matthew 28:9-10)	Saw, heard, touched
6. Peter (#3) (Luke 24:34; 1 Corinthians 15:5)	Saw, heard*
7. Two Disciples (#4) (Luke 24:13-31; Mark 16:12)	Saw, heard, ate
8. Ten Disciples (#5) (Mark 16:14; Luke 24:35-49; John 20:19-24; 1 Corinthians 15:5)	Saw, scars, heard, touched,* ate
9. Eleven Disciples (Thomas present) (#6) (John 20:26-29)	Saw, scars, heard, touched*
10. Seven disciples by Sea of Galilee (#7) (John 21:1-23)	Saw, heard, ate
11. Five hundred disciples in Galilee (#8) (1 Corinthians 15:6)	Saw, heard
12. All the apostles in Galilee (#9) (Matthew 28:18-20)	Saw, heard
13. James (#10) (1 Corinthians 15:7)	Saw, heard
14. All the apostles in Jerusalem (#11) (1 Corinthians 15:7; Mark 16:15-20; Luke 24:46-52; Acts 1:3-9)	Saw, heard, ate
15. Paul (#12) (Acts 9:1-8; 1 Corinthians 9:1; 15:8)	Saw, heard

*implied

Harmony of the Postresurrection Order of Events*

1. Early on Sunday morning after Jesus' crucifixion, Mary Magdalene, Mary the mother of James, Joanna, and Salome went to the tomb with spices to anoint Jesus' body (Matthew 28:1; Mark 16:1; Luke 24:1; John 20:1). Finding the tomb empty, Mary Magdalene ran to Peter and John to tell them someone had taken the body of Jesus (John 20:2).

2. The other women entered the tomb, where an angel (Matthew 28:5) who had a companion (John 20:11-12; Luke 24:4) told them Jesus had risen and would meet the disciples in Galilee (Matthew 28:2-8; Mark 16:5-8; Luke 24:4-8). On their hurried return in trembling astonishment (Mark 16:8) yet with great joy (Matthew 28:8), they said nothing to anyone along the way (Mark 16:8) but went back to the disciples and reported what they had seen and heard (Matthew 28:8; Mark 16:10; Luke 24:9-10; John 20:2).

3. Meanwhile, after hearing Mary Magdalene's report, Peter and John ran to the tomb (John 20:3), apparently by a different and more direct route. John arrived at the tomb first (John 20:4). He peered into the tomb and saw the grave clothes but did not enter (John 20:5). When Peter arrived he entered the tomb and saw the grave clothes (John 20:6). Then John entered, saw the grave clothes and the folded head cloth in a place by itself, and believed (John 20:8). After this, they returned to the place the other disciples were staying by the same route (John 20:10) and so did not encounter the women.

4. Arriving after Peter and John had left, Mary Magdalene went into the tomb (for a second time) and saw the angels (John 20:13). *She also saw Jesus (appearance #1)* and clung to Him and worshipped Him (John 20:11-17). She then returned to the disciples (John 20:18; Mark 16:10).

5. While the other women were on their way to the disciples, Jesus *appeared to them (appearance #2)*. They took hold of His feet and worshipped Him (Matthew 28:9-10). Jesus asked them to tell His disciples that He would meet them in Galilee (Matthew 28:10). Meanwhile the guards were bribed and told to say the disciples had stolen His body (Matthew 28:11-15).

6. When Mary and the women found the disciples, they announced that they had seen Jesus (Mark 16:10-11; Luke 24:10; John 20:18). After hearing this,

---

* There are some key verses on the order of the resurrection events. First Corinthians 15:5-8 lists the order of separate appearances in regard to Peter, the Twelve, 500 brethren, James, all the apostles, and Paul. Luke 24:34 asserts that Jesus appeared to Peter before He appeared to the two disciples on the road to Emmaus and before He later appeared to the Eleven (Luke 24:33-36). John 21:1-13 declares that the appearance to the seven apostles at the Sea of Tiberias (Sea of Galilee—John 6:1) was the third appearance to His disciples as a group (John 21:14). Matthew, Mark, Luke, and John all say the women were at the empty tomb first. Mark 16:9 reports that the first appearance was to Mary Magdalene. John 20:11-18 implies this also.

Peter probably rushed to find Jesus, and *Peter saw Him (appearance #3)* that day (1 Corinthians 15:5; see Luke 24:10).

7. The same day Jesus *appeared to Cleopas and another unnamed disciple (appearance #4)*—perhaps Luke—on the road to Emmaus (Mark 16:12; Luke 24:13-31). He revealed Himself to them while eating with them, and He told them He had appeared to Peter (Luke 24:34; see 1 Corinthians 15:5). [Luke 24:34 may mean either that the two told the Eleven that Jesus had appeared to Peter, or that when the two saw the Eleven, the latter were saying the Lord had appeared to Peter.]

8. After Jesus left the two men, they returned to Jerusalem, where Jesus *appeared to the Ten disciples (appearance #5)* (Thomas being absent—John 20:24), showing His scars and eating some fish (Mark 16:14; Luke 24:35-49; John 20:19-24).

9. After eight days, Jesus *appeared to the Eleven (appearance #6)* (Thomas now present). He showed His wounds and challenged Thomas to believe. Thomas exclaimed, "My Lord and my God" (John 20:28).

10. Jesus *appeared to seven of His disciples (appearance #7)* who had gone fishing in the Sea of Galilee (John 21:1). He ate breakfast with them (John 21:2-13), after which He restored Peter (21:15-19).

11. Then He *appeared to 500 brethren* at one time *(appearance #8)* (1 Corinthians 15:6).

12. After this He *appeared to all the apostles (appearance #9)* in Galilee and gave them the Great Commission (1 Corinthians 15:7; Matthew 28:18-20).

13. Then, He *appeared to James (appearance #10)* (1 Corinthians 15:7), probably in Jerusalem.

14. Later in Jerusalem, He *appeared to all his apostles (appearance #11)* (1 Corinthians 15:7), presenting many convincing evidences to them (Acts 1:3), including eating with them (Acts 1:4). He answered their last question (Acts 1:6-8) and then ascended into heaven (Mark 16:15-20; Luke 24:46-52; Acts 1:9-11).

15. Several years later, on the road to Damascus, Jesus *appeared to Saul of Tarsus (appearance #12)* (Acts 9:1-8; 1 Corinthians 9:1; 15:8), later known as the apostle Paul.

In regard to the above, note first that the initial three events involved no appearances of Jesus, only angels and an empty tomb. Second, Mary Magdalene was the first to see the resurrected Christ. The other women were next, and Peter was third. Third, in all, counting Paul, there were 12 separate appearances. Fourth, the first nine events (1 through 9) were all in and around Jerusalem. Events 10, 11, and 12 were in Galilee, and 13 and 14 were back in the Jerusalem area. The last one (involving Paul) was in Syria, near Damascus (Acts 9:3).

The Evidence for the Historicity of the Resurrection

In all 12 appearances the persons involved saw (with the naked eye) and heard (with their physical ears) Jesus. Four times they saw Him eat. Four times He was touched. The empty tomb was seen at least four times. Twice the grave clothes were seen, and twice His crucifixion scars were viewed. His first 11 appearances occurred over a 40-day period to different groups—including women, the apostles, a doubting apostle, other disciples, an unbelieving half-brother, and over 500 people at the same time. During this time period, Jesus talked with them, taught them, ate with them, and gave them many "indisputable evidences" (Acts 1:3) of His physical resurrection. He literally exhausted the ways in which He could prove to them that He had been physically raised in the same body in which He had died.

One apparent problem is that Luke 24:12 appears to conflict with John 20:3-10. Luke 24:12 mentions only that Peter ran to the tomb after all the women were there and came back and told the apostles. But John says it was both Peter and he who were there, just after Mary Magdalene had been there alone.

However, there is a reasonable response. Assuming that Luke 24:12 is reliable, Luke may have mentioned only Peter because he was the leader of the two men. Likewise, Mary Magdalene may have been singled out because she was the one who spoke first. This seems to be the case also when Matthew mentions only one angel at the tomb (Matthew 28:5) and John mentions two (John 20:12). The "we" (John 20:2) implies that others were with Mary Magdalene. However, Luke 24:12 may be an early copyist error since it is not in some early manuscripts. The RSV omits it. The NASB brackets it and adds, "Some ancient manuscripts do not contain verse 12." The Nestle-Aland Greek New Testament lists many old Italian manuscripts and some old Syriac manuscripts, as well as Marcion, Tatian's *Diatessaron*, and Eusebius (second to fourth centuries) as omitting verse 12.

The Resurrection of the Saints in Matthew 27:52-53

Though not explicitly treated by Ehrman, the historicity of the resurrection of the saints recorded in Matthew's Gospel has been challenged by critical scholars. And of late, this criticism has been endorsed by some Evangelical scholars. Michael Licona's massive (718-page) resource *The Resurrection of Jesus: A New Historiographical Approach*[2] is a defense of the bodily resurrection of Christ, but unfortunately it also denies or casts doubt on the historicity of the resurrected saints mentioned in Matthew 27 and other passages.[3]

The text at issue for Licona is in Matthew 27:50-53, which affirms that when Jesus died, He

> cried out again with a loud voice and yielded up his spirit. And behold, the curtain of the temple was torn in two, from top to bottom. And the earth shook, and the rocks were split. The tombs also were opened. And many bodies of the saints who had fallen asleep were raised, and coming out of the tombs after his resurrection they went into the holy city and appeared to many (ESV).

Licona speaks of the resurrected saints passage as a "strange little text" and calls it "poetic" or a "legend."[4] (He appears to include the angels at the tomb [Mark 16:5-7] in the same category.[5]) He speaks of the event reported in Matthew as similar to Roman legends that employ "phenomenal language used in a symbolic manner," asserting that "it seems to me that an understanding of the language in Matthew 27:52-53 as 'special effects' with eschatological Jewish texts and thought in mind is most plausible."[6] He believes that by this legend "Matthew may simply be emphasizing that a great king has died." Licona further writes, "If he has one or more of the Jewish texts in mind [that contain similar legends], he may be proclaiming that the day of the Lord has come." He concludes that "it seems best to regard this difficult text in Matthew as a poetic device added to communicate that the Son of God had died and that impending judgment awaited Israel."[7]

Then Licona addresses the obvious problem: "If some or all of the phenomena reported at Jesus' death are poetic devices, we may rightly ask whether Jesus' resurrection is not more of the same."[8] This is a very good question, since the two events are connected in the same text. However, his answer is disappointing for many reasons. Most importantly, there exist no good grounds for not taking Matthew 27:51-53 as historical. In fact, there are many reasons that this text in this context should be taken as historical and not as a legend.

Support for the Historicity of the Matthew 27 Resurrection of the Saints

First of all, in this very text the resurrection of these saints occurs in direct connection with two other historical events—the death and resurrection of Jesus (verses 50, 53). There is no reason here to take the resurrection of Jesus as historical and the resurrection of the saints as a legend. Hence, to borrow the subtitle from Licona's book, it appears that this "new historiographical approach," which employs extrabiblical sources to determine the meaning of this text, has led him astray in this case.

Indeed, there are many reasons in the text itself to take these resurrections as literal events, including such terms as "earth," "quake," "temple," "veil," "rocks," "tombs," "bodies," "asleep" (dead), "raised," and "appeared"—all of which speak of physical events elsewhere in the New Testament. Indeed, the crucial word associated directly with the resurrection of these saints ("raised"—*egiro*) is also used of Jesus' resurrection in 1 Corinthians, when Paul speaks of Jesus dying for our sins and being "raised" (*egiro*) again (1 Corinthians 15:3-4). And the word for "appeared" (Matthew 27:53), speaking of the saints after this resurrection, is an even stronger word than usual, meaning "become visible, appear…make known, make clear, explain, inform, make a report esp. of an official report to the authorities."[9]

Second, there is a direct connection between the resurrection of these saints and Jesus' resurrection. For the text is careful to mention that they did not come out of the tombs until "after" Jesus' resurrection (verse 53). Indeed, Paul calls Jesus' resurrection "the first fruits" (1 Corinthians 15:23), so, it is only proper that He should emerge from the dead first. Thus, speaking of the resurrection of these saints after Jesus' resurrection and as a result of it makes no sense if their resurrection, unlike Jesus' resurrection, is a mere legend.

Third, the Matthew text lists the same kind of evidence for the resurrection of these saints as is listed elsewhere for Jesus' resurrection (namely in 1 Corinthians 15): 1) the tombs were opened; 2) the tombs were empty; 3) the dead were raised; 4) there were physical appearances; 5) many people saw these resurrected saints. In brief, if this is not a physical resurrection, then neither was Jesus' resurrection (which preceded and prompted it) a physical resurrection. Or, conversely, if Jesus' resurrection was physical, then so was the resurrection of these saints in Matthew 27. Thus, denying the physical resurrection of these saints undermines belief in the physical resurrection of Jesus.

Fourth, as *Ellicott's Commentary* puts it, "The brevity, and in some sense, simplicity, of the statement differences it very widely from such legends, more or less analogous in character…and so far excludes the mythical element which, as a rule, delights to shows itself in luxuriant expansion."[10] In brief, the typical characteristics of a myth as found in Apocryphal and other literature of that time are not found in this text.

Fifth, some of the elements of this account are confirmed by two other Gospels. Both Mark (15:38) and Luke (23:45) also mention the rending of the veil in the temple (Matthew 27:51) as a result of Jesus' death. Luke's writings in particular have been historically confirmed in nearly 100 details,[11] and there is no reason to believe he is any less historically accurate in mentioning this detail. And if this part of the story is factually confirmed, there is no good reason to reject the rest of it, which Matthew adds.

Sixth, not only is there evidence within the text itself for its historicity; the earliest Fathers of the Christian church took it as historical. Some even used it as an apologetic evidence for Jesus' resurrection. Ignatius of Antioch (c. AD 35–107), a contemporary of the apostle John, referred to the resurrection of these saints as a historical event. Irenaeus (second century), who knew the apostle John's disciple Polycarp, and even Origen (third century), who had a strong propensity to allegorize, considered Matthew 27 to be a literal raising of these saints from the graves.[12] Jerome (fourth century) and Thomas Aquinas (thirteenth century) also held to its historicity.[13]

In short, the cumulative evidence for the historic and nonlegendary nature of this text is strong. In fact, the story is interwoven with the historical evidence surrounding the death and resurrection of Christ in such a manner that the denial of the resurrection of these saints undermines the historicity of the resurrection of Christ reported in the same text.

Paul's Epistles as Forgeries?

Bart Ehrman also makes the claim, in his recent book *Forged*, that many of the books in the canon of the New Testament are forgeries, written under the name of New Testament authors such as Peter and Paul. Ehrman addresses in particular the issue of the authorship of Paul's pastoral epistles, 1 and 2 Timothy and Titus. He mentions the works of Friedrich Schleiermacher in bringing suspicion on these allegedly Pauline epistles. Schleiermacher contends that the ideas presented in these pastoral epistles are in conflict with ideas Paul presents in his other letters. He also notes that the false teachings Paul is refuting in 1 Timothy are connected with the Gnostic teachings that came about in the second century AD, which he believes places the letter in a time period later than Paul; Schleiermacher notes that the "myths and genealogies" opposed by Paul sound much like the mythologies put forth by these second-century AD Gnostics.[14]

While some scholars who doubt Paul's authorship of the pastoral epistles believe that 2 Timothy is distinct from the other two, and some even attribute authorship to Paul, Ehrman believes that, due to the remarkable similarities found between 1 and 2 Timothy, the same forger who wrote 1 Timothy also wrote 2 Timothy. He contends that the phraseology (such as "promise of life," "from a pure heart," and Paul's office of an "apostle, herald, and teacher") used in 2 Timothy is very similar to that of 1 Timothy.

Ehrman states that the reason so many scholars reject the authorship of Paul in these epistles has to do with the vast differences in vocabulary and writing style, which are found to be unique to these letters. Further, the vocabulary used by the writer reflects word usage that was becoming more common after the life of Paul. He points out that, statistically, over one-third of the words of the pastoral epistles do not occur anywhere in the other Pauline letters of the New Testament.

Ehrman does not base his argument on statistics alone, however. There are numerous other factors that form the foundation of his belief in the forgeries of these pastoral epistles. One reason he identifies is the way in which the alleged

This manuscript is a portion of the Gospel of Thomas (composed about AD 140 to 170), which was discovered among the Nag Hammadi (Egypt) manuscripts in 1945. It contains 114 secret sayings (logia) attributed to Jesus, allegedly written by Thomas. Some critics such as the Jesus Seminar have placed the text on par with the four canonical Gospels. However, this is mistaken for several reasons: 1) it contains second-century Gnostic beliefs; 2) it was written in the mid to late second century AD, and the canonical Gospels were written in the first century AD; 3) second-century Church Fathers supported the canonical Gospels, not Thomas; 4) the basic New Testament canon was formed in the first century AD; and 5) Thomas is dependent on truths found in the canonical Gospels, not the reverse. (Photo by Zev Radovan.)

author employs the same words usually used by Paul, but with different meanings. For instance, Ehrman says that the term *faith*, as used in Paul's other epistles, has a connotation of a relationship with another; trusting "in" Christ. In Titus, he points out, the author employs the term *faith* to refer to the body of teachings that form the foundation of Christianity.

Ehrman goes on to explain that some of the ideas and theological statements made in the pastoral letters seem to contradict those of the rest of Paul's letters. He mentions that when Paul confronts the wrong ideas of justification in his letters, he rebukes those who were performing "works of the law" (referring to the Jewish law) in order to gain right standing before God. These works cannot contribute to one's justification; only through faith in the death and resurrection of Jesus Christ can one attain salvation. In the pastoral epistles, however, it seems to Ehrman that the Jewish law is no longer an issue that is dealt with. The author now seems to turn his focus on "good works"—doing good to others. Ehrman states that the author is concerned with the issue that merely being a morally upright person does not earn a person's salvation. He believes that this is completely uncharacteristic of the apostle Paul in his writings, simply because his other letters emphasized correcting those who were trying to use the Jewish law as a means of salvation, not those who were just doing good deeds. On the issue of the doctrine of salvation in these letters, Ehrman goes so far as to refer to 1 Timothy 2 as the author's offer of a way to salvation to women through childbearing.

Additional Evidence to Consider

As an initial critique, D.A. Carson and Douglas Moo are correct in showing that such arguments as Ehrman's fail when we take additional evidence into consideration. The words shared between the pastoral epistles and second-century AD writings are also found in other writings, which date as far back as AD 50.[15] It is virtually impossible to argue that Paul did not know about this kind of vocabulary, because it was apparently used during his time; and it is not at all likely that he simply made up these words.

Now, it is not disputed that there is definitely a change in the way the pastoral epistles are written when compared with Paul's earlier letters. It's just a matter of how to account for it. It must be understood that Paul is writing from a prison cell and awaiting imminent execution; so it is not in the least bit far-fetched to come to the conclusion that these and other circumstances contribute to the way in which he writes—with a sense of urgency not found in his other letters. The issues he addresses in these letters are going to be much different than the ones addressed in his previous ones.

Moreover, the fact that Paul is not addressing an entire church directly but individual church leaders would understandably cause him to use diction that would be different. For instance, a letter that someone writes to their employer requesting time off or inquiring about a raise is going to be vastly different from a letter written to their best friend requesting a small favor. These would be two distinct letters written by the same person, but with different recipients and requests, resulting in different diction and tone. The same can be said of the pastoral epistles: They are a group of letters written under more stressful circumstances than his others, and the requests (or in this case commands) made in these three letters are understandably much different.

In addition, it is important to acknowledge that Paul has written over the course of approximately 25 years and is nearing the end of his life. He is now able to employ years of accumulated wisdom and knowledge gained from his ministry years in ways he would not have been able to in his earlier letters. Paul was continually growing in wisdom and knowledge in the Scriptures and in ministry, so it would be unreasonable to assume that all of his letters, written at different points, would remain the same in terms of rhetorical style, theological articulation, and historical context. It would simply be unreasonable to demand that all of Paul's letters conform to a systematic outline in order to be considered his own writings, for he continually grew intellectually as well as spiritually.

Different Styles and Terminology at Different Times

In light of these factors it is not unreasonable to conclude that the apostle Paul used different rhetorical styles and slightly different terminology at different times. The fact that some of the terms in the pastoral epistles are used in a way that varies slightly from other places may be warranted in light of his unique situation while writing them; these variations would be characteristic of anyone who is writing in different situations. The way in which the term *faith* is used in Titus would be entirely legitimate within this context. Ehrman's difficulty is not legitimate because issues like these have been presented before and dealt with before regarding the passage in 1 Timothy 1:8-9. Here Paul states that the law is not for the righteous but for the lawbreaker. While C.F.D. Maule interprets this passage in such a way as to come to the conclusion of an author other than Paul, Theodor Zahn comments on the same passage, concluding that Paul's theology comes through and is consistent with what he teaches in his other letters. It is not sufficient to draw conclusions of pseudepigraphical authorship of the pastoral epistles from passages of Scripture like these. There is definitely a continuity in Paul's theology that can be shown in the variety of ways he employs his words. It seems that Ehrman does not take these circumstances into account when formulating his argument.

One of the biggest issues preventing Ehrman from accepting the Pauline authorship of the pastoral epistles is that he posits seemingly different historical situations and then takes them for granted. From there he assumes these situations would influence Paul's writing styles in his first ten epistles as well as the pastoral epistles. Ehrman posits that, because Paul thought that Christ would return during his lifetime, it affected the way in which he wrote his letters, even affecting his views of ecclesiology. For instance, Ehrman comes to the conclusion that there is no institution of church leadership in the church at Corinth simply because Paul does not address it specifically. And this, Ehrman assumes, is because Paul saw no need to create such a church government if indeed believers were here in the short term and the Lord would be returning so soon, within his lifetime. However, Ehrman continues, in the pastoral epistles we see the author specifically addressing the leadership of the churches he is writing to, indicating a change in mindset—that the church was here long-term, so leadership needed to be instituted.

These claims put forth by Ehrman are at odds with the accounts of elder leadership appointed in early churches that Paul and Barnabas founded (Acts 14:23). There is also a salutation given to the overseers (or bishops) and deacons in the opening verse of the letter written to the church of Philippi (Philippians 1:1). There is also an extensive account recorded in Acts 20:17-35, where Paul addresses the elders at the church in Ephesus as he is about to leave for Jerusalem; he warns them to guard against the false teachers that will rise up among the church, attempting to bring in false doctrine. It is clear that Paul did in fact have in mind an ecclesiological structure early on in his ministry. Contrary to what Ehrman claims, Paul actually did appoint leaders in the churches that he planted. It is interesting that Ehrman fails to address these instances found in the text.

Ehrman's arguments to support his claim that Paul did not write any of the pastoral epistles are found wanting. Each of his objections can be explained through an understanding of the context of Paul and his writings.

Did Scribes Really Change the New Testament?

Many textual scholars have made the accusation that the scribes who copied the texts of the New Testament actually altered the text to one degree or another, thereby altering the meaning of crucial passages. Again, Bart Ehrman has made his preference for this view clear. The thesis of his book *Misquoting Jesus: The Story Behind Who Changed the Bible and Why* (2005) affirms this very accusation. Ehrman claims that, although some of the scribal variations found in the manuscripts are accidental—careless mistakes on the part of the scribe—there are many instances where scribes actually purposefully altered portions of Scripture in order to satisfy their own agendas.

He argues that these alterations were driven by the scribes' desire to emphasize what they themselves believed on subjects such as the nature and deity of Christ, the role of women in the church, and so on. He points out that the copyists themselves were Christian and that their belief in Jesus Christ created a bias that manifested itself in the preservation of particular doctrines within the Scriptures by altering parts of the text. (It is interesting, however, that he does not provide any evidence for these claims.) The implications this contention has for belief in the inerrancy of the Scriptures are made clear at the outset of *Misquoting Jesus*. Ehrman asks, "How does it help us to say that the Bible is the inerrant word of God if in fact we don't have the words that God inerrantly inspired, but only the words copied by scribes…?"[16]

On the surface this question appears formidable, but upon closer examination one could apply the same way of thinking to Ehrman's books. Namely, *Misquoting Jesus, Forged,* and *Jesus, Interrupted* are only publisher's *copies* and not the words that the author originally penned!

In addition, as we have seen, Ehrman has charged that the New Testament manuscripts are full of errors and that we do not have the originals (autographs). Yet, he forcefully argues based on manuscript evidence that various passages of Scripture were not in the original text.[17] Thus he is essentially arguing his case based on what he considers faulty and unreliable manuscripts, which, he believes, give him assurance of what was, and was not, included in the original text. The question for Ehrman is clear, "If we do not have reliable manuscripts, then how does he know what was in the original text?"

Ehrman's error is actually a very simple fallacy that makes it unnecessary to go through a page-by-page critique of each of his examples.

Finally, as we established in chapter 7, "The Transmission of the New Testament," intentional doctrinal alteration—though a phenomenon that did occur in the ancient world—is only to be used as an explanation for textual variation when other more common unintentional errors cannot explain the data. Yet every single error (we checked!) that Ehrman calls an intentional doctrinal alteration can be easily assessed according to one of the more standard judgments of the canon of textual criticism, such as accidental errors of the eye and human frailty.

13

The Canon of the New Testament

The New Testament canon can be assessed in terms of its early and later development. Most place the emphasis in discussions of the canon on the later centuries of development. However, much canonical activity was taking place in the first three centuries of development as well.

The Earliest Forms of the New Testament Canon: The First Three Centuries

The early church relied heavily upon the words of Christ and the teachings of the apostles as their foundation of doctrine and worship. The traditions that were being taught needed to be handled with utmost care to ensure their accuracy for early Christians as well as for subsequent generations of believers. The book of Acts records much of the history of the early church in the first century AD and how the gospel message was spread throughout the empire of Rome.

At the beginning of church history, the early Christians were able to learn from those who were eyewitnesses of Jesus Christ and His resurrection, and from the apostles. Oral traditions (such as early creeds or confessions) were formed and used as early as a few months to two or three years after the resurrection and ascension of Christ. These traditions were very reliable, being based on heavy repetition and recitation in a culture where memorization was a central part of cultural tradition. It was upon these traditions that Paul relied in his defense of Christ's resurrection in 1 Corinthians 15, when he declares that he is passing on to the church at Corinth the tradition of the teachings of Christ that he received. So it was upon this oral and eyewitness tradition of transmission of the life, death, and resurrection of Christ, as well as upon Jesus' and the apostles' teachings, that the written documents of the New Testament were based.

Some scholars, however, level the accusation that this kind of oral tradition became corrupted during transmission, even going as far as to say that the teachings being transmitted were manipulated by the disciples. However, it must be taken into account that in such cultures, typical oral transmissions are fixed; the accounts of Jesus' life would have been no different. Any deviation from the fixed form of oral transmission of the teachings, life, and work of Christ would have been immediately detected and corrected by the community.

It is also worth considering that, during the early transmission of these teachings, eyewitnesses were still alive to attest to and verify them or refute and correct them. The fact is that these oral traditions were based on firsthand eyewitness accounts. These eyewitnesses were still present during the time when the apostles began to write their epistles and have them circulated among the early Christian communities (more than 250 of them were still alive when Paul wrote 1 Corinthians 15:6, for instance). False accounts of Jesus' life would not have been able to be circulated because of these eyewitnesses.

Furthermore, such accusations of corruption within the oral (and even written) transmission of Jesus' life do not seem to take into account that the disciples were willing to be martyred for their faith in what they proclaimed. Nor do they consider the extrabiblical records that support the claims of Jesus' life and ministry (for example, those of Josephus, Phlegon, Tacitus, Mara Bar-Serapion, Pliny the Younger, the Talmud, Celsus, and Lucian).[1]

The Process of Collection and Recognition

Each of the 27 books of the New Testament was initially a separate literary unit that was written independently of the others. Each of the Gospels was written independently, as were Acts, each of Paul's letters, the general epistles, and the Revelation of John.

Prior to AD 180, there is no evidence that shows that any one community used more than one single Gospel. It was only at this time that evidence has revealed accounts of the existence of single-volume collections of the four Gospels that were regarded as equally authoritative accounts of the gospel story, being widely recognized by authoritative figures in the church. Such collections are mentioned in statements from the Church Father Irenaeus as well as in what is known as the Muratorian Canon, a list from about AD 190 of canonical books. By around this time it was apparently possible to produce books of papyrus that would accommodate the entire text of all four Gospels. One such is P^{45}, which was written at the beginning of the third century AD and originally comprised 55 sheets (or double leaves), equating to 220 pages, and contained all four Gospels with the addition of the book of Acts.

The epistles of Paul were probably the earliest writings that were collected. Not only would the early churches have preserved these letters carefully for their own meetings, but they would have also exchanged copies of these letters with other churches as well, as was the custom. This custom would explain the existence of Paul's letters to churches that did not last very long (such as the church in Galatia). For example, Paul gives explicit instructions in his letter to the Colossians to have his letter be read in their church and in the church at Laodicea (see Colossians 4:16). Moreover, there is record of a letter known as 1 Clement, the earliest Christian document outside of the New Testament, which was sent from the church in Rome to the church in Corinth. This letter dates to about AD 95 and contains references to Paul's letter to the Romans and from 1 Corinthians and

Hebrews. As Kurt Aland recognizes, this indicates the possibility of an existing collection of Paul's letters in circulation among the early churches, although some of the references in this letter from Clement have yet to be identified conclusively.[2]

It is clear that Paul saw himself as authoritative in his apostolic position as is conveyed through his greetings (see Galatians 1:1, among others) and his teachings and writings (as seen in 1 Corinthians, Ephesians 4:17, Colossians 1:25, 2 Thessalonians, and many other passages of Scripture). There is no doubt that Paul viewed the commands he gave to be on the same level of authority as Christ's (1 Corinthians 7:10-11).

The early Church Fathers also attest to the authoritative nature of Paul's letters, as helpfully identified by Peter Wegner. In his above-mentioned letter to the Corinthians, Clement (c. AD 95) refers to Paul's letter to them and even identifies him as an apostle (1 Clement 47.1). Ignatius, bishop of Antioch in the beginning of the first century AD, mentions Paul's concern for the Ephesians in his other epistles. Polycarp, bishop of Smyrna (c. AD 69–155), in a letter to the Philippian church, refers to Paul's letters to them and even equates those letters to Old Testament Scripture, thus attesting to the authority of Paul's words as Scripture. In the mid second century AD, Marcion is noted for recognizing the Gospel of Luke and ten of Paul's letters in his canon. One can infer from this that by this time the epistles of Paul had been collected and circulated among all the early churches.

Of the Gospels, many contemporary scholars believe that Mark was the first Gospel written (c. AD 60), recording the events that occurred years before, and that the other Gospels came out shortly thereafter. However, evidence from the early Church Fathers suggest that the Gospels were written in the order in which we have them, with Matthew first and John last. Colin Hemer provides good evidence that Acts was written before AD 62, which would place Luke before this (see Acts 1:1 and Luke 1:1). This would place Matthew and Mark (possibly referred to in Luke 1:1) in the late 50s. In any event, the synoptic Gospels were composed before AD 62.

The book of Acts, Luke's sequel to his Gospel, which records the history of the early church from about AD 33 to AD 60, is considered a pivotal work by some. The earliest references to its canonicity go back to the end of the second century AD in such documents such as the Muratorian Fragment (c. AD 190) and in its mention by Irenaeus, who states that it was written by Luke. The date range for the circulation of Acts is confirmed by Hemer's *The Book of Acts in the Setting of Hellenistic History* and his conclusion, which, as said, affirms Acts' writing prior to AD 62.

The general epistles were challenged more than the other books because of the seemingly inconclusive evidence for their authorship. It seems there was no consensus about these epistles until around the end of the second century AD.

The canonicity of the book of Revelation was in dispute for many years before it was finally accepted. The earliest documentation of the book's canonical status dates back to the end of the second century AD, being mentioned by Melito, bishop of Sardis (AD 170), who wrote a commentary on it. Justin Martyr and Irenaeus also refer to this book, declaring the apostle John as the author.

Immediate Acceptance vs. Ultimate Recognition

There is an important difference between when a given New Testament book was accepted as canonical and when the Christian church in general eventually recognized it. The following chart reveals that virtually all the New Testament books were recognized and cited by some Father or canon within the first century or so after the New Testament was completed. For instance, by AD 182 to 188, during the time of Irenaeus, every book except the tiny one-chapter book of 3 John was accepted. Of course, since travel and communication was slow, not all the books were recognized everywhere until the Council of Hippo (AD 393).

The New Testament Canon During the First Four Centuries

BOOK	Mt	Mk	Lk	Jn	Acts	Rom	1Cor	2Cor	Gal	Eph	Phil	Col	1Thes	2Thes	1Tim	2Tim	Ti	Phe	Heb	Js	1Pet	2Pet	1Jn	2Jn	3Jn	Jd	Rv
Pseudo-Barnabas (c. 70-130)	x	x	x							x						x	x		x			x					
Clement of Rome (c. 95-97)	x	x				x	x			x					x	x	x		x	x	x	x					
Ignatius (c. 110)	x			x	x				x	x	x									x	x						
Polycarp (c. 110-50)	x	x		x	x	x	x	x	x	x	x	x	x		x	x	x		x	x	x		x				x
Hermas (c. 115-40)	x	x			x		x			x	x				x					x	x		x				x
Didache (c. 120-50)	x		x				x						x	x	x				x								x
Papias (c. 130-40)				x																							x
Marcion (c. 140)			x			x	x	x	x	x	x	x	x	x				x									
Irenaeus (c. 130-202)	x	x	x	x	x	x	x	x	x	x	x	x	x	x	x	x	x		x	x	x		x	x		x	x
Justin Martyr (c. 150-55)	x	x	x	x	x	x	x	x	x	x	x	x	x	x					x	x							x
Muratorian (c. 170)	x	x	x	x	x	x	x	x	x	x	x	x	x	x	x	x	x	x		x			x	x		x	x
Clement of Alexandria (c. 150-215)	x	x	x	x	x	x	x	x	x	x	x	x	x	x	x	x	x		x	x	x		x	x		x	x
Tertullian (c. 150-220)	x	x	x	x	x	x	x	x	x	x	x	x	x	x	x	x	x	x	x	x	x	x	x	x		x	x
Origen (c. 185-254)	x	x	x	x	x	x	x	x	x	x	x	x	x	x	x	x	x	x	x	x	x	x	x	x	x	x	x
Old Latin (c. 200)	x	x	x	x	x	x	x	x	x	x	x	x	x	x	x	x	x	x			x		x	x	x	x	x
Cyprian (d. 258)	x	x	x	x	x	x	x	x	x	x	x	x	x	x	x	x	x	x	x	x	x	x	x	x	x	x	x
Apostolic (c. 300)	x	x	x	x	x	x	x	x	x	x	x	x	x	x	x	x	x	x	x	x	x	x	x	x	x	x	
Cyril of Jerusalem (c. 315-86)	x	x	x	x	x	x	x	x	x	x	x	x	x	x	x	x	x	x	x	x	x	x	x	x	x	x	
Eusebius (c. 325-40)	x	x	x	x	x	x	x	x	x	x	x	x	x	x	x	x	x	x	x	?	x	?	x	?	?	?	x
Athanasius (367)	x	x	x	x	x	x	x	x	x	x	x	x	x	x	x	x	x	x	x	x	x	x	x	x	x	x	x
Jerome (c. 340-420)	x	x	x	x	x	x	x	x	x	x	x	x	x	x	x	x	x	x	x	x	x	x	x	x	x	x	x
Hippo (393)	x	x	x	x	x	x	x	x	x	x	x	x	x	x	x	x	x	x	x	x	x	x	x	x	x	x	x
Carthage (397)	x	x	x	x	x	x	x	x	x	x	x	x	x	x	x	x	x	x	x	x	x	x	x	x	x	x	x
Augustine (c. 400)	x	x	x	x	x	x	x	x	x	x	x	x	x	x	x	x	x	x	x	x	x	x	x	x	x	x	x

Chart from Norman L. Geisler and William E. Nix, *A General Introduction to the Bible*, rev. ed. (Chicago: Moody Press, 1968, 1986); © 2006 Norman L. Geisler. Used by permission of Moody Press. Main source for data: Philip Schaff, indexes to *The Ante-Nicene Fathers*.

x = Citation or allusion; ? = Names are disputed

During this process of the recognition of the New Testament canon several factors were brought into consideration, such as a book's authorship, its apostolic authority or approval, its prophetic voice, and its acceptance in the early church.

The Canon in the Fourth Century and Beyond

Over the first few centuries of the early church the canon of the New Testament came to be recognized by the early Church Fathers. From the time of Clement of Rome in the first century to Athanasius in the late fourth century a consensus formed among the church as to which books were to be accepted as canonical. Athanasius (c. 296–373), the bishop of Alexandria, became the first to have a canon that included all 27 books of the New Testament.

It was during the fourth and early fifth centuries AD that several synods and councils were held to deal with the issue of the New Testament canonical books. It was during these councils that a broader consensus was formed among the church as to which books were to be recognized as divinely inspired and, therefore, canonical. However, it is important to make the distinction that these councils did not *determine* which books were canonical and which ones were not; they merely *discovered* what the church already recognized the New Testament canon to be. The Council of Hippo, held in AD 393 at Hippo, North Africa, confirmed the same 27 books that were generally accepted as canonical by the Synod of Laodicea (AD 363). Next came the Council of Carthage in AD 419, which reaffirmed the 27-book canon of the New Testament Scriptures. In addition, the council placed the book of Hebrews with the Pauline epistles, since it had been separated from Paul's epistles at the Synod of Carthage (AD 397).

The canon of the New Testament, by implication from the factors that formed it, should be viewed as closed. It is a reasonable view that the New Testament canon was completed by the first century AD, by which time all the apostles had died. On dealing with this issue, it is important to consider the passage in Hebrews 1:1-2, which states that God has spoken through Christ as final revelation.

In light of this it must be noted that the apostles did not write any new revelation, but rather explained what had already been revealed in the ministry, death, and resurrection of Jesus Christ. It is clear that there is no new revelation that is to be given from God apart from Jesus Christ, and this means that prophets (such as Muhammad and Joseph Smith) who offer new revelation apart from the work of Jesus Christ are to be deemed false.

PART FIVE

INTRODUCTION TO ARCHAEOLOGY

The term *archaeology* is a compound word (from the Greek *archaios* and *logos*) meaning the "study of ancient things." The early Greeks, Romans, and Jews used the term in their discussions of history. For example, Plato describes the Lacedaemonians as archaeologists since they were fond of people, genealogies, and foundations of ancient cities; Thucydides uses the term to summarize the early history of Greece; Dionysius of Halicarnassus employs the word to describe the history of Rome; and Flavius Josephus employs the term to describe the history (archaeology) of the Jews.[1] It appears that Bishop Hall of Norwich used *archaiologia* in English for the first time in 1607.

The mud brick gate system preserved at Tel Dan dates to the eighteenth century BC and is the only intact arched-gate complex in existence. The structure reaches the height of nearly 50 courses of mud brick and features three massive arches as the primary entrance into the city.

In modern times, when we speak of archaeology, in general we are referring to the discipline typically within the field of anthropology and history that draws upon an investigation of current material human remains in order to understand past customs, cultures, and civilizations. These remains include pottery, graves, buildings, coins, tools, weapons, clothing, jewelry, literature, inscriptions, and more. "Archaeology of the Bible" exists as a specific field of inquiry within this discipline; its primary goal is the excavation of areas associated with the Bible and its societies and cultures, such as Jerusalem, Sodom, Jericho, Egypt, Israel, the Levant as a whole, and Mesopotamia. In this sense, archaeology is classified as "preclassical archaeology."

Archaeology is also an art and science, meaning it is directed by certain fundamental scientific principles universally accepted by archaeologists; and its evaluations draw upon human interpretation, which usually improves with experience and knowledge.

Today, there are numerous academic and popular magazines, journals, and books dedicated to lengthy discussions about the meaning and implications of recent (and some prior) discoveries. This is primarily because many consider archaeology as the intersection between science and faith as well as the overlap between religion and history. The stories of Christianity, and some other religions, provide the background and in some cases the foundation from which one's doctrine emerges. Archaeology digs into those stories to provide illumination, clarification, and understanding, with a goal of discovering truth about the past.

The Rosetta Stone is displayed at the British Museum. Its trilingual text enabled Egyptologists to decipher hieroglyphics. (Photo by Zev Radovan.)

The Rise of Archaeology

For the past 250 years, archaeology has steadily grown into highly developed disciplines in major universities around the world. However, it wasn't always this way. Archaeology originally had its start in treasure-hunting and grave-robbing! This changed quickly after several excavations and discoveries in the eighteenth and nineteenth centuries. For instance, in 1751 after the many finds gathered through the excavations in Italy at the Bay of Naples (1738) and Pompeii (1748), the Society of Antiquaries was formed in London. Archaeology began gaining prominence as a legitimate discipline. Soon after the society was established, their journal was published, with discussions of various archaeological issues and artifacts.

In 1799, this initial period of success was followed by the amazing discovery in Egypt of the Rosetta Stone pictured here (from 196 BC and weighing 1,700 pounds). The astonishing find, a trilingual basalt stone, contained a royal decree (from 196 BC) by Ptolemy V to the priests of Memphis, Egypt, written in Egyptian hieroglyphic (top), a cursive form of hieroglyphic known as Demotic (center), and Greek (bottom). The stone provided the key to deciphering hieroglyphics and was crucial to understanding much of Egypt's history. This crucial find led to the publication of *Description de L'Egypte* (1809-1813), which greatly enhanced our understanding of Egyptian language, customs, and culture.

Archaeology would continue to gain acceptance in the nineteenth and twentieth centuries through the amazing discoveries and research of Paul-Emile Botta (Iraq), Sir Flinders Petrie (Egypt), William F. Albright (Israel), and Austen Layard (Iraq)

Objections to Archaeology and the Discovery of Historical Truth

There are several objections to the knowability of history and to archaeology as a valid discipline. History is indeed a significant *contributing* factor to the discovery of truth. However, rarely, if ever, is it a *determining* factor in establishing a truth. There are several reasons for this:

1. Antiquity (the age of something) does not prove veracity. There are many old errors (for example, earth is the center of our solar system—geocentricity).

2. The evaluator of history is dependent upon fallible human senses that can, and do, often make mistakes. This is not to say that fallible investigators cannot make correct evaluations and draw accurate conclusions; rather, it is a call to humility and an acknowledgment of our limitations when approaching historical issues.

3. The historian is rarely presented with the luxury of possessing a complete, detailed account of past events or viewpoints. Rather, he

or she is offered brief vignettes or isolated portraits, and in some cases, it is secondhand information. Therefore, we must be content with conclusions based on partial knowledge. This should not deter the attempt at an objective investigation, since all disciplines are confronted with similar challenges by historical human frailty. The alternative is complete historical agnosticism, which is not acceptable, and may even be self-defeating.

4. The crucial issue of particular bias or prejudice and its ability to obfuscate objectivity inevitably enters into any discussion involving human historical evaluations. Though bias can be a real problem, we make no attempt to discount or altogether dismiss the presence of bias in this book. This is because all prejudices are not created equal. The question is not whether one *possesses* a certain bias, but whether our prejudices are moral and true. We are biased against murder, rape, lying, and theft, and these prejudices influence our evaluations and decisions in life in a healthy manner.

5. Finally, reminding ourselves of the distant vantage point from which contemporary archaeologists and historians interpret ideas and form conclusions about the past should be a call to academic charity. History can be known, and it is with the above assumptions and understandings that the current book is carried out.

Some would claim that archaeology is not a valid discipline and means for discovering historical truth. Usually these kinds of objections center around two false assumptions. First, the assumption that archaeology is not a science since it cannot *repeat* experiments under controlled conditions in the laboratory. In other words, history is past and cannot be duplicated in real time or tested by any empirical means as can the operation of our solar system. However, this objection confuses the role of *operation* science and *origin* science (as mentioned previously). *Operation* science examines *regularities* (things that occur multiple times and can be empirically studied, like the ocean tides and our solar system). Archaeology is an origin, or forensic, science, which studies *singularities* (things or events that only occur once and cannot be empirically observed in the laboratory, such as a person's birth, and other historical events such as the creation or evolution of the universe, and crimes). Despite this distinction between the sciences, archaeology is nevertheless a legitimate science, similar to any forensic science.

ARCHAEOLOGY AND THE BIBLE

There are fewer disciplines more fascinating than archaeology of the ancient Near East, especially as it touches upon the stories of the Bible. This is because archaeology often brings clarity to the biblical people, places, and events described in the unfolding drama of God's redemption of mankind. Although professional archaeologists remain locked in debate about the role, method, and language of "biblical" archaeology, archaeology and its findings enjoy growing popularity among the laity and armchair archaeologists. This is primarily due to recent successes in unearthing artifacts and cities relating to the stories of the Bible.

Today, nearly 100 biblical figures, dozens of biblical cities, over 60 historical details in the Gospel of John, and 80 historical details in the book of Acts, among other things, have been confirmed as historical through archaeological and historical research. Moreover, the Israeli Antiquities Authority has over 100,000 artifacts (discovered in Israel since 1948) available on their database for perusal. How familiar are you with these finds? Archaeology has been an indispensable tool in the historian's tool kit as well as an aid to the Christian apologist in defending the message of the Christian faith.

The Roman Corinthian columns of the Temple of Hercules located in Amman, Jordan, at Citadel Hill archaeological park, are a vivid reminder of the ancient cities known to us in Scripture as the Decapolis (*deca* = ten; *polis* = city). Amman has been identified as the city of Philadelphia. These ten cities were centers of Greek and Roman culture located east and west of the Jordan River (Mark 5:18-20; 7:31-35).

Archaeology as Biblical "Proof"

Some cite various archaeological finds as "proof" that a particular event really occurred, or that a city or person mentioned in the Bible actually existed. However, the purpose of this book is not to "prove" the

181

stories of the Bible, but rather to show that the narratives of Scripture are historically reliable and consistent with what has been discovered through various excavations and

historical research. With this said, there are traditionally two main approaches to whether archaeology offers confirmation of the Bible.

Introducing the Minimalists

First, some of the more critical scholars are known as *minimalists* and in some cases *revisionists*. They see very little or no historical correspondence between the archaeological data and the biblical text. That is, the Bible is not a reliable source for reconstructing the past. This movement began in the 1980s and 1990s among mostly European scholars in London and Denmark, who questioned the real existence of David and Solomon and whether there actually was a united monarchy; they further questioned the existence of Abraham and the patriarchs, Moses and the Exodus, and Joshua and his conquests.[2]

For the minimalists and their literature,* much of the debate centered on the historicity of David. He was assumed to be a myth, and the existence of the united monarchy in the tenth century BC was considered doubtful. However, this thinking was dealt a setback when in 1993 Avraham Biran of Hebrew Union College discovered a ninth-century BC Aramaic inscription at Tel Dan (northern Israel). The inscription contained a statement (written by an enemy of Israel) referring to a king of the "House of David" (*byt-dwd*). This discovery, along with others such as the Mesha Stele, which contained the same phrase (*byt-dwd*) and excavations at Khirbet Qeiyafa on the Israelite/Philistine border, demonstrated the historicity of David's dynasty and that the southern kingdom of Judah arose between 1100 and 1000 BC. These facts effectively ended the debate of David's historicity and attempts by minimalists to change the dating of the monarchy to the much later Hellenistic period.

In addition, further research into the historicity of Moses has revealed that the names, deities, descriptions of culture, daily life, customs, and language he

This ninth-century BC obelisk illustrates the military victories of Assyrian king Shalmaneser III (858–824 BC). One panel depicts the king of Northern Israel, Jehu (or Joram), bowing before Shalmaneser III, making an alliance or paying tribute (see 2 Kings 8–10). The inscription includes the phrase, "Tribute of Yaua [Jehu or Joram], house of Omri." (Photo by Zev Radovan.)

---

* The leading advocates among the minimalists are Thomas Thompson (*Early History of the Israelite People*—1992), Niels Peter Lemche (*Ancient Israel: A New History of Israelite Society*—1988), and Israel Finkelstein (*The Bible Unearthed: Archaeology's New Vision of Ancient Israel and the Origin of Its Sacred Texts*—2001).

recorded in Genesis and Exodus are consistent with what we know about ancient Egypt and its literature. Bear in mind that responses from conservative scholars regarding the historicity of the Exodus have revealed very little archaeological evidence for it. However, one would not expect to find building structures and permanent artifacts associated with a mobile (nomadic) people group such as the Israelites. We must beware of the fallacy of arguing from silence. Just because little evidence has been found does not mean the Exodus did not occur, or that evidence will not be found in the future. The historicity of Abraham was also denied by the minimalists. However, early- and late-twentieth-century excavations in Mesopotamia have offered strong support for the correspondence of the archaeological data and the Genesis record. These include descriptions of people and places, financial climate, documented names such as "Abraham," treaties, and customs.[3]

Furthermore, minimalist challenges were made to the biblical account of Joshua's conquest of Canaan. These arguments were mostly supported by Kathleen Kenyon's research of Jericho in the 1950s. She concluded that Jericho did not exist by the time Joshua reached the Promised Land in the thirteenth century BC.[4] The Jericho she discovered had fortified walls that were burnt, and most likely existed in the sixteenth century BC—far too early for Joshua to conquer. However, archaeologist Bryant Wood has recently (1990) countered Kenyon's findings with a detailed analysis of pottery and an examination of stratigraphy (rich material layers of occupation), which have shown the walls of Jericho to have collapsed as described in Joshua 6:20-24.[5] What is more, abundant stores of unused grain indicate a short springtime siege as Judges 2:6 and 6:15-20 imply. Wood's analysis of previous excavations of Jericho (by Garstang and Kenyon) has yielded a date of c. 1400 BC for its destruction, which is consistent with the biblical account of the conquest.

The Minimalists and the Use of the Bible

In addition to their theological assumptions, Minimalists have led a campaign among professional archaeologists to abandon the term *biblical archaeology* altogether for the more "scientific"-sounding term *Near-Eastern archaeology*. Their contempt for any title associated with the Bible appears to be driven by its perceived association to biased research, antiquated methodology, rigid ideology, lack of objectivity, and contempt for the scientific method. (However, this notion seems to be shortsighted since it requires archaeologists to discriminate against the Bible as a valid primary-source document originating from the ancient Near-Eastern world.)

More specifically, the minimalists' aversion involves a distaste for those archaeologists who initially consult the Bible in order to locate lost cities or to test various hypotheses. It is said that the Bible should be consulted *after* another Near-Eastern text first mentions the topic under investigation or the location in question is excavated. Otherwise, they say the biblical archaeologist will "see" what he or she wants to see in the data. Certainly, there is always a risk of unhealthy bias in anything we evaluate, and we must guard against it, but unfortunately, these objections fail to realize that one must discriminate against the Bible (which is itself a bias!) as a legitimate text in order to operate this way. Surely, an archaeologist will (and does) consult ancient extrabiblical texts in order to form a hypothesis. They will not always wait for a second source to confirm the first text's information before proceeding. Biblical archaeologists believe there is no problem with first consulting the Bible for information prior to excavating, since the data that is subsequently unearthed must also be analyzed, processed, and published with peer review. Therefore, it does not appear unreasonable for the biblical archaeologist to proceed based on a preliminary analysis of the biblical text, especially if it offers crucial information. In fact, some may consider it irresponsible to proceed without consultation of the relevant biblical material. What is more, the biblical archaeologist adheres to the same generally accepted principles of excavation as do all other Near-Eastern archaeologists, meaning there is no need to be bibliophobic.

The Minimalists' Rejection of Religion

In other cases, the critical archaeologist (and Bible scholar) will reject the Bible as a trustworthy source of historical information since they contend it is a *religious* book about *religion*, written by *religious* people with *religious* purposes; therefore, it cannot be trusted to contain objective information. There are several reasons why this thinking is flawed.

First, to reject information, research, and conclusions because of the source commits the genetic fallacy (a perceived defect in the *origin* of a claim or thing is taken to be evidence that discredits the claim or thing itself). This means we would have to reject all archaeological finds that were inspired by and sourced in the Bible. In addition, this kind of fallacious logic means we would have to reject the model of the benzene molecule, since it was inspired by Friedrich August Kekule's vision of a snake biting its tail. Or what do we make of Nikolai Tesla's idea for the alternating-current motor, which he obtained by a vision while reading a pantheistic poet? Has any philosopher rejected Socrates or his works found in Plato because Socrates' philosophy was inspired by a Greek prophetess?

Second, to reject something because of its religious source confuses the nature of how archaeologists *perceive* and *receive* data. Certainly, any archaeologist can perceive and examine the Bible from a detached, objective, and academic perspective much like a geology professor studies rocks. Even though rocks are religious objects to some, it does not mean we cannot be objective about geology. That is, their *perceiving* the data does not necessarily mean archaeologists *receive* the religious message contained in it.

Third, since all ancient and modern people (including archaeologists) have a religious view, whether they believe in a deity or not (even atheism offers a religious perspective about God), *no* evaluation of the archaeological data would be valid or true.

Fourth, to reject a source because it's religious unfairly discriminates against people of faith in favor of nonreligious positions, assuming the former cannot be objective. In fact, people of faith have contributed in all areas of research including science, biology, art, astronomy, archaeology, philosophy, theology, mathematics, and other fields. Most early scientists approached their studies from religious belief, in most cases through the doctrine of Christianity. These include Kepler (physical astronomy), Pascal (hydrostatics), Boyle (chemistry), Steno (stratigraphy), Newton (calculus, gravitation), Faraday (magnetic theory), Babbage (computer science), Mendel (genetics), Maxwell (electrodynamics), and Pasteur (bacteriology)—among others whose motivation to analyze the natural world was the natural byproduct of a belief in a creator.

Fifth, to reject the reliability of the Bible because it is a religious book destroys the trustworthiness of many ancient Near-Eastern artifacts and literary works; most of them contain religious pronouncements and references to their gods. In fact, we could not consult with any degree of reliability most Egyptian, Babylonian, Hebrew, and Persian archaeological data since most refer to divine actions and belief in pagan deities.

Sixth, if we are to eliminate an object of religious commitment such as the Bible from informing us of history, then we must also set aside artifacts such as idols, religious figurines, altars, and temples and their contribution to understanding the ancient past. Even European art that depicts religious scenes would have to be eliminated since in most cases it was created by people of faith. (One would have to assume the painters were not objective in their painting and therefore could not properly reflect reality.)

Seventh, a rejection of the Bible in archaeological research would in some cases eliminate the *only* data archaeologists possess about a historical event or person. This was the case when scholars had no extrabiblical evidence of Belshazzar (Daniel 5) and David (1 and 2 Samuel); these men were later confirmed through archaeological discoveries in the twentieth century. Time and again the Bible has proven its value in archaeological research.

Originally damaged in an earthquake in the eighth century AD, a Greek mosaic floor map showing portions of Israel, Egypt, and Syria was accidently discovered during the construction of a Greek Orthodox church in 1884. Currently, the map is located on the floor of the St. George Greek Orthodox Church in Madaba, Jordan. It lists the names of important biblical cities and landmarks, including Jerusalem (pictured here), and their orientation in proximity to various geographical features such as the Dead Sea and the Jordan River. It remains the oldest surviving map of the Holy Land, dating to the mid sixth century AD. The value of the map has been confirmed by archaeologists, who utilize its descriptions to locate places of interest. For example, the picture above depicts, in Jerusalem, the central *Cardo* thoroughfare with its pillars and road, the Damascus Gate, and the Nea Church. Other locations such as Ashkelon were found to be in the exact location described by the map. (Photo by Zev Radovan.)

The Maximalists

Those of the second view are known as *maximalists*. These individuals see sufficient correspondence between the archaeological data and the Bible. The biblical text is viewed as a reliable source for reconstructing the past. This group generally assumes that recent digs at ancient Near-Eastern sites confirm the historical narratives recorded in the Bible. For instance, they affirm the historicity of David and Solomon, Abraham and the patriarchs, Moses and the Exodus, and Joshua's conquest of Canaan.

For the maximalist, the Bible is viewed as primary-source literature able to convey helpful information pertaining to customs, cultures, people, ambient life, and the location of cities in the ancient Near East. Some view the archaeological data as strong direct "proof" of the biblical stories; others see a "consistency" or "correspondence," which many believe is the minimal requirement for giving the historical narratives of the Bible the benefit of the doubt. Any archaeologist would agree that there are many difficulties confronting our understanding of the archaeological data, though the maximalist would see few or no contradictions with the biblical record. For the maximalist, the degree of historical certainty is beyond reasonable doubt. As an *origin* science (or sometimes called a *forensic* science), archaeology is viewed as a discipline that offers a collection and review of the material data similar to how a crime-scene investigation is conducted. In some cases, the scientist's findings have the potential and convincing power that allows one to render a verdict about what occurred in the past.

Archaeology and the Bible

The Bible itself is an archaeological document that represents the most complete and substantiated corpus of literature we possess from the ancient world. As we saw in part 1, no other piece of ancient literature comes close to the amount of manuscript attestation necessary for its accurate reconstruction in modern language. Furthermore, the dates between the original writing of the books of the Bible (known as the *autographa*) and their oldest surviving manuscript copies have the least amount of time gap of any piece of literature from the ancient world. This is crucial for archaeology, since the more time that has elapsed between the writing of the original text and the surviving manuscript copy, the greater the possibility that myth and embellishment will be found in the copied text. It is for this reason (that is, the number of manuscripts and their early dating) that many archaeologists confidently scan the biblical text for various clues in their research. The logic of archaeology and its relationship to the Bible becomes clear: If the Bible is marginalized or altogether removed from the archaeological endeavor, one must also marginalize or remove *all* other extrabiblical literature and inscriptions from this same time period due to their weaker textual support. This is not a price most institutions of higher learning should, nor be willing to, pay.

Although the biblical record does not exhaustively document the many cultures, customs, and events of the ancient Near East, it offers us a needed glimpse into this time period. Archaeology can aid how we understand the Bible. For example, the original biblical languages (Hebrew, Aramaic, and Greek) form the linguistic contents of Scripture. However, they are foreign to our modern Western world. The discovery of various extrabiblical inscriptions and literary texts have aided us in clarifying, confirming, and in some cases correcting our understanding of the linguistic meaning and context of the Scriptures.

Such correction occurred in several cases where the Gospel writer Luke was previously thought to be in error. For instance, in Acts 17:6 he described the rulers at Thessalonica with the Greek term *politarcho*. It was thought that since no extrabiblical Greek literature used the term, Luke was mistaken. However, after the discovery of an inscription dating to the first century AD at Thessalonica that used the word *politarcho* in reference to the rulers of the ancient city, there was no longer a debate as to the reliability of Luke's account of those rulers. Through the immense help that archaeology offers, we soon discover that all ancient history directly or indirectly relates in some way to the narrative found in the biblical text. No longer may we safely assert there is an unbroken wall between "secular" and the "sacred." History is all *His*-story.

KEYS TO UNDERSTANDING
ARCHAEOLOGY IN BIBLICAL LANDS

For the novice, archaeology can be a mysterious and confusing discipline. However, in reality the entire process of locating and excavating a particular site is very structured and organized down to the very tools that are used and the personnel who are involved.

Understanding the Process of Archaeological Excavation

In order to begin excavating a site one must identify a *director*, who is in charge of leading the investigation and securing any necessary permits. This person ought to be a qualified (academically and experientially) individual trained in understanding the ancient Near East and possess some familiarity with ancient languages (Hebrew, Greek, Aramaic, and so on). In addition, the director will appoint an administrator, who is in charge of volunteer registrations, scheduling, logistics, travel, food, and lodging. Normally a site will have many supervisors at various areas throughout the excavated area to oversee the volunteer labor. It is not unusual for an investigation to include an official photographer and an architectural specialist to sketch and document areas, features, and artifacts of interest.

Bringing together all the various personnel, logistics, and tools necessary to dig can be an expensive endeavor. Since there is little funding available for archaeological excavation, it is primarily supported through private donations or financed by academic institutions. This means there is a heavy reliance on volunteers (many with no previous archaeological experience) to perform the actual excavation itself. It is common that volunteers undergo a day or two of archaeological training and orientation prior to starting.

Part of this training is familiarization with the tools that are used in unearthing the Bible's most precious treasures. The more basic tools include handheld brushes, trowels, wheelbarrows, picks, rubber baskets, twine, buckets, stakes, hoes, tape measures, and manually operated sifting trays. There are also technical tools utilized, such as cameras, computers, databases, survey transits, ground penetrating radar, and aerial photography, among other things. Usually mechanized equipment such as backhoes, tractors, bulldozers, and the like are forbidden since precious artifacts and building structures that lie just beneath the surface may be damaged or completely destroyed. However, in some rare cases when manual labor is not feasible due to the amount of effort involved, or when the risk to artifacts is greatly reduced, exceptions may be made and heavy equipment used.

In addition to the physical labor involved, time is also allotted for experienced individuals to "read" (interpret) and reassemble pottery and other artifacts to discover their type and date. The corporate review and interpretive process can be lengthy, taking months or years to complete, but is a necessary step to insure the integrity and documentation of the material data. Then various specialists such as epigraphers, architects, anthropologists, scientists, forensic experts, geologists, theologians, and historians should carefully review and examine all (or portions of) the material data to ensure nothing was grossly misinterpreted or omitted.

Once archaeologists are confident they have completed their due diligence in examining the data, their findings are usually published in a scholarly journal and presented at various conferences, where the information can be peer-reviewed and evaluated by the archaeological community at large. Once these important steps have been taken, a body of information is created that usually trickles down for public consumption and evaluation in the form of nontechnical books, much like this one.

Dating Scenarios for Ancient Israel

As the excavation progresses at a given site, it is common to discover several layers (that is, *strata*; singular, *stratum*) of past occupation from various time periods. Usually, the deeper you dig the older the occupation stratum becomes, since more recent settlements are built over older settlements. By collecting and assessing the cumulative data unearthed at various locations around the Near East, archaeologists have developed chronological dating scenarios. These ancient time periods are identified with various civilizations that interacted with ancient Israel (sometimes known as "Palestine") through the centuries. Though not all archaeologists have adopted the same chronological development, there is a general consensus among conservative scholars, with slight variations, about the ages of antiquity and the corresponding civilizations.

Archaeological Ages and Israel[1]		
Neolithic Age	8500–4600 BC	Domestication of plants, animals, and introduction of metals. First evidence of religion (fertility worship) discovered in Israel.
Chalcolithic Age	4600–3600 BC	"Chalcolithic" literally means *copper* and *stone* due to the advances in creating objects made of stone and metal. Denser population with unfortified settlements in Israel. Near the end of the Chalcolithic Age, earliest writing discovered in southern Iraq (Sumer), known as the protoliterate age of logographic writing (in which pictures stand for words).
Early Bronze Age	3600–2350 BC	Increased settlement and urbanization in Israel, which included fortification of outer walls (up to 25 feet across). Cuneiform (*cuneus* = wedge) language emerges in the Near East as the written script produced by wedge impressions in soft clay. However, Egyptian writing used consonantal (no vowels) hieroglyphics in which pictures stood for words and syllables. Written-language illiteracy is high.
EB I	3600–2900 BC	Early Dynastic Period of ancient Egypt.
EB II	2900–2700 BC	Earliest Canaanite high place (Hebrew: *bamah*) discovered at Megiddo. Time of Early Dynastic Period in ancient Mesopotamia.
EB III	2700–2500 BC	Beginning of the Old Kingdom in ancient Egypt.
EB IV	2500–2350 BC	Population decreased, towns destroyed and uninhabited in Israel. End of the Old Kingdom in Egypt.
Intermediate Bronze Age	2350–2000	Urban centers had declined and nomadic lifestyle begins. Natural factors (rain, weather, farming, and so on) lead to highly transient culture.
Middle Bronze Age	2000–1550 BC	Patriarchal period of Abraham, Isaac, Jacob, and his 12 sons. Joseph and the Israelites in Egypt.
MB I	2000–1800 BC	Time of tribal transition and chaos with a declining population living as nomads. Beginning of the Middle Kingdom in Egypt.
MB II	1800–1550 BC	Period of Abraham, Lot, and the destruction of Sodom. (See new evidence emerging from Tall el-Hammam in Jordan.) End of the Middle Kingdom in Egypt.
Late Bronze Age	1550–1200 BC	Period of the Israelite Exodus from Egypt and conquest of Canaan by Joshua. Beginning of New Kingdom in Egypt.

LB I	1550–1400 BC	Time of Moses, Aaron, Joshua, Israelites, and the Exodus.
LB II	1400–1200 BC	Time of the conquest, Judges, and beginning of Hebrew settlement in the Promised Land. (See Bryant Wood's analysis of Jericho and the Merneptah Stele.)
Iron Age	1200–586 BC	Reign of the Judean and Israelite kings from Saul to Zedekiah. This period is ended with the destruction of Solomon's temple by the Babylonian (Nebuchadnezzar II) conquest of Jerusalem in 586 BC.
Iron I	1200–1000 BC	Period of the Judges, King Saul, and beginning of the Davidic dynasty. End of New Kingdom in Egypt.
Iron II	1000–586 BC	Period of the Davidic dynasty and the split of Israel into the Northern and Southern Kingdoms. The Assyrian and Babylonian sieges of Israel and Judah.
Persian Period	586–332 BC	Decline and fall of the Babylonian Empire and the reign of the Persians. Jews freed from Babylonian captivity and Jerusalem rebuilt. Alexander the Great conquers the world, and Hellenistic culture introduced.
Hellenistic Period	332–63 BC	Greek philosophy under Plato and Aristotle (who was the tutor of Alexander the Great) influenced the world's academic and popular thinking on reality, religion, politics, morals, cosmogony (origin of the universe), cosmology (operation of the universe), and the soul. The Septuagint (LXX) was translated for Greek-speaking Jews in Egypt (c. 250 BC). The Jewish revolt (c. 164 BC) under the Maccabees seizes the Jewish temple from the Seleucid King Antiochus IV Epiphanes. By AD 63 Rome ruled Israel as part of the Syria-Israel province.
Roman Period	63 BC–AD 324	Though Roman rule in Israel began in 63 BC when Pompey entered Jerusalem, the Roman Period was inaugurated by Rome's first emperor, Julius Caesar. This period offers biblical archaeologists a glimpse into the rise and spread of early Christianity in addition to the dispersion of the Jews in AD 70.

Basic Archaeological Vocabulary

When archaeologists conduct their excavations and unearth various kinds of material remains, they use special words to communicate about the process and the artifacts themselves. An understanding of this vocabulary (or what we call "archaeologese") is helpful to understanding the archaeological process. The following chart includes a summary of the basic vocabulary (see also the glossary at the end of this book):

Understanding Archaeological Terms
See also "Glossary of Key Terms" following chapter 26.

(Photo courtesy of the Tall el-Hammam Excavation Project [TeHeP].)

Tell (or **tel, tall**)—A *tell* is a mound of earthen debris that consists of layers of buried cities built one on top of the other over time. When a city was destroyed or abandoned, the new inhabitants would construct their own city on top of the previous ruins. Each layer of occupation is called a *stratum*. The study of these layers (*strata*) is known as *stratigraphy*. The analysis of the strata offers a timeline/history of successive cities as well as uncovering precious archaeological artifacts such as buildings, inscriptions, roads, tools, weapons, bones, altars, idols, bricks, and destruction remnants like ash. Archaeologists dig at a tell to slowly expose each successive layer in order to reconstruct the architecture and social aspects of a community. It is also important to note that not all biblical sites are located on or in tells.

Locus—A *locus* refers to a specific area of investigation. Usually archaeologists will mark out their locus as a *square* to be excavated. Often string or rocks can be arranged to mark the dimension of the locus (for example, 5m x 5m square). By marking a boundary the excavators can precisely contain and document all artifacts and information gained from this location, as well as prevent foreign material from being introduced into the area.

Balk—*Balks* refer to unexcavated vertical wall areas within a square. These are necessary in order to observe the soil layers of the area being excavated. These walls (typically 3 feet across) at Megiddo contain an exposed face (pictured left), which is known as a *section*. These sections give the archaeologist a short history of the area being excavated. That is to say, it is a chronological side-view of the area being unearthed. If there are no balks with sections, there can be no history of the square as the archaeologist removes soil and descends deeper and deeper into the square.

Artifacts—When excavators unearth portable items that were made by humans, they call them *artifacts*. These include but are not limited to pottery, jewelry, tools, weapons, knives, artwork, jars, coins, grinding stones, mortar and pestle, and clothing. After these artifacts are washed and examined, some of them are placed on display at museums. Artifacts are important since they tell us about the community, habits, and ambient life.

In situ—As archaeologists unearth artifacts at their dig site that are in their natural setting undisturbed by handling, movement, or transportation, they identify those artifacts as *in situ*. This is unlike some artifacts that surface on the antiquities market or in museums, which have no documented history of discovery in their natural setting or prior location. Although these kinds of objects may be authentic, they are nevertheless without official documentation, which raises concerns about their history and origin. In some cases these sorts of objects turn out to be forgeries.

Features—Unlike artifacts, *features* are nonportable man-made architectural structures such as fireplaces, kilns, walls, hearths, gates, foundations, bricks, amphitheaters, and other permanent items. *Features* convey information about the habits, values, boundaries, and customs of community inhabitants. This large amphitheater (pictured left) was discovered at the biblical city of Beth Shan in northern Israel, the city where bodies of King Saul and his son Jonathan were hung by the Philistines (2 Samuel 21:12).

Mud Brick—In addition to wood and stone, ancient structures were built with clay. *Mud bricks* have been discovered throughout the ancient Near East, like these discovered at Tell el-Hammam (Sodom) in western Jordan. If a community chose to use mud brick, they would begin manufacturing them with local soil, which was poured into a mold (usually 18 inches long by 7 inches wide and 5 inches thick) and left to dry in the sun.

Ecofacts—Those things that are used by the community but not made by humans, including bone, seeds, wood, leather, clay, stone, and other sorts of naturally occurring materials. *Ecofacts* may indicate the availability of materials and the value placed on particular resources. This porous grinding stone (left) found at Sodom was used to grind grain into flour to make bread.

Ossuary—Throughout Israel archaeologists have discovered small (about 18 inch x 12 inch) stone bone boxes, known as *ossuaries*. After the deceased had been in the tomb for some time, family members would collect now uncovered bones and place them into an ossuary with the deceased's name written on it. This was primarily done to make room for more bodies in the tomb. The Israelites were the only culture to use such a burial practice.

Bullae—Ancient *bullae* (singular, *bulla*) are small (nickel-size) clay seal impressions that contain the name, title, or both of the one sealing a particular document or package. Usually kings and persons in authority wore metal rings they could press into a small lump of moist clay, leaving their signature as an authenticating mark. Hundreds of these clay impressions have been discovered, some of which belong to biblical figures.

(Photo by Zev Radovan.)

Potsherd—A *potsherd* is a piece of broken pottery (top). Potsherds are very abundant in Israel as you glance down when walking through a tell. These pieces of pottery are useful to archaeologists because they can provide information on chronology and dating of a community. In other words, designs, shapes, styles, colors, and thickness all change over time and thus can assist the examiner in discovering what particular time this kind of pottery flourished. People groups can also be deciphered based on design. Philistine pottery can be distinguished from Hebrew pottery by discovering the design, shape, and location in which it was found. Certain pieces of pottery (known as *diagnostic sherds*) are set aside for examination, such as handles, rims, and bases, because they offer clearer glimpses into the vessel's style and date (bottom). Pottery reading is the most common and reliable approach to discover chronology.

Ostracon—*Ostracon* (plural, *ostraca*) is a Greek word meaning "potsherd." For the archaeologist, it is a piece of pottery or other hard surface material that contains writing on its surface. Though ostraca are rare, they offer insight into the written language and values of the community, and in some cases may provide a crucial link for understanding history. Ostraca typically contain portions of written receipts, directions, letters, names, descriptions of deities, or anything else that can be communicated in writing.

(Photo by Zev Radovan.)

Glacis—A *glacis* (plural, *glacis*) is a man-made sloping fortification mound of debris that runs from ground level below the tell to the base of a defensive fortification wall on top of the tell. The glacis was used to support the perimeter of the tell and became a crucial aid in defending the community from invasion. The steep slopes, often covered with loose gravel or smooth river rock, would make it difficult for advancing armies to climb up and penetrate the city walls.

Topography, geography—Considering the natural surroundings of a community can aid the archaeologist in locating various cities and events mentioned in the Bible. These natural surroundings include mountains, valleys, caves, rivers, lakes, oceans, and streams. For example, the biblical town of Aroer (bottom), originally built by the Moabites and later captured by Moses, was located on the bank above the River Arnon (above, Deuteronomy 2:36) as shown in this photograph. Aroer is located near other biblical cities in modern Jordan such as Madaba and Dibon (modern Dhibon). The ancient trade route known by its biblical description as the "King's Highway" (Numbers 20:17-21) can also be seen from the town of Aroer.

Stela or **stele / Stelae** or **steles** (plural)—Governments and rulers in the ancient Near East would commemorate important events by erecting stone monuments known as *steles*. Sometimes they are called *monumental inscriptions* and can include dedications, victory, or funerary inscriptions. Notable steles are the Mesha Stele (aka Moabite Stone), the Tel Dan Stele, and the Egyptian Merneptah Stele (pictured left).

(Photo by Zev Radovan.)

Manuscript / codex—A biblical *manuscript* (literally, "manual script") is a handwritten copy of a text written on *papyrus* (plant material), *vellum* (animal skin), or some other paperlike material. A *codex* (plural, *codices*) is a collection of manuscripts *bound* as a book. The *Aleppo Codex* (pictured left) is one of the Masoretic texts from the tenth century AD.

(Photo by Zev Radovan.)

Part Six

Archaeology of the Old Testament

Archaeological Evidence and the Bible

Archaeology of the Old Testament offers us many benefits, such as the ability to clarify and illuminate past events, understand customs and cultures, and historically confirm people and places mentioned in Scripture. As noted in part 5, liberal scholarship has traditionally dismissed the Bible's narratives if they did not have extrabiblical support such as an inscription, literature, or an artifact. Moreover, some scholars (both liberal and evangelical) have allowed extrabiblical materials to determine the historicity of a given passage.

Both approaches appear to unfairly marginalize the Bible, making it a second-class source, while simultaneously elevating extrabiblical materials and literature as primary sources. We must not forget that the Bible is the strongest and most reliably supported piece of literature from the ancient world in terms of its transmission (copy accuracy), number of manuscripts and their early dates, as well as being a historical document itself. Near-Eastern historian Edwin Yamauchi emphasizes the commonness of this fallacy among scholars in his book *The Stones and the Scriptures* (1972).[1] According to Yamauchi, the fallacy in thinking here is reflected in the notion that one cannot believe the biblical narratives unless there is corroborating material evidence sourced outside of Scripture. Though consistency between the two

The Gemariah seal impression was discovered at the City of David. Its paleo-Hebrew inscription reads, "Belonging to Gemaryahu [Gemariah] [son of] Shaphan." Gemariah and Shaphan are mentioned in the books of Jeremiah (36:10-12,25) and 2 Kings (22:3). Shaphan was the scribe under King Jehoiakim. (Photo by Zev Radovan.)

domains (that is, external sources and the Bible) is desirable, it has been made by some to be a *necessary precondition of historicity*.

Those who have adopted this latter approach display a presupposition of biblical skepticism from the outset. This is seen in cases where earlier external evidence (for example, an inscription) is found to overlap a later biblical text. There are occasions when discrepancies between the two sources are discovered and subsequently a later biblical narrative is discarded and the external source is upheld as reflecting earlier, accurate history.

However, Yamauchi correctly notes that one cannot simply demand external corroboration of sources due to the fragmentary nature of the evidence and the *king's vanity* (that is, distortion or exaggeration) often present in earlier ancient inscriptions. Only a fraction of the archaeological evidence has *survived* the ravages of time and then been *surveyed, excavated, examined,* and *published,* according to Yamauchi. Therefore, the demand for corroboration in every instance does not appear reasonable or productive. For example, there are many cases in which biblical persons had no corroboration until recent times. Among these are Pontius Pilate (first external corroboration discovered in 1961), Herod the Great (1965), and the Roman governor Felix (1966). It seems best to assume the Bible is historically reliable until evidence beyond reasonable doubt shows otherwise.

Dealing with the Lack of Data

Scholars who demand corroboration prior to determining historicity have essentially engaged in an argument from silence. That is to say, they will not affirm the historicity of a biblical narrative because the historical record is silent on the issue. We must remember a fundamental principle: *The lack of archaeological data relating to the Bible is not evidence against the historicity of the Bible*. There is no guarantee that future excavations will not turn up corroborating evidence. Successful discoveries, some mentioned earlier in this book, have put to rest numerous debates concerning the historical nature of many biblical passages. These include discoveries relating to the existence of the Hittite civilization, Solomon, David, Balaam, Canaanites, and numerous biblical cities mentioned in Scripture, to name a few.

Archaeology also has its limitations. Although it deals with artifacts, features, measurements, and tangible data, archaeology also involves many interpretive judgments and probabilities. Any interpretations and conclusions must be considered in light of human fallibility and the sparse nature of the data itself. As mentioned above, this is compounded by the fact that only a small amount of the evidence has survived and can be either isolated or disconnected from its in-situ environment. Floods, fires, warfare, natural deterioration, burial, temperature, political climate and time, have all collaborated to make the discovery of biblical artifacts difficult. Therefore, archaeology cannot be classified as an "exact" science; but neither can any empirical science for that matter. Despite its limitations, archaeology is governed by generally accepted principles and methods as a forensic science and is a valuable tool in uncovering the past. Therefore, archaeology has become an indispensable discipline in the historian's tool belt to unearth data supporting the historical reliability of the Bible beyond a reasonable doubt.

Archaeology of the Old Testament

There are a greater number of artifacts that correspond to the Old Testament than those relating to the New Testament. This is not because archaeologists have been unsuccessful in locating New Testament sites, but because the storyline of the Old Testament has a much longer history to cover and for which to accumulate material remains (2500 BC to 400 BC) than does the New Testament (7 BC to AD 100). Naturally, the Old Testament narratives offer more data to process and evaluate. Moreover, the Old Testament communities tended to use permanent materials, such as stone, which gave the artifact a greater chance to survive through the centuries of erosion. In addition, the older remains have been buried and preserved more securely than the more recent New Testament materials, which are nearer the surface. By the time the New Testament arrived, much writing was committed to more easily perishable substances like papyrus, which made for easier transport and storage.

The base of an olive press is visible in the tenth-century BC ruins of the Philistine city of Gath (Tel es-Safi), Goliath's hometown. In approximately 830 BC the city was destroyed by the Aramean king Hazael (2 Kings 12:17), and later conquered by Nebuchadnezzar II on his way to Jerusalem.

There is a growing confidence among many ancient Near-Eastern archaeologists today in the historical nature of many of the cities, people, and stories mentioned in the Old Testament. For example, 50 years ago it was not uncommon for Near-Eastern scholars to suggest that there were over 25,000 sites dating to Old Testament times that had been identified.[2] However, today archaeologists have continued to locate remains from biblical times—a number that should increase anyone's confidence in the descriptions of customs and cultures mentioned in Scripture. This is primarily due to past and recent excavations that are unearthing biblical places such as the Temple Mount Walls and administrative buildings (under Benjamin Mazar and Leen Ritmeyer), the City of David (under Eilat Mazar), the Philistine city of Gath (under Aren Maeir), Sodom (under Steven Collins), Ai (under Bryant Wood), Hazor (under Yigael Yadin), Jericho (under Kathleen Kenyon), Qumran (under Roland de Vaux), and the Pool of Siloam (under Eli Shukron and Ronny Reich) among others, not to mention the Temple Mount Sifting Project (under Gabriel Barkay). Today, all the major biblical cities and geographical features have been located, including Jerusalem, Jericho, the Sea of Galilee, the Galilee region, the Dead Sea, the Jordan River, Caesarea, Dan, Caesarea Philippi, Beth Shan, Gezer, Hazor, Beersheba, Megiddo, Memphis, Alexandria, Luxor, Thebes, Babylon, Nineveh, Athens, Thessalonica, Corinth, Rome, Ephesus, Philippi, Smyrna, and dozens more.[3]

Currently, there are approximately 60 biblical figures in the Old Testament that have been identified through historical and archaeological research. These include Nebuchadnezzar II, Belshazzar, Sennacherib, Darius, Xerxes, Artaxerxes I, Cyrus, Jeroboam, Baruch the scribe of the prophet Jeremiah, Shema the servant of Jeroboam II, David, Solomon, Balaam, and many other kings of Israel and Judea, among others.

Along with these finds comes an increased awareness of the ancient past, and a more informed reconstruction of the people and places of the Bible. However, the discoveries of inscriptions, coins, literature, architectural features, and the like, offer the archaeologist greater challenges in deciphering how these pieces fit together in biblical and extrabiblical history. The reason for this is that in every excavation there is data collected that has to do with the peoples, places, and events that surround the biblical story line, though they are not necessarily mentioned in the Bible. There have been no contradictions demonstrated thus far, though many difficulties indeed remain. This part of the book is dedicated to assisting our readers in understanding some of the more crucial artifacts and remains that have a more direct bearing on validating the historical reliability of the Old Testament.

Front and back view of a first-century AD silver Tyre shekel. Judas would have received 30 of these coins after betraying Jesus.

CREATION AND FLOOD, THE TOWER OF BABEL, AND THE CITIES OF THE PLAIN

The first 11 chapters in Genesis are the most-criticized portions of the Bible. They record extraordinary events such as the creation of the world, Noah's cataclysmic flood, and the confusion of languages at the Tower of Babel. Critics of the nineteenth and twentieth centuries have assumed these events were part of a much earlier Mesopotamian myth tradition, in which one's religion and folklore are merely expressions of fantasy, storytelling, or lessons in which great glory is given to the king or one's gods, rather than actual historical narrative. However, upon closer examination of these extrabiblical accounts in relation to the biblical record, we find that the Mesopotamian accounts provide us with an earlier, independent record containing a core historical theme that corresponds to the events recorded in Genesis.

Creation

The *Enuma Elish,* the major Mesopotamian (Babylonian and Assyrian) creation account, was originally discovered as part of the Assyrian king Ashurbanipal's literary collection, which was unearthed at Nineveh. Other parts of the story were found at Ashur (Assyria) and Uruk. These seven Akkadian cuneiform tablets, taken to the British Museum, were then rediscovered by a young man named George Smith at the British Museum. In 1876 he published their text as *The Chaldean Genesis.* The tablets were originally composed during the early second millennium BC as a mythic creation account featuring the Babylonian god Marduk as its central creative figure. Its similarities with Genesis were immediately recognized by scholars.

The *Enuma Elish* is not the only story of creation to surface in the ancient Near East. Before the time of Abraham, Egypt had their creation account of Ptah (god of Memphis) who became chief of the other gods, assuming the role of First Principle and the giver of life to all other gods. For the most part, the Egyptian myth of creation with Ptah as the primary mover, according to James Pritchard, was a justification for why the First

Dynasty established Memphis as their capital.[1] Naturally, Ptah would be given a promotion as first among the creator-gods of Egypt since the privileged location of Memphis would then be accepted by all. There are some similarities of this account with the Genesis record of creation. First, Ptah is said to be the creator of all things. Second, Ptah is the giver of life. Third, the origin of creation began in the creator's heart and then was spoken by the tongue.

The *Enuma Elish*. (Photo by Zev Radovan.)

In Mesopotamia, not long after Abraham left Ur, a more detailed account of creation emerged known as the *Enuma Elish*. The name of the epic was taken from the opening line of the story, which is translated "When on high...." Here, the story features an assortment of Babylonian gods who represent the physical world such as Apsu (fresh/sweet water), Tiamat (revenge-seeking female deity of oceans/salt water), Ea (the antagonist who kills Apsu), Kingu (son of Tiamat and leader of the revenge-seeking gods), and Marduk (one of many gods in Babylon, who will emerge as the chief creator-god after he promises to vanquish Tiamat and the revenge-seeking others). Marduk emerges as the creator of the constellations (out of the parts of slain Tiamat), firmament, dry land, planets, and human beings. Though creation is one part of the epic, the god Marduk emerges as the myth's main theme. In the end, Marduk is celebrated as the chief of the gods, representing the strength and power of Babylon.

Accounting for Similarities Between Genesis and the Myths

Critical scholars often argue that the similarities found in the Genesis account to the earlier myths are simply a continuation of the kind of stories we find in the Mesopotamian and Egyptian creation records. After all, both Genesis and these myths tell of a chief god who creates through the spoken word; the natural elements of creation are the same (water, firmament, dry land, light, sun, moon, stars, and humans). Since these Mesopotamian accounts are dated much earlier than Moses' account of creation, it is argued, Moses must have borrowed from them.

Though there are few similarities between the Genesis and mythic accounts, they are too close to simply dismiss as outright coincidence. What can be learned from them is not only found in their thematic similarities, but in their crucial differences. Indeed, the differences are the only way to distinguish one thing from another. This standard practice is found in law-enforcement officers' attempts to make a distinction between counterfeit and genuine currency. Besides this, there are several reasons why conservative scholars do not believe Moses was dependent upon these earlier creation myths.

First, the critical scholars' overemphasis on similarities has blinded their eyes to the many differences that set the accounts apart as unique. Unlike the mythic stories, the Genesis account offers one monotheistic God as the creator of all things. The Mesopotamian epic speaks of a pantheon of gods involved in creation. Genesis offers a loving and all-powerful Lord as creator, unlike the *Enuma Elish*, which portrays the gods as conspiring, vengeful monsters who are seeking ill for one another. In the *Enuma Elish*, human beings are created from the blood of a rebel god and are seen as lowly slaves created to serve and feed the gods. This is in stark opposition to the Genesis account, which records that man was made in the image of God and meant to be like His creator—the highest of His creation. Moreover, in the epic, creation was made out of something evil (Tiamat's body) and pre-existing (that is, *ex deo* or *ex materia*), whereas Genesis describes a creation from a good source (that is, God) and out of nothing (*ex nihilo*).

Second, the similarities may be accounted for by the fact that different groups were writing about the same original historical event (creation). If the creation of the world actually occurred, and various civilizations later reinterpreted the story within the contexts of their polytheistic religions and purposes, it would account for the basic similarities in content. Moses would have received his monotheistic creation account directly from God or from oral tradition that was passed down through Noah and his descendants.

Third, we now know the Genesis account is not dependent on or identified with any earlier Mesopotamian, Egyptian, or Assyrian creation tradition because of the recognized *direction* of myth. Near-Eastern scholar D.J. Wiseman and others familiar with myth literature (for example, C.S. Lewis) have understood that an early myth can become even more mythical over time, and that earlier historical events can become embellished with myth over time. But never do we see earlier myth traditions (such as these Mesopotamian and Egyptian creation accounts) become more historical-sounding, believable, and simpler over time. The Genesis record is more simple, historical, natural, and believable than these early myth traditions, and therefore it cannot possibly be dependent on them or classified as just another Near-Eastern creation account. The mythical tone is obvious in the *Enuma Elish*, but it is absent in the Genesis account. The epic tells of Marduk killing Tiamat and splitting her in two parts like a "shellfish" and creating the sky from her body. However, Genesis simply opens with the statement: "In the beginning, God created the heavens and the earth" (Genesis 1:1). It continues with the simple and natural formula, "Then God said, 'Let there be...'" (Genesis 1:3,6,11,14).

Fourth, some critical scholars forget that early creation myths are not necessarily concerned with creation per se; rather, they are attempts to justify or elevate the standing of particular deities or cities in the eyes of the people. For example, creation is not the main story of *Enuma Elish*; it is the relatively unknown Babylonian god Marduk. It appears now that the story is an effort by its author to elevate Marduk as the chief god of Babylon, though prior to this story he was not given prominence among the multitude of other deities. In the above example of the Egyptian account, most scholars recognize that the creation elements present are not the main theme, but the raising of the city of Memphis and its god (Ptah) to prominence in order to justify Memphis as the location of the capital city of Egypt.

For these reasons, we must consider the Genesis account as an independent historical tradition, without dependency on the earlier Mesopotamian or Egyptian myth literature.

The Flood

The Epic of Gilgamesh

The broken tablet pictured here, dated to the fourteenth century BC, is a fragment of the Mesopotamian flood story known as the *Epic of Gilgamesh*. This piece was discovered at Megiddo in the 1950s, and is part of a much older tradition that began in 2600 BC. Fragments of 12 tablets have been recovered at various sites spanning different time periods including neo-Assyrian king Ashurbanipal's (668–627 BC) library at Nineveh, which was destroyed in 612 BC. The extreme popularity of the epic is evident from its wide geographic exposure in lands such as Asia Minor (Anatolia), the Neo-Assyrian Empire, and Babylonia, as well as its translation into Hittite, Hurrian, and Babylonian cuneiform languages.

This fragment of the *Epic of Gilgamesh* was discovered in Megiddo and is a copy of a much earlier version of the flood story. (Photo by Zev Radovan.)

The Gilgamesh flood tradition emerged from the Sumerian literature tradition of myth and legend (third millennium BC), though most scholars are convinced that Gilgamesh (king of the Sumerian city of Uruk/Erech) was a historical person, as attested in other early documents. Eventually, Gilgamesh's search for immortality and special standing as a god led to his popularity among Mesopotamian readers. As George Smith of the British Museum began translation of the texts in the late nineteenth century, he discovered a story line of a great flood that highly resembled at many points the biblical account of Noah's Flood recorded in the book of Genesis. For example, tablet XI of the epic says the gods were displeased with humans; a god (Ea) warns Utnapishtim (the Babylonian "Noah") to build a square ship with pitch inside and out and to bring animals and family aboard; a weeklong deluge ensues; all of humanity is killed in the flood except the inhabitants of the boat; the boat came to rest on Mount Nisir in Kurdistan; the waters subsided and dry land emerged; the last of three birds sent out did not return; Utnapishtim offers sacrifices to the gods; the gods are saddened; and they grant Utnapishtim divine immortality.

The Atrahasis Epic

This kind of flood story line is also found in the seventeenth-century BC Babylonian *Atrahasis Epic*. Like the Gilgamesh account, humans have displeased the gods, causing alienation; a god (Enki) warns Atrahasis of the coming flood; the gods instruct Atrahasis how to survive the deluge; Atrahasis builds a boat and gathers animals and birds into it; all mankind is destroyed except Atrahasis, who makes an offering to the gods in order to restore divine-human relations. As the god Enki speaks to Atrahasis concerning the flood the epic reads,

> Flee the house, build a boat, Forsake possessions, and save life. The boat which you build,…be equal…. Roof her over like the depth, so that the sun shall not see inside her, Let her be roofed over fore and aft. The gear should be very strong, the pitch should be firm, and so give (the boat) strength. I will shower down upon you later a windfall of birds, a spate of fishes.[2]

Then, Atrahasis brings his family and the animals on board the boat, bolts the door shut, and seals it with pitch. It reads,

> He brought pitch to seal the door. Adad was roaring in the clouds. The winds were furious as he set forth. He cut the mooring rope and released the boat…the flood [came forth], its power came upon the peoples [like a battle]. One person did not see another, they could [not] recognize each other in the catastrophe. [The deluge] bellowed like a bull, the wind [resound]ed like a screaming eagle. The darkness was dense, the sun was gone….[3]

Other Flood References

Other references to the Flood have been found in the literature of nearly two dozen civilizations worldwide, including the Chinese, Jewish, Greek, Mexican, Hawaiian, Babylonian, Sumerian, and Algonquin Indian traditions.

One particular reference to the Flood has been noted in the Sumerian King List, which is dated to the late third millennium BC. The list records pre- and post-flood kings, life spans and length of reigns, reading, "These are five cities, eight kings ruled them for 241,000 years. (Then) the flood swept over the earth. After the flood swept over (the earth) (and) when kingship was lowered (again) from heaven, kingship was (first) in Kish."[4] Moreover, the kings prior to the flood are said to have lived extremely long lives—thousands of years. After the flood the life spans were drastically reduced, mostly to hundreds of years. The parallels to Genesis 6–9 in the epics and worldwide presence of flood narratives are striking, which have led some to believe that 1) the story of the great flood is altogether legend, or 2) that the Genesis account simply borrowed from these earlier myth records, or 3) that the Genesis Flood is confirmed by these texts.

The Eridu Genesis

Thorkild Jacobsen identified an additional flood story written in the Sumerian language, *The Eridu Genesis*, which most likely took form about 2000 BC. In this account, which is supported by discoveries of flood texts at Ashurbanipal's library in Nineveh and other similar Sumerian and Babylonian documents dated to the seventeenth century BC, the god Enlil sends the flood upon the world. Due to mankind's multiplication of cities and growing population on the earth, there was an increase in "noise" that disturbed the gods' sleep. Enlil decides to end this disturbance with a catastrophic deluge in which only Ziusudra, his family, and the animals he is instructed to bring aboard a boat survive. As with the other Babylonian and Sumerian records, the stories have a familiar order—creation of man and animals, the establishment and growth of kings, people, and cities, and then the flood. The order is identical in the biblical account offered in Genesis. The similarities can be seen when the god Enki informs Ziusudra of the coming flood.

> May you he[ed] my advice! By our hand a flood will sweep over (the cities of) the half-bushel bas[kets, and the country;] [the decision,] that mankind is to be destroyed, has been made. A verdict, a command of the assemb[ly cannot be revoked],....

At the point when Ziusudra is instructed by Enki to build a boat to survive the coming deluge, the text is lost. Then the account starts again at the flood:

> All the evil winds, all stormy winds gathered into one and with them, then, the flood was sweeping over the cities...for seven days and seven nights. After the flood had swept over the country, after the evil wind had tossed the big boat about the great waters, the sun came out spreading light over heaven and earth.[5]

After the waters subside, Ziusudra emerges from the boat and offers a sacrifice to the gods. Because of this, he is promptly rewarded with divine immortality.

Analysis of the Myths vs. Genesis

Though the Mesopotamian flood accounts read much like myth, the historical reality of such an event behind them cannot easily be dismissed for several reasons.

First, there are numerous flood stories from different geographical regions and ethnic backgrounds. If the Flood actually occurred, this is what one would expect to see in the historical-archaeological record. Such an event surely would leave a lasting impression on the human psyche and demand an explanation from those who heard about it.

Second, it has been recognized by Near-Eastern scholars (such as Jacobsen) that accounts such as these are part of a mytho-historical tradition in which historical narrative is interwoven with legendary elements that take on the form of the religious culture in which it is written.[6] Therefore, we must be careful not to dismiss the historical nature of these accounts, though we must simultaneously recognize myth when it presents itself.

It has also been widely recognized that the biblical Flood narrative found in Genesis 6–9 cannot be dependent on or a product of these mytho-historical accounts; rather, Genesis emerges from its own tradition. There are five reasons for this conclusion.

1. *The worldviews are opposed to each other.* The Mesopotamian records reveal a polytheistic or henotheistic (worshipping one main god among others) religious culture—unlike Genesis, which portrays a monotheistic religious environment. In the former, the gods are arbitrary, unduly concerned with selfish desires, and at war with each other. The latter reflects an unchanging and uncompromising divine mind that is concerned for His creation.

2. *The focus of the divine characters is different.* In the Mesopotamian accounts, the gods finally realize they need man (for example, the gods become hungry and thirsty because mankind has not made offerings) and what he has to offer the gods. However, Genesis records the opposite: Man is to realize his need for God, and without Him we are prone to wicked selfishness.

3. *Genesis has a worldview progression diametrically opposed to the myth accounts.* The Mesopotamian accounts begin with a positive view of existence— mankind originally is dysfunctional and in need of organization, but steadily progresses to a state that becomes better than it originally was. In the end, the survivor of the flood is either immortalized or given divine status. By contrast, Genesis begins with portraying man as "good" in the Garden of Eden, then the situation steadily worsens over time through the sinful and wicked character of mankind. By the end of the account, the survivor (Noah) is rebuked and chastised for inappropriate action. The former account holds to an optimistic view of life, whereas the biblical narrative reflects a pessimistic view of life. The contrast is made clearer when we recognize that the Genesis account is morally corrective, whereas the

Mesopotamian stories are preoccupied with personal immortality and the anger of the gods.

4. *The reasons for the flood are different.* In the Mesopotamian records the problems that precipitated the flood were nonmoral actions that disturbed the gods (for example, making noise, multiplying population, and so on). Unlike the Mesopotamian stories, Genesis makes clear that the reason for the Flood was due to man's immoral actions and wicked character.

5. *The direction of myth makes literary dependency unlikely for Genesis.* As we discussed previously, the earlier Mesopotamian accounts are most certainly mythological in tone, but the later Genesis story possesses a natural and simple tenor. Though earlier myth can be transformed into a more elaborate mythological story line, it certainly does not become more natural, simple, and believable through time as we find in the later Genesis account. For example, compare the earlier Sumerian Kings List, which records the life spans of kings at tens of thousands of years. The later Genesis narrative notes long lives for many antediluvian individuals, yet they are believable because they are within several hundred years. The direction of myth principle eliminates the later Genesis account from being dependent upon the earlier legends.

For these reasons it is best to classify Genesis within its own historical tradition and as a historical account rather than as part of the Mesopotamian mytho-historical tradition. The following chart will assist in clarifying the differences in the two traditions.

Differences in Mesopotamian and Genesis Flood Accounts	
Mesopotamian	Genesis
Earlier (third millennium BC)	Later (fifteenth century BC)
Mythological tone with some history	Historical narrative without mythical tone
Polytheistic or henotheistic worldview	Monotheistic worldview
Gods are arbitrary and ill-tempered	God is unchanging, patient, moral
Focus is upon gaining immortality (survival)	Focus is upon abolishing evil (moral)
Originally man is wretched	Originally man is good
Optimistic view of existence	Pessimistic view of existence
The problem is growing population and noise	The problem is sin and wickedness
The solution to the problem is government or king	The solution is right relationship to God

Mesopotamian	Genesis
Exaggerated antediluvian life spans	Believable antediluvian life spans
Survivor is hero of the story	God is Hero of the story
Survivor becomes divine or immortal	Survivor is rebuked and chastised
Survivor offers sacrifice of appeasement	Survivor offers sacrifice of thanksgiving
The land was replenished by the gods	The land was replenished by human activity

See chart and description found in Alfred J. Hoerth, *Archaeology and the Old Testament* (Grand Rapids, MI: Baker Books, 1998), 53; see also K.A. Kitchen, *On the Reliability of the Old Testament* (Grand Rapids, MI: Eerdmans, 2003), 425; Thorkild Jacobsen, "The Eridu Genesis," *Journal of Biblical Literature*, vol. 100, no. 4 (December 1981), 527-529.

Historical and Doctrinal Nature of the Flood

For Christians, the historical nature of Noah's Flood is well-established by the New Testament Scriptures, as well as being connected to crucial doctrines of salvation and Christ's second coming. Jesus and Peter refer to the Flood as a historical event and link the story (Matthew 24:37; Luke 17:26) to baptism, a type or picture of what saves us (1 Peter 3:18-22; 2 Peter 2:5), and to the future wicked conditions that immediately precede Christ's second coming (Matthew 24:37-39). This is seen in Peter's statement: "Baptism, which *corresponds to this* [the waters of the Flood], now saves you" (ESV). The Flood provides the historical illustration type for actual salvation. It would make no sense for these statements to be used in support of Christian doctrine if they were actually mythological. It would be absurd to say, "Just as Noah and the Flood are myth, so also this corresponds to real baptism, which is a picture or type of what saves us."

The Tower of Babel

The record of the tower of Babel is preserved for us in Genesis 11:1-9. There it states that the inhabitants of Shinar were building a city and a tower and spoke one language, but later these languages were confused by God. According to most critical scholars, this event found in Scripture is mythical and certainly could not have taken place in Mesopotamia, where it is said to have occurred. Originally, support for this notion was found in the fact that no extrabiblical Mesopotamian record existed that documented such an incredible event. However, archaeological and canonical sources discovered in Mesopotamia give evidence of the historical nature of the Genesis account of the Tower of Babel. There are several reasons why the Genesis account should be viewed as historical.

Ziggurats

First, there have been at least 30 *ziggurat tower* remains found throughout the Mesopotamian region, the oldest of which was located at Eridu, dating to the late fifth to mid fourth millennium BC (the Ubaid period). Ziggurats are built in an ascending stair-stepped pyramid structure similar to the Egyptian pyramids. Though there is still much debate about the function of the ziggurat in Mesopotamian culture, they did include at the top a temple or shrine to a god or gods.

Excavations conducted between 1922 and 1934 by Sir Leonard Woolley at Abraham's birth city of Ur have located the Ziggurat of Ur-Nammu, which was dedicated to the moon-god Nanna. This structure dates to the late third millennium BC. The ziggurat tradition continued down through the Neo-Babylonian and Persian period as attested through excavations conducted at Babylon, where the city's ziggurat was discovered. The timing and multiple remains throughout the Mesopotamian region confirm there actually existed towers of the sort mentioned in Genesis 11.

The Great Ziggurat of Ur was constructed in ancient Sumer in the late third millennium BC in honor of the god Nanna/Sin. (Library of Congress, LC-matpc-13205/www.LifeintheHolyLand.com.)

Building Materials

Second, the building materials described in Genesis are consistent with those used to build Mesopotamian ziggurats. Genesis 11:3 reports that the builders sought to use "bricks" that were thoroughly "burnt" as well as "bitumen for mortar" (ESV). Near-Eastern scholars have recognized that sun-dried bricks were in use within the area of Canaan by the eighth millennium BC (Neolithic Period); by the sixth millennium BC sun-dried bricks appear in Mesopotamian sites such as the Samarran area. The Ziggurat of Ur-Nammu at Ur is an example of a tower structure that originally rose over 200 feet high, with its outer walls built of sun-dried mud bricks and bitumen mortar. This type of mortar was expensive; it was reserved for government and cultic buildings of importance, and stands in contrast to the mud mortar used in Israel during earlier periods. In contrast to sun-dried bricks, fired/baked bricks appear in the fourth millennium BC and are used with bitumen mortar, making the wall structure extremely strong.[7]

The Confusion of Languages

Third, Mesopotamian literature reflects the biblical account of the confusion of languages. For example, the fourth-millennium BC* Sumerian legend known as *Enmerkar and the Lord of Aratta* appears to contain allusions to a unified language and the subsequent diversifying of language by the gods. The larger story is composed around two main figures, Enmerkar, who is the priest-king who ruled in Uruk, and the lord of

---

* Though reflecting a tradition of the fourth millennium BC, the extant copy was most likely *composed* in the late third millennium BC.

Aratta, who ruled a city (Aratta) located far to the east of Uruk, and their love for the woman Inanna. Inanna is the lord of Aratta's wife; however, it appears that Inanna loved Enmerkar more than she did her husband. A series of intellectual challenges between the two men is designed so one can gain the upper hand. The portion of the epic that contains the reference to the languages makes up part of a subsection called "The Spell of Nudimmud." Jacobsen's translation reads,

> In those days, there being no snakes, there being no scorpions, there being no hyenas, there being no lions, there being no dogs or wolves, there being no(thing) fearful or hair-raising, mankind had no opponents— in those days in the countries Subartu, Hamazi, bilingual Sumer* being the great country of princely office, the region of Uri being a country in which was what was appropriate, the country Mardu lying in safe pastures, (in) the (whole) compass of heaven and earth the people entrusted (to him) could address Enlil, verily, in but a single tongue....Enki, lord of abundance, lord of effective command, did the lord of intelligence, the country's clever one, did the leader of the gods, did the sagacious omen-revealed lord of Eridu estrange the tongues in their mouths[†] as many as were put there. The tongues of men which were one.[‡8]

Some have suggested that these statements refer to the confusion of languages as an actual historical event that has been embedded in mythic language, similar to what we have seen with the Flood and creation accounts.[§] This appears to be the case since the god Enki is involved, the deity associated with the historical peoples of Eridu. The confusion of language is an event the memory of the people would not soon forget. It may very well be a recounting of the story of what happened in Shinar in terms of the causal connection between their god(s) and the confusion of language.

The Word Babel

Fourth, it is also interesting to note that the word *Babel*,[¶] the term associated with this event by God (Genesis 11:9) is still used today to refer to unintelligible speech. (*What*

---

* Samuel Kramer translates this as "harmony-tongued" in Samuel Noah Kramer, "The Babel of Tongues: A Sumerian Version," in *Journal of the American Oriental Society* 88, no. 1: 108-111.

† In "The Babel of Tongues" Kramer translates "estrange the tongues in their mouths" as "changed the speech in their mouths."

‡ In "The Babel of Tongues" Kramer translates "The tongues of men which were one" as "Into the speech of man that (until then) had been one."

§ As was the case for creation and the Flood, the presence of widespread testimony to the confusion of languages is expected to emerge from various people groups. For more on the confusion of language from other cultures see James George Frazer, *Folk-Lore in the Old Testament; Studies in Comparative Religion, Legend and Law* (New York: Macmillan Company, 1923), 384ff, in which he mentions cultures in Kenya (the Wasania), Australia, California (the Maidu), Guatemala (the Quiche Maya), and the Tlingit of Alaska, to name a few.

¶ Though the term means "the gate of God," it sounds like the Hebrew word for "confused" (*balal*). For more on the word association of "Babel" see Mark L. Howard, "Therefore it was called Babel," *Journal of Creation* 23 (3) 2009, 56-57.

are you babbling about?) It is also interesting that the Mesopotamian city (and area) of Babylon adopted this name from early times; Babylon is in the general vicinity of the land of Shinar, where the events originally took place. It is not only Babylon's beginnings that have been associated with the confusion of language; its fall as an empire is associated with unintelligible writing on the wall to the last Babylonian king, Belshazzar (Daniel 5).

Theories of Language Origin

What is more, of the two main theories of the origin and development of language—namely, the *monogenesis theory*, which holds that all people come from a common genetic and linguistic source and the language evolved over time into diverse languages, and the *candelabra theory*, which holds that languages began in different separate geographical locations and developed based on the social grouping of the population—neither can adequately explain the diverse linguistic phenomena we experience today. The former theory does not allow enough time for the linguistic evolution to take place. The latter theory cannot explain the presence of similar words and speech, which implies a common original language and not a radical division in geographical groups. However, the Genesis account of the Tower of Babel episode appears to overcome these problems, since all people spoke the same language originally, and the time needed to diversify the world's languages is explained by the supernatural and immediate confusion of languages. Furthermore, the fact that there are today multiple languages utilized around the world is a consistent modern testimony to the *result* of such an extraordinary historical event. Despite our limited understanding of how the diversity of language occurred, the effects described in Genesis 11 are consistent with what we experience as a phenomenon in our modern world.

Though external evidence for the confusion of languages in Genesis 11:1-9 is admittedly thin, certainly it is consistent with the biblical account offered in the Scriptures.

Ancient Sodom

Discovery

The famed biblical "cities of the plain" (Genesis 10; 13:10-13; 19) were once thought by critical scholars to be merely legendary places used by biblical authors to explain a moral metaphor. In 1924, William F. Albright set out to explore the southern end of the Dead Sea, looking for the city of Sodom. As a result, he posited that the city lay beneath the Dead Sea waters, since the water level must have risen over the centuries. Later investigations of the southern sea floor revealed that the waterline had indeed

The stone and mud-brick ruins of Bab edh-Dhra located southeast of the Dead Sea.

risen as Albright suspected; however, no ancient structures were found. Albright began to survey an area near the southeast shores of the Dead Sea in modern Jordan, the city of Bab edh-Dhra pictured here, which he dated to the Early Bronze Age (3150–2200 BC). Bab edh-Dhra was later excavated, in the mid-1960s, by Paul Lapp and again in 1973 by Walter Rast and Thomas Schaub. Evidence shows this well-settled and fortified city was equipped with a massive cemetery, homes, building structures, monoliths, cultic structures—enough infrastructure to house a large number of inhabitants. The examination of the cumulative data has revealed that the city was destroyed by an enormous fire, which is confirmed by an extremely thick layer of ash present at the site. In view of these facts, many scholars (including Bryant Wood) have identified Bab edh-Dhra as the biblical city of Sodom.

However, more recent ongoing research conducted by Dr. Steven Collins at the northeastern end of the Dead Sea region (in Jordan) has offered promising evidence supporting the northern location of Tall el-Hammam as the city of Sodom.[9]

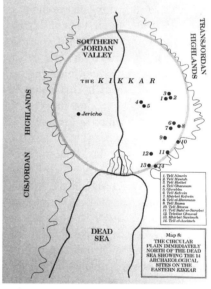

Background and Setting

Sodom and the other "cities of the plain" are referenced early within the table of nations (Genesis 10) and extend to the period of Abraham (Genesis 13; 19). Genesis 19:28 describes Sodom at the time of its destruction as existing in the "land of the valley [plain]." Collins argues for the location of Sodom based on 40 salient points about the geography of the cities of the southern Jordan valley. When referencing the biblical data, Collins noticed the word used for "plain," or in some translations "valley," is the Hebrew *kikkar*, which means "disk" or "circle." The word is used in Old Testament Hebrew over 50 times to refer to "a talent of metal" or a "circular flat loaf of bread," but none of these usages employ the definite article to convey a sense of location (geography).

However, there are 13 rare geographical usages of *kikkar* (found only in the Old Testament); 10 of these are found in the context of the Sodom story, which

(Photo courtesy of Tall el-Hammam Excavation Project [TeHeP].)

Tall el-Hammam, southwest view of the upper tell surface.

places the location of Sodom in the eastern disk of the southern Jordan valley (Genesis 13:1-12; immediately north of the Dead Sea).

Collins notes that there are many other standard Hebrew terms for "plain" and "valley," but these are always avoided when the Bible speaks of the *kikkar* of the Jordan or the "cities of the *kikkar.*" From an aerial map looking down on the *kikkar* it reveals that Jericho resides at the western edge of the disk, southeast of Bethel/Ai, where Abraham was positioned when he saw the smoke rising from Sodom after its destruction (Genesis 13:3-4). Genesis tells of Lot separating from Abraham; Lot saw that the Jordan *kikkar* (valley) was well-watered, like the Lord's garden and the land of Egypt (Genesis 13:10), so he travelled *east* and lived in the cities of the valley and pitched his tent near Sodom (Genesis 13:12). The Scriptures say that Lot viewed the entire Jordan disk with his naked eye, something that would be impossible when looking south toward Bab edh-Dhra. Moreover, Sodom was considered one of the cities of the plain, and no city south of the "mouth of the Jordan" (*hayarden*), like Bab edh-Dhra, would be considered as belonging to the cities of the *kikkar*. To include Bab edh-Dhra in the cities of the disk would force an unnatural meaning on the term *kikkar*. The "*kikkar* of the Jordan" appears to refer only to the disk-shaped alluvial plain directly east of Bethel/Ai and north of the Dead Sea; thus Sodom must be located on the eastern side of the Jordan disk. This conclusion is confirmed by Genesis 10:19 , which describes the cities of the plain as the eastern extent of the Canaanite clans.

Collins has identified Sodom's location as Tall el-Hammam, which is situated on the eastern edge of the Jordan disk, eight miles northeast of the mouth of the Jordan (*hayarden*). It is the largest tell in the southern Levant, measuring 1,000 meters long and containing within its walls 85 acres, a much smaller area than the general occupational spread beyond the walls of 240 acres. The tell itself is comprised of a massive upper and lower area that most likely dates to the

Tall el-Hammam is the largest tell in the southern Levant, with the upper tell alone measuring over 80 acres. (Photo courtesy of Tall el-Hammam Excavation Project [TeHeP].)

Early Bronze Age. The enormous size of the area was anticipated since 1) it is represented by the Bible to be the largest Bronze Age urban center in the eastern *kikkar*, much larger than Jericho, Jerusalem, and any other city in the southern Jordan valley; 2) it is the only *kikkar* city mentioned by itself; 3) King Bera of Sodom is the only spokesperson within the military coalition formed by the cities of the plain (Genesis 14:17-24); 4) Lot was accustomed to sitting in the gates of the city (Genesis 19:1), thus implying defensive fortification; 5) it was situated in close proximity to a major east-west trade route; 6) it had access to abundant fresh water and rich agricultural soil; 7) it had excellent sight lines into the Jordan valley; and 8) it is always mentioned first when speaking of the eastern cities of the plain.

Key Confirmations of Tall el-Hammam as the Site of Sodom

Human remains discovered at Sodom in the Middle Bronze Age destruction layer. (Photo courtesy of Tall el-Hammam Excavation Project [TeHeP].)

In addition to other high-heat indicators unearthed at Tall el-Hammam such as the thick layer of ash and debris, charred human remains, and destruction debris, this 4.5-inch-long piece of a melted Middle Bronze Age storage jar (in left of photo) was discovered. Its "frothy" and "glassy" melted appearance reveals that the sherd was briefly exposed to temperatures that far exceeded 2,000° F. (which is about the same heat as volcanic magma). Additional melted sherds have been discovered at various locations across the site, indicating that the city was destroyed in a sudden, intense, high-heat catastrophic event. A similar "melting" phenomenon resulting from brief high-heat exposure is found in the two small greenish pieces of Trinitite (or "desert glass," pictured in right of photo) taken from ground zero at the United States atomic weapon test area in New Mexico. Astoundingly, analysis of some soil and sand samples from Tall el-Hammam shows they possess qualities similar to Trinitite. (Photo by Michael C. Luddini. Courtesy of Tall el-Hammam Excavation Project [TeHeP].)

After eight seasons of excavation at the site, Collins has discovered several key indicators that confirm the city as Sodom. First, an abrupt occupational gap of several centuries immediately after the Middle Bronze Age II (1800–1550 BC) offers a perfect fit for the timing of the destruction of Sodom. For some reason, the city was no longer inhabited, which appears strange since it was located on a major trade route, had freshwater springs, possessed fortifications, and was located close to the Jordan River. Sodom had location, location, location! However, during the time of Moses and Joshua (1400 BC) the eastern Jordan disk ("plains of Moab") is called "the wasteland" below Pisgah (Numbers 21:20), which is consistent with the timing of its destruction and the lack of Late Bronze Age (1550–1200 BC) and Iron Age I (1200–1000 BC) material at the site.

Excavators at the tell, this author (Joseph Holden) being one of them, have noticed the transition from the Middle Bronze Age directly into the sudden appearance of occupation that begins in the tenth century BC (Iron Age II). An example of this abrupt transition can be seen in Field D on the upper tell. Our excavation team uncovered a massive Iron Age II defensive wall built over the Middle Bronze Age mud-brick fortification rampart. It appears the city lay in ruins for several centuries after the conflagration, until it was possibly rebuilt as one of the largest cities in the area under Solomon, as his administrative capital of the Gilead district (1 Kings 4:19).

Second, Tall el-Hammam contains a massive destruction and ash layer (one meter thick in some areas) distributed at various locations of the Middle Bronze Age layer of the city. The site reveals extensive destruction by fire of architectural features such as roofs, dwellings, walls, fortification barriers, as well as personal items such as jewelry, tools, and pottery. In addition to these, one of the most sobering and striking features involves human remains that depict catastrophic destruction. It appears that many of the inhabitants' bones are charred and distorted, like those pictured, and are situated in a way that indicates a violent high-heat flash event that may have thrown inhabitants to the western side of their dwellings, showing that the destruction could have originated from the east.

Theories positing an earthquake, accompanied by natural gas and bitumen released into the air, as responsible for the destruction have been largely dismissed since the nature of the destruction is not consistent with architectural collapse or lurching, nor is there evidence of pressurized gas and bitumen in the northern Dead Sea area. Besides, if an earthquake were responsible, the city would have simply been rebuilt immediately, as any city at a prime location such as this would have been.

Third, in addition to the architectural destruction, distorted human remains, and pottery, environmental analysis of the site has revealed high-heat indicators that are consistent with the biblical description of Sodom's fiery destruction. For example, one sample of Middle Bronze Age pottery had its surface transformed into glass. After visual and scientific testing of the shard, its transformation could only be explained by an extreme high-heat flash event; only a temperature of thousands of degrees Fahrenheit (much hotter than kilns of that day could heat pottery) could achieve such a process. Related to this, samples of area soil and sand have been examined. These samples give evidence of a high-heat event that was hot enough to turn desert sand into "desert glass," a phenomenon more associated with lightning, airbursts, or atomic explosions in the deserts of New Mexico than the once fertile Jordan River valley. Collins describes the high-heat catastrophic remains when he says,

> The latest Middle Bronze Age layer at Tall el-Hammam consists of 1.5 to 3 feet of heavy ash and destruction debris. A fortified town was then built atop the upper tall in the tenth century B.C.E. All of Tall el-Hammam and associated eastern kikkar sites also lay in ruins for this same period of time—approximately seven centuries. The terminal destruction layer at Tall el-Hammam lies across both the upper and lower tall and consists of a matrix of heavy, dark ash mixed with fragments of pottery, mudbricks, a wide range of object fragments and human bone scatter. Numerous pottery fragments of this matrix lie across the site and have outside surfaces melted into glass, with some bubbled up like "frothy" magma, indicating they were burned in a flash heat event far exceeding 2,000 degrees Fahrenheit. The conflagration must have yielded extremely high heat and effected catastrophic damage.[10]

In support of these archaeological finds are the many geographical reasons why Tall el-Hammam fits the biblical account of Sodom. As mentioned, Dr. Steven Collins has compiled a massive assortment of geographical data, some of which is adapted in the chart below. (For a complete listing of Collins's points, see appendix B, "Ascertaining the Geography of the Cities of the Plain: 40 Points.")

Which Location of Sodom Accounts for the Biblical Geography of Genesis 13:1-12?		
Geographical Criterion	Bab edh-Dhra	Tall el-Hammam
Located on the *kikkar* of the Jordan River	No	Yes
Located on kikkar that is visible from Bethel/Ai	No	Yes
Located on the farthest edge of the Jordan disk (perhaps easternmost of *kikkar* cities)	No	Yes
In area watered like the Garden of Yahweh	Maybe	Yes
In area of *hayarden* watered like Egypt	No	Yes
In area of annual delta (*hayarden*) inundation (watered like Egypt)	No	Yes
In lands east of Canaan boundary	Yes	Yes
Accessed by traveling eastward from Bethel/Ai	No	Yes
Likely located on major east-west trade route	No	Yes*

From Steven Collins, "40 Salient Points on the Geography of the Cities of the Kikkar," in *Biblical Research Bulletin*, vol. 7, no. 1: 5ff. Used by permission.
*See Steven Collins and Latayne C. Scott, *Discovering the City of Sodom* (New York: Simon and Schuster/Howard Books, 2013).

Biblical Significance

Ancient writers in the Near East, whether they were writing myth or history, always used actual geographical markers familiar to them to adequately communicate their story. In the case of Tall el-Hammam, the geographical information appears to have exceeded the customary criteria needed to typically consider an ancient ruin a confirmed biblical city. Many existing biblical sites have been confirmed based on much less geographical evidence than that offered for Tall el-Hammam. Indeed, after reviewing the still-increasing amount of archaeological, biblical, and geographical evidence, if one denies that Tall el-Hammam is the biblical city of Sodom, every biblical city that has been confirmed on less than epigraphical evidence must be called into question.

The Tall el-Hammam location seems to possess everything needed to be consistent with the biblical data and the historical context of the Middle Bronze Age, including the following:

1. It is confirmed by Middle Bronze Age chronology based on pottery reading, stratigraphy, and architectural design;

2. it displays catastrophic destruction of infrastructure with high-heat indicators;

3. pottery and human remains depict massive destruction with high-heat indicators;

4. it evidences an occupational hiatus for several centuries after its destruction as attested by Numbers 21:20 and absence of Late Bronze Age materials;

5. 40 points attest to Sodom's geographical location within the eastern *kikkar* (see appendix B, "Ascertaining the Geography of the Cities of the Plain: 40 Points");

6. at least a dozen ancient cities exist in close proximity, none of which are major urban centers in the eastern Jordan disk;

7. the enormous size of the tell fits with the biblical descriptions of the site as a massive urban city-state;

8. the mud-brick sloping fortifications (glacis) descending approximately 100 feet from the outer walls of the upper tell down to the surface of the lower tell match the biblical account of Sodom's gates;

9. it is located east of Bethel/Ai; and

10. the site would be within view of Abraham while he was at or near Bethel, so he would have been able to see the smoke rising from Sodom after its destruction.

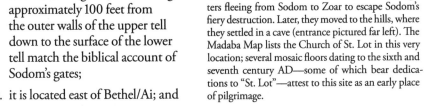

These sixth- to seventh-century AD ruins (located near the Dead Sea in Jordan) of a Byzantine monastery and church mark the traditional site of Lot's cave. Genesis 19:30-38 tells of Lot and his two daughters fleeing from Sodom to Zoar to escape Sodom's fiery destruction. Later, they moved to the hills, where they settled in a cave (entrance pictured far left). The Madaba Map lists the Church of St. Lot in this very location; several mosaic floors dating to the sixth and seventh century AD—some of which bear dedications to "St. Lot"—attest to this site as an early place of pilgrimage.

Bab edh-Dhra does not appear to fit with the Middle Bronze Age dating or the geographical details mentioned in Scripture. The site is much too early (2600 BC) to fit with the Middle Bronze Age lives of Abraham and Lot.

Worthy of note is the fact that Sodom is the only *major* Bronze Age urban center mentioned in the Bible located on the eastern Jordan disk, and that Tall el-Hammam is the only major Bronze Age urban center on the eastern Jordan disk. There are a handful of other cities; however, they are much too small to be considered major urban centers by any means. In other words, Tal el-Hammam appears to be in the right place, in the right time, with the right stuff.

EXODUS AND CONQUEST

The biblical Exodus and the preceding story of the ten plagues have been regularly challenged by critical scholars due to the alleged nonexistence of archaeological and historical evidence. When approaching this subject it is important to remind ourselves that a major regional event like the Exodus as described in the Bible would leave massive amounts of historical and archaeological evidence. This is in contrast to the customary apologetic approach that sees little or no evidence for the Exodus event and therefore tries to find reasons to explain why none would be found. Regrettably, some apologists underestimate the size, impact, and circumstances of the Exodus and think of it as a "minor" event. This appears to be used often as an excuse for why the Egyptians would make no record of it—but in the process these apologists also diminish or eliminate the miraculous nature of the Exodus (more on this faulty apologetic below).

If this was the greatest destruction of an ancient civilization in historical times, as the Bible seems to describe, then we should expect the discovery of hieroglyphic documents and archaeological evidence consistent with the plagues and Exodus event, and not just some evidence but a lot of it. That the Bible describes a mass destruction event in Egypt in association with the Exodus is clear from the following passages:

- The Pharaoh's officials pleaded with him, "Do you not realize that Egypt is *destroyed*?" (Exodus 10:7; see also NIV, KJV).

- There was "not a house without someone dead" (Exodus 12:30b NIV); "all the livestock of Egypt [left in the fields] died" (Exodus 9:6).

- "Nothing green remained on tree or plant in all the land of Egypt" (Exodus 10:15b NIV).

- "All the water that was in the Nile was turned to blood…so that the Egyptians could not drink water" (Exodus 7:20-21; see also 7:24).

- Later, Moses reminded the Israelites about what the Lord "did to the army of Egypt…and how the Lord has destroyed [the army] to this day"

(Deuteronomy 11:4 ESV; compare RSV, NASB, NIV) and therefore for nearly 40 years—"to this day" (Hebrew '*ad yom*)—the Israelites had no fear from any Egyptian forces.

• Pharaoh drowned with the army (Psalm 136:15).

It is regularly asserted by some well-meaning apologists that slaves always remained invisible in the background of Egyptian life, not dominating the royal archives of Pharaoh. But the Exodus consisted of more than a mere escape of slaves, since the entire nation was "destroyed" (Exodus 10:7). Instead it is very reasonable to expect that much material, especially documentary writings as well as indirect events relating to the Exodus, will be visible. It is often said that those who write their own country's history will disregard embarrassing and traumatic details, choosing rather to develop themes that depict strength and wealth. Though this does occur in lesser events on occasion, it is not convincing when this way of thinking is applied to the mass destruction of an entire country. Such an event cannot be covered up by some palace conspiracy or missed through some scribal oversight. Despite the idiosyncrasies of ancient ways of recording history, and no matter how good a nation is in keeping things secret, there is bound to be someone who records such major events in some fashion.

In view of this, our present section will address several literary and historical aspects of the Exodus that support its historical nature, in an attempt to narrow the gap between what some suppose to be myth and historicity.

Egyptian Documentary Evidence for the Exodus

Though the evidence for the Exodus has been slow to be gathered, there is good reason to believe that it actually occurred as described in the Bible. This thinking is based on the biblical testimony, Egyptian extrabiblical sources, and archaeological excavation in Egypt and neighboring regions.

For example, one of the most well-known documents in Egyptology is the Ipuwer papyrus (officially known as Papyrus Leiden 344), which records an account remarkably similar to the plagues described in the book of Exodus. The papyrus was obtained by Swedish diplomat, Giovanni Anastasi, and sold to the Leiden Museum in Holland in 1828. No one realized the exact significance of the contents of the document until the first full translation was done in 1909 by

The Ipuwer Papyrus. (Photo: Erich Lessing/Art Resource, NY.)

a British Egyptologist, Alan H. Gardiner, under the title *The Admonitions of an Egyptian Sage from a Hieratic Papyrus in Leiden*. In addition, there have been many later full translations made, including an Oxford edition (2009).

Currently, the document is stored at the National Museum of Antiquities in the

Netherlands. Its contents are widely regarded by Egyptologists as a lamentation over the catastrophic conditions in Egypt written by a high Egyptian official named Ipuwer sometime prior to the thirteenth century BC (which is consistent with either an early or late chronology for the Exodus).* Ipuwer was known as one of the great wise sages in Egyptian history. His astonishing description of the conditions, to the surprise of Egyptologists, appeared remarkably similar to the biblical account of the ten plagues recorded in the book of Exodus.

The date of the Ipuwer manuscript approximately fits the Exodus date. The hieratic script style was in use at that time period, the events described are remarkably similar to the plagues, the location of the events (Egypt) matches the setting of the Exodus, and the odds of all these calamities occurring at the same time make them more than coincidental. There is no scientific, linguistic, or historical fact that Egyptologists can point to that would decisively preclude the content of the papyrus being a lament over the Exodus plagues. A simple comparison of the content in both the book of Exodus and the Ipuwer papyrus leaves little doubt to their similarities (see table below):

The Book of Exodus and the Ipuwer Papyrus: Comparison	
Exodus*	Ipuwer Papyrus (P. Leiden 344r)†
Events occurred fifteenth century BC	Copied in thirteenth century BC
Ten plagues in Egypt	Lament over catastrophe in Egypt
The Nile river was turned to blood....Blood is throughout the land (7:20-21).	The Nile river is blood...(2:10). Blood is everywhere (2:6).
All the Egyptians dug along the Nile for water to drink, for they could not drink the water of the Nile (7:24).	Men shrink from the (Nile) water...and thirst after water (2:10).
The LORD sent hail mingled with fire, and fire walked along the ground (9:22-26).	Behold, the fire has gone up on high, and its burning should go forth against the enemies of the land (7:1).
Hail struck down every plant of the field and stripped every tree (9:25).	Trees are destroyed and branches stripped off....There is no food (4:14–5:2).

---

* This papyrus copy can be dated to the thirteenth century BC, even though the vast majority of Egyptologists believe that the original composition (autograph) was written to record the chaotic times in Egypt sometime between the end of the 6th Dynasty and the Second Intermediate Period (c. 1800–1550 BC). Of course, this chronology would make the Ipuwer account rather early for the Exodus event (though some advocates of the Theran volcanic explosion theory would date the Exodus to c. 1600 BC). However, there appears to be no good reason to doubt that its descriptions reflect the plagues upon Egypt. There is nothing in the document itself that has been conclusively shown to necessitate a pre-Exodus date before the 1500s or 1400s BC. There are no dates at all in what we have of this damaged document (about one quarter of it is missing). The Egyptians had no chronological eras such as we do, namely BC and AD. Nor do any chronological markers, such as names of established pharaohs, appear in the portion of the papyrus that we have (the missing portions may have named the pharaoh).

Exodus*	Ipuwer Papyrus (P. Leiden 344r)†
Locusts covered the land of Egypt and ate all the plants and fruit of the trees left by the hail. Nothing green remained on tree or plant in all the land of Egypt (10:15).	Grain has perished on every side (6:3).
A severe plague on the livestock in the field (9:3).	The cattle weep and moan (5:5).
There was pitch darkness in all the land of Egypt (10:22-23).	The day does not dawn…and there is terror because of it [darkness] (9:11; 10:1).
The LORD struck down all the firstborn in the land of Egypt from the firstborn of Pharaoh to the firstborn of livestock (12:29). There was not a house without one dead…. There was a great cry (loud wailing) throughout Egypt (12:30).	The children of princes are dashed against the walls. The chosen [firstborn?] children are laid out dead…(4:3-4; 5:6-7). He who places his brother in the ground is everywhere (2:13-14). It is groaning throughout the land mingled with lamentations (3:13-14).
The women of Israel…asked the Egyptians for silver and gold jewelry and for clothing….Thus they plundered the Egyptians (3:22; 12:35-36)	Gold, lapis lazuli, silver, malachite, carnelian, (bronze), and our finest stones are fastened to the necks of female slaves (3:2-3).
The Israelites left Egypt headed for the eastern desert then the Sinai (chapters 12–17).	Poor people [slaves] flee into the desert like nomads who live in tents (9:14–10:2).

© Joseph M. Holden, 2013

* Composite of several leading translations (NASB, NIV, KJV, RSV, ASV) checked against interlinear Hebrew translations.

† Composite of Gardiner 1909, Faulkner 1965, and Oxford 2009 translations and commentaries (in-depth technical commentaries often add nuances of meaning to the formal translation).

Both the biblical account of the Exodus and the Ipuwer papyrus are consistent with the Exodus-like themes and parallels contained in other Egyptian literature, including tomb inscriptions, emerging from Egypt's New Kingdom period (c. 1550–1100 BC).

For example, as recently pointed out by archaeological researcher Brad C. Sparks, eminent Egyptologists have found an early Egyptian document from c. 1300 BC, called the *Destruction of Mankind*. It contains reference to the full Hebrew divine name, I AM THAT I AM, in the Egyptian root word *YWY* (or *Yawi*). These Egyptologists specifically cite Exodus 3:14—when the name I AM THAT I AM was revealed to Moses at the Burning Bush.[1] Sparks further notes that the *Destruction of Mankind* tells of a non-Egyptian people who flee from the eastern Nile Delta, the biblical Land of Goshen, only to be pursued by the Egyptian army. Respected Egyptologists have already identified *dozens* of Egyptian texts with what *they* call Exodus parallels, describing Exodus-like events and themes, which Sparks has compiled and which will soon be published.[2]

The National Trauma of the Exodus

The presence of Exodus-like events and parallels in a wide array of Egyptian documents should not be surprising. It was a traumatic event for the nation, and it haunted succeeding pharaohs. Just think of it—Egypt's pharaoh, a "god" with powers of the sun-god in human form, had drowned (Psalm 136:15). The army was destroyed, the labor force (slaves) had escaped; the nation was plundered of its wealth, its water supply poisoned, its agriculture and livestock wiped out, with ensuing mass famine. Death, darkness, destruction, and despair must have filled the land.

This national catastrophe would surely have left an indelible mark on the soul and religious life of the country for centuries. Future Egyptian pharaohs would have been highly motivated to record these events in some manner so they too would never forget, and so they would also know the deepest secrets of the catastrophe. The accounts of the Exodus were recorded not because the pharaohs wanted to advertise the humiliation of their gods and the past pharaoh to succeeding generations and foreign nations, but because they wanted to remember—so they could try to avoid such a terrifying series of events like this again.

Nor, it would seem, would these pharaohs have wanted to reopen old wounds from the Exodus trauma through the public reopening of records. This could tear apart the fabric of society since it was the Egyptians' central belief that it was the "great" pharaoh and their "strong" gods that held the heart and soul of Egypt together. Therefore, it would be reasonable to assume that great care was taken to preserve the records of the Exodus in a way that cloaked the event in secrecy, as a carefully guarded state secret. Nobody in Egypt except the pharaohs would have been allowed to read these sacred books during the New Kingdom period. The Exodus was also often dressed in mythological or religious clothing, which carried great significance to the Egyptians' polytheistic mindset, just as we might expect.

Naturalistic Explanations for the Egyptian Plagues

Though the similarities between the biblical Exodus account of the plagues and the Egyptian sources appear to be more than coincidence, there are some who continue to offer naturalistic explanations. For example, one such argument says that the Nile could have overflowed its banks and carried red earth from the highlands of Ethiopia, thus turning the Nile red in color.[3] But such silt is brown, not red, and it cannot poison the water; the Egyptians normally let the silt settle out or used filters to remove it before drinking. The Nile is brown, not red, in color; it never turns red naturally; no one has ever taken photos of the Nile made red from natural occurrences. Every Egyptian tourist guidebook and brochure in the world would be plastered with photos of the "Red Nile" to induce tourists to come see the "Biblical Plagues" for themselves if this were an annual "natural" occurrence!

An even more popular idea holds that a form of red algae poisoned the Nile and triggered a domino effect of subsequent plagues. This notion continues to be espoused despite the complete lack of any scientific evidence of any red algae ever occurring in the Nile or anywhere in Egypt or East Africa.[4] This idea claims further that, as a result of the red algae killing the fish, the fish contracted anthrax; an infestation of frogs then swarmed the banks of the river in search of a better life. (Except anthrax cannot infect fish or frogs, only land animals such as sheep, and rarely cattle.) Moreover, the story goes, the overflow of the Nile would bring about the perfect conditions for an insect epidemic that could spread the anthrax from the frogs to the livestock (except, as we just noted, anthrax cannot attack frogs). The locusts, hail, fire, and darkness that covered the land are said to be merely natural occurrences, though more severe than usual due to the alleged chain reaction kicked off by the excessively high Nile flood and the red algae (which do not naturally occur in Egypt and, as Sparks observes, would be killed by the torrential Nile floodwaters as the normal algae are killed every year).

Again, no one can show photos of the Nile made red from any natural causes, so there is no "naturally occurring" phenomenon of silt or algae that turns the river red. And these naturalistic explanations are not convincing for several circumstantial and theological reasons in addition to the scientific contradictions and impossibilities pointed out above (see the table below).

Scientific and Factual Errors in the Red Algae/Red Mud Theory of the Exodus Plague of Blood and Ensuing Plagues	
Scientific Facts Showing Errors	Comments
No photos of a "naturally" occurring "red" Nile	"Natural" occurrences of "red" algae or "red" mud in the Nile must *naturally occur sometime* in order for anyone to know that they "naturally occur." They thus must be seen and be able to be photographed—but that never happens.
Nile is brown not red at flood season	Scientists say the river is *brown* during the annual summer flood season, not red, and their photos prove it.
Wrong season of the year	Popular theories claim that the red algae must come at flood season to add redness to the alleged "red" mud, but that is when the Nile *kills all algae* due to turbulence smashing algal cells, disrupted habitats, and darkness of the waters.
Nile kills algae as they stick to mud particles	Algae stick to mud particles and sink, thus removing them from the water and killing them (death by flocculation).
Nile blocks sunlight, killing the algae by stopping photosynthesis	The same alleged "red" mud often theorized to enhance the redness of the water containing "red" algae will *block sunlight and thus block plant photosynthesis,* killing any algae of any color—red, green, blue, or something else.
Wrong habitat	Red algae are never found by scientists occurring naturally anywhere in the Nile, or Egypt or East Africa. In fact the usually named species (*Haematococcus pluvialis* and *Euglena sanguinea*) are fragile cold-climate or ice-water species unsuited for the tropical heat of the equatorial Nile.

Scientific Facts Showing Errors	Comments
Supposed "red" algae are actually green	The usually named species of supposedly "red" algae (*H. pluvialis* and *E. sanguinea*) causing the Exodus plague of blood are in fact *green*, not red.
"Red" algae are nontoxic, nonpolluting	The usually named species of supposedly "red" algae (*H. pluvialis* and *E. sanguinea*) are not toxic, are nonpolluting, are not on water-pollution lists; they actually help clean the water, and in fact are used for human and animal food supplements.
Supposed "red" algae never cause "red tides" and never kill fish	The usually named species of supposedly "red" algae (*H. pluvialis* and *E. sanguinea*) never cause harmful (or harmless) "red tides," never kill fish, and are in fact used as food for fish (as well as food for animals and humans).
"Red tides" occur in salt-water oceans not fresh-water rivers	Red tides almost always occur in salt-water oceans, not freshwater rivers, and only *extremely rarely* in *stagnant* lakes and *stagnant* rivers—and *never* in the very nonstagnant, high-volume, turbulent Nile, the second-longest river system in the world.
Anthrax does not infect frogs or fish	The "domino theory" of "red" algae/mud blood plague claims that anthrax first infected fish and frogs, then cattle. But in fact anthrax infects only *land mammals* like sheep and rarely cattle. Anthrax does not infect in the water, does not infect *non*-mammals like frogs or fish in water (or on land), and must be dry to form infectious spores. The Israelites would have been the hardest hit by anthrax sheep-disease (from their blood sacrifices of sheep in the Passover), not the Egyptians.
Biting flies cannot breed in winter when they hibernate	The popular "domino theory" of the plagues claims that when the Nile floodwaters receded in the winter, biting stable flies bred and spread anthrax, thus causing the plague of boils. But flies hibernate in the winter and cannot breed then.

Brad C. Sparks, "Red Algae Theories of the Ten Plagues" [Parts 1, 2, 3], *Bible and Spade,* vol. 16, no. 3 (Summer 2003) , 66-77; vol. 17, no. 1 (Winter 2004), 17-27; vol. 17, no. 3 (Summer 2004), 71-82.

It is highly unlikely that all these natural factors described above converged on Egypt at the same time. In fact some cannot occur at the same time as they would nullify the alleged effect. For example, natural high floodwaters also kill natural algae; red mud or mud of any color brought by floodwaters kills algae too; receding floodwater cannot breed flies because it is winter (a regular seasonal occurrence) and flies would be in hibernation then; excess floodwater would prevent the hypothesized extra silt from drying out quickly and being drawn into the air by wind to cause darkness; and so on.

It may be believable that two or three conditions came together by random chance—but nine or ten in the same setting and in just the right sequence? It is utterly unlikely. Clever attempts to link the alleged natural plagues in a "chain" so as to avoid the extreme improbability of all happening by random natural chance at exactly the same time frame have failed. This is acknowledged even by the authors of such theories (several plagues always remain unaccounted for in the "domino" chain); and, as just noted, some such plagues would actually nullify or prevent other "natural" plagues.

Naturalistic explanations do not account for how the Hebrew slaves were spared from the catastrophic conditions but the Egyptians who lived among or near them were not. Moreover, sandstorms and Nile floods do not discriminate based on whether you are an Egyptian (ethnic origin) or a slave (social status)! Unfortunately for the critics' view, this type of selectivity is necessary to make the scenario believable.

Besides, none of these natural causes satisfactorily address the death of Egypt's first-born. Natural forces do not discriminate based on the *order* of one's birth. The theory also leaves unaddressed the historical narrative of Moses calling down these plagues at precisely the same time as these "natural" conditions are appearing in Egypt. That is to say, the presence of a moral and theological dimension with a clearly defined purpose and timing within the Exodus passages demonstrates that the plagues were more than simply a *natural* phenomenon; rather, they meet the criteria of a miraculous event.

The real problem here seems to be the critics' antisupernatural presupposition, and unfortunately even some apologists follow suit for different reasons (as we noted previously). Why can't we simply read the text in a straightforward way? Critics assume what they are supposed to prove. They *assume* supernatural events cannot possibly occur, and then dismiss any account of a supernatural event they may find, deeming it noncredible since it describes a supernatural occurrence—then they turn around and complain there is no evidence for the supernatural event! This is a classic circular argument and a fallacy. Similarly, the critics *assume* that God does not exist, since if He does exist, then miracles (which are acts of God) are possible.

Archaeological Evidence for the Exodus and Conquest

Evidence from the Nile Delta

Archaeological excavations carried out since 1966 in the northeastern Nile Delta region have suggested the presence of western Semites. Manfred Bietak of the University of Vienna has investigated the area known as Tell el-Dab'a (originally called Avaris, which became the Hyksos capital during the Hyksos period in the 1700s to 1500s BC). Here, as well as in surrounding territories, Bietak has discovered dwellings built in Syro-Palestinian fashion (also used by the Israelites) dating to the time when the Hebrews are believed to have been in Egypt prior to the Exodus.[5] According to Bietak, those who settled at Tell el-Dab'a (which is near the Land of Goshen) were people from Canaan, though these individuals became highly Egyptianized. Bietak has concluded that beginning under Pharaoh Senusret (Sesostris) III (c. 1800 BC), the settlements at Tell el-Dab'a went through a massive expansion during the late twelfth and thirteenth Egyptian dynasties, which would be consistent with Exodus 1:12 that says the more Egypt afflicted their Hebrew slaves the more they multiplied.

What is most striking about the excavation is the evidence that work on the palace in the Eastern Nile Delta was suddenly stopped. Bietak says that pots of paint, plumb lines, and instruments were simply dropped to the floor! The palace was suddenly abandoned. This is what one would expect to see if a Hebrew Exodus abruptly occurred in the eastern Nile Delta (Goshen) in this time frame.

Though archaeological evidence for the Exodus has been slow in its development, what we do possess is consistent with an Israelite presence in Egypt immediately prior to the time of the Exodus. There still remain problems with reconciling the archaeological material with commonly accepted Egyptian chronology, though some have argued that this chronology should be revised downward by some 200 to 300 years or even more. The physical evidence unearthed at Tell el-Dab'a fits nicely with the Exodus account, but the interpretation of the evidence itself is colored by the dating and the philosophical presuppositions of the interpreter. The details from Tell el-Dab'a are very promising but need further research with additional data from surrounding regions.

The Balaam Inscription

In addition to excavations by Bietak and the Egyptian documentary parallels, the discovery of the Balaam inscription adds an important historical support for the Exodus and its ensuing events. In the text of Numbers 22:22-40, the Balaam story appears in direct connection with the historical events of the Exodus and the Conquest. There is no reason here to discriminate and take Balaam as historical or semi-legendary but the Exodus and Conquest as pure myth. Though critical scholars have long dismissed Balaam and his talking donkey as sheer fiction, this view began to shift after 1967 when a crumbled plaster Aramaic text was discovered within the rubble of an ancient building in Deir 'Alla (Jordan). The c. 800 BC inscription is contained within 119 fragments written with 50 lines of text in faded red and black ink. It is written in red ink for emphasis, and reads,

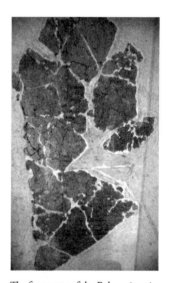

The fragments of the Balaam inscription reflect the earliest archaeological data of any biblical prophet or his prophecies. The inscription is currently on display at the Citadel Museum in Amman, Jordan.

> Warnings [Sayings] from the Book of Balaam the son of Beor. He was a seer of the gods [line 1a; see lines, 2-4; see similarly Numbers 22:5; Josephus 24:9].

Balaam's reputation as a prophet is consistent with the biblical account that has Balak the king calling upon Balaam to pronounce curses on the Israelites (Numbers 22:6).

Though the building in which the text was found was most likely destroyed in the great earthquake around the time Uzziah reigned as king (Isaiah 6:1), the plaster text appears much older due to the extremely worn and faded color condition of the ink, and it is believed that it was part of an already circulating text. It appears that people in Deir 'Alla admired Balaam, who later became a sort of icon to the inhabitants of the area. The time required for such reverence to grow adds support to a much earlier dating of the original text, thus placing it closer to the time of the Exodus. Moreover, the building in which the text was found is located less than 30 miles from the area Balaam is said to have engaged Israel prior to their crossing the Jordan River, in the plains of Moab (Numbers 22–24). The find has posed a problem for Exodus skeptics and revisionists since the text apparently places a historical Balaam in the same geographical area as the Israelites during the Exodus and Conquest.

The Merneptah Stele

Attempts to date the Exodus forward to the thirteenth century BC appear to contradict Egyptian records indicating that Israel had already been established in Canaan by that century. If the Exodus had occurred much later, then the Egyptian Exodus-parallels mentioned above would be much too early to refer to an Exodus-like event. The hieroglyphic stele found by Sir William Flinders Petrie in Pharaoh Merneptah's funerary temple in western Thebes is the earliest known mention of Israel from any ancient document outside the Bible, and it dates to c. 1210 BC, based on the generally accepted date of Merneptah. It is also the only known mention of "Israel" in ancient Egyptian writing (a possible second and earlier example has turned up in a Berlin museum but is still under study).[6] The stele's contribution comes in the form of a eulogy to a victorious Merneptah:

Merneptah Stele (Photo by Zev Radovan.)

> Hatti is pacified; plundered is the *Canaan* with every evil; carried off is Ashkelon; seized upon is Gezer; Yanoam is made as that which does not exist; *Israel is laid waste, his seed is not*; Hurru is become a widow for Egypt! All lands together, they are pacified;[7]

There is no doubt that Israel was in the land by the thirteenth century BC, though not established as a nation with a king or kingdom as yet. "Israel" is written with an Egyptian *determinative symbol* in the Merneptah Stele, which indicates Israel was a *people* at this time and not a *land*.[8] Apparently, this refers to a time when Israel was without rulers, such as during the four-century-long time of the judges prior to the establishment of a national infrastructure and the united monarchy under David and Solomon in the tenth century BC. Israel's listing along with the other established cities and biblical lands (Ashkelon, Gezer, and so on) implies that Israel was comparable in importance and not an insignificant wandering tribe of Bedouins. The dating for Israel's presence in the land supplied by the Merneptah Stele fits well with the timing of the Exodus from Egypt and the subsequent conquest of Canaan in about 1400 BC.

Indirect Support for the Exodus

Archaeology has also provided us with discoveries that indirectly support the Exodus narrative.

The Writer's Familiarity with Egypt's Language and Culture

First, a linguistic and cultural knowledge of Egyptian life is reflected in the Hebrew language used to pen the book of Exodus. The one individual who had the knowledge, experience, and education necessary to account for these details is Moses who "was instructed in all the wisdom of the Egyptians" (Acts 7:22 ESV). (See chapter 4 for arguments about the Mosaic authorship of Exodus and the other books of the Pentateuch.) Many scholars recognize that these Egyptian features must have come from an author intimately acquainted with Egyptian slave-labor practice and who had an understanding of the Egyptian royal court, was familiar with the Egyptian flora and fauna (Genesis 13:10; Exodus 9:31-32),* and possessed a command of Egyptian language and geography.† In fact, the name "Moses" seems to be an Egyptian name much like the Pharaohs' dynastic name Thut*mose*. This extensive familiarity with Egypt in the book of Exodus, rather than with Babylonia,‡ thus supports the belief that the writer could have been an eyewitness of the Exodus and the plagues, not an individual far-removed from the actual events. The critical scholars who postulate anonymous Jewish authors of the Pentateuch say that they allegedly wrote or compiled the book of Exodus in exile in Babylonia a thousand years after the Exodus—a very great distance in space and time from Egypt in the second millennium BC.

---

* Note that the crop sequence, trees, and animals in these passages are indigenous to Egypt rather than the Palestinian region.

† The Pentateuch has more Egyptian loan words than any other section of the Bible.

‡ The exception might be the Pentateuch author's seeming familiarity with Mesopotamian law codes such as the Code of Hammurabi (Hammurapi)—which, however, may have been widely known throughout the ancient Middle East, unlike the details of Babylonian geography and culture. But Mesopotamian geography and culture are not reflected in the book of Exodus, which is, as one might expect, heavily Egyptian, not Babylonian, in coloring. Mesopotamian language does not appear in the book of Exodus either. An exception to the expected lack of knowledge of Mesopotamian culture in distant Egypt would be that the cuneiform Amarna tablets in Egypt prove the Egyptian fluency in the Mesopotamian language (*Akkadian*—that is, "Babylonian") as a diplomatic language, in the *fourteenth* century BC. However, the early date of the Exodus in the *fifteenth* century BC would predate the development of this diplomatic language, so there is no discrepancy.

The Law-Code Question

Second, the law code described in the book of Exodus displays a comfortable fit with the form and structure of law codes dated to earlier periods. Previous to recognizing this fit, critics had argued that Moses could not write at all, let alone have written a sophisticated law code such as seen in Exodus and Leviticus, and that the Hebrews did not learn the art of writing until after they settled in Canaan.

However, the discovery of a diorite stele containing a much earlier law code (now known as the Hammurabi Code) created by the Babylonian king Hammurabi (or Hammurapi, c. 1700 BC), all but silenced the critics.

Archaeologists have since unearthed thousands of cuneiform clay tablets in central Mesopotamia, known as the Nuzi letters, that date to the fifteenth century BC. These letters reflect societal laws and codes relating to norms, private contracts, adoption, and inheritance, laws and codes that were in place for centuries prior to their writing. For instance, the law permitted a man to remarry if his wife could not bear children, or the wife could provide a surrogate mother to give birth, such as a slave woman (see the example of Abraham, Sarah, and Hagar, Genesis 16:1-3). If a couple could not have a child, adoption of another individual to carry on the family name and inherit the wealth was acceptable according to the Nuzi tablets. However, if the couple had a son born to them, then the son would take priority over the former adoptee (see Isaac's position over Eliezer, Genesis 15:4). What is more, after the child was born of surrogacy, that child could not be expelled from the family or sent away (see Sarah's request to send Hagar and Ishmael away, Genesis 21:10).

This seven-foot stele known as the Code of Hammurabi contains 282 law codes dealing with various situations. The picture on top depicts Hammurabi facing the seated god Marduk. Beneath them are the written codes themselves. (Photo by Zev Radovan.

Based on these finds and their consistency with laws and customs found in Exodus and the other books of Moses, it seems reasonable to believe the author of Exodus was well-acquainted with Egyptian culture and Mesopotamian law in the second millennium BC. Despite these helpful parallels supporting the context of the patriarchal narratives in Genesis, some evangelical scholars have recognized the limitations inherent in these examples and some defects in these parallels. Thus they caution against excessive reliance on indirect evidences such as parallels of customs, laws, societal norms, and so on.

Issues with Historical Investigation of the Exodus

Historians must *investigate* ancient literature, not prejudge it, to try to objectively assess whether it is credible and reliable or composed of fabrication, myth, and legend, or is otherwise untrustworthy. If the ancient document "passes the test" or survives the investigation, then its credibility will be high and one can rely on it as telling the truth to the degree that depends on how extensively it was tested.

Historical investigation is not a 100 percent certain procedure with absolutely guaranteed results. Nevertheless, the Bible remains the one outstanding piece of ancient literature that excels in passing historical investigations mounted by even its harshest critics. This does not mean we have given the Bible a free pass regarding its trustworthiness. The free-pass approach uses the faulty logic that declares, for example, "We don't know what the ancients knew, so who are we to criticize the eyewitness or author of the book?" In other words, the free-pass approach maintains that critics cannot criticize because they are looking back in time some 3,500 years; supposedly, our day cannot provide a superior vantage point in any way to that of the one who experienced the events at the actual time.

But this tired truism, which may not be true, cannot answer factual questions! Yes, as a general rule, we normally prefer contemporaneous eyewitness evidence over that of later material. But in some cases we today might well know more than what an ancient author knew about his own time. Rapid electronic communications did not exist 3,500 years ago. It is possible that someone in one town might not know what had occurred in a neighboring town or surrounding geographical area, given the isolation imposed by older methods of communication. By excavating a library of clay tablets covering a thousand years of history, we might well know more than an average person living back then or even the average temple scholar, who did not have access to or could not read the language used in the tablets (for example, the Sumerian language used in some tablets in later Babylonia, which was a language not known to the general population or to any but the inner circle of scribes and specially-trained priests).

On the other hand, it is also possible that an ancient scholar or eyewitness 3,500 years ago could indeed have had a clearer view of his own history than we do today, in spite of technological limitations. We just cannot prejudge the question one way or the other and then use the prejudgment to entirely sweep away critical objections to the Bible's historicity. We need to address the fundamental issues straight on. And in the case of the Exodus we have an abundance of evidence.

The Argument from Silence

There are times when critical scholars appear to argue from silence—that is, they dismiss the historicity of the Exodus because no supporting material has been discovered. It is also asserted by some well-intentioned apologists that critics cannot argue that the "absence of evidence is evidence of absence." If there is no evidence discovered for the Exodus, it is argued, this "absence of evidence" doesn't prove the absence of the Exodus event from history.

One must guard against two extremes when approaching the argument from silence.

One should recognize that the absence of evidence—when there has been a diligent search for it—*is* evidence of the absence of the event in the area searched. How could it be otherwise? How else does one establish that an alleged event or fact is "absent"? How does one come to this conclusion *except by searching for the event diligently and not finding it?* It certainly is not positive proof that the event did not occur, but it is evidence (of absence) that is as strong as the thoroughness of the search that was designed to look for it.

For instance, if search teams looking for a child missing in the forest cannot find him in one area, they don't tell themselves this "absence of evidence" of the child proves nothing and they must keep futilely searching the same area over and over again instead of expanding the search to a wider area. No, they say they *do* indeed have evidence of absence of the child in that one area, and then they *continue* the search in the *next* area, and the next area after that, until hopefully searchers find him or her. This is just common sense.

On the other hand, the finding of "no evidence" does *not* automatically carry the same weight as its exact opposite (hard evidence)—in this case the total *contradiction* of the Exodus event. The "no evidence" finding may warrant a merely *neutral* or ambiguous conclusion, or even the more preferred approach of giving the historical details surrounding the Exodus event the benefit of the doubt as the search continues.

In the case of the Exodus, there has never been a diligent search for Egyptian documentary evidence for it until now. The scattered hieroglyphic text evidences known so far have been uncovered by Egyptologists by accident in the normal course of their work, not because of a special search for Egyptian records of the Exodus, and even the accidentally uncovered evidences have never been collected together in one place until now.[9] Even Christian scholars have failed to conduct a diligent search for Egyptian records of the Exodus, and no such exhaustive search is known from any published source, secular or not.

In modern history there has never been a full-time scholar dedicated to investigating the Egyptian records for evidence of the Exodus, at least until now. No professorship of Exodus studies is known of anywhere in the world, in any Christian or Jewish seminary, Bible college, or secular university at any time, past or present. No "Department of Exodus Studies" exists in any university or college or seminary anywhere in the world, now or in the past. (And even if such an Exodus professorship or department did exist, it might not be dedicated to searching for Egyptian documents on the Exodus—documents that so many believe do not exist.) No archaeological excavation along the shores of the Red Sea has ever looked for signs of the

Stone and mud-brick dwelling foundations unearthed in Jericho at Tell es-Sultan. (Photo by Abraham Sobkowski, PD.)

Exodus. Simple due diligence would call for these minimal efforts to be made before any scholar declares the Exodus either disproven or "unnecessary to be proven" ("unnecessary" because the alleged lack of Egyptian records is supported only by tenuous arguments or excuses, such as reducing the Exodus to a minor event that is easily overlooked).

Jericho as Evidence of the Exodus and Conquest

Modern excavations conducted at Jericho (Tel es-Sultan) have been offered by some as archaeological evidence supporting the conquest of Canaan and therefore, by implication, the Exodus event some 40 years before the conquest. These excavations are purported to demonstrate that the city was destroyed around the time of the Exodus (c. 1440 to 1400 BC) *if the archaeological data are reinterpreted to fit the Bible,* which creates some problems and raises some issues.

Archaeological data have demonstrated that Jericho is one of the oldest continuously inhabited cities in the world, dating back thousands of years before Christ. It is located nine miles north of the Dead Sea and five miles west of the Jordan River, adjacent to the arid Judean wilderness. Teams of archaeologists have excavated Jericho in four major campaigns since the early twentieth century and they continue to do so to the present day. Except for the first campaign, these efforts were unable to match the archaeological data to the biblical chronology of the conquest of Canaan by Joshua (Joshua 6).

A Questionable Attempt to Reconcile Evidence and Dates

In 1990, Bryant Wood of the Associates for Biblical Research revisited much of the previous data collected by Kathleen Kenyon in the 1950s and others, including the pottery data. By reinterpreting the data, Wood concluded that the destruction of the city must have occurred c. 1400 BC, thus appearing to bring the archaeological data at Jericho more in line with the biblical text and supporting an early chronology for the Exodus and conquest. Despite the chronological issues, by redating certain c. 1600 BC Middle Bronze pottery remains found at Jericho to c. 1400 BC, the end of the first period of the Late Bronze Age (LB I), Wood claims to have identified several archaeological features that confirm biblical descriptions of the city at the time of its conquest by Joshua. (See the chart "Archaeological Ages and Israel" in chapter 15.) These include the collapse of fortification walls (Joshua 6:20); grain storage indicating that the conquest was in the spring (Joshua 2:6; 3:15; 5:10); the city being destroyed by fire (Joshua 6:24); the grain stored in the city not being consumed by its inhabitants, thus indicating a short siege (Joshua 6:15,20); and the grain never being used by the attackers (the Hebrews were not to take anything from the city: Joshua 6:17-18).[10]

Attempts to lower the date of the end of the Middle Bronze age throughout the entire Israel region (by John Bimson of the University of Sheffield, Great Britain) or on a localized basis at Jericho only (Wood) have been met with criticism. Some believe this reinterpretation of the earlier data, which claims errors in the original excavators' archaeological analysis, is unnecessary. This is because the first Jericho excavation actually matched the biblical chronology of the Conquest with the archaeological data found, without having to reinterpret the data or attribute errors to the original archaeological analysis in order to create a match. Subsequent studies that have ignored those results did so mainly because the *dates* of the archaeological periods (Early Bronze, Middle Bronze, Late Bronze, Iron Age) had been radically changed in the interim so that there was no longer a match with the Bible. The *analyses* of the archaeological *artifacts* and the archaeological periods to which they were assigned remain valid and unchanged today—only the dates of the periods have changed.

Critics of Wood's efforts to redate some of the Jericho pottery unearthed by Kenyon have questioned his attempts to reinterpret the data and to claim that Kenyon misinterpreted and hence "misdated" Jericho's archaeology. Wood claims that the Middle Bronze Age destruction of the city must have actually occurred c. 1400 BC in the Late Bronze Age, which brings the archaeological data at Jericho in line with the biblical text. Thus Wood redates the Middle Bronze Age destruction of Jericho to the Late Bronze Age.

Problems with the Jericho Pottery Redating

Unfortunately, as appealing as Wood's redating of *pottery* may seem to be at first glance, it is very unclear whether he has succeeded in redating the Jericho *wall destruction* to c. 1400 BC and thus the time of Joshua's conquest. His "detailed study of the pottery of the Middle Bronze–Late Bronze I period at Jericho"—which is crucially important to his argument—as of 1990 admittedly "has not yet been published." And over 20 years later it apparently still had not been published (no mention of its publication in the 2008 online edition of his original article, for example, or in 2010 postings).[11] In 2009, Wood's research update on Jericho still insisted that Kenyon had "erred," but nevertheless admitted, "It remains for me to publish a critique of Kenyon's theories and an in-depth study of the pottery from the various expeditions, to demonstrate that Kenyon's conclusions were incorrect...."[12]

When Wood's initial publication was severely criticized by another archaeologist, Wood softened his argument somewhat from his original claims. In his original article, Wood stressed how several types of pottery found by earlier excavators at Jericho, in what is normally considered to be the Middle Bronze Age walled city (which was destroyed by fire), were absolutely unique to the Late Bronze Age period. Thus the Middle Bronze Age dating by Kenyon was wrong because of her "methodologically unsound and, indeed, unacceptable" errors, and work that was "especially poorly founded." He claimed she "inexplicably...ignored" supposedly "obvious" Late Bronze Age pottery from the walled city.

So in the original article, this supposedly "obvious" and uniquely Late Bronze Age–dated pottery, it was confidently asserted, could be "found only" in the Late Bronze Age, "confined to" the last part of the Late Bronze I period, and "all characteristic" of (unique to) the Late Bronze Age.

But *after* the published criticism, Wood responded by painting a rather different picture. He conceded that Late Bronze Age pottery is so similar to Middle Bronze Age pottery that the "subtle differences" are difficult to distinguish and require "careful study":

It is important to recognize that the pottery of the Late Bronze I period is *very similar* to that of the final phase of the Middle Bronze period. In fact, the material culture of the Late Bronze I period is *simply a continuation* of that of the Middle Bronze period. As a result, many Middle Bronze forms *continue* into Late Bronze I. There are *subtle* differences in a number of types, however, and several new forms are introduced. With careful study of the pottery evidence, therefore, it is possible to distinguish the Late Bronze I period from the terminal phase of the Middle Bronze period.[13]

However, the first example of pottery, which Wood for some reason chose to extensively discuss, is not a conclusively "uniquely" dated item. It is called the "flaring carinated bowl" and was found in the city mound by Kenyon. Wood was forced to admit that the "subtle differences" in the "slight crimp" in the bowl require a "discerning eye" to see and "*One could argue this point, however, since the difference is slight*" (emphasis added). The change in this "slight crimp" over time from Middle Bronze Age to Late Bronze Age is undocumented by any drawings illustrating the change. This Late Bronze Age dating has of course been vigorously disputed.[14]

Where Is the Evidence?

All this inspires little confidence in what is supposed to be a revolutionary redating of Jericho. With several other bowl and pot types, Wood claims "strong" indicators for a "unique" (or "diagnostic") Late Bronze Age date. This should be Wood's crucial evidence, the clincher, but he had already warned in advance (see quote above) that these are all "subtle" differences that may be arguable. And then he goes on with weak examples (instead of the strongest evidence) of other pottery that are merely "*more* in the Late Bronze *tradition*" (emphasis added) than in the Middle Bronze tradition, but not absolutely unique to Late Bronze Age. This pottery should be more or less irrelevant if it does not uniquely determine the date. In still other examples he is nebulous about whether the Late Bronze Age date carries uniqueness or not. Although everything hinges on this pottery evidence, these examples evidently all remain *undocumented and unpublished* by Wood to this day.

In short, none of Bryant Wood's equivocal, unpublished evidence convincingly proves that a biblical-style conquest of a formidable walled city—as famously depicted in the book of Joshua—occurred in the Late Bronze Age period. Wood might still be right, and we hope he publishes the evidence to prove it in the near future. As mentioned before, though, there are other alternatives.*

---

* Brad C. Sparks, forthcoming manuscript on Exodus-like parallels in Egyptian literature. Proponents of the redating of Jericho pottery from the Middle Bronze Age to the Late Bronze Age like to cite several archaeological features as confirming the biblical descriptions of the city at the time of its conquest by Joshua (destruction by fire in the spring, collapse of the walls, abandonment of the city afterward, and so on). But these are not unique to the supposed "Late Bronze Age" destruction of Jericho (actually the Middle Bronze Age destruction) nor are they unique to the biblical conquest of Jericho (Ai was also destroyed by fire and left abandoned). The Early Bronze Age city of Jericho was also heavily fortified with walls and was destroyed by fire, with total wall destruction on the east side, and was left abandoned for centuries. Moreover,

Biblical Significance

We do not need to rely on weak evidence or faulty arguments to support the Exodus event or the subsequent conquest of Canaan. We do not have to make excuses for the Bible or rewrite the miraculous out of it so that what remains will somehow withstand scientific and historical scrutiny better. We can argue from a position of strength, not weakness. The archaeological and documentary data powerfully corroborate the Exodus account as described by Moses. The intimate knowledge of Egyptian life, language, slave labor, and customs recorded in the book of Exodus reflect firsthand knowledge of Egyptian society by the author. The interweaving of miracles with various historical figures and geography throughout the Pentateuch makes it difficult to separate them—showing that the author intended them to be understood as historical and literal.

The difficulties that still remain in aligning archaeological data with biblical chronology may yet be resolved. It appears that scholars are associating the archaeological data with the right archaeological periods but assigning the wrong dates to those periods (or to the Egyptian dynasties usually used to date the archaeological periods). This is seen in, among other things, the fact that those period dates continue to shift around (as shown by, for example, the long-running debate between Amihai Mazar and Israel Finkelstein over Iron Age dates and the continual slide toward later dates for Egyptian dynasties).

The evidence for the Exodus is strong and extensive, as we would expect from the mass destruction event recounted in the Bible, the destruction of the nation of Egypt. In the end, faith supplies the final measure of certainty for those seeking God. But the powerful Egyptian evidences for the Exodus in its most miraculous aspects go a long way toward supporting the historicity and credibility of the Bible.

---

unlike the alleged Late Bronze Age destruction, the Early Bronze Age city was destroyed by invaders crossing the Jordan River from the east who were organized in at least eight distinguishable "tribes"—no such "tribal" attack occurred with the Late Bronze Age (Middle Bronze Age) destruction.

Some reputable archaeologists have argued that it was in fact the Early Bronze Age city of Jericho that was destroyed in the Israelite conquest, despite the apparent six- or eight-century dating problem (Rudolph Cohen, Emmanuel Anati, et al.). Cohen and Anati point to the very early date of the Ipuwer papyrus as supporting Egyptian evidence that links up precisely with this archaeological evidence of the tribal destruction of Early Bronze Age Jericho.

THE AMARNA LETTERS, THE HITTITES, AND THE CITY OF MEGIDDO

The Amarna Letters

Several of the Amarna Letters were discovered in 1887 by a peasant woman sifting through the ancient Egyptian ruins at the palace of Akhenaten. Four years later, in 1891, the Egyptologist Sir William Flinders Petrie excavated Tell el-Amarna for two years and recovered the remaining tablets.

Background and Setting

Tell el-Amarna (the "hill of Amarna"), a plain located on the east bank of the Nile River between Cairo or Memphis and Luxor in central Egypt, was the site where the ancient Egyptian pharaoh Amenhotep III (1390–1352 BC) and his reformer son Akhenaten (meaning "the splendor of Aten") with his wife Nefertiti made their new capital, Khut-Aten. Akhenaten (Amenhotep IV) is remembered for his abandonment of the old religious practice of Egypt (the worship of Amun, as facilitated by the priests located at Thebes). He instituted a new religious practice (some have referred to it as the first Egyptian attempt at monotheism) that exclusively worshipped the visible sun disk, Aten.

The 382 Amarna Letters consist of clay tablets written on both sides in Akkadian

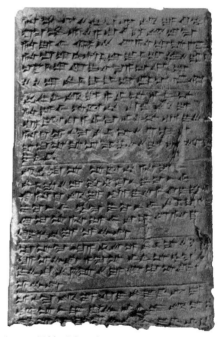

Amarna Tablet (Photo by Zev Radovan.)

cuneiform (from *cuneus*, which means "wedge" and refers to the shape of the characters), the international political language of that day. The letters measure from as small as 2 by 2.5 inches to as large as 3.5 by 9.5 inches. The tablet pictured here is a letter from the king of Cyprus (Alashiya) to Amenhotep III, Akhenaten's predecessor. It seems to be a response to Egypt regarding some Cypriot raiding of Egyptian villages.

The letters found at Amarna describe the political conditions and turmoil present in the Egyptian-controlled Canaanite (Syro-Israelite) territories during the time Israel was settling the Promised Land under Joshua (c. 1400 to 1300 BC). Some of the letters contain myths or legends, news about various cities, diplomatic correspondence, requests for supplies (food), and communication about the exchanging of gifts between kings. However, most are correspondence from the princes and vassal kings of Syria, Israel, Babylonia, Hatti (Hittites in Asia Minor), and Assyria to the Egyptian government, usually containing desperate pleas for economic and military help to combat invading armies and marauders threatening these kingdoms.

Although Moses subdued the land to the east of the Jordan River, the territories west of the Jordan were disintegrating into a state of chaos and desperation. Egypt was too weak to support and control its northeastern territories due to its own internal political and religious problems. It appears that the Israelites seized this opportunity under Joshua to establish themselves in Canaan, defeating one city after another. One particular correspondence on tablet 287 records that 'Abdi-Heba, prince of Jerusalem (Urusalima), sent desperate news to Egypt that many officials in Jerusalem had joined the '*Apiru* and the lands of the King of Egypt were lost to his enemies. The prince's plea for archers, protection, and even protective sanctuary in Egypt for his family appear to have fallen on deaf ears.

Scholars have agreed that '*Apiru* (also *Hapiru* or *Habiru*) is etymologically equatable to *Hebrew*.[1] This has led some to believe that the '*Apiru* references in the letters are to the Hebrews under Joshua's command. However, further research has indicated that this term may not have been referring to an ethnic group; rather, it may be a derogatory word applied to all kinds of enemies (or outlaws) who harassed these territories. It seems the Canaanites used the term as a disdainful descriptive, and that the Babylonians employed the term to refer to some within their own military. Furthermore, it has been demonstrated that the word was also used before and after the conquest of Canaan. Nevertheless, it may be possible that since the Hebrews were known as Egyptian slaves, as "outlaws and marauders," and were comprised of loosely connected nomadic individuals in their wanderings out of Canaan and into Egypt, with no ties to a settled community (that is, they were immigrants), this derogatory byword's origin may have been connected to an ethnic stereotype of dislike (for example, Joshua or Abraham "the Jew/Hebrew," meaning the "traveler" or "migrant") long before the conquest.

The Biblical Significance of the Amarna Letters

The Amarna Letters have contributed to the historical reliability of the Old Testament in general, and they support the trustworthy nature of the descriptions found in the Bible relating to the time of the conquest (1400 BC to 1300 BC) under Joshua in particular. This is evident for several reasons.

First, the presence of geographical markers is numerous. The collection of letters contains references to cities mentioned in the Bible, most of them being located along the Syrian and Canaanite coastal region. These include Ashkelon (Asqaluna), Gaza (Hazzatu), Gezer (Gazru), Hazor (Hasura), Joppa (Yapu), Lachish (Lakisa), and Megiddo (Magidda), among others.

Second, the tablets reveal a settled Canaan territory as the book of Joshua describes. Critics of the Bible previously believed that Canaan was not settled earlier during the patriarchal period, and therefore, Joshua could not have conquered fortified cities like Jericho and Ai centuries later. However, the Amarna Letters ended this debate with their descriptions of villages, towns, camps, cities, provinces, and fortifications, as well as thriving agricultural production.

Third, many of the people groups described in the Bible have been identified in the letters. These include the Hittites, Amorites, Perizzites, Canaanites, Egyptians, Babylonians, and Assyrians, to name a few.

Fourth, the Amarna correspondence offers clarification of biblical passages. For example, tablet 287 records the words of the prince of Jerusalem (Urusalima), 'Abdi-Heba, when he writes to Egypt: "It was not my father and not my mother but the arm of the mighty king that placed me in the house of my father." This statement seems to offer illumination as to how the office of king-priest in Jerusalem was obtained by the mysterious king of Salem (Jerusalem), Melchizedek (Genesis 14:14-20). The phrase "not by father and not by mother" is reminiscent of Melchizedek's description by the author of the book of Hebrews when he writes of him, "He is without father or mother or genealogy" (Hebrews 7:3 ESV). This indicates that the occupant did not inherit the office (king-priest) by means of lineage, but only by appointment. This also offers us information on how to understand Jesus' relationship to Melchizedek in Hebrews 7:1-28. That is to say, Jesus was *appointed* a priest after the order of Melchizedek (7:15-17); His office was not inherited by lineage as was the Levitical priestly order.

Fifth, the Amarna Letters confirm that the language of Canaan in Abraham's day is the ancestor of the peasant speech of Israel today. This is obvious in various Canaanite words, names, and phrases (forms of speech) that persist in modern-day Israel and surrounding territories. This phenomenon confirms the prophet Isaiah's reference to the "language of Canaan" (Isaiah 19:18).

The historical value of the Amarna letters cannot be underestimated. Though as yet no undisputed direct reference to biblical figures or events have been discovered in the texts, they are rich indirect witnesses to the linguistic, historical, and political climate of those countries and cities mentioned in the Bible during the time of Joshua's conquest.

The Hittites

For decades, the Hittite civilization remained an enigma to many, prompting nineteenth-century critical scholars to refer to them as a legendary people. This conclusion grew from the fact that though the Bible mentions the Hittites nearly 50 times, there were no extrabiblical sources confirming them. For those who believe in the historical reliability of the Old Testament and the benefits of archaeological research in the ancient Near East, this posed a challenge.

However, this dilemma was quickly solved by discoveries made in the late nineteenth and early twentieth centuries. In 1834, French archaeologist Charles Texier began researching an area about 100 miles east of Ankara, Turkey, near the modern city of Bogazkale, where he noticed the remains of large stone structures. Though these remains were not fully understood, progress was made when A.H. Sayce (in 1876) investigated an unknown language written on stones in Turkey and northern Syria, and when Ernest Chantre (in 1893 and 1894) located several fragments of undecipherable clay cuneiform tablets. These preliminary investigations came to a climax when, in 1906, Hugo Winckler began seven years of excavation that turned the

Hittite tablets. (Photo by Rex Geissler.)

Hittite debate upside down with his discovery of more than ten thousand clay tablets of the royal Hittite library! This discovery was pivotal in establishing the historical presence of the Hittite people and the historical reliability of the Old Testament narratives.

Background and Setting

Throughout the Old Testament the Hittites are named in well-known events, including the reference to Bathsheba's husband as Uriah the Hittite (2 Samuel 11) and that Abraham bought a cave from Ephron the Hittite (Genesis 23). Though much is still unknown, it now appears that sometime in the early second millennium BC the Hittites migrated from Europe to Anatolia (the peninsula of Asia Minor). They spoke an Anatolian form of Indo-European language.

Hittite soldiers carved on rock relief at the Hittite capital city of Hattusha. (Photo: Rex Geissler.)

The first Anatolian Hittite kingdom (which some call the Old Kingdom) seems to have begun in the seventeenth century BC at their capital city, known as Hattusha (also called Hattusas), under their first king, Labarnas I. The population was mostly comprised of a mixture of people groups indigenous to Europe, Hatti, and northern Syria. A series of tough battles with the Mittani (a rising power located east of the Euphrates) resulted in the Hittites losing control of northern Syria and much of their empire; subsequently the Old Kingdom was brought to an end in about 1400 BC.

The New Kingdom started where the Old Kingdom ended, locked in war with the Egyptians and Mittani over the valued region of northern Syria. Ultimately, the Hittite king Suppiluliuma I succeeded in bringing the Hittites the long-desired control of Syria, which expanded the kingdom from the Euphrates River in the east, to the Mediterranean Sea in the west, to Hattusha and Anatolia in the north. In the ensuing years, the Hittites saw more war, and a series of peace treaties were signed with surrounding nations, including Egypt, in order to keep the growing Assyrian army to the east in check. However, the placating and political positioning was short-lived; in the twelfth century BC Hattusha was destroyed by invading tribes from the west, leaving the surviving remnant of the people, known as the "Neo-Hittites," to live in the southeastern region of the former kingdom. By the ninth and eighth century BC, the Assyrian army pushed west toward Syria, and soon after, Tiglath-pileser III put an end to the remaining Hittite influence in the region.

The arched Lion Gate at Hattusha is one of five Hittite gates attached to the city walls. (Photo by Rex Geissler.)

The archaeological discoveries at Hattusha and other Anatolian locations of Hittite influence reveal their unique and elusive language was an adaptation of indigenous languages such as Akkadian, Hattic, and Sumerian, using the cuneiform script. In addition, Hittite inscriptions have revealed that the Hittites were accustomed to using a unique form of hieroglyphics like the one shown in this hieroglyphic Hittite seal, which dates from the period of 1400 to 1200 BC.

Most of the tablets discovered, however, were written in the cuneiform script, which has allowed scholars to reconstruct the origin, development, and law codes of the Hittite people.

There is no doubt that the Hittites have a prominent role in the Old Testament, appearing among Solomon's wives (1 Kings 11:1) and horse trading partners (1 Kings 10:29). Esau's wives (Judith and

Hittite seal ring. (Photo by Zev Radovan.)

Basemath) were Hittites (Genesis 26:34); however, a problematic passage emerges as Abraham (2000–1850 BC), who lived prior to the establishment of the Hittite kingdom (1650 BC), is said to have purchased the cave of Machpelah from Ephron the Hittite. Harry Hoffner Jr. has offered a solution to this apparent historical anachronism by recognizing that the words *Hittite* and *Hethite* are written identically in consonantal Hebrew. Therefore, the Genesis 23 passage should be understood as referring not to the Hittites of

Anatolia and northern Syria, but the Hethites indigenous to Hebron (see the NET translation of this passage, which has adopted "Hethites"). What is more, it appears that references to "Hittites" throughout the Scriptures can have many usages, as they can mean Canaanites (Genesis 15:20), Hurrians, or Horites.

The Biblical Significance of Discoveries About the Hittites

No longer can one accept the critical belief that the Hittites are a mythical people conjured up in the fertile imagination of the Old Testament writers. Though much more could be learned about Hittite law, language, and culture, the discoveries at Hattusha and other areas of Hittite influence have silenced the most ardent Bible skeptics. The once insurmountable dilemma involving the Hittites has now been turned into a victory for archaeology as a discipline and for Bible-believing Christians.

Ancient Megiddo

Megiddo is a strategically located ancient city in the Jezreel Valley (also known as the Plain of Esdraelon) with a long embattled history and a future, according to prophecy, as the place known as *Armageddon* (literally, "mountain of Megiddo"—Revelation 16:12-16; 19:19). Its proximity to the international trade highway that connected ancient merchants from Mesopotamia to Egypt made Megiddo the ideal setting for prosperity and power.

The city was first examined in 1903 to 1905 by the German explorer Gottlieb Schumacher, of the Society for Oriental Research (on behalf of the Deutscher Palästina-Verein). There he discovered various Egyptian and Hebrew artifacts as well as some 20 layers of occupation dating back to the Chalcolithic period. Subsequent excavations by the University of Chicago (1925 to 1939), Yigael Yadin (1960 to 1971), and David Ussishkin and Israel Finkelstein (1992 to 2002), have unearthed several more layers of occupation, bringing the total number of strata to 25.

Background and Setting

Megiddo is mentioned in the Bible and attested in extrabiblical sources, the earliest of which recounts the military exploits of Thutmose III (1468 BC) in his attempt to subdue the Canaanite-

Tel Megiddo. (Photo by Todd Bolen/BiblePlaces.com.)

occupied Megiddo. During the time of Joshua, it was a city far away from Egypt's control and easily conquered by the Hebrews in their invasion of Canaan (Joshua 12:21). It also comprised part of the territory given to Manasseh (Joshua 17:11), though it remained occupied by its former inhabitants (Judges 1:27). By the tenth century BC, the city had become one of Solomon's administrative capitals along with other major cities such as Hazor and Gezer (1 Kings 4:7-12). Extrabiblical sources such as the Amarna Tablets (fourteenth century BC) describe Megiddo as the center of conflict. The tablets record that the prince of Megiddo wrote to Egypt in order to request military aid to overcome an attack from the king of Shechem wishing to expand his territory. In addition, Tiglath-pileser III (Assyria) mentions that his armies captured Megiddo in 732 BC. The valley of Megiddo has been the site of many battles both ancient and modern. In ancient times, Ahaziah and Josiah, kings of Judah, were killed there (2 Kings 9:27; 23:29-30). In the modern era, General Allenby defeated the Turks in the same area during World War I.

Apparently, Megiddo's settlement activity commenced sometime in the period from 4000 BC to 3000 BC, though the presence of flint implements suggests even earlier Neolithic activity at the site. Megiddo's growth by the third millennium BC became apparent when archaeologists uncovered massive for-tifications in some places measuring 25 feet across and nearly 18 feet high. More-over, an elaborate religious or sacred pre-cinct that featured a circular shaped stone Canaanite altar and several temples was discovered. The sacred area was most likely enclosed by a low wall. The presence of animal bones in the surrounding area and cult paraphernalia reveal that the high place was used for sacrificing animals.

Megiddo stone altar—Early Bronze Age (3200–2200 BC).

In the Middle Bronze Age, Megiddo was expanded to include an increased num-ber of dwellings, and the city once again appeared to prosper under Egyptian control, though Egypt's influence may have been limited, as reflected in the Amarna Tablets. Soon after, Megiddo experienced a period of decline that began in the Late Bronze Age and continued until the time Joshua conquered the city. From the time of its conquest until Solomon acquired the city as one of his provincial administrative sites in the tenth century BC, it was destroyed several times. During this period, the infrastructure was poorly kept and construction was below par.

The biblical and extrabiblical description of the city and its activities appears to be consistent with the testimony of Scripture. Namely, 1) it was an early urban center, 2) it was destroyed during the time of Joshua's conquest of the city, 3) it reflects people groups mentioned in the Bible (for example, Canaanites, Hebrews, and so on), 4) the presence of gods, goddesses, altars, cult figurines, and offering stands reflect the practice of pagans and Israel alike, and 5) the architectural signature pattern of the fortifications reflects the work of Solomon.

Megiddo's Confirmation of the Biblical Record

There are several features and artifacts related to Megiddo that confirm the reliabil-ity of the biblical record.

First, Solomon fortified Megiddo (1 Kings 9:15-17) by making improvements in the defensive walls, palace, and gate systems. Yigael Yadin, of Hebrew University in Jerusa-lem, first recognized Solomon's architectural signature by relating the similar gate systems he found while excavating Hazor and revisiting the archaeological records at Gezer, which contained the same trademark gate design. According to 1 Kings 9:15, Solomon was the fortifier of these three cities.* Archaeologists have shown that these gates are nearly identical in their dimension, architecture, and materials used, thus reflecting a single individual behind their construction. This detail is indirect confirmation of the biblical record of Solomon's activity at these locations and his historical presence. Most likely, by the end of the tenth century BC Megiddo was destroyed by Egypt's Pharaoh Shishak, as it was then under the control of the northern kingdom of Israel.

Solomon's casemate gate complex at Megiddo.

Second, during Gottlieb Schumacher's expedition to Megiddo in the early twentieth century, he recovered a seal belonging to the servant of Israel's king Jeroboam II (793–753 BC). It reads, "Belonging to Shema, servant of Jeroboam." Second Kings 14:23-29 offers us details concerning Jeroboam: He reigned 41 years from Samaria, had a son named Zechariah, who eventually became king, and was an idolater who did evil in the eyes of the Lord. The seal was eventually lost, but fortunately, impressions were made like the one pictured here.

The Shema seal mentioning Jeroboam II. (Photo by Zev Radovan.)

Third, archaeologists have discovered that Megiddo's water-tunnel system was most likely carved out around the ninth to eighth century BC, at least in part (the shaft) by Israel's King Ahab. The shaft descends some 120 feet and is connected to a freshwater spring by over 200 feet of tunnel (pictured below) that was carved by two work parties, one at each end, similar to Hezekiah's tunnel construction in Jerusalem. The tunnel system was necessary due to the frequent sieges levied against the inhabitants of Megiddo and the location of the spring. Because it lay outside the fortification walls, Megiddo's water supply was vulnerable to enemy attack or discovery. Previous to the tunnel's construction, residents would have to leave the safety of the city defensive walls to retrieve water. However, the tunnel allowed for easy access from within the city confines as long as the spring itself was concealed from enemy sight.

Fourth, in the 1950s a portion of a Mesopotamian flood narrative, known as the *Epic*

---

* In 1969, excavators at Gezer discovered an ash layer in which Hebrew, Egyptian, and Philistine artifacts were found, suggesting all the three cultures had converged at the site at the same time. For some time archaeologists were unsure of how to make sense of the finds, then 1 Kings 9:16 helped them understand exactly what they had come across. The text says that the pharaoh of Egypt captured and destroyed Gezer with fire, killing the Canaanites who dwelt there. Subsequently, Pharaoh gave Gezer as a dowry to one of Solomon's wives, who happened to be Pharaoh's daughter!

of Gilgamesh, was discovered at the site. As mentioned in chapter 16, the widespread presence (in nearly two dozen civilizations) of the Flood story, despite the traditional stories' legendary tone, leaves little doubt that the account of Noah's Flood recorded in Genesis 6–9 describes actual historical events. The various flood accounts emerging from different areas of the world, such as China, Greece, Israel, Sumer, Babylonia, Assyria, and the New World, among others, are consistent with what scholars would expect if the key elements of the story were true.

For example, the crucial elements of the story are present in the various accounts, which imply or directly state that 1) the gods were alienated from man, 2) the gods became angry and plan to send a flood, 3) a Noah-like figure is warned of the flood and builds a boat, 4) various kinds of animals and his family are brought aboard, 5) the catastrophic deluge occurs, 6) the boat comes to rest upon a mountain as the waters subside, and 7) the Noah-like figure and his family disembark from the boat safely. After recognizing the key elements in the stories, it is tempting to claim that the later Genesis account borrowed from or is literarily dependent in some way on the earlier mythical accounts of the Flood. However, again as previously mentioned, after comparing both traditions, many Near Eastern scholars have recognized that the similarities between the Mesopotamian and Hebrew accounts of the Flood cannot be easily explained by literary dependence. This is because there are significant key differences within both traditions that are contradictory, as well as problems relating to the progression of myth over time.*

Megiddo water tunnel. (Photo by Zev Radovan.)

The Biblical Significance of Megiddo

Megiddo eventually came under the control of the Assyrians in the late eighth century BC as an administrative center and was later destroyed by Pharaoh Necho in 609 BC. The city continued to exist through the reigns of biblical kings Darius, Xerxes, and Artaxerxes I during the Persian period, only to be abandoned during the Hellenistic period in the mid fourth century BC.

It is not difficult to recognize and appreciate the value of Megiddo in confirming the historical reliability of the Bible. First, the location itself has been discovered to be the biblical city of Megiddo that is mentioned in six books of the Bible. Second, Solomon has been confirmed as the architect of the Iron Age II gate systems that feature a unique casemate pattern (which features a series of chambers between the walls) identical to

---

* For the details of the similarities and difference in both accounts as well as why we reject literary dependence, see the section in chapter 16 on the Gilgamesh epic and *Enuma Elish*.

Hazor and Gezer. Israeli archaeologist Yigael Yadin has also recognized that a palace in the city was built during the reign of Solomon, as well as several fortifications. Third, the biblical king of Israel Jeroboam II has been confirmed as a historical figure due to the discovery of his servant Shema's seal by Gottlieb Schumacher. Fourth, the water shaft at Megiddo has been credited by many to Israel's King Ahab. Fifth, the Babylonian account of the flood recovered at the site, the *Epic of Gilgamesh*, supports the Genesis account of a catastrophic flood. In addition to these, the cumulative data unearthed at Megiddo support the biblical account of the peoples and events surrounding the region, including the involvement of the Canaanites, Egyptians, Babylonians, Assyrians, and Hebrews, confirming the city of Megiddo as a valued piece of evidence confirming the biblical record.

KING DAVID AND HIS DYNASTY

K ing David's existence and kingdom have been the crucial topic of debate for Bible critics of the past century. If David existed at all, they argue, he certainly did not have a dynasty of kings that followed after him, nor was the influence or territory of his kingdom widespread. Israel under David, according to critics such as Israel Finkelstein of Tel Aviv University, was little more than a tribal chiefdom, not a bustling tenth-century BC kingdom.

However, nineteenth- and twentieth-century discoveries in northern and southern Israel, Jerusalem, and Jordan have made it extremely difficult for critics to sustain these views. David is now considered to be a historical king who ruled over a unified Israel that covered a vast territory. He was the father of an eternal dynastic line of kings that extended through his son Solomon and that would ultimately culminate in Christ inheriting David's throne (Luke 1:32). For Christians, the battle for David's historicity is crucial since he is mentioned

The Valley of Elah is the location where David and Goliath fought their historic battle around 1000 BC (1 Samuel 17).

over 1,000 times in the Old and New Testament, is the key figure in Christ's genealogy, is the writer of nearly half the psalms, and is the father of the kings of Judah. If he didn't exist, then neither do the spiritual benefits that flow out from him.

David's Story

Our picture of David begins with his youth, when his father, Jesse, marches his seven older sons before Samuel the prophet in order to discover which of these would be Israel's next king. When none of these young men are chosen, Jesse promptly sends for his eighth and only remaining son. Upon David's arrival, Samuel follows the Lord's instructions and anoints David as the future king of Israel (1 Samuel 16:1,12). Soon after, as the Philistines sought to encroach on the hill country south of Jerusalem, David found himself in the Valley of Elah (near Azekah and Socoh, 17:1), disturbed by what he encountered. The Philistine giant, Goliath of Gath, continued to blaspheme the God of Israel every day for more than a month. Therefore, the Bible records that David, armed with a sling and five smooth stones, accepted Goliath's challenge (1 Samuel 17:40).

Slings were lethal weapons, being able to propel objects up to nearly 100 miles per hour and accurate up to nearly 100 yards. Goliath, armed with a spear, javelin, and sword, met David in the valley for the decisive duel. During this period of time, opposing armies would often either taunt the opposition until one side attacked, or send out a champion as a representative of each army who would fight to the death. The loser's army would retreat, while the opposing army would attack. The story ends with David slinging a stone that lodges in Goliath's forehead, thus defeating the Philistine aggression (1 Samuel 17:50).

The famed story of David and Goliath has been thought by some to be a moral metaphor on which the historicity question should not be imposed. Very little in the way of historical evidence has surfaced in the past supporting the events recorded about these two individuals, much less the battle itself. However, archaeological research in the southwestern region of Israel has supported the historical dimension of this ancient battle scene.

Archaeology Sheds Light on David's Kingdom

Tell es-Safi (The City of Gath)

Ongoing excavations conducted since 1996 by Aren Maeir of Bar-Ilan University at Tell es-Safi have unearthed the biblical city of Gath, Goliath's hometown (1 Samuel 17:4). The location, situated halfway between Jerusalem and Ashkelon, is identified with Canaanite, Philistine, and Crusader Blanche Garde inhabitants, though the site also contains remains from the later Middle Ages. According to Maeir, it is the largest preclassical site in the southern Levant, and it has been settled continually from the Chalcolithic period (fifth millennium BC) up to modern times, its occupation thus spanning six millennia. Several features and artifacts discovered at the site confirm its historical connection to David, Goliath, and the city of Gath.

Excavations led by Professor Aren Maeir have revealed that Gath (Tell es-Safi) was a thriving Philistine city during the tenth century BC, at approximately the same time 1 Samuel 17 says David fought Goliath.

First, through the use of aerial photography at the site, Maeir noticed a previously unknown man-made trench that circles the site, measuring 8 meters wide and 2.5 kilometers long. After further review, the trench was found to be the earliest siege system in the world, designed to contain the inhabitants of the city and keep them from fleeing. Analysis of the trench system has confirmed an Iron Age II dating, which has subsequently been associated with the Aramean siege of Gath by King Hazael (2 Kings 12:17). This find as well as evidence of destruction supports the current location of Tell es-Safi as being ancient Gath.

Second, the discovery of destroyed dwellings that preserved hundreds of pottery vessels, utensils, cooking implements, jewelry, ivory, metal weapons, and cultic objects have confirmed the city of Gath was well-established in the ninth century BC. This represents the crucial time immediately after Solomon's reign, in which the separation of the northern kingdom of Israel and the southern kingdom of Judah took place. Bible critics have long dismissed the biblical portrait of life in Israel during this time period due to the lack of archaeological support. However, these finds support the biblical view that Gath and the Philistines played a prominent role prior to David's time, making the battle between the two warriors historically plausible. It is now understood that the Philistines are Indo-European (Aegean) peoples who migrated to Israel by about 1200 BC and figured prominently as Israel's antagonists, as the Bible records.

Third, in 2005 while a team of archaeologists were excavating through a debris layer of pottery shards and animal bones, they unearthed an inscribed ostracon (pottery fragment) containing two Philistine names.[1] The secure context in which the object was found has established a date of approximately 950 BC, making it the earliest known alphabetic inscription from a Philistine site. The inscription itself is difficult to discern and was likely made by a sharp instrument such as a flint point or metal needle or peg; it is incised in a proto-Canaanite script and reads *alwt / wlt*. According to Maeir, the names on the inscription do not enable comprehensible reading in a Semitic language, though they are scrawled in a local alphabetic script. The names themselves are indeed Philistine names possibly related to Greek or Anatolian names— and remarkably, they are similar to the name *Goliath*!

The tenth-century BC Gath inscription discovered at Tell es-Safi (Gath) contains two Philistine names written in Proto-Canaanite script, which offers cultural, chronological, and linguistic details consistent with the biblical account of David and Goliath. (Photo by Zev Radovan.)

Maeir notes that there is no *direct* connection between the two inscribed names and the name *Goliath*, and perhaps what is more appropriately noted here is the *indirect* relationship between the ostracon and Goliath. That is, the accumulation of evidence such as the tenth-century BC date of the shard and the location and dating of the ruins of Gath, coupled with Philistine names written in proto-Canaanite alphabetic script,* would make the David and Goliath story entirely plausible. In other words, Tell es-Safi yields the right time, the right material data, and the right location. Additional pottery shards and the many reconstructed colorful vessels reminiscent of Mycenaean pottery gathered from the excavation, as well as visible surface pottery material, indicate that the Philistines lived in Gath in the late eleventh or early tenth century BC, during the time Goliath fought David.

David a Tribal Chieftain?

Soon after the battle, David's fame and popularity grew, but so did the number of his enemies. King Saul summoned David in order to bring comfort to his tormented life, yet David found himself on the run from the angry and jealous king. He would spend the next several years hiding from Saul while navigating the desolate caves and wilderness of En-Gedi near the shores of the Dead Sea and fighting the Amalekites (2 Samuel 1:1).

Things changed soon after Saul and his sons were killed in battle (2 Samuel 1) by the Philistines on Mount Gilboa (1 Samuel 31). David tore his clothes and mourned their deaths (2 Samuel 1:11-12). The book of 2 Samuel records that he was anointed king and subsequently ruled Judah from Hebron for seven years and six months, and then ruled over all Judah and Israel in Jerusalem for thirty-three years (2 Samuel 5:5; 1 Kings 2:11; 1 Chronicles 12). Though critical scholars such as Finkelstein and Silberman have adopted the notion that David's kingdom was more or less a loosely associated group of tribes without urbanization, fortified cities, or centralized authority, archaeological finds from this period reveal just the opposite.

The Evidence of Khirbet Qeiyafa

An example of a find that demonstrates the high level of David's kingdom is found in the recent (2007) excavation of Khirbet Qeiyafa by Yosef Garfinkel, who currently holds the Yigael Yadin Chair of Archaeology at Hebrew University in Jerusalem, and Saar Ganor of Hebrew University.[2] They have uncovered a fortified city near the Valley of Elah that covered an area of nearly six acres and held a population of nearly 600 people. The city has been dated to the period from 1025 to 975 BC (Iron Age), during the reign of David. The dating has been supported by extensive pottery reading and the radiocarbon testing of olive pits (by Oxford University) found at the site.[3]

Critics originally assumed the site was a Philistine city due to its close proximity to Gath, which is a short distance away; thus the Khirbet Qeiyafa site would not fall

---

* In 1996, Seymour Gitin and Trude Dothan unearthed a seventh-century BC inscription at the biblical city of Ekron that provided the names of two kings, Achish and Padi. First Samuel 21:11; 27:2 tells of David fleeing from Saul and joining Achish, the king of Gath. Though the Achish of the Ekron inscription is not the same person as Achish that lived earlier during David's time, it shows a remarkable continuity of names that spans centuries within Philistine culture. The other individual whose name is contained in the inscription, Padi, is mentioned several times in the Taylor Prism (Sennacherib's annals of his campaigns in Judah in 701 BC) by Sennacherib as the one he made king over Ekron. The annals of Sennacherib also mention that King Hezekiah had placed Padi under arrest for a short time (between 705 and 701 BC) prior to the latter's assuming his role as Assyria's vassal king in Ekron.

under David's authority or be considered part of the Davidic kingdom. However, further research into the style of pottery and architectural features such as the massive fortified walls of the city refute this notion. The construction resembles the fortified cities of Gezer and Hazor, as do the dwelling structures and pottery samples that do not appear in Philistine culture or cities.

It would appear that the sheer size of this city would, by extension, refute the notion that David's capital city of Jerusalem was simply an unsettled community of nomads.[4] The construction of the fortifications and many of the building structures at Khirbet Qeiyafa would have required cooperation with an organized city-state network; it would seem impossible for a mere chiefdom to accomplish such a feat. Some of the huge stone ashlars that comprise the construction of the four-chambered gate complex of the city weigh an extraordinary five tons![5] The sophistication of culture and complexity of its architecture alone would appear to severely damage Finkelstein's tribal-chiefdom theory, since no mere tribe or chief would have the technology to achieve such a project. What is more, the strategic fortified location of the Khirbet Qeiyafa site, between the much larger city of Gath and the capital city of Jerusalem, may reflect an attempt by David to defend against Philistine incursions into the Jerusalem area.

In addition to these, objects unearthed at the site reveal a diet consistent with the Israelites. Most noticeable is the lack of pig bones, unlike Philistine cities, which commonly show evidence of the raising and consumption of pigs (and dogs) as a dietary staple. Unlike the Philistines, the Israelites only ate bread, vegetables, olives, grain, fish, lamb, and beef, a diet in line with the Mosaic law.*

Even more telling in identifying the city's inhabitants is its location in proximity to another biblical city of Judah dating to the same time period (Iron Age), namely, Khirbet Gudraya (known as Gederah). We see these two sister cities mentioned in 1 Chronicles 4:23 as the place where the descendants of Judah lived and were called "potters" in the "king's service." The reference in Chronicles to the king's employment centers, and the archaeological remains found at both sites, suggest that they were the administrative cities on the Philistine boundary known as Netaim (Khirbet Qeiyafa) and Gederah respectively.

This identification could be supported by the discovery of an early alphabetic script inscription on a piece of pottery at Khirbet Qeiyafa dating to the eleventh to tenth century BC. Recent analysis of the inscription does not give a certain conclusion as to the identity of the script or the language used, but most scholars[6] involved believe its language could be Hebrew, while its script is early alphabetic (perhaps Canaanite, Phoenician, or Hebrew).[7] Some have suggested that if the inscription was written in the Hebrew language and script, it would confirm Khirbet Qeiyafa as a Judahite site, thus strengthening the argument for a thriving Davidic kingdom. However, others have pointed out that even if the script or language turns out to be other than Hebrew it would not preclude the site from being designated as Judahite. This is because there is precedence for

---

* There are some Israelite sites that reflect the eating of pigs, but these are primarily found in cities that were destroyed by the Assyrians and Babylonians, and they reflect the backslidden religious and moral condition of the population, as expressed in the messages of the prophets Isaiah and Jeremiah.

the use of a diplomatic language other than one's own native language and script. The ostracon may have been carried to Khirbet Qeiyafa by a scribe or written there in a diplomatic language by Judahite scribes. Its contents were analyzed by Gershon Galil of the University of Haifa and said to reflect a high caliber of scribal work and culture at the city, which is consistent with the site being identified as one of David's administrative/provincial outposts, namely Netaim.[8]

The Convincing Nature of the Khirbet Qeiyafa Discoveries

It now seems there is no reason to reject the biblical descriptions of David's kingdom based on lack of evidence for urbanization or centralized authority. Based on the scriptural, epigraphical, and archaeological remains, Khirbet Qeiyafa could be a late eleventh- or early tenth-century BC fortified administrative center, most likely inhabited by descendants of Judah, that possessed a high level of scribal and cultural activity and is attested in the biblical text (1 Chronicles 4:23 or 4:31). It would seem reasonable then to assume that David's kingdom, especially at Jerusalem, had achieved a high urbanized functional level and technology during his (and Solomon's) reign.

The identification of the city as Netaim by Galil is not certain; Garfinkel and Ganor believe that the discovery of two gates at the site suggest that the city should be identified as *Shaaraim* (1 Chronicles 4:31), since that Hebrew name means "gates" or "two gates." * This would be a notable feature, since not even larger cities would have two gates; most operated with a single gate system.

Khirbet Qeiyafa has dealt a severe blow to the minimalist critics of David's kingdom since it has effectively demonstrated that Judah possessed the technology and development during David's reign to establish a well-developed urbanized kingdom.[†] In a recent

---

* The distinction between Netaim and Shaaraim appears to be of little consequence to the argument we are making for the authority, development, and comprehensive nature of David's kingdom. The archaeological evidence can apply to both name identifications. For discussion on the Garfinkel and Ganor position see Yosef Garfinkel and Saar Ganor, "Khirbet Qeiyafa: Sha'arayim," in *The Journal of Hebrew Scriptures*, vol. 8, art. 22 (2010): 2-10. Access at www.arts.ualberta.ca/JHS/Articles/article_99.pdf.

† Supporting this thesis is Jane M. Cahill's excellent article responding to Margreet Steiner's contention that during David and Solomon's reigns Jerusalem was only a small town of a few administrative buildings (see Margreet Steiner, "David's Jerusalem: Fiction or Reality? It's Not There: Archaeology Proves a Negative," in *Biblical Archaeology Review* 24:04 [July/August 1998]). Cahill bases her critique of Steiner on her research as a member of Yigal Shiloh's staff responsible for publishing the results of his excavations in Area G, which is the area in which she investigated the famous Stepped-Stone Structure and the soil- and stone-filled terraces (Jane M. Cahill, "David's Jerusalem: Fiction or Reality? It Is There: The Archaeological Evidence Proves It," in *Biblical Archaeology Review* 24:04 [July/August 1998]). Also see the more recent Ronny Reich, *Excavating the City of David: Where Jerusalem's History Began* (Jerusalem: Israel Exploration Society, 2011) for more information on the various stages of excavation in the City of David.

From a textual perspective, Nadav Na'aman demonstrates through a closer look at the Amarna letters (fourteenth century BC) that six of them were sent by 'Abdi-Heba, king of Jerusalem (Urusalima), thus refuting Margreet Steiner's notion that there was no city or town prior to the Israelite settlement (Nadav Na'aman, "David's Jerusalem: Fiction or Reality? It Is There: Ancient Texts Prove It," in *Biblical Archaeology Review* 24:04 [July/August 1998]). Worthy of note is Na'aman's discovery of phrases that indicate Jerusalem was indeed in existence and under rule. For example, one Amarna letter refers to "house(s)" in Jerusalem and a "town belonging to Jerusalem."

In addition, a more recent artifact discovered by Eilat Mazar through sifting revealed Jerusalem's earliest writing in the form of an Akkadian cuneiform clay fragment that was dated to the fourteenth century BC. Yuval Goren, a clay petrologist from Tel Aviv University, has confirmed that the clay used in the fragment came from Jerusalem, thus indicating high-level scribal activity in a thriving Jerusalem prior to the Davidic kingdom. Confirming the Amarna letters, this

article responding to Welsh scholar Philip Davies, Garfinkel summarizes the evidence supporting Khirbet Qeiyafa as a Judahite city and also spells out the death of minimalism as a viable option.[9] The article responds to the minimalist "Mythical Paradigm" (that is, the Hebrew Scriptures are products of the Hellenistic era and are only late literary compositions, not describing historical events); the "Low Chronology Paradigm" (that is, lowering the transition time from agrarian to urbanization from c. 1000 BC to c. 925 to 900 BC, casting David and Solomon as tribal agrarian leaders living in tents, not urbanized kings); and the "Ethnic Identification of Khirbet Qeiyafa" (that is, was the city Judahite, Canaanite, or Philistine?). Garfinkel answers these minimalist ideas with the archaeological evidence from Khirbet Qeiyafa that has been detailed above—evidence that supports the site as an urbanized Judahite city that dates to c. 969 BC (within the reign of David), too early for Solomon's reign (965–930 BC).[10] This dating refutes the minimalist notion that urbanization in the southern Levant began c. 925-900 BC.[11]*

The evidence from Khirbet Qeiyafa, combined with that of the "House of David" inscription (discussed below), attests to an urbanized and organized state in the region capable of supporting such material characteristics. The notion of David and Solomon being tent-dwelling tribal chiefs of an agrarian society is quickly fading away in light of the mounting evidence uncovered at Khirbet Qeiyafa.

Evidence for the "House of David"

In addition to the urban evidence supporting David's well-developed kingdom, there is also evidence in the form of monumental inscriptions that confirm his historical existence and God-given dynasty (his throne would last forever—2 Samuel 7:8-17).

The Tell Dan Stele

One of these inscriptions mentioned above is an Aramaic-inscribed stele found in 1993 and 1994 by Avraham Biran at Tell Dan in the northern territory of Israel.[†] Most believe it was originally erected as a memorial inscription by Syria's King Hazael (1 Kings

---

find offers evidence that Jerusalem had an organized government that employed scribes to correspond at a high diplomatic level (see Hershel Shanks, "Jerusalem Roundup: Sifting Project Reveals City's Earliest Writing," *Biblical Archaeology Review* 37:02 [March/April 2011]).

* Garfinkel cites recent evidence to support Khirbet Qeiyafa as an urbanized Judahite city based on 1) its location (strategic); 2) its new settlement and its importance in late eleventh century BC; 3) its massive stone and casemate wall fortifications (not present in Philistine brick construction or Late Bronze Age Canaanite construction in Israel); 4) its two identically sized gates with four chambers; 5) its urban planning, which included dwellings incorporated into the city wall, already present in the eleventh century BC and consistent with other later Iron Age II Judahite sites such as Beersheba, Beth-Shemesh, Tell Beit Mirsim, and Tell en-Nasbeh; 6) its pottery vessels and their place of origin (stamped handles; Khirbet Qeiyafa area is their place of origin); 7) its diet and food preparation (no pig bones, pottery usage, and carbon-14 dating on olive pits dates to eleventh to tenth century BC); and 8) the script/inscription (the 70-letter inscription contains words associated with Hebrew language; epigraphist Haggai Misgav agrees that most likely the language of the inscription is Hebrew (for example, based on *ta'as,* meaning "to do"). (These are a sampling of the 14 points in Yosef Garfinkel, "A Minimalist Disputes His Demise: A Response to Philip Davies," *Biblical Archaeology Review,* online article accessed at www.bib-arch.org/scholars-study/minimalist-response-garfinkel.asp on July 2, 2012.)

† Excavations at Tell Dan have unearthed the altar erected by King Jeroboam I (reigned 931–910 BC) when he established calf worship at the city (and at Bethel) during the beginning of the divided kingdom (1 Kings 12:25-33).

19:15) in the ninth to eighth century BC to boast of his military campaigns over Israel. It is possible that the stele commemorates Hazael's campaign against Jehu (2 Kings 10:32-33), and it is probable that Dan was part of the territory that Jehu lost.

The Tell Dan Stele measures 13 inches high but originally stood nearly 3 feet tall. It contains the first extrabiblical mention of David, thus confirming the historicity of the biblical king. The highlighted portion of the Aramaic text reads "house of David" (*bytdwd* or *Beth-David*). (Photo by Zev Radovan.)

When it was discovered, the basalt stele was being reused in three separate pieces as building stone in structures securely dated to the eighth century BC; however, its Aramaic script dates comfortably to the late ninth century BC. Alan Millard has provided a translation as follows:

> Then my father lay down and went to his [fathers]. There came up the king of I[s]rael beforetime in the land of my father, [but] Hadad [ma]de [me] king....Hadad went before me [and] I went from...of my king(s) I killed ki[ngs] who harnessed...[ch]ariots and thousands of horseman... son of...king of Israel and kill[ed] yahu son of [I overthr]ew the *house of David*. I set/imposed [tribute]...their land to [ ]...other and to [was/ became kin]g over Is[rael]...siege against.[12]

The presence of the dynastic title "house of David" (*bytdwd* or *Beth-David*) on an inscription written by an enemy of Israel in the context of Israelite kings speaks volumes in support of the Davidic dynasty. That is, Israel's enemies viewed the Israelite kings collectively as being of the house of David, thus supporting the biblical concept of David's kingly lineage. What is more, the inscription is the first extrabiblical mention of King David found anywhere.

Criticism of the Tell Dan Find

Due to the Tell Dan discovery, biblical critics have found it difficult to deny the historicity of David, though as expected there are some who still challenge the reading. Because there are no dots (word spacers) in between *byt* and *dwd* (which would look like *byt • dwd*), it is argued that the phrase refers to a eponymic place name (a location or city such as *beth-Haran* or *Beth-el*) that has been drawn from the larger-than-life legendary hero known as "David" in the Hebrew narrative and included in the stele as a revered location with an honorable title.

This interpretation is unlikely for several reasons. First, those familiar with Aramaic inscriptions have rejected this idea, including British scholar Alan Millard, since there are instances in which word dividers are not present, such as the ostracon from Tell Qasile (excavated 1948 to 1950 and 1971 to 1974), which reads *bythrn*, meaning "Beth Horon," without a word divider.* According to Anson Rainey, the absence of word dividers is appropriate especially if the combination of words is a well-established proper name,† which certainly is the case with the house of David since it was a familiar political title to surrounding nations for at least 150 years prior to the stele. Rainey also points out that the same construction is seen in the "Balaam son of Beor" inscription, where no word dividers are present between the phrase "son of" and "Beor."

Second, there is a complete absence in ancient Near-Eastern literature or inscriptions of a place name with the title "Beth-David." Third, the phrase "House of David" appears nearly two dozen times in the Hebrew Scriptures, thus providing the phrase the context appropriate for its usage and understanding when it presents itself in extrabiblical sources. It is not good hermeneutical or historiographical practice to transfer a phrase that obviously finds its meaning and context informed by the Hebrew Scriptures to something alien to its common usage. To force *bytdwd* to designate a place name when the stele clearly uses the phrase in the context of the kings of Israel—and the Old Testament uses it in the context of a dynastic title—is something the text simply cannot support.

It is also important to note that two additional pieces of the stele were later recovered;

---

* The Hebrew-inscribed ostracon is clearly a commercial document; it reads, "Ophir gold to *bythrn* (Beth Horon), 30 shekels" (see 1 Kings 9:28). See Benjamin Maisler [Mazar], "Two Hebrew Ostraca from Tell Qasile," in *Journal of Near Eastern Studies*, vol. 10, no. 4 (October 1951), 265-267.

† Anson Rainey, "The House of David and the House of the Reconstructionists," *Biblical Archaeology Review*, vol. 20, no. 6 (November/December, 1994). Rainey offers an additional example of the ancient Aramaic personal name BRRKB (Bir-Rakib) from Zenjirli (Zincirli) in southern Turkey, where the absence of word dividers does not hinder a proper two-word rendering.

they offered several biblical names such as Jehoram (son of Ahab), Ahaziah, and Ben Hadad (1 Kings 15:20; 2 Kings 8:7-26; 9:6-10) that nicely fit the context and time period described.

The Mesha Stele (Moabite Stone)

In addition to the Tell Dan Stele, more evidence has emerged supporting David's dynasty and the political and military climate surrounding the events of the ninth century BC. In 1868, F.A. Klein discovered (then purchased for about $400) a ninth-century BC monument known as the Mesha Stele (also called the Moabite Stone) east of the Dead Sea in the biblical city of Dibon (in present-day Jordan). The inscribed basalt monument originally stood over 3 feet tall and 2 feet wide; it records the military victories of the Moabite king Mesha over the Israelite kings' territory east of the Jordan River (see 2 Kings 3:4). The stele is written in the first person (by King Mesha) and is the longest monumental inscription yet recovered in Jordan, though parts of the text have been reconstructed. Originally, the stele was complete, but due to later unfortunate circumstances in the negotiations with Bedouin to secure the artifact it was smashed into separate pieces. Fortunately, an impression of the stone inscription was made by Charles Clermont-Ganneau (1846–1923) prior to these events.

The ninth-century BC Mesha Stele was discovered at the biblical city of Dibon in 1868. The smooth portions of the stele are reconstructions of the text based on the paper impressions taken of the original inscription by Clermont-Ganneau. (Photo by Zev Radovan.)

The value of the stone is seen in the damaged portion of line 31 of the inscription. Through an analysis of the paper impression and the stone itself (which is housed at the Louvre Museum in France) by epigrapher Andre Lemaire, a reconstructed translation reveals yet another "house of David" phrase.[13] The stone reads *b*[—]*wd*; however, through additional independent analysis by several scholars (for example, Mark Lidzbarski and Rene Dussaud) traces of a *t* were discerned after the *b*, thus making the inscription read *bt*[-]*wd*. Lemaire was then able to confidently supply the last remaining letter as a *d*, giving the complete phrase *bt*[*d*]*wd* ("House of David").[14] What is interesting, and a cause for objection for some, is that "house" is spelled with the shortened *bt* instead of the Tel Dan Stele spelling of *byt*. However, Lemaire answers this concern by explaining that the stone's Moabite inscription appears to spell "house" both ways; five times it is spelled as *bt* and once as *byt*. The *y* may have been an optional consonant or an archaic spelling of the word.[15]

The Mesha Stele provides us with a remarkable extrabiblical reference to the dynasty of David, a view into the political and military climate of the ninth century BC (2 Kings 1–3), the names of surrounding geography (Moab, Israel, Dibon, Arnon, Madaba, Aroer, territory of Gad), and personal names mentioned in Scripture (Yahweh, Mesha, Omri,* Omri's son [Ahab], David). It also provides us with information not stated explicitly in the Bible—how Moab repossessed the land that was for so long controlled by David and Solomon. We now know that King Mesha wrested control of the region from Israel soon after the beginning of the divided kingdom.

The City of David

After more than seven years of rule from Hebron, David began making plans to move the capital to Jerusalem. Its central location and topography of mountains and valleys offered good natural defenses; however, the area was occupied by the Canaanites.

The particular piece of land that interested David, known today as the City of David, was occupied by the Jebusites. Fresh water was supplied by the Gihon Spring on the east side of the Jebusite-occupied territory, though by David's time the Jebusites had carved a tunnel to channel water into the city itself. It appears from the biblical text (2 Samuel 5:8) that Joab conquered the city by going into the tunnel and up a shaft (known as Warren's Shaft) and into the city (1 Chronicles 11:6). Subsequently, David used the stronghold as his central location to rule Israel, and began building his city and house that he collectively called the "city of David" (2 Samuel 5:9-11). Soon after, he would purchase the threshing floor of Araunah the Jebusite located on the top of Mount Moriah, where he would offer burnt sacrifices to the Lord (2 Samuel 24:18-25; see Genesis 22:2; 2 Chronicles 3:1).

The narrow walled slice of land known as the City of David is represented here in a reconstructed model at the Israel Museum. It shows the territory being located south of the Temple Mount (background) and immediately west of the Kidron Valley ravine. Its geographical orientation made it a desirable defensive position. It was seized from the Jebusites by David's military commander, Joab. Later, David would purchase the threshing floor of Araunah the Jebusite to build an altar (2 Samuel 24:18-25); the floor would later become the land on which Solomon would build the first Jewish temple.

---

* According to Alfred J. Hoerth, *Archaeology and the Old Testament* (Grand Rapids, MI: Baker Books, 1998), 308, Assyrian records from the ninth to seventh century BC often mention Israel as *mat-Omri* (land of Omri) or *bit-Omri* (house of Omri). Omri's descendant Joram (or possibly Jehu) is also depicted and inscribed on the Black Obelisk of Shalmaneser III (858–824 BC) as paying tribute or making an alliance with Shalmaneser III (2 Kings 9–10).

Major Finds

Excavations at the city of David have spanned parts of three centuries, beginning in 1867 with Charles Warren and continuing to the current excavations begun in 2007 by Doron Ben-Ami and Yana Tchekhanovets. Through the decades of excavation many features alluded to or explicitly mentioned in the Old Testament have been located. These include Hezekiah's water tunnel, the Siloam inscription, architectural remains of a large stone structure that some (for example, archaeologist Eilat Mazar) believe to be the palace of King David, Warren's Shaft, the Canaanite tunnel, the royal steward inscription,* the typical Israelite four-room house of Ahiel, Gihon Spring, the Spring and Pool Towers, tombs, the tenth-century BC retaining wall to David's palace known as the Stepped-Stone Structure, and much more. What is more, the high concentrations of ceramic storage jars found in the area (and at other locations mostly in the Judean territory) containing stamped impressions bearing the Hebrew words *L'melech* (*LMLK*, "belonging to the king")† testify to the city's location as the royal seat of Israel's and then Judah's government.

LMLK Storage Jar Handle reads "Belonging to the king." (Photo by Zev Radovan.)

This eighth-century BC seal impression (with fingerprint—see left side) reads, "Belonging to Ahaz, [son of] Jehotham, king of Judah." (Photo by Zev Radovan.)

Stamp-Seal Impressions Confirm David's Dynasty

Among the finds more closely associated with the dynasty of kings descending from David are the many small stamp-seal impressions (called *bullae*; singular, *bulla*)‡ found at the city, as well as some unprovenanced seals. During the excavation of

---

* The royal steward inscription is a lintel tomb inscription written in paleo-Hebrew discovered by French translator Charles Clermont-Ganneau (1870) in the modern Arab village of Silwan (ancient Siloam), which is located directly across the steep valley from the City of David. Nahman Avigad later deciphered a biblical name in the inscription as "[Shebna]yahu," the royal steward over the house of King Hezekiah. The prophet Isaiah prophesies against Shebna for hewing out a tomb and living above his means (Isaiah 22:15-25; 1 Kings 4:6; 16:9). The entire inscription is dated to the seventh century BC and reads, "This is the [sepulchre of ...]yahu who is over the house. There is no silver and no gold here but [his bones] and the bones of his amah with him. Cursed be the man who will open this!" The rock containing the inscription was cut out by Clermont-Ganneau and transported to the British Museum, where it resides to this day.

† A high concentration of these kinds of stamped storage-jar handles was discovered at various sites in Judah, most of which have the city to which they correspond stamped on the handle. These include cities such as Sochoh, Ziph, Hebron, and *MMST* (perhaps referring to Jerusalem), which were most likely administrative centers Hezekiah established to store rations for an anticipated Assyrian military response to his revolt. Archaeologists have excavated layers at various sites dating to the Assyrian invasion of Judah in 701 BC and have located a high number of these types of stamped handles.

‡ *Bullae* (singular, *bulla*) are tiny nickel-sized impressions left by the pressing of a seal or ring into a piece of moist lump of clay. These would seal documents and small packages identifying the sender's name and usually their position, if any, as well as ensuring that only the recipients would open the correspondence. Hundreds of these impressions have been located,

the city of David by Yigal Shiloh in 1978, perhaps the greatest discovery was the nearly 50 seal impressions made by officials working in Jerusalem during the seventh century BC. The high concentration of seals near David's palace indicates the presence of an archive. The documents are no longer attached—most likely they were burned as a result of the Babylonian attacks on Jerusalem in the late seventh and early sixth century BC.

The presence of multiple official bullae within the city confines attests to the Bible's portrayal of David and his central government structure being located at the city of David. That is, if his successors had their administrations at the city, there is good reason to believe David did as well. The following chart is a summary of bulla impressions relating to persons mentioned in the Old Testament, though not all are from the city of David; some of them refer to people of the "house of David."

King Uzziah's (Azariah's) burial plaque was found in 1931 by E.L. Sukenik of the Hebrew University (2 Chronicles 26; Isaiah 6:1). Second Chronicles 26:16-23 tells of Uzziah's inappropriate action of burning incense in the temple, something prohibited by the Mosaic Law. As a result, he was struck with leprosy and isolated until the day he died. The funerary inscription reads, "To this place were brought the bones of Uzziah, king of Judah, do not open!" The first-century AD plaque was copied from an earlier eighth-century BC inscription. (Photo by Zev Radovan.)

Seal Impressions of People in the Old Testament

Biblical Person	Inscription	Scripture
Jezebel (873–852 BC)	Jezebel ([I']yzbl)*	1 Kings 16:29–22:40; 21:25
Azariah/ Uzziah (788–735 BC)	Abiyah the servant of Uzziah Shebaniah the servant of Uzziah	2 Kings 14:21-22 2 Chronicles 26:1-23
Jeroboam II (790–749/50 BC)	Belonging to Shema, the servant of Jeroboam †	2 Kings 14:23-29

some of which through excavations such as the Yigal Shiloh expedition and others through the antiquities trade market. For a scholarly treatment and cataloging of western Semitic bulla see Nahman Avigad, *Corpus of West Semitic Stamp Seals* (Jerusalem: The Israel Academy of Sciences and Humanities, The Israel Exploration Society, The Institute of Archaeology—The Hebrew University of Jerusalem, 1997).

* Jezebel, the Phoenician daughter of King Ethbaal, was accustomed to sealing documents for her husband, Ahab (see 1 Kings 21:8).

† After the seal impression was discovered by Gottlieb Schumacher in the early twentieth century at Tell Megiddo, it was lost. Fortunately, impressions were made of the artifact prior to its disappearance.

Biblical Person	Inscription	Scripture
Jotham (758–741 BC)	To Jotham	2 Kings 15:32-38 2 Chronicles 27:1-9
Ahaz (742–726 BC)	Belonging to Ahaz, [son of] Jehotham, king of Judah / Belonging to Ushna, the servant of Ahaz	2 Kings 16:1-20 2 Chronicles 28:1-27
Hezekiah (726–697 BC)	Belonging to Hezekiah, [son of] Ahaz, king of Judah / Belonging to Jehozarah son of Hilkiah, servant of Hezekiah / Azariah son of Jehoshaphat, servant of Hezekiah / Belonging to Domia, the servant of Hezekiah / ...servant of Hezekiah	2 Kings 18:1–20:21 2 Chronicles 29:1–32:33
Eliakim and Hilkiah (726–697 BC)	Belonging to Eliakim the son of Hilkiah	2 Kings 18:18
Amariah (726–697 BC)	Belonging to Amariah [son of] Hananiah, servant of Hezekiah	2 Chronicles 31:15
Hoshea (732–722 BC)	Belonging to Abdi, the servant of Hoshea	2 Kings 17:1-6
Shebna (8th century BC)	...Shebna, servant of the king	Isaiah 22:15-25
Manasseh (697–642 BC)	Belonging to Manasseh, son of the king / Belonging to Manasseh son of Hezekiah	2 Kings 21:1-18 2 Chronicles 33:1-20
Asaiah (late seventh century BC)	Belonging to Asayahu (Asaiah), servant (minister) of the king	2 Kings 22:12,14 2 Chronicles 34:20
Joezer and Igdaliah (late seventh century BC)	Belonging to Yehoezer son of Yigdalyahu	Jeremiah 35:4 cf. 1 Chronicles 12:7
Azaliah and Meshullam (621 BC)	Azaliah the son of Meshullam	2 Kings 22:3
Nathan-melech (640–609 BC)	Nathan-melech, servant of the king	2 Kings 23:11
Ahikam and Shaphan (640–609 BC)	Belonging to Ahikam, the son of Shaphan	2 Kings 22:12
Baruch and Neriah (627–586 BC)	Seal of Baruch (Berekyahu) son of Neriah the Scribe*	Jeremiah 36:32

---

* This bulla was identified by the late bulla specialist Nahman Avigad as bearing the name of the prophet Jeremiah's scribe, Baruch, who penned the book of Jeremiah (Jeremiah 36:1-32)

Biblical Person	Inscription	Scripture
Priestly family name of Immer	[Ga'a]lyahu…[son] of Immer*	Jeremiah 20:1-18
Seriah and Neriah (627–586 BC)	Seraiah son of Neriah	Jeremiah 51:59
Malchiah (627-586 BC)	Malchiah son of the king	Jeremiah 38:6
Hananiah and Azzur (627–586 BC)	Hananiah the son of Azariah (Azzur)	Jeremiah 28:1
Gemariah and Shaphan (627–586 BC)	Gemariah son of Shaphan	Jeremiah 36:10-12
Jerahmeel (627–586 BC)	Jerahmeel son of the king	Jeremiah 36:26
Elishama (627–586 BC)	Elishama servant of the king	Jeremiah 36:12
Jehucal and Shelemiah (627–586 BC)	Jehucal son of Shelemiah	Jeremiah 37:3; 38:1
Gedaliah and Pashhur (627–586 BC)	Gedaliah son of Pashhur	Jeremiah 38:1
Azariah and Hilkiah (6th–5th century BC)	Seal of Azariah, the son of Hilkiah (the high priest?) / Seal of Hanan, the son of Hilkiah the priest	2 Kings 22:4-14; 23:4 1 Chronicles 6:13; 9:11; Ezra 7:1
Jehoahaz (or Shallum) (609 BC)	Jehoahaz the son of the king	2 Kings 23:31-34 2 Chronicles 36:1-4
Pedaiah (598–586 BC)	Pedaiah the son of the king	1 Chronicles 3:18
Seraiah and Neriah (598–586 BC)	Seraiah son of Neriah	Jeremiah 51:59
Ba'alis (586–580 BC)	Baal-yasha king of the [Ammonites] / Milcom the servant of Ba'alis	Jeremiah 40:14
Jaazaniah (597–580 BC)	Jaazaniah servant of the king	2 Kings 25:23
Shelomith was the "amah" (sister) of Elnathan (510–490 BC)	Belonging to Shelomith / Belonging to Elnathan the governor	1 Chronicles 3:19 Ezra 8:16

---

* This bulla was discovered by the archaeologist Gabriel Barkay as a result of sifting the Temple Mount dirt discarded from recent renovations of the Al Aqsa Mosque. Immer is the name associated with the priestly family that had oversight of the Temple Mount during the time of Jeremiah. Pashhur, the son of Immer, is described in Jeremiah 20:1-18 as the individual who beat Jeremiah and placed him under arrest.

Biblical Person	Inscription	Scripture
Sanballat, Governor of Samaria	(Belonging) to [...]iah * son of [San-] ballat, Governor of Samar[ia]	Nehemiah 2:10

© Joseph M Holden, 2013.

The Biblical Significance of Discoveries About David

The archaeological remains attesting to David's historicity have removed him from the realm of myth and legend and placed him in a well-established role as a historical king of Israel, as the Bible declares. The discovery of the Tell Dan Stele has provided a solid link in establishing David among the major contributors to the Israelite nation, as well as informing us of the political and military climate of the ninth century BC.

Though debate continues over how influential and widespread David's kingdom was during the tenth century BC, initial archaeological data (Tell es-Safi, Tell Rehov, Khirbet Qeiyafa) appear to indicate that his kingdom was extremely centralized and widespread.

King Hezekiah

Nineteenth- and twentieth-century research in Jerusalem and Nineveh has turned up various materials relating to the historicity of the Judean king Hezekiah (726–697 BC) and the events surrounding him. Evidence of Hezekiah's preparation for the Assyrian siege (701 BC) has been discovered at the south end of the City of David and in Jerusalem's Jewish Quarter.

The Pedaiah seal reads "Pedaiah, the son of the king." Pedaiah was the son of King Jehoiachin (Jeconiah) (1 Chronicles 3:17-18). (Photo by Zev Radovan.)

Furthermore, excavation at Nineveh in the early nineteenth century recovered detailed Assyrian records that mention Hezekiah by name and describe Assyrian military exploits in Israel.

Background and Setting

Immediately prior to the death of King Ahaz (741–726 BC), Judah stood alone as the sole remaining kingdom to survive the Assyrian takeover of Israel by Sargon II. Hezekiah, the son of Ahaz, reigned during the tumultuous times of the late eighth and early

---

* Confirmation of this bulla is found in the collection of fifth-century BC Jewish manuscripts known as the Elephantine Papyri. The correspondence was written from the Jewish community living at Elephantine Island located in the midst of the Nile River near Nubia. One particular letter, known as the "Passover letter" (now on display at the Egyptian Museum of Berlin), contains a reference to "Delaiah and Shelemiah, the sons of Sanballat, the governor of Samaria." These letters also confirm that the Persian king Darius was involved in the authorization to rebuild Jerusalem; they confirm as well the Israelites' participation in its construction, as the Bible states in the book of Ezra and Nehemiah.

seventh century BC. Born to an ungodly father who tolerated the worship of pagan gods, Hezekiah was a reformer diligent to bring Judah back into line with the law of Moses (2 Kings 18:4-5; 2 Chronicles 29:25-30). He extended this offer of reform to those in Israel (the Northern Kingdom) who had not gone into Assyrian captivity by encouraging their return to the feasts of the Lord at Jerusalem (2 Chronicles 30:1-26).

As the reforms in Jerusalem increased, so did the power of Israel's enemy Assyria. By this time, the Northern Kingdom of Israel no longer existed, but Sargon II (722–705 BC) continued to have a military presence in these vassal territories. When Sargon died in 705 BC, Hezekiah appears to have stopped paying the Assyrian vassal taxes (2 Kings 18:14-16), reflecting what many believe to be an economic revolt by the remaining cities in Judea. In 701 BC, Sennacherib sought to crush the rebellion by conquering all the fortified cities of Judea, including Lachish* (2 Kings 18:13-14). Hezekiah understood that in order for Jerusalem to survive the coming Assyrian siege, he would need to strengthen his fortification defenses and make sure the people had access to water. According to 2 Chronicles 32:5, Hezekiah strengthened the walls that had been broken down and built another outer wall to reinforce the existing wall structure. In addition, he stopped the flow of water that came from the Gihon Spring, which lay outside the city walls, and diverted its water to the west side of the City of David. This would ensure that the people would have access to water during a lengthy siege. We now know that both feats were accomplished with remarkable efficiency and engineering.

Hezekiah's Preparations for Assyrian Attack

A 13-year excavation that began in 1969 of Jerusalem's Jewish Quarter by Israeli archaeologist Nahman Avigad led to the discovery of an outer defensive wall section built by Hezekiah immediately prior to the Assyrian siege in 701 BC. The wall fortification has been measured at a massive 23 feet wide and nearly 27 feet high, earning it the name "Hezekiah's *Broad* Wall." Hezekiah clearly understood that the Assyrian battering rams were powerful weapons to be reckoned with and that his fortifications and repairs to the wall had to withstand them. The

The remains of Hezekiah's broad wall in Jerusalem. The lower right side of the wall runs through the foundations of an eighth-century BC Jerusalem home.

---

* Archaeologists have discovered Assyrian records and palace wall reliefs at Nineveh documenting the brutal destruction of Lachish. Excavations at Lachish have exposed earthen siege ramps piled against the city walls and high quantities of Assyrian arrowheads. One mass grave contains nearly 1,600 skeletal remains, testifying to the carnage experienced.

Scriptures imply that the wall and water tunnel projects were hastily completed due to the imminent threat of Sennacherib's army. This haste is confirmed by analyzing the construction of Hezekiah's broad wall. Avigad noticed that the stones used to build the wall were smaller than the usual stones used for such projects. It now appears that Hezekiah's hastily constructed wall utilized the stones from Jerusalem homes for its construction. In fact, a portion of the wall runs directly through people's dwellings. This is confirmed by Isaiah 22:9-10, which says, "You counted the houses of Jerusalem, and you broke down the houses to fortify the wall" (ESV).

In order to address the city's need for water, Hezekiah had to figure a way to route the water from the Gihon Spring outside the city walls to the inhabitants within Jerusalem. In what is considered to be an engineering marvel to this day, he stopped up the spring and dug a tunnel using two work parties digging from each end to reroute the flow of water to the Pool of Siloam (2 Kings 20:20). Discovered in 1838 by Edward Robinson, this tunnel measures 1,748 feet long and about 2 feet wide in most places.

After an examination of the tunnel by archaeologists had concluded, youths travel-ing up the tunnel area in 1880 discovered a Paleo-Hebrew inscription that the archaeologists had missed, describing the dramatic final moments of the work parties. The Siloam inscription reads in part, "The axes were against each other and while three cubits were left to cut...and on the day of the tunnel (being finished) the stonecutters struck each man towards his counter-part, ax against ax and flowed water from the source to the pool for 1200 cubits." Dating to the eighth century BC, it remains one of the oldest Paleo-Hebrew inscrip-tions of its kind ever found.

Hezekiah's water tunnel.

The Bible records that Hezekiah's efforts to fortify the walls and bring water to the inhabitants of Jeru-salem, along with his prayers, were successful. Sen-nacherib's siege of the Judean cities succeeded until he came to Jerusalem, where 185,000 Assyr-ian troops were killed overnight by the angel of the Lord (2 Kings 19:35-37; Isa-iah 37:36-38).

According to 2 Kings 19:36-37, this event prompted Sennacherib to return to Nineveh in disgrace, and 20 years later (681 BC) he was killed by his sons Adrammelech and Sharezer while wor-shipping his god Nisroch. This assassina-tion was a fulfillment of Isaiah's prophecy directed to Hezekiah that Sennacherib

Replica of the Siloam inscription found in Hezekiah's water tunnel. The original is displayed at the Istanbul Archaeological Museum.

would return home and fall by the sword in his own land (Isaiah 37:7). Sennacherib's death is also confirmed in the Babylonian Chronicles.

Critical scholars have argued that a plague was the cause of the Assyrian deaths. However, this is not convincing since it requires one to dismiss the supernatural element at work here and to assume the disease could attack only the Assyrians and not the Jews. Either way it requires a miracle!

Confirmation by Assyrian Sources

The discovery of the Taylor Prism (a hexagonal clay prism written in Akkadian cuneiform) in 1830 at Sennacherib's palace in Nineveh, along with a second identical record known as the Prism of Sennacherib (or Annals of Sennacherib), historically confirms the biblical account of the Jerusalem siege. The annals, dating to 701 BC, read as follows:

As to *Hezekiah, the Jew, he did not submit to my yoke,* I laid siege to 46 of his strong cities, walled forts and to countless small villages in their vicinity, and conquered (them) by means of well-stamped (earth-)ramps, battering-rams brought by (thus) near (to the walls) (combined with) the attack by foot soldiers, (using) mines, breeches as well as sapper work. I drove out (of them) 200,150 people, young and old, male and female, horses, mules, donkeys, camels, big and small cattle beyond counting, and considered them booty. *Himself [Hezekiah] I made a prisoner in Jerusalem, his royal residence, like a bird in a cage. I surrounded him with earthwork in order to molest those who were leaving his city's gate.* His towns which I had plundered, I took away from his country and gave them (over) to Mitinti, king of Ashdod, Padi king of Ekron, and Sillibel, king of Gaza....Hezekiah himself, whom the terror-inspiring splendor of my lordship had overwhelmed....*

The Annals of Sennacherib. (Photo by Zev Radovan.)

The annals continue on to describe how Hezekiah had sent tribute to Sennacherib in an effort to buy peace, something Isaiah had warned him not to do.

The Hebrew-inscribed seal impression of King Hezekiah reads, "Belonging to Hezekiah, [son of] Ahaz, king of Judah." Its blackened color is due to burning, which also hardened and preserved the inscription. (Photo by Zev Radovan.)

---

* James Pritchard, *Ancient Near Eastern Texts Relating to the Old Testament* (Princeton, NJ: Princeton University Press, 1969), 288, emphasis added. The Taylor Prism records that Sennacherib brought a man named Padi back to Ekron and established him as king over the people there. This is confirmed in the Ekron inscription discovered in 1996 at Ekron, which lists Padi as the king.

However, we understand several things from Sennacherib's account contained in the annals of the siege that correspond to the biblical record: 1) Hezekiah did not submit to Sennacherib's army. 2) Sennacherib laid the Judean cities waste. 3) Sennacherib surrounded Jerusalem. 4) Sennacherib's boasting and splendor appears to have negatively affected Hezekiah. 5) Neither the Bible nor the annals record that Jerusalem was conquered. If in fact Sennacherib had conquered Hezekiah at Jerusalem he surely would have written about it, as he did in regard to the lesser 46 cities. For Sennacherib not to boast over his destruction or conquering of Jerusalem is to go against what we know about Mesopotamian/Assyrian kings. They liked to boast! The conquering of Jerusalem would have been something to boast about, but mention of it is strangely lacking in the annals. How could a world superpower like Assyria have conquered all the fortified cities in Judea, including Lachish, and then have somehow come to a complete halt when encircling Jerusalem? There appears to be no *natural* explanation in either the Assyrian records or the Bible.

The Biblical Significance of Discoveries About Hezekiah

Challenges to the historicity of Hezekiah and his position among the kings of Judah have largely vanished due to these extrabiblical sources. The events surrounding Hezekiah's reign and Assyrian military exploits in Israel during this period are now well-established facts. The discovery of Hezekiah's broad wall, the Siloam tunnel, the Annals of Sennacherib, and more recently Hezekiah's royal clay seal impression (bulla) has solidified his historical place alongside other ancient figures.[16]

NEBUCHADNEZZAR II AND THE PERSIAN KINGS

Discoveries Involving King Nebuchadnezzar II

Several excavations during the past two centuries have yielded enough archaeological data to construct an accurate portrayal of the Babylonian Empire in general, and of the life of Nebuchadnezzar II in particular. These finds have all but silenced the critics' claim that the history described in Scripture is in conflict with actual ancient Near-Eastern history.

Background and Setting

As the Assyrian Empire began to weaken in the late seventh century BC, the Babylonians (also called the Chaldeans or Neo-Babylonians) increased in strength through their many successful military campaigns in the west. By 626 BC, the Assyrians were fighting a losing battle with the seminomadic Scythians and Cimmerians from the north, who were successful in wresting vast western regions from Assyrian control. In that same year, Nabopolassar (626–605 BC) captured Babylon and all its territories in southern Mesopotamia. By 612 BC, the Chaldeans under Nabopolassar had allied with the Medes (north of the Tigris River) to defeat the Assyrians at Nineveh and bring an end to their empire (see Nahum 1:1–3:19).

By the late seventh century BC, the fall of Assyria had left a power vacuum that several of the surrounding nations sought to fill, including Egypt. Even before Nabopolassar's death in 605 BC, his son Nebuchadnezzar II (605–562 BC) had ambitiously moved his armies to the west in an attempt to establish his Babylonian kingdom as the new world power. In 609 BC, Nebuchadnezzar defeated Pharaoh Necho's Egyptian army at Carchemish near the Euphrates River (see Jeremiah 46:1-2). In pursuit of the Egyptians, Nebuchadnezzar had to travel through Israel toward Egypt, thus he swept into Jerusalem, making its king, Jehoiakim (also known as Josiah's son Jehoahaz), a vassal leader. At this time, Daniel, along with many other Judeans, was deported to Babylon where he and his people would spend the next 70 years in captivity.

In the first decade in the sixth century BC, Jehoiakim rebelled against Babylon and stopped paying tribute, which only invited a siege of Jerusalem by Nebuchadnezzar's army a short time later. Upon Jehoiakim's death during the siege, Jehoiachin was established as the new king; he offered his surrender to Nebuchadnezzar three months later. As a result, Jehoiachin and his family, royal officials, and 7,000 craftsmen, as well as some 10,000 captives, were deported to Babylon (2 Kings 24:1-17). (After he had spent 37 years in a Babylonian prison, Babylonian king Evil-merodach [562–560 BC] would release Jehoiachin from prison to sit at the king's table and provide him with an allowance of rations according to his needs for the rest of his life—2 Kings 25:27-30.)

Nebuchadnezzar installed Josiah's son Zedekiah (597–586 BC, also known by his Hebrew name Mattaniah) as his new vassal king. Zedekiah reigned nine years before he rebelled against Babylon, thus provoking Nebuchadnezzar to bring his armies west to Jerusalem for a third time (2 Kings 25:1-7). On his way, Nebuchadnezzar had to decide whether to attack the rebellious Ammonites or to proceed to Jerusalem; thus according to Ezekiel (21:21-29), Nebuchadnezzar consults the divining power of his gods by "shaking the arrows" and "reading the liver," a common occult practice in Babylon. It then becomes clear he must proceed to Jerusalem first. En route, he overruns Lachish, Azekah, and the Judean military outposts along the way (Jeremiah 34:7), finally coming to Jerusalem where he will besiege the capital for nearly 18 months (Jeremiah 52:4).

In 586 BC, Zedekiah's refusal to heed the words of Jeremiah (Jeremiah 27; 34:2-7) brought a fiery destruction upon the city, the execution of his own sons at Riblah (2 Kings 25:7), and the destruction of the Jerusalem population and Solomon's temple. The rule of the Davidic dynasty and the Hebrew nation had come to an end. Nebuchadnezzar looted Jerusalem of its valuables, including the precious vessels from the temple, which he carried back to Babylon (2 Kings 25:13-17).

Prior to his death in 562 BC, Nebuchadnezzar had engaged in a massive building campaign that is preserved in the archaeological record—features that today are spread over several hundred acres (Daniel 4:30). The city of Babylon is said to have covered an area of over 3,000 acres, with defensive walls wide enough for at least two chariots to travel side by side. Its splendor is reflected in the Ishtar Gate (entrance to the city) and the city's architecture, which are unrivaled in detail and beauty; the supporting walls that ringed the city were an impressive ten miles long! The city was divided in half by the north-south flow of the Euphrates River. The outer walls of the inner city were circled by a moat that was filled from the Euphrates, making its defensive fortifications even more difficult for a potential enemy to penetrate.

After the brief reigns of Evil-merodach (2 Kings 25:27), Nergal-Sharezer (Jeremiah 39:3), and Labashi-Marduk (556 BC), in 556 BC a high royal official known as Nabonidus (and his co-regent son Belshazzar) came to the throne (Daniel 5:1,22). According to historical records, Nabonidus was driven by his desire to rebuild the temple of his god Sin in Haran, thus he was most often away from Babylon, leaving his son Belshazzar as king. The more aggressive and strengthened Persian army under Cyrus II (559–530 BC) was slowly capturing more territory in southern Mesopotamia and eventually claimed Babylon itself in 539 BC. Herodotus explains that the capture of Babylon occurred with little violence because the Persians diverted the Euphrates and entered through the riverbed. The well-known story recorded in Daniel 5 of Belshazzar's banquet feast, and the mysterious writing on the wall, is said to occur on the same night the city fell to the Persians and Belshazzar was killed (Daniel 5:30). Because of Daniel's interpretation, he was promoted to third ruler in the Babylonian kingdom (Daniel 5:29). As a result of the fall of the city, the Babylonian Empire came to an end.

There are good reasons to accept the biblical account of Nebuchadnezzar II and his dealings with Israel during the late seventh and early sixth centuries BC. The following discussion includes several of those reasons.

The Babylonian Chronicles

First, support for Nebuchadnezzar's existence and military exploits in Israel and Mesopotamia can be seen in both Babylonian and Israelite extrabiblical records. The series of cuneiform tablets known as the Babylonian Chronicles describe the principal events each year from 747 BC to about 280 BC. One of these tablets (pictured) recounts Nebuchadnezzar's first decade as king along with his second siege of Jerusalem in March 597 BC (Isaiah 39):

> He [Nebuchadnezzar] camped against the city of Judah [Jerusalem] and on the second day of the month of Adar he took the city and captured the king [Jehoiachin]. He appointed a king of his own choice there [Zedekiah], took its heavy tribute and brought them to Babylon.

This cuneiform tablet is part of the series of Babylonian Chronicles that detail Nebuchadnezzar's exploits from 605–594 BC. It records his siege of Jerusalem in 597 BC and is currently displayed at the British Museum. (Photo by Todd Bolen/ BiblePlaces.com.)

The chronicles speak of Nebuchadnezzar's replacement of King Jehoiachin and the establishing of his vassal king, Zedekiah. These activities correspond to the prophecies and histories recorded about him in the book of Jeremiah, 2 Chronicles 36, and 2 Kings 24. The tablets themselves are straightforward historical accounts that do not employ a mythical tone or grandiose inflations; therefore, there is no reason to believe that embellishments have been introduced into the texts.

Unfortunately, not all of Nebuchadnezzar's exploits in Jerusalem have been recovered through the chronicles, though several other related finds offer us confirmation of the biblical record, especially that of his final invasion of Jerusalem (587 BC) and destruction of the temple in 586 BC. These include 21 hastily scribbled letters that record brief lists of names and correspondence between Judean military outposts and the city of Lachish immediately prior to Babylonian invasion of Judea (589 to 588 BC). The first 18 of the 21 letters were discovered in 1935 by J.L. Starkey in the gate tower at Tell ed-Duweir (Lachish); three more were discovered in 1938. The more legible letters were first published in 1938 by Harry Torczyner as *The Lachish Letters*; the rest of them are not legible enough to translate. The notes themselves are inscribed on small pieces of pottery (ostraca). One such letter shows that, among the cities still withstanding Nebuchadnezzar's armies were Lachish and Azekah, the same two cities attested in the words of Jeremiah the prophet (Jeremiah 34:7). The desperate tone contained in Letter IV reads in part:

> I have written on the door according to all that my lord hath written to me. And with respect to what my lord hath written about the matter of *Beth-haraphid,* there is no one there.
>
> And as for Semechiah, Shemaiah hath taken him and brought him up to the city. And as for thy servant, I am not sending *anyone* thither, but I will send tomorrow morning.

The Lachish Letter—sixth century BC. (Photo by Zev Radovan.)

And let (my lord) know that we are watching for the signals of Lachish, according to all the indications which my lord hath given, for we cannot see Azekah.

King Jehoiachin's Ration Record

Second, while excavating at Babylon near the Ishtar Gate in the early twentieth century, Robert Koldewey recovered an official Babylonian administrative document containing the food rations given to Judean prisoners, including King Jehoiachin and his sons. As mentioned earlier, according to 2 Kings 24 and 2 Kings 25:27-30, Jehoiachin was taken captive by Nebuchadnezzar and deported to Babylon, though some time later while in prison Nebuchadnezzar's son Evil-merodach had ordered the release of Jehoiachin and subsequently provided him with a daily allotment according to his needs. The Babylonian text is consistent with these passages when it records, "10 sila of oil to Jehoiachin, king of Judah…and to the sons of the king."

The Jehoiachin Ration Record is a cuneiform document that dates from the period from 595 to 570 BC, spanning the time the Bible says Jehoiachin was taken captive to Babylon by King Nebuchadnezzar II. (Photo: Bildarchiv Preussischer Kulturbesitz, Berlin/Vorderasiatisches Museum, Staatliche Museen, Berlin/Olaf M. Tessmer/Art Resource, NY.)

Stamp Seals Found at the City of David

Third, dozens of stamp seals (*bullae*) discovered at the City of David near what is known as the stone House of Ahiel, and located through the antiquities trade, demonstrate the historicity of biblical figures mentioned during the time of Nebuchadnezzar's conquest of Jerusalem[2] (see also the chart "Seal Impressions of People in the Old Testament" in chapter 19). For example, a seal was found at the City of David in a well-documented context (area G) that contains the paleo-Hebrew inscription "Belonging to Gemaryahu [Gemariah] [son of] Shaphan." Gemariah and Shaphan are both mentioned throughout the books of Jeremiah (36:10-12,25-26) and 2 Kings (22:12). Shaphan was the scribe under King Jehoiakim, and Gemariah owned the home in which Baruch read the book of Jeremiah to the people of Jerusalem (Jeremiah 36:10). In addition, an unprovenanced seal (pictured) has emerged bearing the name "Belonging to Berekyahu [Baruch], son of Neriyahu [Neriah], the scribe," who is none other than the prophet Jeremiah's personal scribe Baruch (Jeremiah 36:1-32).

The Baruch Seal (Photo by Zev Radovan.)

Other biblical figures have been located such as "Jerahmeel, the king's son" (Jeremiah 36:26), who was the individual sent by King Jehoiakim to arrest Jeremiah and his scribe. Further, a seal impression that reads, "Belonging to Yehuchal [Jehucal] ben Shelemiyahu ben Shovi" identifies the person sent by King Zedekiah to ask Jeremiah for prayer (Jeremiah 37:3; 38:1). In addition, the sixth-century BC seal bearing the name of King Jehoiachin's son Pedaiah reads, "Belonging to Pedaiah son of the king"(1 Chronicles 3:18-19). Apparently, many of the stamp seals found at the City of David, the pie-slice-shaped piece of land that lies immediately south of the Temple Mount, were baked hard by the Babylonians' fiery destruction of Jerusalem (take, for example, the blackened King Hezekiah seal).

As noted in chapter 19, one such seal was discovered by archaeologist Gabriel Barkay during a sifting

The ruins of a typical Israelite four-room house known as the House of Ahiel lie opposite the Arab village of Silwan above the Kidron Valley in the City of David, where many stamp seals (bullae) were discovered. The home, named after a piece of pottery with the name "Ahiel" on it, was destroyed during Nebuchadnezzar's siege of Jerusalem in 586 BC. Discovered by Yigal Shiloh of Hebrew University, it is the best preserved home from the First Temple Period.

project of precious Temple Mount soil discarded in a Jerusalem dump and later in the Kidron Valley as a result of renovations to the Al-Aqsa Mosque. The blackened seal contained wavelike lines on the back, implying it was attached to a bag or sachet of some kind, while the front gave an inscription that, though incomplete, can be confidently reconstructed as "Ga'alyahu [Gedeliah] son of Immer." Jeremiah records that the name *Immer* belongs to a family of priests who had oversight of the temple (Jeremiah 20:1), and with whom the prophet was well-acquainted (Jeremiah 20:1-6). Pashhur the priest and son of Immer was responsible for the beating and imprisoning of Jeremiah (Jeremiah 20:2) immediately prior to Nebuchadnezzar's invasion. Jeremiah prophesied that Pashhur would be taken captive and deported to Babylon, where he and his family would die (Jeremiah 20:6). Apparently, Gedaliah was Pashhur's son (Jeremiah 38:1).

The Sarsekim Tablet

Fourth, a small (about two-inch-long) cuneiform tablet discovered in the late 1800s near Baghdad, but only recently deciphered (2007) at the British Museum by Assyriologist Michael Jursa of Vienna, was found to contain the name *Sarsekim.**

Sarsekim was the *rab-saris* (chief officer and eunuch) to Nebuchadnezzar II during his siege of Jerusalem in 586 BC (Jeremiah 39:3) and was among the group of Babylonian officers who saw Zedekiah flee for his life toward the Arabah (Jeremiah 39:4). The Sarsekim Tablet dates to 595 BC and tells of Sarsekim giving a substantial amount of gold (about 1.5 pounds) to the temple of Esagila (the

The sixth-century BC cuneiform Sarsekim Tablet confirms the historicity of Nebuchadnezzar's chief officer who accompanied him at the siege of Jerusalem (Jeremiah 39:3). Josephus in his *Antiquities of the Jews*, VIII, mentions Sarsekim as one of Nebuchadnezzar's generals who took Jerusalem in 586 BC. (Photo © The Trustees of the British Museum.)

temple of the chief god Marduk in Babylon) in the tenth year of Nebuchadnezzar's reign (595 BC). The tablet records his Babylonian name as *Nabu-sharrussu-ukin*, which becomes *Nebusarsekim* in English. This small relic's testimony to the historicity of an insignificant figure in the Bible lends support to the historicity of the major biblical figures and events with whom he is mentioned. The deciphering of this tiny tablet led Irving Finkel of the Department of the Middle East at the British Museum to assert,

This is a fantastic discovery, a world class find. If Nebo Sarsekim existed, which other figures in the Old Testament existed? A throwaway detail in the Old Testament turns out to be accurate and true. I think that it means the whole of the narrative [of Jeremiah] takes on a new kind of power.[3]

* The cuneiform East India House Inscription at the British Museum provides additional support, clearly expressing Nebuchadnezzar's achievements and acknowledgment of the Babylonian god Marduk.

Nebuchadnezzar's Building Projects

Fifth, ancient building materials that identify Nebuchadnezzar as the chief architect of Babylon have been identified. Immediately after the defeat of Nineveh in 612 BC, Nebuchadnezzar began large-scale building projects in order to beautify and fortify hundreds of acres of his capital city. Archaeologists have learned that Babylon contained magnificent gate structures, massive walls built in triplets, an impressive ziggurat, temples, the enduringly famous Hanging Gardens, administrative buildings, and palaces among others. Though the Euphrates River that originally bisected the city in Nebuchadnezzar's day has submerged one side of the city, remains from the other side leave a fingerprint unmistakably traceable to Nebuchadnezzar himself. It is estimated that more than 14 million baked bricks were made, many of them stamped (or hand-inscribed) with a cuneiform inscription that identifies Nebuchadnezzar. The mention of Esagila and Ezida on the brick is a reference to, respectively, the temple of the chief god Marduk and the temple of Nabu (the god of writing).

Nebuchadnezzar brick identifying the king as the builder. The brick reads, "Nebuchadnezzar, king of Babylon, who cares for Esagila and Ezida, eldest son of Nabopolassar, king of Babylon." (Photo © The Trustees of the British Museum.)

In addition to this, the Cylinder of Nebuchadnezzar II (British Museum), recovered from the ruins of Babylon, describes him as the builder and renovator of three palaces in the city, includ-

The Babylonian Ishtar Gate, reconstructed of blue-glazed brick, at the Pergamon Museum in Berlin. The ornamented gate contains an inscription written in the first person by Nebuchadnezzar taking credit for its building. (Photo © Fotolia.)

ing his father's (Nabopolassar's) older palace and a summer palace along the Euphrates River. These kinds of cylinders were usually buried underneath the foundations of buildings as records and testimony (for future kings) of a particular structure. A similar record known as the Barrel Cylinder of Nebuchadnezzar II (Israel Museum) was written in the first person to commemorate the rebuilding of the Lugal-Maradda temple in central Babylonia. It boasts of the discovery of inscriptions within the foundations of the temple itself identifying Naram-Sin (king of Akkad), who reigned some 1,600 years prior to Nebuchadnezzar.

Babylon's famous and beautiful Ishtar Gate (600 BC), located during excavations conducted at Babylon from 1899 to 1914, has preserved 60 lines of dedicatory inscription that identifies Nebuchadnezzar as its builder. According to most scholars, the Ishtar Gate was the eighth gate that provided northern access to the inner city of Babylon. The Akkadian cuneiform text is written in the first person and reads in part,

> Therefore, I [Nebuchadnezzar] pulled down these gates and laid their foundations at the water-table with asphalt and bricks and had them made of bricks with blue stone on which wonderful bulls and dragons were depicted. I covered their roofs by laying majestic cedars length-wise over them. I hung doors of cedar adorned with bronze at all the gate openings. I placed wild bulls and ferocious dragons in the gateways and thus adorned them with luxurious splendor so that people might gaze on them in wonder.[4]

The gate provides solid historical confirmation of Nebuchadnezzar's title as king, his historical existence, Babylon as the place of his reign, and his architectural affinities. The collective archaeological records and inscriptions are in accord with the prophet Daniel's account of Nebuchadnezzar's boast: "Is not this great Babylon, which I have built by my mighty power as a royal residence and for the glory of my majesty?" (Daniel 4:30 ESV). It was during this prideful moment (see verse 31) that Nebuchadnezzar heard a voice from heaven telling him that his kingdom had been taken from him and that he had been afflicted with the disorder known as *boanthropy* (verses 32-33—the belief that one is an ox and must conduct one's life accordingly). Apparently, Nebuchadnezzar later came to his senses and acknowledged the sovereignty of the Most High God (verses 34-37).

Confirmation of the Existence of the Babylonian King Belshazzar

Sixth, while inspecting the ancient ruins at Ur (Tell el-Muqayyar), J.E. Taylor (the British Consul in Basra) discovered four cuneiform capsules known as the Cylinders of Nabonidus (554-540 BC).* These important records not only confirm the historicity of Belshazzar, the king of Babylon who had Daniel interpret the writing on the wall, they also added historical details that help explain Daniel's rise to third-highest rank in the Babylonian kingdom (Daniel 5:29).

Critics had long dismissed the book of Daniel as mythological embellishment since he had recorded the name *Belshazzar* as the reigning king of Babylon (5:1); however, there were no extrabiblical records or Babylonian kings lists that reflected Belshazzar as being part of the Chaldean dynasty. In fact, critics claimed Belshazzar did not exist— that is, until a similar discovery was made, bolstering Taylor's earlier find.

---

* Interestingly, an Aramaic document was recovered from among the Dead Sea Scrolls (4Q242). Known as "The Prayer of Nabonidus," it was most likely copied from an older version of the prayer sometime during the first century BC. It is written in the first person and tells of Nabonidus's affliction with an ulcer for seven years while he was at Tema. The prayer mentions that it was an exorcist Jew from among the exiles of Judah who ultimately forgave his sins. He begins to recount the story of his approach to the gods and then the rest of the text is missing. At very least, we see here an independent corroboration of the books of Daniel (Daniel 9:2) and Jeremiah (Jeremiah 29:10-12) when they affirm that the Jews were in Babylonian captivity during the sixth century BC.

The Cylinder of Nabonidus contains the name of King Belshazzar, mentioned in Daniel 5. (Photo © The Trustees of the British Museum.)

The prevailing critical belief was overturned when excavations led by Hormuzd Rassam (1826–1910) at the temple of Shamash in Sippar (southern Iraq) recovered a mid-sixth-century BC cylinder that describes Nabonidus's reconstruction of pagan temples in Harran (for example, that of the moon god Sin) along with his discovery of ancient Mesopotamian kings' inscriptions, including those of Naram-Sin (2254–2218 BC) and Shagaraki-shuriash (1245–1233 BC). It is from this text that we understand that Belshazzar (*Bel-shar-usur*) was the son and co-regent of the Babylonian king Nabonidus. Apparently, when Nabonidus was away from Babylon on various expeditions and temple renovation projects he left his son in charge as king. Support for this is found in the cuneiform Nabonidus Chronicle (dated to about 530 to 400 BC) that records the events in Babylon from 556 to the 530s, telling of Nabonidus's hiatus for at least ten years in Arabia (he established a base at the Oasis of Teima) in his effort to forge trade alliances with the Arabs. It further explains why Belshazzar could offer Daniel only the third-highest position in the kingdom after he had interpreted the writing on the wall. Since Nabonidus was the king and Belshazzar his co-regent, Daniel could naturally occupy no greater than the "third ruler" position.

The Biblical Significance of Discoveries About Nebuchadnezzar

There is very little doubt among scholars today about the existence and exploits of Nebuchadnezzar II. This is primarily due to the growing body of material evidence that has been accumulated from more than 150 years of research in Mesopotamia and Israel. The Bible has accurately recorded the events relating to the final days of the Davidic dynasty and the destruction of Solomon's temple. In addition to its rich commentary on the seventh and sixth centuries BC, the Bible has helped to fill in gaps in the archaeological record with data that are not supplied in any extrabiblical source. In fact, the material data have vindicated those who had placed their trust in the historical record the Bible contains, especially as it pertains to the historicity of King Belshazzar and the exploits of Nebuchadnezzar II.

The Persian Kings

Persia and its kings figure prominently in the Bible. The books of Esther, Ezra, and Nehemiah offer a glimpse into this time period and the Hebrews' dealings with the Persian kings and culture. Since several key discoveries are related to Persia and its kings it seems best to discuss this information as we address those discoveries below.

Background and Setting

The Persians and their territory (modern Iran) developed late relative to other surrounding countries. We learn from cuneiform texts found in Mesopotamia dating to the third millennium BC that northeast of the Tigris River various groups (Elamites, Kassites) engaged in trade. By the late second millennium BC, European tribes began migrating into the area, two of which were the Medes and the Persian tribes. The Medes eventually allied with the Chaldeans (Babylonians) to the south to make war on the mighty Assyrian empire, defeating Assyria at Nineveh in 612 BC. By the eighth cen-

The ruins of Persepolis (in modern-day Iran) date from the late sixth century BC and attest to the power and wealth of the Persian Empire. The name *Persepolis* (in Old Persian the name is *Parsa*) literally means "The City of the Persians;" its name today is *Takht-e Jamshid.* (Photo © Fotolia.)

tury BC Medes and Persians had consolidated their strength in the area known as Media and Elam. Media lay northeast of Assyria while Elam resided in the south, immediately north of the Persian Gulf.

The Cyrus Cylinder. (Photo by Zev Radovan.)

Cyrus the Great

By the late seventh century BC, the Persians' close alliance with the Medes resulted in a marriage between the royal families of the Medes and Persians. Cyrus II (559–530, also known as Cyrus the Great) was born of this union between the two royal households. After becoming king, Cyrus II forged alliances to consolidate his power and developed Persia into the stronger of the two tribes. It was in the northern Media territory that the biblical city of Ecbatana (Ezra 6:2—the modern city at the site is Hamadan) was founded as the capital of the Medes until Cyrus conquered it in the mid sixth century BC. Soon after his conquest of Ionia, a Greek-speaking region on the Aegean Sea in Asia Minor, Cyrus established the Persian city of Pasargadae in the southeast region of Persia. Other Persian cities would also be established, such as Persepolis (pictured on previous page) and Susa. Scholars are convinced that Pasargadae was not used much after Cyrus's death. Cyrus's ambition and military savvy stretched his kingdom to what is now western Turkey (Anatolia) and east into India.

Eventually, Cyrus pushed his armies west into Chaldean territories; in 539 BC the Persians conquered Babylon itself without a battle while the Chaldean king Nabonidus (556–539 BC) was away, having left his co-regent and son Belshazzar in charge (Daniel 5:1-30). The Bible mentions a prophecy about King Cyrus in Isaiah 45:1-7, over 100 years prior to his birth. Cyrus did not appear to know the God of Israel (Isaiah 45:4) since his description of the victory over Babylon gave credit to the Chaldean god Marduk. However, Cyrus was indeed used by God to bring release to the Jews being held in Babylonian captivity for the previous 70 years (Daniel 9:2; Jeremiah 25:11-12).

The sixth-century BC Cyrus Cylinder, which many have recognized as the first charter of human rights, is a clay record written in Babylonian cuneiform of Cyrus's victory over Babylon. Worthy of note, the cylinder gives permission to worship freely and to rebuild destroyed cities and worship centers. Though the Jews were not mentioned by name in the cylinder, they were free to return to their homeland that lay in ruins. Later some did under Ezra, Nehemiah, and Zerubbabel, but many stayed and lived within

Tomb of Cyrus in Pasargadae (Iran). (Photo © Fotolia.)

Persian society (see the book of Esther). In addition to the Cyrus Cylinder, Ezra 1:2-4 and 6:3-5 state that Cyrus believed he had been charged and authorized by God to rebuild the ruined temple in Jerusalem, and that the Jews should return to pursue the endeavor. Cyrus lived nearly a decade longer, only to be killed in a battle he personally led in 530 BC. His stone tomb pictured here, which was looted prior to its discovery, resides about one mile outside the palaces at Pasargadae.* It stands over 30 feet tall; its

---

* The tomb of Cyrus is mentioned by Strabo (15.3.7) in the first century BC and Plutarch (Alexander 69.4) and Anabasis of Arrian (6.29) in the second century AD. Strabo mentions that Alexander the Great visited the tomb prior to his death in 323 BC.

interior measures only 80 square feet. Cyrus as a historical figure has been confirmed through a variety of material remains, including palace wall reliefs, his tomb, and building bricks that bear his name.

The Reign of Darius the Great

After Cyrus died, his son Cambyses II (529–522 BC), who reigned only seven short years, failed to realize his plan of adding Egypt to the Persian Empire. After his death, the biblical king Darius the Great (522–486 BC) occupied the throne for 36 years. Ezra 6:1-13 tells of Darius and his search for the royal document that authorized the Jews to rebuild their temple and city. Ezra tells us that Darius not only gave permission to continue the building, but that he also gave aid to the restoration project. Several monuments have been discovered that attest to the historicity of this biblical king. First, the Behistun Relief was found carved into the side of a high rock face near Ecbatana and the Zagros mountains. It depicts Darius and his soldiers leading his defeated enemies by a rope. Fortunately for archaeologists and epigraphers, the relief was accompanied by Akkadian, Elamite, and Per-

This clay brick from the sixth century BC bearing Cyrus's name was discovered in Ur and is written in Babylon cuneiform (Ezra 6:14). It reads, "Cyrus king of the world, king of Anshan...the great gods delivered all the lands into my hands and I made this land dwell in peace." (Photo by Zev Radovan.)

sian inscriptions that chronicle Darius's achievements and ascendancy to power, which helped scholars eventually read the cuneiform language. Moreover, excavations at Susa have revealed that Darius is attested in palace wall reliefs and inscriptions; one that is housed at the Louvre Museum reads, "This palace which I built at Susa."

Xerxes I and Artaxerxes I

Upon Darius's death in 486 BC, his son Xerxes I (486–465 BC) quickly put down revolts in Egypt and Babylon and set his sights to subdue the rebellious Greeks in 480 BC. This unsuccessful campaign led to the complete loss of control of Greece itself and eventually western Asia Minor.

The book of Esther (1:1-3) opens during the third year of the reign of Xerxes I while he was occupying the capital city of Susa northeast of Babylon and the Tigris River. The book of Esther uses the king's Hebrew name of Ahasuerus (from the king's Old Persian name, Khshayarsha) instead of his Greek name, Xerxes. Some have identified Esther through an examination of Persian archaeology and records as Queen Amestris, who was enthroned as a replacement of Queen Vashti during the seventh year (c. 479 BC) of Xerxes's reign (2:16-17). By and large, most scholars have accepted the historicity of the book of Esther. Its identification of a major Persian city (Susa) and king (Xerxes) as well as its familiarity with Persian culture and language (shown in the loan words used) has been verified through excavations at major Persian sites such as Persepolis, Susa, and Pasargadae.

When Xerxes was assassinated in 465 BC, his brother Artaxerxes I (464–424 BC) took the throne by force and reigned from Susa in the north. The Bible mentions that in the seventh year of the reign of Artaxerxes, Ezra the scribe was given a letter from the king authorizing him (and others) to return to Jerusalem with the king's silver, gold, and provisions (Ezra 7:1-26).

In addition, Nehemiah declares he was in the capital city of Susa in the twentieth year of the king's reign (Nehemiah 1:1; 2:1) when his burden for Jerusalem prompted him to pray and soon after petition the king. Nehemiah records that Artaxerxes granted him permission to restore and rebuild Jerusalem in the king's twentieth year (444 BC).*

The rock-cut tombs of Persian kings Darius, Xerxes, and Artaxerxes are set in a row in Persepolis. (Photo © Fotolia.)

Artaxerxes was the last Persian king mentioned in the Old Testament. By the end of his 40-year reign in 424 BC, he had ruled longer than any Persian king who came before or would come after him. The Persian Empire would fall to the swift Greek armies of Alexander the Great just about 100 years later. There is little doubt among scholars of the historicity of Artaxerxes I. This is due to the multiple citations of his life and works we find in the historical record, such as his tomb at Persepolis, the palace wall reliefs, his role in the Bible, and his attestation in the fifth-century BC royal silver bowl/cup that bears his name. The bowl inscription reads,

> Artaxerxes, the great king, king of kings, king of countries, son of Xerxes (who was) son of Darius the king, the Achaemenian, in whose house this silver drinking cup (was) made.

What is more, a collection of correspondence written on papyrus from the Jewish community at Elephantine Island in Egypt mentioned Darius, Xerxes, and

The silver bowl of Artaxerxes I dates to the fifth century BC. The inscription around the rim of the bowl mentions three biblical kings of the postcaptivity era who are also mentioned in Esther, Ezra, and Nehemiah. They are Darius, Xerxes, and Artaxerxes I. (Photo © The Trustees of the British Museum.)

---

* This event begins the countdown of Daniel's prophecy of 70 weeks (Daniel 9:24-27) decreed for the Jewish nation. The end of the sixty-ninth week would be marked by the Messiah's death, with the final week (seven-year period) to be fulfilled in the future.

Artaxerxes by name in association with the rebuilding of Jerusalem and the second Temple. For example, the Passover Papyrus mentions "the fifth year of king Darius"; the Settlement of Claim by Oath Papyrus mentions "in the year 25 of King Artaxerxes"; and the Petition for Authorization to Rebuild the Temple of Yaho Papyrus includes the phrases "...give you favor before King Darius...in the 14th year of King Darius...year 17 of King Darius."*

This massive limestone wall relief unearthed at the treasury in Persepolis pictures Darius seated on the throne speaking with a Median figure. Darius's son Xerxes I is standing behind the throne. The cupbearer appears behind Xerxes (Nehemiah 2:1). On each end of the relief are the immortal guard troops. (Photo by Zev Radovan.)

The Biblical Significance of Discoveries About the Persian Kings

The confirmation of the Persian kings is important to biblical studies since their existence and acts form the cultural and political background to the books of Esther, Ezra, and Nehemiah; knowledge about the kings adds information about what prompted the rebuilding of the Jewish Temple. In addition, the unambiguous confirmation of the decree of Artaxerxes to rebuild Jerusalem in 444 BC offers a clear historical beginning to Daniel's prophecy of the 70 weeks. The date is easily confirmed by simply calculating (using the lunar calendar) backward from the time of Christ's crucifixion.

---

* James Pritchard, *Ancient Near Eastern Texts Relating to the Old Testament* (Princeton, NJ: Princeton University Press, 1969), 491-492. Also, the seal of Darius I, whose reign spanned the prophetic periods of Haggai and Zechariah, can be seen at the British Museum. The seal depicts Darius in his chariot (with a driver) shooting a lion with his bow and arrow. Above them is the winged Persian national god, Ahura Mazda.

OLD TESTAMENT PERSONS CONFIRMED BY ARCHAEOLOGY

Person	Scripture	Dates	Reference
King Ahab	1 Kings 16:28-33; 21:1,21; 22:39	9th century BC	Mesha Stele Kurkh Monolith Palace in Samaria
King Ahasuerus (Xerxes I)	Esther 1:1-2	5th century BC	Silver Bowl of Artaxerxes I Palace wall relief at Persepolis (Iran) Elephantine Papyri Tomb at Persepolis
King Ahaz/Achaz	2 Kings 16:2 Matthew 1:9	8th century BC	Stamp seal (bulla)
Ahikam	2 Kings 22:12	7th century BC	Stamp seal (bulla)
Amariah	2 Chronicles 31:15	8th to 7th centuries BC	Stamp seal (bulla)
King Artaxerxes I (Longimanus)	Ezra 4:7; 7:1-21; Nehemiah 2:1; 5:14; 13:6	5th century BC	Silver bowl inscription of Artaxerxes I Elephantine Papyri Tomb at Persepolis
Asaiah	2 Kings 22:12,14 2 Chronicles 34:20		Stamp seal (bulla)
King Ashurbanipal (Osnapper)	Ezra 4:10 2 Chronicles 33:10-13	7th century BC	1,200 texts from the library of Nineveh Stele of Ashurbanipal Nineveh palace reliefs

Person	Scripture	Dates	Reference
Azaliah	2 Kings 22:3	7th century BC	Stamp seal (bulla)
Azzur	Jeremiah 28:1	7th to 6th centuries BC	Stamp seal (bulla)
King Ba'alis	Jeremiah 40:14	6th century BC	Stamp seal (bulla)
Balaam	Numbers 22–24 Jude 11; Revelation 2:14	15th to 14th centuries BC	Balaam Inscription (1967)
Baruch (Jeremiah's scribe)	Jeremiah 32:12-16	7th century BC	Stamp seal (bulla)*
King Belshazzar (son of Nabonidus)	Daniel 5; 7:1; 8:1	6th century BC	Nabonidus Chronicle Cylinder of Nabonidus
Ben Hadad II	2 Kings 8:7-13; 13:1-3	9th century BC	Tell Dan Stele Black Obelisk of Shalmaneser III
King Cyrus II	2 Chronicles 36:22-23 Ezra 1:1-8 Isaiah 44:28; 45:1	6th century BC	Tomb at Pasargadae Cyrus Cylinder Cyrus Brick Inscriptions
King Darius I (son of Hystaspes)	Ezra 4:5,24	6th to 5th centuries BC	Tomb at Persepolis Behistun Inscription Elephantine Papyri
King Darius (the Persian)	Nehemiah 12:22	5th century BC	Silver Bowl of Artaxerxes I Behistun Inscription Palace wall relief at Persepolis (Iran)
King David	1 Samuel 16:13 2 Samuel 5:3-7	10th century BC	Tell Dan Stele Mesha Stele
Eliakim	2 Kings 18:18-37; 19:2	6th century BC	Stamp seal (bulla)
Elishama	Jeremiah 36:12-21	6th century BC	Stamp seal (bulla)

---

* This bulla was identified by the late bulla specialist Nahman Avigad as bearing the name of the prophet Jeremiah's scribe, Baruch, who penned the book of Jeremiah (Jeremiah 36:1-32).

Person	Scripture	Dates	Reference
Elnathan	Ezra 8:16	5th century BC	Stamp seal (bulla)
King Esarhaddon	2 Kings 19:37 Ezra 4:2 Isaiah 37:38	7th century BC	Royal Brick Inscription Esarhaddon Chronicle Stone Prism of Esarhaddon Stone Lion's head with inscription Wall relief of Esarhaddon and Queen Mother Letters of Esarhaddon
King Evil-merodach (Amel Marduk)	2 Kings 25:27 Jeremiah 52:31	6th century BC	Jehoiachin Ration Record
Gedaliah (son of Ahikam)	2 Kings 25:22-25 Jeremiah 39:14; 40:5-16; 41; 43:6	6th century BC	Stamp seal (bulla)
Gedaliah (son of Pashhur)	Jeremiah 38:1	7th to 6th centuries BC	Stamp seal (bulla)
Gemariah	Jeremiah 29:3; 36:10-12,25	6th century BC	Stamp seal (bulla) Lachish Letters?
Name similar to Goliath	1 Samuel 17	11th to 9th centuries BC	Gath Inscription
Hananiah	Jeremiah 28:1	7th to 6th centuries BC	Stamp seal (bulla)
Priestly family name of Immer	Jeremiah 20:1; 38:1	7th to 6th centuries BC	Stamp seal (bulla)*
King Hazael	2 Kings 8:7-15; 12:17	9th century BC	Tell Dan Stele Black Obelisk of Shalmaneser III Gath siege trench Ivory decoration inscription at Khadatu

* This bulla was discovered by archaeologist Gabriel Barkay as a result of sifting the Temple Mount dirt discarded from recent renovations of the Al-Aqsa Mosque. Immer is the name associated with the priestly family that had oversight of the Temple Mount during the time of Jeremiah. Pashhur, the son of Immer, is described in Jeremiah 20:1-18 as the individual who beat Jeremiah and placed him under arrest.

Person	Scripture	Dates	Reference
King Hezekiah	2 Kings 16:20; 18:1-2	8th to 7th centuries BC	Stamp seal (bulla) Annals of Sennacherib Taylor Prism The Azekah Inscription Jerusalem broad wall Water tunnel system
Hilkiah (high priest)	2 Kings 22:4-14; 23:4,24	7th century BC	Stamp seal (bulla)
Pharaoh Hophra (Apries)	Jeremiah 44:30	6th century BC	Herodotus's Histories Tablet reliefs from Abydos Palace at Memphis Babylonian Chronicles
King Hoshea	2 Kings 15:30; 17:1	8th century BC	Stamp seal (bulla) Assyrian records of Tiglath-pileser III
Son of Immer	Jeremiah 20:1	7th to 6th centuries BC	Two stamp seals (bullae)
Jaazaniah	2 Kings 25:23 Jeremiah 40:8	7th to 6th centuries BC	Stamp seal (bulla)
King Jehoahaz (or Shallum)	2 Kings 23:30-34 1 Chronicles 3:15 2 Chronicles 36:1f	7th century BC	Stamp seal (bulla)
King Jehoiachin (Coniah)	2 Kings 24:8-15 2 Chronicles 36:8f Jeremiah 22:24,28; 37:1	6th century BC	Jehoiachin Ration Record Babylonian Chronicles Jar handles stamped with his name at Tell Beit Mirsim and at Beth-Shemesh
King Jehu (or Joram)	1 Kings 19:16-17 2 Kings 9:20; 10:31	9th century BC	Black Obelisk of Shalmaneser III
Jerahmeel	Jeremiah 36:26	7th century BC	Stamp seal (bulla)
Jehucal	Jeremiah 37:3; 38:1	6th century BC	Stamp seal (bulla)
King Jeroboam II (son of Jehoash)	2 Kings 13:13 1 Chronicles 5:17 Amos 1:1; 7:9-11	8th century BC	Stamp seal (bulla)

Person	Scripture	Dates	Reference
Queen Jezebel	1 Kings 16:31; 21 2 Kings 9	9th century BC	Stamp seal (bulla) Palace in Samaria
Joezer and Igdaliah	Jeremiah 35:4 see 1 Chronicles 12:6	7th century BC	Stamp seal (bulla)
King Jotham (son of Uzziah)	2 Kings 15:32	8th century BC	Stamp seal (bulla)
Malchiah	Jeremiah 38:6	7th to 6th cen- turies BC	Stamp seal (bulla)
King Manasseh (son of Hezekiah)	2 Kings 20:21; 21 2 Chronicles 33:10-11	7th century BC	Stamp seal (bulla) Prism B of Esarhaddon
King Menahem	2 Kings 15:14-23	8th century BC	Assyrian records of Tiglath- pileser III
King Merodach- baladan (Babylon)	2 Kings 20:12 Isaiah 39:1	8th century BC	Marble Boundary Stone Annals of Sargon of Assyria Sennacherib Prism
King Mesha (Moab)	2 Kings 3:4	9th century BC	Mesha Stele (a.k.a. Moabite Stone)
Meshullum	2 Kings 22:3	7th century BC	Stamp seal (bulla)
Nathan-melech	2 Kings 23:11	7th century BC	Stamp seal (bulla)
King Nebuchadnezzar (Babylon)	2 Kings 24:1-11 Daniel 1:1; 2; 3; 4:34-37; 5	7th to 6th cen- turies BC	Royal Brick Inscriptions Ishtar Gate Babylonian Chronicles Behistun Inscription East India House Inscription
Pharaoh Necho	2 Chronicles 35:20- 22; 36:4	7th to 6th cen- turies BC	Statues of Necho Herodotus Histories Necho's name removed from monuments by his son Psam- metichus (Psamtik) II
Neriah	Jeremiah 36:32	7th to 6th cen- turies BC	Stamp seal (bulla)

Person	Scripture	Dates	Reference
King Omri	1 Kings 16:16-30 2 Kings 8:26 2 Chronicles 22:2 Micah 6:16	9th century BC	Black Obelisk of Shalmaneser III Mesha Stele
Pedaiah	1 Chronicles 3:18f	6th century BC	Stamp seal (bulla)
King Pekah	2 Kings 15:27	8th century BC	Assyrian records of Tiglath-pileser III
Tiglath-Pileser III (Pul)	2 Kings 15:19,29 1 Chronicles 5:6 2 Chronicles 28:20	8th century BC	Palace wall relief Assyrian records of Tiglath-pileser
Sanballat	Nehemiah 2:10	5th century BC	Elephantine Papyri Stamp seal (bulla)
King Sargon II	Isaiah 20:1	8th century BC	Winged Bull of Sargon II Palace of Sargon (Khorsabad) Annals of Sargon Royal Brick Inscription
Sarsekim	Jeremiah 39:3	6th century BC	Cuneiform tablet at British Museum
King Sennacherib (Assyria)	2 Kings 18:13; 19:16-36 2 Chronicles 32 Isaiah 36:1; 37	8th to 7th centuries BC	Royal Brick Inscriptions Annals of Sennacherib Taylor Prism Sargon's palace reliefs
Seriah	Jeremiah 51:59	7th to 6th centuries BC	Stamp seal (bulla)
Shaphan	2 Kings 22:12	7th century BC	Stamp seal (bulla)
Shebna	2 Kings 18:18-37 Isaiah 22:15-25	8th century BC	Royal Steward (tomb lintel) Inscription
Shelemiah	Jeremiah 37:3	7th to 6th centuries BC	Stamp seal (bulla)
Shelomith	1 Chronicles 3:19	5th century BC	Stamp seal (bulla)

Person	Scripture	Dates	Reference
Pharaoh Shishak (Shoshenq I)	1 Kings 11:40; 14:25 2 Chronicles 12:2-9	10th century BC	Karnak Temple of Amun reliefs
Pharaoh Tirhakah (Taharqa)	2 Kings 19:9 Isaiah 37:9	7th century BC	Statues and Sphinx of Tirhakah Esarhaddon documents
King Uzziah (Azariah)	2 Kings 15:13-34 2 Chronicles 26; 27 Isaiah 6:1	8th century BC	Uzziah Burial Plaque Stamp seal (bulla)
Yahweh	Numbers 6:24-26	9th to 6th centuries BC (dates of references)	House of God Ostracon Ketef Hinnom Amulets (Silver Scrolls) Mesha Stele

© Joseph M. Holden, 2013.

PART SEVEN

ARCHAEOLOGY OF THE NEW TESTAMENT

~

As we have seen, archaeology has contributed much to our understanding of the customs, cultures, laws, practices, events, persons, and lifestyles mentioned in the Old Testament. In like manner, those who approach the New Testament seriously will find that archaeological fieldwork carried out in ancient biblical lands during the past two centuries has provided historical "color" for modern Bible readers. These contributions are seen in several areas relating to apologetics and New Testament studies.

First-century AD Ephesus was one of the largest cities in the Mediterranean world, with a population of possibly up to 500,000. It was known for the worship of the goddess Diana and for its great Temple of Artemis (Diana) and its massive theater (pictured here). Acts 19:21-41 describes the riot that occurred here because of Paul's preaching and the ensuing mob scene in the theater. (Photo by Norman Herr, PD.)

First, *the discovery of cities and landmarks described in the New Testament has firmly secured the historical-geographical reliability and setting for the New Testament narratives*, which supports the believability of the doctrines that grow out of them. For as Jesus said to Nicodemus, "If I have told you earthly things and you do not believe, how can you believe if I tell you heavenly things?" (John 3:12 ESV). If the New Testament had said that Jesus went "up" to the waters of the Dead Sea from Jerusalem, we would not consider the text a credible geographical description, since Jerusalem is nestled in the hill country and the Dead Sea is nearly 1,300 feet below sea level (it is the lowest place on earth). Whenever the Bible mentions mountains, hills, rivers, wilderness, valleys, cities, lakes, and seas, archaeology has in many cases confirmed them. Cities such as Capernaum, Caesarea Philippi, Jerusalem, Caesarea, Philippi, Corinth, Thessalonica, Athens, and a multitude of others have been excavated sufficiently to offer us corroboration of biblical place names and a glimpse of everyday life in the first century and earlier.

Second, *archaeological data has helped limit the critical theories that dismiss the New Testament as mythological*; instead, the data has placed the biblical text squarely within a historical framework. Discoveries such as the Pool of Siloam (John 9) and Pool of Bethesda (John 5:2), the Temple Mount, the Mount of Olives; inscriptions of the names of various biblical rulers such as Tiberius, Pontius Pilate, Herod, Quirinius (Luke 2:2), Gallio (Acts 18:12), Sergius Paulus (Acts 13:6-7), and Erastus (Romans 16:23); and Emperor Claudius's expulsion of the Jews from Rome (Acts 18:2) continue to be facts that keep the New Testament anchored in a historical-geographical setting. No longer can the fertile imaginations and theories of critical scholars run unchecked by the archaeological data.

The apostle Paul's first missionary contact on the European continent was at Philippi (Acts 16:11-40), located about ten miles east of the ancient seaport of Neapolis (Acts 16:11; modern-day Kavalla). The sprawling city at Philippi, named after the father of Alexander the Great, Philip II, attests to a thriving Roman colony in the eastern territory of Macedonia. The ruins pictured here boast an amphitheater (in background) that was used during Paul's day and a masonry crypt that is believed, though without support, to be the prison of Paul and Silas.

Third, *our understanding of the religious climate immediately prior, during, and after the New Testament period has been greatly enhanced by the documentary finds unearthed in the 1940s.* These include the Nag Hammadi (Gnostic) texts discovered in Egypt, the Dead Sea Scrolls found in 11 caves at the Dead Sea Settlement of Qumran, and the hundreds of early Greek New Testament texts. The assortment of finds have touched on various areas relating to biblical studies, shedding light on the development of Judaism during the intertestamental period (that is, the time between the end of the Old Testament and the beginning of the New Testament), Christianity during the first century, and Gnostic beliefs in the second century. These finds have contributed to knowledge of Jewish sectarian belief and messianic expectations prior and during the time of Christ, early Christian belief and distinct messianic portraits found in the Gospels, and the heretical development of Christian belief in the Gnostic texts. Moreover, the Hebrew and Greek texts of these documents have significantly aided researchers in their linguistic analysis of the Bible texts.

Archaeological research in Bible lands has been very slow to accumulate. Of the nearly 5,500 sites in Israel that are candidates for excavation, only a few hundred have been excavated. Moreover, there are thousands more sites in the Fertile Crescent (Mesopotamia) that have been considered valuable candidates for archaeological research. However, time, politics, and funds are always key factors that determine where and when (and if) these sites can be examined in any systematic way. Despite these slow advances, the material data unearthed to date has shown a remarkable consistency with the New Testament, corroborating people, places, structures, customs, ruling figures, and their official titles. The remainder of this part will survey numerous finds relating to Jesus and the people of the New Testament.

Jesus and Other New Testament Persons in Non-Christian Sources

Though Jesus dominates the pages of the New Testament there is little *direct* hard archaeological data mentioning His name or ministry. This has led some critical scholars in the past to dismiss Him as a historical figure. Still others, such as the English logician and philosopher Bertrand Russell in his *Why I Am Not a Christian*, believe that Jesus lived but did not accomplish all the things mentioned about Him in the Gospels. Russell adds that Christ was not the best and wisest of all men, but would grant Him a very high degree of moral goodness.

For the most part, Russell's opinion characterizes the vast majority of opinions concerning the historicity of Christ. Despite these attempts, arguments denying the existence of Jesus of Nazareth have fallen out of favor due to the growing body of documentary evidence from Jewish and Greco-Roman sources that speak of Jesus and the events surrounding His life and ministry. From these early non-Christian sources (Flavius Josephus, the Babylonian Talmud, Pliny the Younger, Tacitus, Mara Bar-Serapion, Suetonius, Thallus, Lucian, Phlegon, and Celsus) we may reconstruct the salient features of the life of Christ without appealing to the New Testament. These features include the following:

1. Jesus lived during the reign of Tiberius Caesar.
2. He lived a virtuous life.
3. He was a wonder-worker.
4. He had a brother named James.
5. He was claimed to be the Messiah.
6. He was crucified under Pontius Pilate.
7. He was crucified on the eve of Passover.

8. Darkness and an earthquake occurred when He died.

9. His disciples believed He rose from the dead.

10. His disciples were willing to die for their belief.

11. Christianity spread as far as Rome.

12. Christian disciples denied the Roman gods and worshipped Jesus as God.

If Jesus was an actual figure of history, we would expect some evidence to be left behind by early historians and chroniclers. Indeed, this is exactly what scholars have discovered. From these discoveries emerge over 30 New Testament individuals (including Jesus) mentioned in Scripture who have been corroborated as historical figures by non-Christian sources, some of which, naturally, have more credibility than others.

Documentary References to Jesus

Following is a survey of the more prominent documentary references to Christ.

Titus Flavius Josephus

The first-century AD Jewish historian was educated in law and history. After surrendering to Vespasian's Roman army in AD 70 at Jotapata, Josephus was quickly employed by the Roman government to be the spokesman and translator for Emperor Titus. In the early 90s, Josephus wrote his *Antiquities of the Jews*, which contain several statements about Christ, including a passage describing the judicial session convened by "Annas" where James "the brother of Jesus the so-called Christ" was charged before the Sanhedrin "and handed over to be stoned to death."[1] Josephus adds another reference to Christ, known as the "Testimonium Flavianium," when he writes,

> About this time arose Jesus, a wise man (if indeed it be right to call him a man). For he was a doer of marvelous deeds, and a teacher of men who gladly receive the truth. He drew to himself many persons, both of the Jews and also the Gentiles. (He was the Christ.) And when Pilate, upon the indictment of leading men among us, had condemned him to the cross, those who had loved him at the first did not cease to do so (for he appeared to them alive on the third day—the godly prophets having foretold these and ten thousand other things about him). And even to this day the race of Christians, who are named from him, has not died out.[2]

It is important to note that the genuineness of Josephus's words has been challenged by some, since it would be doubtful that a non-Christian Jew would write about Jesus in this manner.* Some have suggested the passage as it stands above contains interpolations by later Christian writers. It is argued that descriptions such as "if indeed it be right to call him a man," "he was the Christ," and "for he appeared to them alive on the third

---

* See Origen's *Contra Celsum*, 1:47, which tells us that Josephus did not believe Jesus to be the Messiah.

day—the godly prophets having foretold these and ten thousand other things about him" are uncharacteristic of Josephus.

Analysis of the passage has confirmed the core historical nature of the Testimonium, though some scholars still believe there has been a slight degree of tampering. After an examination of the text by Josephan scholars such as Steven Mason and Christopher Price,[3] and by historical apologist Gary Habermas,[4] there emerge several reasons why the genuineness of the passage can be maintained:

1. There is no precedent for Christian copyists fabricating whole stories.

2. An examination of the Syriac, Arabic, and Greek, and the texts of Ambrose and Jerome, affirm the passage as possessing an authentic core. According to Schlomo Pines, the tenth-century AD Arabic text titled *Kitab al-Unwan* contains the core passage without the disputed phrases.[5]

3. There is no textual evidence against Josephan authorship of the passage since it is written in the style of Josephus.

4. Josephus makes no connection between John the Baptist (also mentioned in *Antiquities of the Jews,* 18) and Jesus, an association Christian interpolators would certainly do.

5. Even if the disputed phrases identified above were removed from the text, there would still remain a core historical passage identifying Jesus that is supported by most scholars.[6]

6. The passage fits the context both historically and grammatically.

7. The mention of Jesus in *Antiquities of the Jews,* 20 in relation to James seems to presuppose an earlier mention of Jesus, which one would assume to be the Testimonium in *Antiquities of the Jews,* 18.

Distinguished New Testament scholar F.F. Bruce said of the text, "There is nothing to say against the passage on the ground of textual criticism; the manuscript evidence is as unanimous and ample as it is for anything in Josephus."[7]

The Testimonium Flavianum is a valuable witness to Christ's life, death, and remarkable influence. It clearly declares, despite the Christian interpolations, that Jesus was known to be wise and of good moral conduct (virtuous); that He had Jewish and Gentile disciples, that Pilate condemned Him to be crucified, and that His disciples reported that Jesus had risen three days later, and that this was something the prophets had foretold.

The Babylonian Talmud

In addition to the Jewish writers of the New Testament and Josephus, the Talmud is another early Jewish, but non-Christian, witness to Jesus. Compiled between AD 70 and 200 during what some call the *Tannaitic Period* (from *Tannaim,* the scribal group responsible for transmitting the Scripture at the time), the Talmud mentions Jesus in an early tractate (*Sanhedrin* 43a). It declares that "Jesus was hanged on Passover Eve" and "he [Jesus] practiced sorcery and led Israel astray and enticed them into apostasy." Also, it asserts, "As nothing was brought forward in his defence, he was hanged...." It continues in the same tractate that "Jesus...was near to the kingship" (probably a reference to His descent from David) and early rabbis taught that "Jesus had five disciples...."

Some rabbis have attempted to argue against the historical features in this tractate as referring to the Jesus of the New Testament, claiming that the compilers of the Talmud were simply reacting to the much earlier Gospel portrayals of Jesus as receiving an unfair trial, and the tractate has actually nothing to do with Jesus' historicity.[8] According to these critics, many of the features do not line up with the biblical record, such as Jesus being "hanged" rather than crucified. However, these arguments seem unconvincing for several reasons.

First, Jesus is attested in at least nine other historical documents besides the Gospels, and therefore, independent historical corroboration exists that Jesus was indeed historical.

Second, if the descriptions of Jesus were not historical, the Talmud could have simply denied the historical nature of the "unfair trial." But such a denial is absent from the Talmudic text.

Third, Habermas explains that "hanged" is used of Christ's crucifixion (Galatians 3:13, *kremamenos*) and is the same root term applied to the two malefactors crucified with Jesus (Luke 23:39, *kremasthenton*).[9] Though *stauros* is the more common word used for crucifixion (Matthew 27:31), *kremamenos* (hanged) is an adequate term for the same manner of death.[10]

Though other references to Jesus in the Talmud are of much later origin and of questionable historical value, the mentioning of Jesus in this early tractate of the Talmud by those who opposed His ministry offers corroboration of the biblical testimony.

Cornelius Tacitus

A Roman historian, Tacitus (c. AD 56–117) wrote concerning the affairs of several Roman emperors in his *Annals of Imperial Rome* (AD 108). He is best known for his record of how Emperor Nero responded to Christians after the great fire in Rome—specifically, how Nero attempted to extricate himself from a report that he was responsible for the fire. Some of his entries record events involving Christians, including Christ Himself. He writes of this event in the *Annals*, 15.44:

> To suppress this rumour, Nero fabricated scapegoats—and punished with every refinement the notoriously depraved Christians (as they were popularly called). Their originator, Christ, had been executed in Tiberius' reign by the governor of Judea, Pontius Pilate. But in spite of this temporary setback the deadly superstition had broken out afresh, not only in Judea (where the mischief had started) but even in Rome. All degraded and shameful practices collect and flourish in Rome. First, Nero had self-acknowledged Christians arrested. Then, on their information, large

numbers of others were condemned—not so much for incendiarism [that is, arson] as for their anti-social tendencies. Their deaths were made farcical. Dressed in wild animal skins, they were torn to pieces by dogs, or crucified, or made into torches to be ignited after dark as substitutes for daylight. Nero provided his gardens for the spectacle, and exhibited displays in the circus, at which he mingled with the crowd—or stood in a chariot, dressed as a charioteer. Despite their guilt as Christians, and the ruthless punishment it deserved, the victims were pitied. For it was felt that they were being sacrificed to one man's brutality rather than to the national interest.[11]

In addition to providing the rich body of information that confirms the life of Christ, as well as His death at the hand of Pontius Pilate during the reign of Tiberius, Tacitus apparently possessed knowledge of the destruction of Jerusalem in AD 70 by the Romans. According to Habermas, this information was originally penned in Tacitus's *Histories* but, having unfortunately been mostly lost, is now found in the records of Sulpicius Severus (*Chronicles* 2:30.6).[12]

Gaius Suetonius Tranquillus

As the leading secretary of Emperor Hadrian (AD 117–138), the Roman historian known commonly as Suetonius wrote two brief statements referencing Christ and Christians. First, "Because the Jews at Rome caused continuous disturbances at instigation of *Chrestus*, he [Emperor Claudius] expelled them from the city."[13] This historical nugget is consistent with Acts 18:2, where we are told that Priscilla and Aquila were among those expelled from Rome by Claudius.* In addition, Suetonius refers to Nero's persecution of Christians: "Punishments were also inflicted on the Christians, a sect professing a new and mischievous religious belief."[14]

From these statements we understand that there was an acceptance of the existence of a man named *Chrestus* (Christ) in the first century; that some Jews caused disturbances related to Christ (severe enough for Claudius to expel every Jew from Rome in AD 49); that Christianity was unique (new); and that Christians were persecuted (see Acts 26:9-11).

Pliny the Younger (Gaius Plinius Secundus)

Pliny was an imperial legate in the Roman province of Bithynia (in Asia Minor at the southwest corner of the Black Sea). One of his letters (c. AD 112) to Emperor Trajan describes the economic and social problems involving Christians, along with some of their unique worship practices. In *Letters,* 10:96, Pliny writes,

They [Christians] were in the habit of meeting on a certain fixed day

---

* Suetonius, "Claudius," 25:4, in *The Twelve Caesars*, tr. Robert Graves (Baltimore, MD: Penguin, 1957). *Chrestus* is an alternative spelling of *Christ*; Habermas agrees and views it as the same Latinized spelling that Tacitus uses. H. Wayne House sees *Chrestus* as a Latin variant of the Greek *Christos*.

before it was light, when they sang in alternate verses a hymn to Christ, as to a god, and bound themselves by a solemn oath, not to do any wicked deeds, but never to commit any fraud, theft or adultery, never to falsify their word, nor deny a trust when they should be called upon to deliver it up; after which it was their custom to separate, and then reassemble to partake of food—but food of an ordinary and innocent kind.

We learn from Pliny's passage that Christianity had reached Bithynia, that Christians regularly met together, that worship was offered to Christ in recognition of His deity, and that the Christians were bound to a high moral code and regularly partook of a common meal. Later in Pliny's letter we learn there was a rapid increase in the Christian population in Bithynia and Pontus (the province to the east); this growth threatened the pagan temples, which were mostly going unpatronized, and those who profited from the sale of pagan religious images; and that genuine Christians could not be made to renounce their faith even under the penalty of death.

Emperor Trajan's reply to Pliny asserted that "no search should be made" for Christians, but when guilty Christians are discovered they are to be punished for not worshipping the Roman gods. In support of the historical events found in these letters, the early Church Father Tertullian mentions the interaction between Pliny and Trajan, recounting essentially the same information found in Pliny's letters.[15] Those who repented of their Christianity by worshipping Roman gods might be pardoned and released. Only when Pliny has punished (executed and imprisoned) enough Christians does he write of the people's return to the pagan worship system in his province.

Further, we learn from fourth-century Christian historian Eusebius that Emperor Hadrian wrote to his representative in the province of Asia, Minicius Fundanus, allowing the punishment of Christians in a more temperate way.[16]

Mara Bar-Serapion

Sometime between the late first and early third century, the Syrian Mara Bar-Serapion writes to his son Serapion describing the senselessness of the Jewish plot to kill Jesus when he asserts, "What advantage did the Jews gain from executing their wise king? It was just after that their kingdom was abolished."[17] From this text we learn that Jesus was considered by many to be the king of Israel, that He was killed by His own countrymen, and that the Jews were dispersed from their land.

Thallus, Phlegon, and Lucian

Thallus (*Histories*), Phlegon (*Chronicles*), and Lucian (*The Death of Pelegrine*) write of the various cosmic disturbances, earthquakes, and darkness and the crucifixion and Jesus' postresurrection appearances.

Though the works of Thallus (who wrote a history of the eastern Mediterranean world from the Trojan War to his own time—AD 52) are no longer extant, Julius Africanus (AD 221) preserves the words written in the third book of Thallus's *History*:

On the whole world there pressed a most fearful darkness; and the rocks were rent by an earthquake, and many places in Judea and other districts were thrown down. This darkness Thallus, in the third book of his *History* calls, as appears to me without reason, an eclipse of the sun.[18]

Both Julius Africanus (*Extant Writings*, 18) and Origen in his *Against Celsus* confirm Phlegon's record of Christ's death and resurrection in the latter's no longer extant *Chronicles*. Origen states of the resurrection,

Jesus, while alive, was of no assistance to himself, but that he arose after death and exhibited the marks of his punishment, and showed how his hands had been pierced by nails.[19]

Origen continues with his description of the cosmic disturbances at Christ's crucifixion when he reports, "And with regard to the eclipse in the time of Tiberius Caesar, in whose reign Jesus appears to have been crucified, and the great earthquakes which then took place, Phlegon too, I think, has written in the thirteenth or fourteenth book of his *Chronicles*."[20]

Lucian of Samosata, a second-century AD Greek writer critical of Christianity wrote in *The Death of Peregrine*,

The Christians, you know, worship a man to this day—the distinguished personage who introduced their novel writes, and was crucified on that account....You see, these misguided creatures start with the general conviction that they are immortal for all time, which explains the contempt of death and voluntary self-devotion which are so common among them; and then it was impressed on them by their original lawgiver that they are all brothers, from the moment they are converted, and deny the gods of Greece, and worship the crucified sage, and live after his laws. All this they take quite on faith, with the result that they despise all worldly goods alike, regarding them merely as common property.[21]

Toledoth Jesu

This late-fifth-century anti-Christian document contains an early Jewish tradition that describes thwarting of the disciples' attempt to move the body of Jesus. This document tells of the preemptive reburial of Jesus in a newly dug grave prior to the disciples stealing the body by an individual who later gave the body to the Jewish religious leaders. The common notion that Jesus' body was stolen was one of the earliest explanations of the resurrection (Matthew 28:11-15). Second-century apologist Justin Martyr (AD 150) and Tertullian (AD 200) confirm the fact that the Jewish leaders had sent special envoys of trained individuals to further the Toledoth Jesu theory even as far as Rome and surrounding territories.[22]

The Acts of Pontius Pilate

Writing about AD 150, Justin Martyr refers to Christ in his *First Apology* and sources the facts surrounding His crucifixion to a now-lost government document known as the *Acts of Pontius Pilate*:

> And the expression, "They pierced my hands and my feet," was used in reference to the nails of the cross which were fixed in His hands and feet. And after He was crucified they cast lots upon His vesture, and they that crucified Him parted it among them. And that these things did happen, you can ascertain from the Acts of Pontius Pilate.[23]

Later in the same work, Justin again mentions the *Acts of Pontius Pilate* as a source to confirm the miraculous signs foretold by the prophets and performed by Christ. He writes,

> ...and that it was predicted that our Christ should heal all diseases and raise the dead, hear what was said. There are these words: "At His coming the lame shall leap as an hart, and the tongue of the stammerer shall be clear speaking: the blind shall see, and the lepers shall be cleansed; and the dead shall rise, and walk about." And that He did those things, you can learn from the Acts of Pontius Pilate.[24]

It is important to note that Pilate's records mentioned here are not to be confused with a later document that bears a similar name. Since there are no surviving manuscripts of this earlier, imperial document and it is not widely referenced, we would naturally be reserved in our use of this source.

Other Non-Christian References to New Testament Individuals

Other New Testament individuals besides Jesus are also mentioned in early non-Christian sources. (Some of these persons are discussed in more detail in the chapters that follow.) The following chart concludes this chapter by summarizing these sources, including those for Jesus discussed above and others mentioning Him.

New Testament Persons Cited in Ancient Non-Christian Sources

Person	Scripture Reference	Source
Herod Agrippa I and II	Acts 12; 23:35 Acts 25:13-26; 26	Philo, Josephus Coin inscriptions Nabatean Inscription Beirut Museum Inscription
Ananias (high priest)	Acts 23:2; 24:1	Josephus
Annas (high priest)	Luke 3:2; Acts 4:6; John 18:13,24	Josephus
Herod Antipas	Matthew 14:1-6 Mark 6:14-22 Luke 3:1 Acts 4:27; 13:1	Josephus Coin inscriptions that read "Herod the Tetrarch"
Herod Archelaus	Matthew 2:22	Josephus
King Aretas IV (Damascus)	2 Corinthians 11:32	Josephus Madaba Map Inscription Coins with Aretas bust
Caesar Augustus (Octavius)	Luke 2:1	Priene Inscription announcing birthday Coin Inscriptions Funerary Inscription (*Res Gestae Divi Augusti*)
Bernice	Acts 25:13-15	Josephus Suetonius Beirut Museum Inscription
Caiaphas (high priest)		Josephus Ossuary inscription
Emperor Claudius	Acts 11:28; 18:2	Josephus Suetonius Tacitus Coin inscriptions
Drusilla	Acts 24:24	Josephus Suetonius
Erastus	Romans 16:13-23; 2 Timothy 4:20	Erastus Inscription at Corinth
Marcus Antonius Felix	Acts 23:24-26; 24; 25:14	Josephus Suetonius Tacitus

Person	Scripture Reference	Source
Porcius Festus	Acts 24:27; 25; 26:24,32	Josephus
Gallio	Acts 18:12-17	Gallio Inscription at Delphi Pliny the Younger Suetonius
Gamaliel	Acts 5:34; 22:3	Josephus Jewish Mishnah Talmud
King Herod (Judea)	Matthew 2:1-22; Luke 1:5	Josephus Tacitus Coin inscriptions Herod's tomb at the Herodium Latin wine jug inscription Herodian architecture (for example, Temple Mount, Masada, Machaerus, the Herodium, and so on)
Herodias	Matthew 14:3; Mark 6:17	Josephus
James (son of Mary)	Acts 12:17; 21:18; epistle of James	James Ossuary
James (son of Zebedee)	Matthew 4:21; 10:2; Mark 5:37	Josephus
Jesus (of Nazareth)	Gospels	Josephus Tacitus Suetonius Pliny the Younger Lucian Babylonian Talmud Mara Bar-Serapion Toledoth Jesu James Ossuary Inscription Megiddo Mosaic Floor Inscription Alexamenos Graffito (picture)
John the Baptist	Matthew 3:1-13; Luke 1:7-39	Josephus Baptismal site (and steps) in Jordan at Jordan River
Joseph (adoptive father of Jesus)	Matthew 1:20	James Ossuary
Judas the Galilean	Acts 5:37	Josephus

Person	Scripture Reference	Source
Lysanias	Luke 3:1	Josephus Stone Inscription at Abila (northern Morocco)
Herod Philip I (of Iturea)	Luke 3:1	Josephus
Herod Philip II (of Galilee)	Matthew 14:3; Mark 6:17; Luke 3:19	Josephus Coin inscriptions
Pontius Pilate	Luke 23:7,22; John 18:31	Josephus Tacitus Philo Coins minted during his reign Pilate Dedication Stone Inscription
Quirinius (Publius Sulpicius)	Luke 2:2	Josephus Tacitus Res Gestae Inscription at Antioch Pisidia
Salome ("daughter of Herodias")	Matthew 14:6	Josephus
Sergius Paulus	Acts 13:7	Two stone inscriptions (Cyprus and Rome) L. Sergius Paulus Inscription (Pisidian Antioch, Turkey)
Theudas	Acts 5:36	Josephus
Tiberius Caesar	Luke 3:1	Josephus Tacitus Suetonius Marcus Velleius Paterculus Coin inscriptions Mentioned on Pilate dedication stone (Caesarea)

23

JESUS AND ARCHAEOLOGICAL SOURCES

The strong documentary evidence offers formidable support for the existence, life, death, and ministry of Jesus. However, *direct* archaeological corroboration for Jesus is admittedly rare. Despite this, recent finds have added valuable confirmation of Christ in various ways.

The Megiddo Mosaic Inscription

In 2005, inmates at the maximum security prison located at Megiddo, Israel, accidently unearthed an ancient church-floor mosaic measuring 16 x 32 feet. Its inscription

Greek mosaic floor inscription mentioning "the God Jesus Christ," discovered in Megiddo. (Photo by Zev Radovan.)

describes a table offered to Christ by a female worshipper named "Akeptous." The ornate Greek inscription, laid out in small mosaic tiles, makes reference "to the God Jesus Christ" and that the table was offered to Jesus "as a memorial." The phrase "God Jesus Christ" has been over-lined (instead of the traditional underlining) for emphasis, and confirms the notion that early Christians affirmed the deity of Christ. This find has also attested to the spread and acceptance of Christianity within the borders of Israel and the surrounding Mediterranean regions. Astonishingly, the mosaic floor with its inscription has been dated to the third century AD, making it part of what many believe to be the oldest church yet discovered in the Holy Land.

The Alexamenos Graffito

A carving depicting the manner in which early Romans viewed Christianity and its Jewish savior, Jesus, was found in 1857 on Palatine Hill in Rome.* An instance of graffiti (known as a *graffito*) depicting a Christian worshipper of Jesus on the cross was discovered, though its original exact location is somewhat uncertain. Everett Ferguson in his *Backgrounds of Early Christianity*, says it was "scratched on a stone in a guard room on Palatine Hill near the Circus Maximus in Rome."[1] Orazio Marucchi, in the *Catholic Encyclopedia*, says, "On a beam in the *Pædagogium* on the Palatine there was discovered a *graffito* on the plaster, showing a man with an ass's head, and clad in a perizoma (or short loin-cloth) and fastened to a *crux immissa* (regular Latin cross)."[2] Last of all, Graydon Sny-

Alexamenos Graffito. (Photo from Rodolfo Lanciani:, *Ancient Rome in Light of Recent Discoveries*, 1898; PD.)

der, in *Ante Pacem: Archaeological Evidence of Church Life Before Constantine*, places the location of discovery "in the servants' quarters of the Imperial Palace."[3] The exact location is thus uncertain, though the original guardroom may have been used later for a school; thus the individual authors may be referring to the same location.

This *graffito*, which is now located in the Kircherian Museum in Rome, depicts an early Christian named Alexamenos worshipping at the feet of a man on a cross who has the head of a donkey. There is what appears to be the Greek letter Y (upsilon). At the left of the drawing is a young man who apparently is Alexamenos; his name is scrawled on the plaster. His hand is raised in an act of worship, it is assumed. The reading of the *graffito* is as follows:*

---

* This discussion of the Alexamenos Graffito is adapted from material provided by Dr. H. Wayne House. Used by permission.

ΑΛΕ (ALE)

ΞΑΜΕΝΟΣ (XAMENOS)

ΣΕΒΕΤΕ (SEBETE)

ΘΕΟΝ (THEON)

A literal translation is problematic if σεβετε (*sebete*) is understood as a second-person imperative, because it would need to be translated "Alexamenos, worship God!" though it could be a second-person indicative, therefore "Alexamenos, you are worshipping (your) God." If the word is spelled incorrectly,[4] and should read σεβεται, it could be a third-person middle indicative and be translated "Alexamenos is worshipping (his) God."[5] Why the word for *worship* is written as a plural rather than a singular is uncertain, but most agree that the text should read "Alexamenos worships God" or "Alexamenos worships (his) God."

That Christians were accused of worshipping an ass's head may be seen in the words of the late second-century apologist Tertullian. He indicates that both Christians and Jews were accused of worshipping a god with a donkey's head,[6] and even mentions that a certain Jew carried a caricature around Carthage that had a Christian with a donkey's ears and hooves, entitled *Deus Christianorum Onocoetes* ("the God of the Christians begotten of a donkey"). *

This graffito is an important attestation to the fact that early Christians worshipped Jesus as God, were the targets of slander and ridicule, and used the crucifix in their worship, at least by the third century. This latter, crucial aspect supports the Gospel statements describing crucifixion as the manner by which Christ died, a method of capital punishment that has been previously disputed.[7] As Marucchi rightly says, "It would not have been possible for Alexamenos's companion to trace [draw] the *graffito*

The Yehohanan Ossuary with inscription contained the ossified bones of a first-century crucifixion victim. (Photo by Zev Radovan.)

of a crucified person clad in the *perizoma* (which was contrary to Roman usage) if he had not seen some such figure made use of by the Christians."[8]

---

* Tertullian's text reads, "But lately a new edition of our god has been given to the world in that great city: it originated with a certain vile man who was wont to hire himself out to cheat the wild beasts, and who exhibited a picture with this inscription: The God of the Christians, born of an ass. He had the ears of an ass, was hoofed in one foot, carried a book, and wore a toga. Both the name and the figure gave us amusement. But our opponents ought straightway to have done homage to this biformed divinity, for they have acknowledged gods dog-headed and lion-headed, with horn of buck and ram, with goat-like loins, with serpent legs, with wings sprouting from back or foot" (Alexander Roberts et al., *The Ante-Nicene Fathers,* vol. III: "Translations of the Writings of the Fathers Down to A.D. 325" [Oak Harbor, WA: Logos Research Systems, 1997], 31).

The Yehohanan Ossuary

That Christ died by crucifixion, and that the Romans practiced this form of capital punishment in the first century AD during the life of Christ, is now well-attested. This is supported by our understanding of history spanning from the sixth century BC to fourth century AD; namely, that this type of punishment was used by the Persians, Carthaginians, and the Romans, only to be abolished in the fourth century by Emperor Constantine.

First-century AD ossified heel bone with Roman crucifixion nail, belonging to a crucifixion victim identified as Yehohanan ben Hagkol. (Photo by Zev Radovan.)

Moreover, a limestone ossuary (an 18-inch-long stone box for the storing of bones of the deceased) was discovered in Jerusalem in 1968 that contained the bones of a first-century AD crucifixion victim named Yehohanan ben Hagkol. Upon examination, the right heel and wrist bone still contained the Roman seven-inch spikes intact, thus attesting the Roman practice during the first century when Christ was reported to have been crucified (Matthew 27; Mark 15; Luke 23; John 19; see also Psalm 22).

The James Ossuary

One of the earliest and most important discoveries relating to the historicity of Jesus and members of his family is the limestone bone box (called an *ossuary*) made known to the public in October 2002.[9] Ossuaries were used in Israel from about the second

James Ossuary. (Photo by Zev Radovan.)

century BC until the fall of Jerusalem in AD 70. Over 10,000 such ossuaries have been discovered, but only about 100 contain inscriptions. Of these, only two have an identification similar to the one etched in the now famous and somewhat controversial "James Ossuary." The entire Aramaic inscription reads, "Jacob (James), son of Joseph, brother of Jesus" (*Ya'akov bar Yosef akhui di Yeshua*).

If, in fact, the inscription in its entirety is recognized as authentic (which we believe to be the case), we have clear first-century AD testimony of Jesus, His father, Joseph, and brother James. James (*Ya'akov*) is given in the Gospel accounts as a brother of Jesus (Matthew 13:55), but he is also one of the most important figures in the New Testament. The book of Acts reveals that he was the leader of the Jerusalem church and the moderator of the Jerusalem Council in Acts 15; he also penned the epistle of James. He is also spoken of a number of times in the writings of Josephus. He was put to death by certain Jewish leaders in AD 62, so if the James Ossuary is the one in which his bones were placed, then the dating of the bone box would be approximately AD 62 or 63, allowing time for the reburial of the bones after the decomposition of the flesh, according to Jewish practices.

Aramaic inscription that reads, "James, son of Joseph, brother of Jesus." (Photo by Zev Radovan.)

In December 2004, the Israeli Antiquities Authority (IAA) and the State of Israel brought an indictment against Oded Golan, an antiquities dealer and owner of the James Ossuary, claiming that the second part of the inscription, the portion which reads "brother of Jesus," was a forgery. This indictment seems to have come to nothing after five years of court proceedings, which concluded in March 2010 after 116 hearings involving 138 witnesses, 52 expert witnesses, over 400 exhibits, and more than 12,000 pages of court transcripts!* According to Golan's written summary of the trial (supported by the 474-page Hebrew-language opinion handed down by Jerusalem District Court Judge

---

* Oded Golan, "The Authenticity of the James Ossuary and the Jehoash Tablet Inscriptions—Summary of Expert Trial Witnesses" (March 2011), 1. The trial was brought to an end on March 14, 2012, when Jerusalem District Court Judge Aharon Farkash cleared the defendants (Oded Golan, Robert Deutsch, et al.) of *all* forgery charges (see Judge Farkash's 474-page opinion in the case). The clearing of the forgery charges shows that the prosecution failed to demonstrate that the inscription was a forgery. As a result, there is no reason to doubt that the inscription in its entirety is an authentic description of Jesus and His family. This conclusion is supported by dozens of expert witnesses and the script analysis offered by Andre Lemaire (Sorbonne) and Ada Yardeni (Hebrew University of Jerusalem), which gave them no reason to doubt the authenticity of the inscription (see appendix C for a summary of the expert witness testimony). There is yet to be offered a reputable paleographical challenge to their conclusions on the matter. See Hershel Shanks, ed., *James Brother of Jesus: The Forgery Trial of the Century* (Washington DC: Biblical Archaeology Society, 2012).

Aharon Farkash on March 14, 2012), many high-level scholars with expertise in ancient epigraphy, paleography, biogeology, and other crucial disciplines relating to examining the inscription have testified that there is no reason to doubt that the phrase "brother of Jesus" was engraved in the first century AD by the same hand that engraved the rest of it. In view of this, it is very likely that we may have a very early and important historical witness to Jesus and His family.* A summary of the arguments for and against the authenticity of the inscription is given below.

Arguments Against the Authenticity of the James Ossuary

1. The ossuary was not discovered in situ, within a secure archaeological context, but rather obtained through the antiquities trade.

2. Though the bone box itself and the first half of the inscription are not contested, arguments that the second half of the inscription ("brother of Jesus") was recently engraved (forged) and was not completed by the same hand have been posited due to the absence of natural occurring patina.† (Patina is a thin layer of biogenic material expected to be present on most, if not all, ancient artifacts to some degree. It is caused by the continuous secretions and activities of microorganisms such as bacteria, fungi, algae, and yeast on the stone and inside some of its grooves. If the same consistency of patina is equally distributed on the ossuary and found within the engraved grooves, it would suggest the authenticity of the inscription. The absence of patina within the disputed portion of the inscription would suggest a forgery or modern engraving of letters.)

3. The foundation of the IAA's case against Oded Golan was based on an eyewitness (Joe Zias, an anthropologist formerly employed by the IAA) who claimed to have previously seen the ossuary without the "brother of Jesus" portion of the inscription.

Arguments for the Authenticity of the James Ossuary[10]

1. The size of the ossuary indicates that the bones belonged to an adult male, thus being consistent with James.

---

* Only Protestants would consider James to be the half-brother of Jesus through Joseph and Mary, since both the Roman Catholic Church and Eastern Orthodox Churches believe that Mary remained a perpetual virgin. Roman Catholics consider James and the other brothers and sisters of Jesus in the Gospels to be cousins of Jesus through a supposed brother of Joseph. On the other hand, the Eastern Church believes that James and the other siblings were stepbrothers and stepsisters of Jesus born to Joseph from a former wife.

† After testing the ossuary, clay specialist Professor Yuval Goren of Tel Aviv University initially championed the idea that ancient patina was missing from the second half of the inscription and that the forger must have used some other bonding substance or else this was a result of cleaning the inscription. However, subsequent examination of the inscription by Orna Cohen of the prosecution team revealed ancient patina in the word *Jesus*, thus discrediting Goren's testimony; this led Goren to reverse his initial conclusions.

2. In 2004, while the ossuary was in IAA possession, the forensics department of the Israel police (Mazap) made a silicon impression (cast) of the inscription that contaminated and mutilated it. When the silicon was removed it also removed the naturally occurring patina, but despite this action, traces of the patina were still present in several of the letter grooves, indicating that the inscription is indeed ancient.

3. The name on the ossuary (James) reveals that the person was a male.

4. Ossuaries were used by Jews only in the area of Jerusalem and from the end of the first century BC until AD 70, the same time period that Josephus tells of the death of James at the hands of the Jewish religious leaders.

5. Of those ossuaries bearing an inscription, almost all speak of the deceased occupant's father, and occasionally of the person's brother, sister, or other close relative if that person was well-known. The rare presence of a sibling's name (Jesus) would indicate that Jesus was a very prominent figure.

6. Specialist and archaeologist Professor Amos Kloner dates the ossuary to between AD 45 and 70, thus consistent with the death of James in AD 62 according to Josephus.

7. Though the names Joseph, James, and Jesus are common names in the first century, the combination "James, son of Joseph" is rare and unique to this ossuary, meaning that it is highly probable that the bone box belongs to James, Jesus' brother, even without the second half of the inscription mentioning this.

8. Professor Camil Fuchs, head of the statistics department at Tel Aviv University, researched deceased males in Jerusalem in the first century AD. He concluded (based on conservative estimates of a growing Jerusalem population between AD 6 and 70, minus all women, minus children who would not have reached manhood by the time of James's death, minus non-Jews, and considering the fame of Jesus as a brother to warrant the inscription, time of death, and literacy) that with 95 percent assurance there existed at the time in Jerusalem 1.71 people named James who had a father named Joseph and brother named Jesus.[11]

9. Golan affirms that he purchased the ossuary from an antiquities dealer who said it was found in the Silwan (Kidron Valley area) in Jerusalem. James the Just, leader of the Jerusalem church and half-brother of Jesus,* was

---

* The evidence appears clear that James was truly the half-brother of Jesus and son of Mary. The perpetual virginity of Mary was not taught at the earlier periods of the church and even was rejected by Augustine. The word for *brother* in Greek is ἀδελφός (*adelphos*), while the word for *cousin* is ἀνεψιός (*anepsios*) (Frederick W. Danker, Walter Bauer, and William Arndt, *A Greek-English Lexicon of the New Testament and Other Early Christian Literature* [Chicago: University of Chicago Press, 2000], 78). Louw and Nida say, "The interpretation of ἀδελφός in such passages as Mt 12.46; Mk 3.31; and John 2.12 as meaning 'cousins' (on the basis of a corresponding Hebrew term, which is used in certain cases to designate masculine relative of various degrees) is not attested in Greek nor affirmed in the Greek-English lexicon edited by Arndt, Gingrich, and Danker. Such an interpretation depends primarily on ecclesiastical tradition" (J.P. Louw and Eugene

stoned and thrown from the pinnacle of the Temple, according to Josephus. According to Christian tradition, he was buried in a rock-cut tomb in the Kidron Valley, and one year later, in accordance with Jewish tradition, his bones were interned in an ossuary.[12]

10. Expert witnesses have confirmed that the inscription in its totality was inscribed by the same hand in the first century, though this was a much disputed item (especially by Yuval Goren and Avner Ayalon) until experts were put under oath at trial.

11. Experts have confirmed the presence of microbial patina on the ossuary and on both parts of the inscription: "James, the son of Joseph" and "brother of Jesus," demonstrating the unity and antiquity of the inscription. In addition, this patina is generally deemed ancient, without the possibility of it occurring naturally in less than 50 to 100 years, making a recent forgery impossible. The world's leading expert in biogeology and the patination process, Wolfgang Krumbein of Oldenburg University in Germany, affirmed that the patina on the ossuary and inscription most likely reflects a development process of thousands of years. He added that there is no known process of accelerating the development of patina. In addition, he concluded that the patina covering the inscription letters is no less authentic than the patina covering the surface of the ossuary (which the IAA says is authentic). Other researchers from the Royal Ontario Museum in Toronto confirmed that the patina within the letter grooves is consistent with the patina on the surface of the ossuary, thus legitimizing the entire inscription's antiquity.

12. According to expert paleographers Andre Lemaire and Ada Yardeni, who authenticated (and dated) the inscription based on the shape and stance of the letters, the Aramaic is fully consistent with first-century style and practice.[13] No credible challenge to their findings has yet to be published.

13. The addition of the words "brother of Jesus" is exceptional among the ossuaries found in Jerusalem.[14] During the trial, it was revealed that what eyewitness Joe Zias, who does not read Aramaic, thought he saw (the James Ossuary) was actually a different but similar ossuary with three Aramaic inscribed names (Joseph, Judah, Hadas), known as the "Joseph Ossuary."[15] Prior to the pronouncement of the final verdict by Judge Farkash, apparently Zias said to Hershel Shanks, editor of *Biblical Archaeology Review,* that

---

Albert Nida, eds., *Greek-English Lexicon of the New Testament* [New York: United Bible Societies, 1999], 118). The relationship is confirmed by the second-century Church Father Hegesippus when he distinguishes James and Jude as brothers. Moreover, Jude in his letter says that he is the brother (ἀδελφός) of James. Matthew 1:25 is plain that the abstention from sexual relations between Joseph and Mary was only until the birth of Jesus. It was morally proper for Jewish husbands and wives to have sexual relations and bear children, in contrast to some of the extreme ideas of celibacy practiced in some segments of the patristic period. The church historian Eusebius says that James was the head of the Jerusalem church and was brother of Jesus.

he was "joking" when he said that the "brother of Jesus" portion of the inscription was missing from the ossuary![16]

So extensive and strong is the support for the authenticity of the ossuary and its inscription that, according to Golan, the prosecutor said in his closing arguments that the state would probably dismiss the charges that the ossuary inscription is a forgery.[17] In fact, many of the IAA witnesses who initially claimed that the inscription was a forgery appeared to have changed their minds after closer analysis and scientific testing.[18] What is more, many prosecution witnesses (witnesses for the IAA/state, who argued that the inscription is a forgery) confirmed the authenticity of the inscription based upon careful analysis of the patina and the engraving. (See appendix C for a survey of numerous expert witnesses and their conclusions about the ossuary inscription.)

Summary and Conclusion

Oded Golan summarizes the outcome of extensive scientific tests performed on the ossuary and its inscription when he writes,

> Neither the prosecution nor the IAA presented even a single witness who was an expert on ancient stone items or patina on antiquities and who ruled out the authenticity of the inscription or any part of it. On the contrary, the findings of all the tests, including those of prosecution witnesses Goren and Ayalon, support the argument that the entire inscription is ancient, the inscription was engraved by a single person, and that several letter grooves contain traces of detergent/s that cover the natural varnish patina that developed there over centuries, and was partially cleaned (mainly the first section), many years ago.[19]

The apologetic and historical implications following from this ossuary are far-reaching. It informs us that 1) James, Joseph, and Jesus have historical corroboration as individuals and a family in the first century; 2) early Christians, like James, may have been buried according to Jewish custom; 3) Aramaic was used by early Christians; and that 4) early Christianity emerged from its Jewish roots, making it extremely difficult to divorce Christianity from its Jewishness. As such, the inscription's primary apologetic value rests in this: After the most intense interdisciplinary expert scrutiny according to the rules of law, the James Ossuary can be considered the most authenticated and most scrutinized artifact in history. We now can appreciate the ossuary as an authentic artifact that provides the earliest direct archaeological link to Jesus and His family.

The Tomb of Jesus

Two sites are in competition as the burial place of Jesus of Nazareth—the Church of the Holy Sepulchre and the Garden Tomb, which is located near the Damascus Gate. The former site has ancient tradition supporting it but lies within the confines of a church that obscures a place of crucifixion and burial; the latter has a more visible tomb near what is alleged to be the location of the crucifixion. Determining which of these two is, in fact, where Jesus rose from the dead is important for the Christian faith, since Christianity is tied to history. Regarding the resurrection of Jesus, Paul said that if He has not risen ("in the flesh" is understood), then we are yet in our sins and the apostles are liars (1 Corinthians 15:13-17).

The Garden Tomb

In the late nineteenth century British general Charles Gordon discovered a site outside the Damascus Gate that is now called Gordon's Calvary, or Skull Hill, where he believed that Jesus was crucified. Near this site was also a tomb within a garden that he believed to be the tomb of Jesus. Unlike the traditional site located in an ancient church and surrounded by ornate crosses and incense thuribles, which obscure a former location of garden and rock quarry from which tombs were carved, the Garden Tomb is in the open, easily recognized as a place of burial, and in a beautiful garden.

The Garden Tomb resides in a beautiful, quiet setting and is frequented generally by Protestant Christians who find the surroundings of an ancient church too steeped in ritual. The Garden Tomb satisfies many of the requirements of the place of Jesus' burial and resurrection, including its situation in a garden, outside the city walls, and near what is arguably a place of crucifixion. The mystical manner in which Gordon sought to connect the place of crucifixion and burial with the Temple Mount and Pool of Siloam has been a point of criticism. He placed a skeleton with its head at Skull Hill, its backside on the Temple Mount, and the feet at the Pool of Siloam, viewing this as a confirmation of its identification. This notion is highly speculative, and is not argued by staff at the Garden Tomb.

The Garden Tomb (Jerusalem).

The Church of the Holy Sepulchre

The ancient and traditional site of the crucifixion and burial of Jesus has many points of support also, but there is no tomb to observe. The tomb there, which early had been separated from other tombs in the stone quarry and made into a place of homage, was destroyed in the early eleventh century AD by order of Muslim caliph Al-Hakim bi-Amr Allah.[20]

In spite of there being no tomb—a structure called an edicule stands where the tomb once stood—the tradition for this site is very strong, going back to the second century AD. When the Emperor Hadrian had defeated the Jews after the Bar Kokhba revolt (AD 132–135) and banished them from Jerusalem, in his attempt to replace Judaism and

Christianity he built a temple to Venus over the site where the Church of the Holy Sepulchre now stands, a temple to Jupiter over where the Temple once stood, and a shrine to the god Adonis at the location of the Church of the Nativity. This was a standard practice to emphasize the triumph of one religion over another in the ancient world (a practice that has continued in Islam through the centuries). The Church of the Holy Sepulchre (known as the Church of the Resurrection by the Greek Orthodox) satisfies many requirements defined in Scripture for Jesus' tomb—outside the city wall, near a place of crucifixion, and within a garden. This was the place that early Christians took Queen Helena when she came to Jerusalem and requested to know the location of Jesus' death and resurrection.

Church of the Holy Sepulchre (Jerusalem).

Which Is the Tomb of Jesus?

In order for a site to be the historical location of the burial and resurrection site of Jesus, certain factors must be present. Both of the two competing sites fulfill conditions, but only one fulfills them all. The conditions for the correct tomb are as follows:[21]

1. It had to be near the site of the crucifixion.

2. It had to be located in a garden.

3. It had to be outside the city walls of Jerusalem when Jesus was crucified in the early AD 30s.

4. It had to be hewed out of a stone quarry.

5. It had to be an exceptional tomb since it was a rich man's tomb.

6. It had to have a rolling stone.

7. It had to have an outer chamber and inner chamber, in view of the biblical accounts regarding the women, apostles, and angels at the tomb.

8. It had to be a new tomb, thus hewed in the first century AD.

The Garden Tomb satisfies items 1 through and 7.[22] Item 5 is questionable since there are larger tombs than the small Garden Tomb. Item 6 is uncertain since a rolling stone was not found at the site, and the trough in front of the Garden Tomb is not a groove for a rolling stone but is rather a water trough going all the way across the front of the tomb. Item 8 is the most significant since there is no doubt that the Garden Tomb is a First Temple tomb, created hundreds of years before Jesus and part of a quarry containing eighth-century BC tombs; consequently, it cannot be the correct tomb, since Jesus was placed in a newly created tomb.[23]

The Church of the Holy Sepulchre satisfies items 1 through 4. The tomb resided near a place of crucifixion, and evidence of a garden has been found. The city walls at the time of Christ did not extend beyond the site of the tomb, and there are several other tombs found near where the tomb of Christ stood before the Muslim caliph destroyed it. Since there is no tomb to investigate, there is no way to substantiate items 5, 6, or 7, but one would expect that the tomb of Jesus would have the features of other first-century AD tombs. An outer chamber of a tomb is found just a few feet away from the current commemorative site of the tomb, which was built on the place of the former tomb. The tombs in the Church of the Holy Sepulchre are first-century AD tombs, so this would satisfy number 8.

The varying burial practices of the Jewish people make it very easy to determine whether a tomb is from the first century BC and AD (Second Temple) or the eighth century BC (First Temple).

Burial practices of the First Temple Period are as follows. The deceased was placed in the tomb, after preparation, on a raised slab or narrow platform, with a stone headrest. Generally each burial chamber had three such slabs. Under these raised slabs there was a compartment in which bones of the deceased were placed after approximately a year, when the flesh had all decayed. Thus they were "gathered to their fathers." The caves in which the deceased were placed had an outer room for preparation and visitation by relatives and an inner room or rooms with three stone platforms.

During the first century BC and first century AD, until the fall of Jerusalem in AD 70, deceased persons were wrapped from head to toe, and their bodies were then placed in niches in the wall and on the floor. Often there were several burial niches in the same room. After the body had decayed, there was a second burial, with the bones broken and placed in a bone box called an ossuary. The length of the box would be based on the length of the longest bone, the femur. Sometimes another person might be placed in a person's ossuary at a later time if insufficient ossuaries were available. These boxes were then kept in the tomb for times of commemoration of the dead.

A first-century rolling-stone tomb similar to the tomb of Jesus is visible from the roadway near Mount Carmel, Israel. (Photo used by permission of H. Wayne House.)

We cannot know for certain the location of the death, burial, and resurrection of Jesus, but most of the evidence, including Hadrian's early marking of the spot, points to the traditional site as the correct location.[24] It was long remembered in the minds and hearts of the Christians of the first century and afterward, and it is the place that has been accepted by Christians of all faiths for nearly 2,000 years.

Is Jesus' Hometown of Nazareth a Myth?

For the past 2,000 years first-century Nazareth was unquestionably considered the historic hometown of Jesus.[25] The Gospels make it abundantly clear that Jesus was "of Nazareth" (John 1:45; 19:19; Mark 1:24; Luke 18:37). However, religious researcher Rene Salm has challenged the historical Nazareth in his *The Myth of Nazareth: The Invented Town of Jesus* (American Atheist Press, 2008). According to his view, ancient Nazareth did not emerge prior to AD 70, and the settlement of Nazareth did not exist earlier than the second century AD, long after Christ's crucifixion.

To substantiate these claims, Salm appeals to, among other things, 1) late-dating Roman and Byzantine artifacts (for example, oil lamps); 2) the Gospel of Luke, which tells us that Jesus' hometown was Capernaum, not Nazareth; 3) "problematic" biblical passages (for example, Matthew 2:23: "He went and lived in a city called Nazareth, so that what was spoken by the prophets might be fulfilled, that he would be called a Nazarene" [ESV]) that have no prophetic reference in the Hebrew Scriptures; and 4) the fact that Josephus and the Jewish Talmud do not mention Nazareth in their lists of Galilean cities.

However, there are several reasons why Salm's argument against Nazareth should be rejected.

1. Limited archaeological work has been completed in the Nazareth area since most of the ancient city lies under the modern city of Nazareth (with a population of about 60,000). The sparseness of materials and current cumulative data should not be stretched into a theory of Nazareth's nonexistence; the alleged absence of material data and the presence of *later* Roman and Byzantine evidence is not "contradictory" evidence that disproves Nazareth's first-century existence. This sort of thinking displays the logical fallacy of arguing from silence. Besides, the archaeological data from excavations in the Nazareth area demonstrate that Nazareth was used up until the destruction of Jerusalem in AD 70.*

2. The location of Sepphoris in relation to Nazareth is consistent with the social and economic milieu of Jesus' day. Sepphoris, rebuilt in 4 BC by the tetrarch of Galilee, Herod Antipas, was located about an hour's walk from modern-day Nazareth. This is strong evidence that villages like Nazareth were set within a short distance from this major hub, implying they were not "isolated" from the rest of the Galilee. The labor

---

* Nazareth archaeologist Yehudah Rapuano mentions that some Hellenistic and early Roman artifacts—sherds, a storage jar, cooking pots recovered from tombs, and lamps—found at Nazareth over past excavations "fit comfortably within the first century CE." For example, Rapuano refers his readers to several artifacts (the Jar of Fig. 217:6; pots in Fig. 192:18,26; lamps in Fig. 192:6,15) in the record of Bellarmino Bagatti's excavations (1969). Rapuano says, "Salm's personal evaluation of the pottery, which he rehearses from his book *The Nazareth Myth*, reveals his lack of expertise in the area as well as his lack of serious research in the sources. By ignoring or dismissing solid ceramic, numismatic and literary evidence for Nazareth's existence during the Late Hellenistic and Early Roman period, it would appear that the analysis which Rene Salm includes in his review, and his recent book must, in itself, be relegated to the realm of 'myth'" (Stephen J. Pfann and Yehudah Rapuano, "On the Nazareth Village Farm Report: A Reply to Salm," *Bulletin of the Anglo-Israel Archaeology Society*, vol. 26, (2008), 107-108.

force (masons and carpenters) most likely could not afford, or did not need, to live in the large, opulent cities, so they settled in nearby villages. Since Joseph and Jesus were masons/carpenters, with no indication that they were wealthy, it would make sense that they settled close by Sepphoris.

There is evidence of first-century agricultural infrastructure in Nazareth and a nearby roadway system connecting the port city of Caesarea Maritima to Tiberias.[26] In addition, during the summer of 2009, excavations at Nazareth revealed several first-century artifacts such as a house and clay and chalk vessel remains. According to the then Israel Antiquities Authority director of excavations, Yardenna Alexandre, archaeologists have discovered the remains of a wall, a hideout, courtyard, and a water system that collected water from the roof dating to the time of Jesus.[27] Moreover, in 1997 and 1998, excavations at Mary's Well in Nazareth closer to the basilica, conducted by Alexandre, yielded coin evidence dating from the late Hellenistic and early Roman periods.[28] All of these remains imply a self-sustaining first-century community intricately connected with the rest of northern Israel.

3. Although Salm rejects Matthew 2:23 due to its lack of specific reference among the prophetic books of the Old Testament, this conclusion is mistaken for several reasons: 1) Matthew did not say a single prophet made the statement; rather, it was of the prophets (plural)—meaning that Matthew was not quoting any specific prophet but was instead referring to the general consensus among the prophets that Jesus would be called a "Nazarene." The fulfillment of this title can be understood in several ways. For example, the prophets said the Messiah would be despised and rejected (Isaiah 53:3; Daniel 9:26; Zechariah 12:10) much in the way Nazareth was despised during the early first century (John 1:46; 7:41,52). 2) Though Jesus never took the vow of the Nazirite (the word is spelled differently than Nazareth), He fulfilled it by perfectly keeping the Law and separating Himself to the Lord, which was the essence of the Nazirite vow (Numbers 6:2; Judges 13:5). 3) Others have indicated that the Hebrew word *netzer* (meaning "branch") is the word from which Nazareth was named (since it sounds similar).

4. Salm ignores the numerous independent statements in the New Testament that identify Jesus with Nazareth. At His crucifixion Pontius Pilate placed a government-authorized sign (a *titulus*) above Jesus' head that read, "Jesus of Nazareth…" (John 19:19). It is worthy of note that the religious leaders did not dispute truthfulness of Jesus' hometown written on the placard when they petitioned Pilate to change the writing; they only challenged His claim to be "the King of the Jews" (John 19:20-22)! Also, the New Testament writers often referred to "Jesus of Nazareth" (Mark 1:24; Luke 18:37), and those among the early church were identified as the "Nazarene sect" (Acts 24:5 NIV). Moreover, even the foes of Jesus referred to His hometown as "Nazareth" (Luke 4:33-34). Never is Jesus identified with any other city; He is never called "Jesus of Caesarea," "Jesus of Capernaum," "Jesus of Bethlehem," or "Jesus of Jerusalem"; only "Jesus of Nazareth."

5. **The absence of historical notation among early literature (Josephus and the Talmud) does not prove that Nazareth is a myth.** Lack of identification does not mean lack of *existence*; it's a logical fallacy to argue from silence. There are plausible reasons why Nazareth is not found in Josephus and the Talmud's list of Galilean locations: 1) It is possible that Josephus and the Talmud omit it because the lists are not intended to be exhaustive; 2) it may be because Nazareth (due to its despised reputation and size) was such an insignificant village at the time it warranted no mention; and 3) by the time Josephus wrote his list of Galilean cities in the late first century, Nazareth may have been known by another name or may not have been occupied. What is more, Jewish religious leaders may have refrained from listing Nazareth out of disdain for Jesus and His claims to be the Messiah. None of these reasons preclude Nazareth from being the historic village of Jesus.

6. **Salm's theory forgets the fact that Old and New Testament writers always layered their narratives over real geographical locations.** Never have we discovered otherwise. It is strange hermeneutical practice to accept the historicity of the Galilee region (as Salm apparently does) but reject the existence of Nazareth, which is located within it. Nazareth and Galilee are often mentioned coupled together, in a nonmythical tone. Salm often asserts that instead of Nazareth being Jesus' hometown, the Scriptures place the home of Jesus in Capernaum. However, this notion is fraught with problems, the most crucial of them is that Salm is either unaware or simply ignores that the same grammatical coupling is associated with Capernaum as well: "Capernaum, a city of Galilee" (Luke 4:31).

7. **Several of Salm's criticisms of the pottery report of the Nazareth Village Farm excavations (for example, "double dating") have been shown to be in error** and based on misnumbered exhibits within the published report. Stephen Pfann and Yehudah Rapuano explain Salm's confusion:

> The errors pointed out by Salm in the pottery report of the Nazareth Village Farm excavations were not the result of "double dating" as he supposed, but rather of misnumbering. Originally, the part of the article dealing with the pottery was prepared in a different layout. At some point before the article was sent to the editors, it underwent a change in the format, presumably for reasons of spacing and for the reader's greater convenience. The plates were reorganized and the drawings were given new numbers. In the process, some of the connections between the drawings and the text were lost or changed. In a few cases the same figure number was erroneously repeated. It is to these occurrences that Salm referred.[29]

Regarding the pottery and dating they maintain,

The numbering errors in the article do not, however, change the date of the pottery.[30]

In the "Nazareth Village Farm Report" are examples that belong to the Hellenistic period (for example, figures 40:5-8) and to the subsequent early Roman period (for example, figures 37:5 and 7). The dates for parallels of the pottery of Roman period Galilee are usually expressed according to a range reflecting the time period that the forms were in production and use. The early Roman period is usually considered to date from the mid first century BC to the first half of the second century AD. Pfann and Rapuano conclude, notably,

> While early Roman sherds were found in different parts of the site, we noted that the pottery forms in Area 1, Locus/Layer 2, as a group fit comfortably within the first century CE.[31]

8. Salm's theory favors the interpretations of liberal biblical scholarship without questioning their philosophical assumptions or methodology; nor does his theory seriously interact with conservative evangelical scholarship on the matter. Most notable is his unwarranted rejection of the reliability of the biblical text. There is simply no reason to reject the integrity of the Gospel records, which, as seen throughout this book, are supported by credible eyewitnesses and thousands of early manuscripts.[32]

THE TEMPLE MOUNT

The Jewish Temple was the center of Israel's national and religious life, being located in Jerusalem on a prominent crest overlooking the Kidron Valley known as Mount Moriah. The religious value of the Temple Mount (that is, the location where the First and Second Temples stood) is recognized by all three Abrahamic religions (Judaism, Christianity, and Islam) as being the location of significant events described in the Bible and in Islamic tradition.

For Judaism, it is the holiest place—where Abraham offered up his son Isaac (Genesis 22:2,9) and where two Jewish Temples stood, built during the time of Solomon, during the time of Zerubbabel, and during the time of Herod the Great. For Christians, it is the place where Abraham offered his son Isaac, the area where Christ taught and ministered to the people, and the mountain crest on which Christ was crucified outside the city gates in the first century. For Muslims, the Temple Mount is the third holiest site in Islam (after Mecca and Medina), to which it is believed that Muhammad and his winged horse (El Burak) made his "Night Journey" (Surah 17:1) from Mecca; Jerusalem is where Islamic tradition says Muhammad ascended to heaven and spoke with Allah concerning prayer.

In the Hebrew language, the approximately 38-acre platform and its surrounding walls today called "Temple Mount" is known as *har ha-bayit* (the Mountain of the House). The same location is known in the Arabic tongue as *haram al-sharif* (the Noble Sanctuary).

History of the Temple Mount

From Abraham Through the Babylonian Destruction

The long history of the Temple Mount begins in Abraham's day (2050–1850 BC), when he is told by God to offer his son Isaac as a sacrifice on a mountain in the land of Moriah (Genesis 22:1-14). Abraham traveled to his destination and built an altar on which he laid the wood and his son Isaac, but when Abraham was about to plunge the knife into his son, God intervened to halt the sacrifice.

Temple Mount in Jerusalem is the location of the silver-domed Al-Aqsa Mosque (bottom) and the gold Dome of the Rock (center). Some propose that the First and Second Jewish temples were located in the same location as the Dome of the Rock. (Photo by Todd Bolen/BiblePlaces.com.)

This location would again factor in prominently in the eleventh to early tenth century BC, when we are told in 2 Samuel 24 that God was angered by David's decision to take a census of the people of Israel and subsequently punished him with national pestilence, which killed about 70,000 Israelites in three days. In order to avert God's plague from Jerusalem, David was commanded by Gad to purchase the threshing floor of Araunah the Jebusite located on what is now the Temple Mount in order to erect an altar of sacrifice to the Lord (2 Samuel 24:15-25). Therefore, David purchased the parcel of land and the oxen for 50 shekels of silver (2 Samuel 24:24).

Soon after, David would begin collecting the materials that his son Solomon would use to build the first Temple for the Jewish nation (1 Chronicles 22:5), near the location of David's altar. First Kings 5 tells of Solomon's need of lumber and his request to Hiram (the king of Tyre, also known as *Eiromos*) for building materials such as cedar and cypress trees. Hiram's existence has been confirmed by a bronze bowl inscription discovered in

Cyprus that bears his name and title as "Hiram, king of the Sidonians." Josephus also refers to Solomon and Hiram and some letters that were exchanged between them, letters that may have still been in existence during the first century AD.[1]

First Kings 6:1 describes the very year that Solomon began his construction of the First Temple: It was 1) 480 years after Israel left Egypt, 2) in the fourth year of Solomon's reign, and 3) in the month of Ziv (second month of the fourth year). In 586 BC, some 400 years later, during the reign of Babylonian vassal king Zedekiah, the Babylonian Chronicles tell of King Nebuchadnezzar II's (605–562 BC) capture of Jerusalem (2 Chronicles 36:17) in which Solomon's Temple would be destroyed (2 Chronicles 36:19).

The First Temple: Archaeological Support

Lending additional support to the existence, dating, and function of the First Temple are the "Three Shekels" and "House of God" ostraca (clay pottery fragments). The former ostracon surfaced on the antiquities market during the 1990s and consists of a ninth- to seventh-century BC receipt containing a Hebrew inscription describing three shekels of silver that were donated to Solomon's Temple—literally "the House (or Temple) of Yahweh" (*Beyt Yhwh*). The artifact has been confirmed for authenticity by independent sources, who have examined the pottery, ink, language, and even the patina—the microscopic microbial residue that covers most ancient objects.[2] Though some have suggested that the text could be referring to another Jewish temple location than the one in Jerusalem, it nevertheless is consistent with the existence, date, and function of a Jewish Temple.

The "Three Shekels" Ostracon. (Photo by Zev Radovan.)

The "House of God" Ostracon is a similar text discovered in Arad (an ancient Jewish city in the Negev) among dozens of similar shards dating to the early sixth century BC. Arad served as a fortress of the Judean monarchy and an administrative center in the Negev for some 300 years (from the ninth to the sixth century BC). The text, written in ink by a professional scribe using Hebrew script, is addressed to "Elyashib" at Arad; in the text the "House of God" (presumably in Jerusalem) is mentioned. Besides the "Three Shekels" Ostracon, this inscription is one of the earliest archaeological finds referencing the Jewish Temple outside the Bible.

The "House of God (Yahweh)" Ostracon discovered in Arad. (Photo by Zev Radovan.)

Reconstruction Under Zerubbabel and Herod the Great

After Israel's 70 years of Babylonian captivity came to an end (Daniel 9:2) when the Medes and Persians under Cyrus (see Isaiah 45:1-7) conquered Babylon,* efforts led by Zerubbabel and Jeshua the priest to rebuild "the altar of the God of Israel" (Ezra 3:2–6:18) marked the beginning of the Second Temple's construction. The Second Temple structure would be finished in the sixth year of the reign of the Persian king Darius (c. 515 BC), leaving the Temple Mount platform and city walls to be rebuilt by Nehemiah (c. 444 BC).

The Arch of Titus was built in Rome adjacent to the Roman Forum by Titus's brother, Emperor Domitian, to commemorate the victories of Titus, which included the successful siege of Jerusalem in AD 70. The sculpture on the inner panels of the arch depicts Roman soldiers carrying away temple treasures such as the priestly trumpets, golden menorah, and other valuable articles.

This reconstructed Temple would serve the Jewish nation until Herod the Great began his ambitious project to remodel the Temple structures (c. 20 BC; John 2:20) and greatly expand the Temple Mount platform and its retaining walls. This enormous project would enlarge the Temple Mount area to twice its size by building outward toward the north, south, and west. Eastern expansion was not possible since Solomon's eastern wall was already perched atop the Kidron Valley crest. Josephus mentions Herod's work on the Temple as an "extraordinary"

Herod's renovated and expanded Temple Mount looked much like this replica displayed at the Israel Museum.

---

* The Cyrus Cylinder (see Isaiah 45:1-7), written after the capture of Babylon by the Medes and Persians under Cyrus in 539 BC, tells of the freeing of all captives. This decree brought an official end to Israel's 70 years captivity in Babylon (see Daniel 9:2). See more in chapter 20.

undertaking that Herod hoped would ensure his legacy and for which he would be remembered by future generations.[3] This newly remodeled structure would eventually become the largest man-made structure in the world by the time of Christ.

Roman Destruction and New Construction

Only 100 years after Herod began his remodeling project, the Jewish revolt against Rome (AD 66–70) would lead to the destruction of the Temple and its buildings (Matthew 24:1-2) in AD 70 by the Roman army under Titus. The Roman destruction was total; it involved the violent dismantling of all structures upon the sacred platform.

The Dome of the Rock resides at the center of the Temple Mount complex and marks the spot revered by Muslims as the place from which Muhammad ascended to heaven.

After the Temple's destruction and the subsequent diaspora of the Jews, the Temple Mount structures and the old city walls would lie in ruins for the next 700 years. However, the Temple Mount area would again change in the Islamic era, in the late seventh and eighth century AD. The construction of the Dome of the Rock took place in the late seventh century AD under the Umayyad caliph Abd al-Malik.* Al-Malik desired to pattern the gold-domed structure after a fourth-century AD Christian building (located on the adjacent Mount of Olives) that was dedicated to the ascension of Christ. The rock protruding from the floor beneath the dome is the tip of Mount Moriah and is revered by Muslims as the place where Muhammad ascended to heaven to receive instructions from Allah concerning prayer.

The Al-Aqsa Mosque, built in AD 705, is located on the southern Temple Mount platform where the Royal Stoa (also known as the Royal Colonnade or Royal Basilica) once stood as part of Herod's renovated Temple Mount.

The significance of the domed structure is found in the fact that caliph Abd al-Malik

---

* The Dome of the Rock structure has been restored several times in the twentieth century by the Hashemite kingdom (Jordan). In 1922 to 1924 the outer wooden dome was replaced with an aluminum gold-coated dome in order to stop water leakage. In 1952 to 1964 the earlier restoration to stop water leakage failed and was remedied again along with restoring the lost luster to the dome itself. In 1969: emergency repair and restoration were made to the twelfth-century AD stepped platform (minbar) inside the structure after it was set on fire by an Australian tourist in 1969. In 1992 to 1994 King Hussein spent nearly nine million dollars for an Irish construction company to refurbish the building and strengthen its supporting structure. This included adding thousands of glittering gold plates to the dome, rebuilding the roof supports, restoring the minbar, and fireproofing the Temple Mount compound. See the Jordanian government report on these restorations in "The Hashemite Restorations of the Islamic Holy Places in Jerusalem," accessed at www.kinghussein.gov.jo/islam_restoration.html.

intended the site to be 1) a rival sacred location to Mecca and Medina, 2) a sacred location commemorating Muhammad's ascension to heaven as equal to or greater than Christ's ascension, and 3) a direct challenge to Christianity and its assertion that Jesus Christ was the Son of God.* To the south of the Dome of the Rock is located the silver-domed Al-Aqsa Mosque (meaning "the farthest"), which was initially built in AD 705 and then improved with the addition of its dome in AD 1035. According to Islamic tradition, the mosque was built on the southernmost site of the Temple Mount where Muhammad stood. Today, the Al-Aqsa Mosque, including its outdoor surrounding space, can accommodate over 300,000 people at one time kneeling in prayer.

Archaeological Features Around the Temple Mount

The Southern Wall and Gates

Additional improvements were made during the Islamic and Crusader eras (seventh to twelfth century AD) to the surrounding areas below the Temple Mount, especially to the southern wall and southwest corner beneath the Al-Aqsa Mosque. Here were located the Umayyad and Crusader administrative centers, as well as visible remnants from Herod's expansion of the Temple Mount platform and walls. For example, in the southern wall (directly beneath the Al-Aqsa Mosque) there remains Herodian architecture in the form of a double gate that would allow worshippers to access the Temple Mount from the south. Once through these gates the worshipper would be led gradually up to the Temple Mount platform through a long subterranean passageway with arched ceilings. Though the gate itself was filled in with a stone wall during the Crusader period, a subtle lintel and relieving arch can still be seen. At the base of the exposed portion of the double gate, a Herodian master course of stone supports the structure; it originally also provided the gate with a doorjamb.

The remains of the Double Gates can be seen immediately above the protruding arch in the form of a half lintel and subtle arch. The wall made of small stones located to the left of the arch was constructed by the Crusaders in about AD 1099.

Moreover, archaeologists have exposed 30 steps at the base of the southern Temple Mount wall that were carved out of the natural stone ascent to the Mount. These steps,

---

* The second and third points are supported by the style of the architectural structure and the story line of the ascension, which was said to have occurred nearly 700 years after Christ's ascension. In addition, Arabic literature embedded in the inner decorative walls of the Dome of the Rock structure attests to its theological challenge to Christianity and the deity of Christ. The inscription reads: "There is no God but God; Muhammad is his Prophet; Jesus is also his Prophet, but God has no Son: He neither Begets nor is Begotten." It is also debatable whether the caliph intended the Dome of the Rock structure to commemorate the ascension of Muhammad, since no inscription or dedication to Muhammad or the ascension story was ever found there. It would seem strange to have omitted reference to the "Night Journey" and ascension story from its structure if this had been one of the primary reasons for revering the site and building the structure. To explain this omission, the story of Muhammad's ascension to heaven was most likely created at a later time within Muslim tradition.

The rock from which the southern steps were carved can still be seen, along with modern stone additions toward the upper steps. These are the same steps Jesus and His disciples would have climbed to access the Temple from the south through the Double Gates.

The Triple Gates.

Herodian masonry featured in the Temple Mount construction regularly displays finely crafted margins with a smooth raised boss (face). (Photo by Zev Radovan.)

dating to the time of Christ, were used to bring worshippers up to the double gates, where they could access the Temple Mount platform. They are still visible today, but the visible portion represents only a part of their total width, which has been estimated to be over 200 feet.

Further Herodian remains can be seen in the eastern section of the Temple Mount's southern wall (the same wall that contains the double gates).* Located about 200 feet to the east of the double gates are the triple gates. Though the three stone arches and their gates have since been filled in with stone, most likely during the Crusader period, one can view the beveled Herodian door jamb, which is set in a master course of stone laid by King Herod.

The Herodian identification of the many gates and structural features of the Temple Mount was fairly simple to make due to Herod's masonry style. Archaeologists noticed a signature pattern in the courses of stone used, which contain nicely embossed borders with a smooth finished (or sometimes unfinished) raised face. Depending on where and how the stone was used, ornamented detail such as beveling would be used, especially as the stones adjoined gates as doorjambs.

Evidence from Wall and Platform Stones

One significant find at the southwest corner of the Temple Mount was a large angular corner stone that had been thrown down from the top of the Temple Mount wall (perhaps by the Romans in AD 70). The stone, found among other Temple Mount stones dating to

---

* Josephus mentions that there were gates facing south in the middle of the southern wall (*Antiquities of the Jews*, 15.4111). These are most likely the current double and triple gates located by archaeologists at the same location.

the first century, was handcrafted as a parapet (that is, a special beveling that provides a small level niche that prevents one from falling over the rail). This rare stone has been called the "Trumpeting Stone" since a partial Hebrew inscription was found on its rail that reads: "to the place of trumpeting…." Apparently, this stone was designated by Herod's masons to be placed in a specific location on the Temple Mount so it would not be confused with other stones designated for a similar location. The inscription indicates that the priests were to announce with the trumpet the beginning and ending of Sabbath and holy days, as well as using various blasts to announce other important times relating to the Jewish religious calendar. According to Josephus, the priest would communicate with the people of Jerusalem through specific trumpet blasts in order to give notice of when to cease working and when it was time to resume labors.[4] The Mishnah speaks of dozens of trumpet blasts throughout the day as warnings related to the Sabbath and other crucial time periods.[5] What is more, the trumpets (along with other Temple implements, including the menorah) used by the priest are depicted on the first-century AD triumphal Arch of Titus located southeast of the Roman Forum near the Coliseum in Rome.

Additional building stones and debris were uncovered at the base of the western side of the southwest corner of Temple Mount; some of these stones bear testimony to Jesus' prophecy in Matthew 24:1-2 that not one stone would be left upon another. These include stones from a first-century AD street, vendor shop niches that served as the supporting piers

The Trumpeting Stone with its Hebrew inscription was most likely toppled from the top southwest corner of the Temple Mount.

Evidence of the Roman destruction of the Temple Mount structures (AD 70) are still visible under the protruding stub of Robinson's Arch in piles of stones discovered on the pavement of a first-century street.

The southwest corner of the Temple Mount features some of the largest Herodian stones visible above ground. As the builders placed these massive stones one upon another, they carefully made sure that each stone was set back about one inch from the lower stone it rested upon. This ensured that the enormous weight and pressure from the fill material placed on the other side of the wall would not cause the wall to collapse.

for Robinson's Arch* (a stepped arch leading from the street level that would offer an ascending entrance into the Royal Stoa located on the Temple Mount), stones from ritual baths for purification (*mikva'ot*), massive Herodian Temple Mount retaining wall stones, and discarded building stones (found in situ at street level); all these were thrown down by the Romans in their destruction of the Temple in AD 70.

Jesus' prophecy of Jerusalem's destruction also came with a warning—namely, to flee Jerusalem and run for the mountains when the city was facing imminent siege by the Romans (Matthew 24:15-22; Mark 13:14-20; Luke 21:20-24). According to church historian Eusebius of Caesarea (c. AD 260–340), Jesus' Jewish followers acted on His warning and fled to the mountainous area known as Pella prior to the Roman destruction in AD 70.[6]

The ruins of Pella, located about 20 miles south of the Sea of Galilee in modern-day Jordan. Pella served as the place of refuge during the Roman siege of Jerusalem and total destruction of the Temple in AD 70. Though some Roman buildings still remain (bathhouse, necropolis, odeon, and so on), the site is dominated by Byzantine-era construction.

In regard to the Temple Mount, of architectural importance is the discovery of huge ashlar stones (hewn or squared stones), still clearly visible today, that were placed by Herod at the southwest corner of the Temple Mount wall. Some of these enormous stones were cut to nearly 40 feet in length, nearly 8 feet wide, and over 3 feet tall. The extraordinary weight of some of these well-placed stones reaches 50-plus tons. Further excavations along the western wall of the Temple Mount (accessed through the rabbinic tunnels) near the Antonia Fortress (and Herod's rock quarry) have unearthed some of the largest set stones known to date, which were used in Herod's expansion of the Temple Mount. These include stones measuring more than 44 feet long and standing over 10.5 feet high!

The Western Wall

A vast portion of this western retaining wall section (known as the "Wailing Wall") has been exposed and reserved as a place for Jews desiring to pray and study the Hebrew Scriptures.[†] Currently, this tightly guarded sacred location is partitioned into two areas,

---

* Refers to the remains of a protruding arch (50-plus feet wide) on the western side of the southwest corner of the Temple Mount wall discovered by American archaeologist Edward Robinson in 1838. The remains of the arch bulge from the wall at about 30 feet above street level.

† The Wailing Wall Plaza (that is, the western retaining wall of the Temple Mount), as well as all of Jerusalem, was under the control of foreign powers until the final hours of the Six-Day War in 1967, when Israel's army once again took control of Jerusalem after bitter fighting with Jordanian and Arab forces. Soon after Israel's victory, nearly 250,000 Jews visited the site for the first time since the Temple's destruction in AD 70. Currently, Israel has reserved this sacred location for the study and practice of Judaism, while simultaneously allowing the Temple Mount precincts to be administered by the Islamic Waqf.

one side for men and the other for women.* Since religious Jews rarely, if ever, enter the Temple Mount area for fear of unknowingly treading upon the holy place and sparking violent reactions from Muslims, who despise their presence, they have found the Western

The Western "Wailing Wall" with its two partitioned areas for men and women. Today, the western wall remains one of the many archaeological confirmations of King Herod's architectural renovations of a massive structure the Bible describes as the Jewish Temple.

Wall Plaza to be a more appropriate place of meditation. It is the closest one can come to the Temple and conveniently gather with others without actually entering the Temple Mount itself.

Prior to the 1967 war, Christian pilgrims and Jews visited the remains of the wall in small numbers to pray. The narrow confines and dilapidated abandoned dwellings located at the base of the wall greatly limited the number of visitors at the site. This was remedied by Amihai Mazar after the Six-Day War by removing the abandoned structures, leveling the plaza area, and considerably lowering the street level. This move exposed multiple courses of large, precisely carved stones placed by Herod to give the western side of the Temple Mount support. Each stone has about a one-inch setback from the stone below it, giving the wall added strength.

---

* Non-Jews and tourists are welcome to enter both sections with a head covering and appropriate attire.

Archaeological Artifacts and Features on the Mount

Up until this point, we have surveyed some of the more significant features surrounding the Temple Mount area, all of which appear consistent with the biblical statements concerning the existence, function, and destruction of the Jewish Temple. The architectural remains, coinage, ritual purification baths, inscriptions, historical records (Josephus, Mishnah, Babylonian Chronicles, and so on), Roman triumphal monuments (Arch of Titus), and destruction debris are all consistent with the cultural and religious climate described in Scripture.

However, we must also ask whether there is evidence from the Temple Mount *itself* or its surrounding area to support the Bible's statements concerning the existence and location of the Temple. This evidence has been difficult to obtain since it is not legal to carry out archaeological digs on the Temple Mount itself. However, from time to time excavations occur that are not supervised by an archaeologist, such as the recent expansion of the lower portions of the Al-Aqsa Mosque; the digging of trenches for utilities (with heavy equipment) on the surface of Temple Mount; and other controversial restoration and construction projects. These types of unsupervised construction projects have been criticized due to the risk of destroying high-value artifacts and structures.

Among the Temple Mount rubble from a construction project, archaeologists Gabriel Barkay and Zachi Zweig discovered a charred stamp-seal impression that bears a partial Hebrew inscription. When translated it reads, "Belonging to Ga'alyahu son of Immer." The well-known priestly family of Immer is mentioned in the Bible as living during the end of the First Temple period (Jeremiah 20:1; Ezra 2:37,59; 10:20; Nehemiah 3:29; 7:40,61; 11:13; 1 Chronicles 9:12; 24:14). (Photo by Zev Radovan.)

Stamp Seals

The risk of destruction was especially acute when Temple Mount authorities (and the Israel Antiquities Authority—IAA) allowed the unsupervised expansion (that is, no senior archaeologist present) of the Al-Aqsa Mosque and the careless discarding of rich archaeological soil. Jerusalem archaeologists Gabriel Barkay and his then student Zachi Zweig petitioned for a permit to retrieve the abandoned soil; it is currently being carefully examined by the Temple Mount Sifting Project (located on Mount Scopus) staff and volunteers for artifacts of high historical value. Among the fascinating finds are a bronze coin minted during the Jewish war with the Romans (AD 66–70) that bears the inscription "Freedom of Zion," arrowheads, mosaics, jewelry, Egyptian scarabs dating to the second millennium BC, and a Hebrew stamp seal (*bulla*), among other items.[7]

Of particular importance is, as described in chapter 20, a sixth-century BC Hebrew-inscribed stamp seal that contains the name of the biblical priestly family *Immer*, who had administrative power over the Temple Mount during the tumultuous days of the prophet Jeremiah (Jeremiah 20:1) and who was responsible for the beating and imprisoning of the prophet (Jeremiah 20:2-3). The seal itself was not in this case attached to a letter as was customary, but rather was fixed to a cloth sachet, as the wavy pattern impressed on the back of the seal indicates. The seal is important in at least two ways: 1) It offers support to Jeremiah's record of a family named Immer who existed in Jerusalem during his time period; and 2) it confirms that the Temple Mount was an important administrative center at the end of the First Temple period as indicated in the biblical text. Other individuals mentioned by Jeremiah who are associated with the Temple Mount and are mentioned in Scripture have been historically confirmed through the identification of their personal stamp-seal impressions such as Jeremiah's scribe, Baruch, who penned the book of Jeremiah (Jeremiah 36:4-32). Moreover, the seals have been identified of both "Gemaryahu (Gemariah) ben Shaphan" who was an official secretary described in Jeremiah 36:10-12, and "Yehuchal (Jehucal) ben Shelemyahu" who was sent by King Zedekiah to Jeremiah in order to ask him to pray (Jeremiah 37:3; 38:1).*

Locating Solomon's Temple Mount

Examinations of structures and features open to the naked eye can offer fruitful results, as seen in the previous discussion of the Herodian reconstruction of the Temple. For example, visible at the base of the northwestern steps are large pre-Herodian stones that some (such as Leen Ritmeyer, 2006) propose to be the northwesternmost edge of Solomon's raised Temple Mount platform. Moreover, Herodian platform paving stones are visible; these would have provided adequate space for worshippers and non-Jews as they circulated around the open Temple Mount area. In addition, cisterns for washing and ritual cleansing and the Temple Mount retaining walls themselves (though most of the middle and upper courses of stone contained in the walls were placed during the Islamic and Crusader periods) are visible.

This final landing step includes pre-Herodian stone set at an angle parallel to the central portion of the current eastern wall (which is located in the same place as Solomon's eastern wall). This has led archaeologist Leen Ritmeyer to believe that this stone course forms the western wall boundary of Solomon's square temple platform.

---

* See our chart "Seal Impressions of People in the Old Testament" in chapter 19 for a listing of various individuals mentioned in the Hebrew Scriptures whose stamp seals have been found.

Perhaps the most telling feature involving the Jewish Temple is the sacred rock that is covered by the Dome of the Rock structure, known as *es-Sakhra* (Arabic for *rock*), where Muhammad is said to have ascended to heaven. Recent analysis (from 1968 to 2006) of the Temple Mount data by leading expert and archaeological architect Dr. Leen Ritmeyer has led him to identify the location of the Solomonic and Herodian Temples as the place where the Muslim Dome of the Rock stands today. Among other theories of where the First and Second Temples were located, dating back to Melchior de Vogue's northern theory in 1864, Ritmeyer's proposal is distinguished by hard literary and archaeological research. His participation with Israeli archaeologist Benjamin Mazar of the Hebrew University in Jerusalem in excavations from 1968 to 1978 of the southwest corner and surrounding areas of the Temple Mount have made him the world's foremost expert on the Temple topic; he possesses the most current archaeological research pertaining to the location of both Temples. His research on this important and fascinating topic was published in *The Quest: Revealing the Temple Mount in Jerusalem* (2006).

Ritmeyer explains that according to the measurements of the size of the Temple Mount found in Josephus and the second-century AD Mishnah,[8] combined with current archaeological data, the original raised Temple platform constructed by Solomon was 500 cubits by 500 cubits (approximately 750 feet by 750 feet) square. According to Ritmeyer, confusion exists as to the location of Solomon's square Temple Mount because of the misapplication of key texts in Josephus and the Mishnah *Middot*:

> The principal error made by most researchers is to equate the square Temple Mount, described by both Josephus and Middot, with that built by Herod the Great. Such a position cannot be maintained, as neither of the measurements given in these two sources can be reconciled with the dimensions of the present-day Temple Mount [constructed by Herod].[9]

Ritmeyer has established these measurements not only from the literature, but from hard facts on the ground, specifically the bottom step comprised of a line of pre-Herodian stones (laid in a north-south direction) located at the northwestern corner descending from the current raised platform. His identification of their unique angle—that is, that they are parallel to the central section of the eastern wall that overlooks the Kidron Valley (which is believed to be in its original location from the time of Solomon), and end exactly at the northern edge of the current raised platform—has led him to believe that these large step stones formed one of the three sides of Solomon's square Temple Mount.[10] Ritmeyer proposes that these step stones, which sit on bedrock, form part of the 500-cubit *western wall* course of Solomon's Temple Mount. From this data it is easy to mark out the 500 cubits by 500 cubits square mentioned in the *Middot*.

The Possible Site of the Temple

In addition to his discoveries of the proposed pre-Herodian western wall boundary and surrounding Temple Mount walls and structures, Ritmeyer has on various occasions sought to research the relationship between the protruding rock (*es-Sakhra*) covered by the Dome of the Rock structure and the Temple itself. In order to achieve this, he carefully examined the markings found on the rock, which has helped to offer archaeological evidence supporting the site as the location of both the First and Second Temples.

First, Ritmeyer noticed flat areas forming the foundation trench carved into the southern side of the rock itself, and a rock scarp on the northern end, which he proposes to be the foundation locations for the northern and southern walls of the Holy of Holies. The surface of the northern scarp, according to Ritmeyer, was cut down in size by Crusaders, forming a flat area on which to place two shrines that would complement the Crusader altar built on the rock. According to 1 Kings 6:20, Solomon's inner sanctuary was 20 royal cubits long by 20 royal cubits wide by 20 royal cubits high. Ritmeyer measured between the two trenches a distance of 34 feet, 5 inches, which is exactly 20 royal cubits.[11]

Es-Sakhra is also known as the "Rock of Binding," referring to Abraham's offering of his son Isaac. (Photo by Zev Radovan.)

Second, Ritmeyer discovered a natural rock edge (scarp) on the western side of the rock, which would provide the natural back end and western support structure for a western wall of the innermost sanctuary.

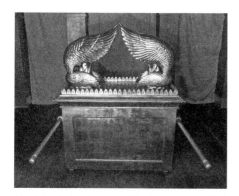

The Ark of the Covenant (Exodus 25:10-22; 37:1-9), which was placed in the Holy of Holies, was the most revered artifact ever made. It was a rectangular wooden chest measuring 2.25 feet wide by 3.75 feet long made of *shittim* wood (acacia) that was overlaid with gold. Its lid (called the mercy seat or atonement cover) was made of solid gold, with golden cherubim fashioned from the same piece of gold sitting atop the lid with outstretched wings. It was from between the two cherubim on the mercy seat that God would speak to Moses (Exodus 25:22; Numbers 7:89). Since the Ark was not to be touched, special poles (wood overlaid with gold) were used to transport it from location to location until it was placed in its final, permanent location in Solomon's Temple. Inside the Ark were placed the two tablets of the Law given by Moses (Exodus 25), Aaron's rod that budded (Numbers 17:10; Hebrews 9:4), and finally the golden jar of manna (Exodus 16:33; Hebrews 9:4). The model shown is from the "Wilderness Tabernacle," located in Kibbutz Almog, near the Dead Sea. (Photo by Zev Radovan.)

Third, if the northern, southern, and western walls could be identified, there should be no foundation markings 20 royal cubits to the east side of the Holy of Holies, since the Scriptures say Solomon used a wooden partition made of olive wood and overlaid with gold (1 Kings 6:31) between the inner sanctuary and the Holy Place. The later Herodian Temple used a curtain (veil), according to the Bible (Matthew 27:51), Josephus, and Jewish sources (Mishnah *Yoma* 5.1ff). After examining the rock, Ritmeyer discovered the presence of Crusader quarry marks but found no evidence of trenches on the eastern side of the inner sanctuary!

Fourth, Ritmeyer noticed a rectangular depression in the exact center of the Holy of Holies area.* After measuring the dimensions (1.5 cubits/2.25 feet wide by 2.5 cubits/3.75 feet long) of the depression he discovered it was the same dimensions as the Ark of the Covenant (Exodus 25:10)! First Kings 6:19-21 is consistent with these markings since it describes the innermost sanctuary as the location where Solomon *prepared* a special place for the Ark.

This special preparation is also confirmed in 1 Kings 8:6-8,20-21, where it says, "There I have *set* a place for the ark...." According to Ritmeyer, the Hebrew verb *sim,* translated "set," can

---

* Leen Ritmeyer, *The Quest: Revealing the Temple Mount in Jerusalem* (Jerusalem: Carta Jerusalem and the LAMB Foundation, 2006), 247. Ritmeyer treats objections to his proposals in a convincing manner (pages 247-250), offering literary, geological, and archaeological evidence supporting his claims. He indicates that the construction of the Dome of the Rock in the late seventh century AD—and the extreme reverence with which the Muslims (and Christians for a short time during the Crusades) have treated the site—has protected the rock through the centuries from the natural elements and vandalism, making these Temple markings discernible. Even during the Crusader period, the rock (and its markings) appeared to have been protected since the entire western half of the rock was overlaid by stone steps and a platform that served as part of the Crusader Church.

also mean "put" or "make," which would fit the archaeological evidence visible on the rock itself.[12] In this case, Ritmeyer suggests translating *sim* as "made," rendering the Solomon's statement as "I have *made* there a place for the Ark...." The preparation made by Solomon to stabilize the Ark on Mount Moriah's rocky surface ensured that the Ark would not tilt, wobble, or slide to one side in an undignified manner.[13] The value of the biblical passages cannot be underestimated, for without their descriptions we would not have recognized the rock markings and dimensions (1 Kings 6:20) for what they really were.

Features of and Surrounding the Temple Proper

After identifying the Holy of Holies, Ritmeyer's proposal for the location of the sacrificial altar is relatively simple to mark as immediately east and southeast of the Holy Place. Some have suggested the altar was located on the rock (*es-Sakhra*) itself. However, Ritmeyer has eliminated this location. Since the altar was originally located on the threshing floor of Araunah, which was most likely a flat circular area, it would not have made sense to place it on the top of the rock (or the tip of a mountain). This would not

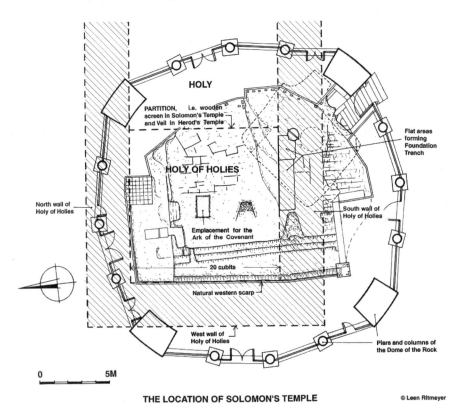

THE LOCATION OF SOLOMON'S TEMPLE   © Leen Ritmeyer

(© Ritmeyer Archaeological Design.)

have been practical for oxen to walk on nor for the separation of wheat and chaff. On the Mount itself, the topography in relation to the bedrock and an analysis of the Mishnah *Middot* (chapter 3) favor Ritmeyer's placement of the altar as east and off-center, slightly to the south of the Holy Place and the current Muslim Dome of the Chain.

As one begins to move east from the Holy Place through Herod's Temple, beyond the Temple Court (Azarah) and the altar of sacrifice are two narrow areas known as the Court of the Priests and the Court of the Israelites. Moving eastward through the Nicanor Gate one would encounter the 15 semicircular steps where the Levitical choir would sing out into the Court of the Women (the Treasury); there four giant lamp stands would illuminate the area. From here moving east the worshipper would exit the Temple compound through the Eastern Gate into the Temple Mount plaza/platform area.

According to the *Middot* (2.3), the space immediately surrounding the Temple sanctuary was a protected area that allowed the presence of only Jews. No Gentiles were allowed past the *soreg*, which was a low-lying wall (about three to five feet tall) marked with warnings in Greek, Hebrew, and Latin that no Gentile was allowed to pass through the *soreg*, upon penalty of death.[14] At least two Greek-language warning markers have been discovered in secondary use, like the one pictured here. The typical warning reads, when translated,

No Gentile may enter
beyond the dividing wall
into the court around the
   Holy Place
Whoever is caught
will have himself
to blame for his
subsequent death

This Greek-inscribed Temple warning marker and others like it would be placed at each entry point along the *soreg* boundary surrounding the Temple sanctuary. (Photo by Zev Radovan.)

The *soreg* line marked the innermost boundary between the outer retaining walls of the Temple Mount built by Herod and the Temple sanctuary itself, located at the center of the Mount. The area between the *soreg* boundary wall and the outer Temple Mount walls is known as the Court of the Gentiles (outer court); non-Jews could freely move about there through the colonnades and open expanse. Interestingly, Acts 21:28-31 appears to be consistent with the existence of the *soreg* and its strict penalty when it describes the riot that ensued after Jews mistakenly believed that the apostle Paul had taken a Gentile into this forbidden area. Paul's letter to the Ephesians (2:13-14) portrays this kind of separation barrier as having been overcome by Christ's finished work on the cross: "Now in Christ Jesus you who once were far off have been brought near by the blood of Christ. For He Himself is our peace, who has made both one, and has broken down the middle wall of separation" (NKJV).

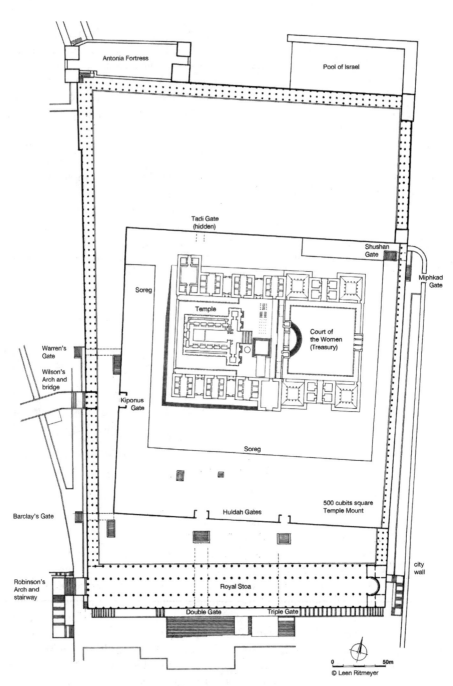

First-century Temple Mount structure. (© Ritmeyer Archaeological Design.)

The archaeological and literary evidence supporting the biblical record of the existence, location, function, and personnel associated with the First and Second Temples are strong, especially in light of the recent archaeological data provided by Ritmeyer, Mazar, and others.* Any attempt to dismiss the Jewish presence or the religious functions held sacred by Israel appears to be at odds with a mountain of data that confirms the reliability of the biblical statements about the Temple Mount, its religious and administrative functions, and the renovations and reconstructions through the centuries.

---

* Even minute details are being uncovered which are confirming the historical nature of the Scriptures. For example, in June 2012, Ronny Reich and Eli Shukron discovered a tiny gold bell measuring about one-half inch in diameter while excavating in Jerusalem adjacent to the Temple Mount. The bell has curved vertical ridges and a loop at the top for fastening. The excavators suggest that it may have been worn by a high official or attached to the priestly garments as described in Exodus 28:33-35.

HEROD, PILATE, AND CAIAPHAS

Herod the Great

Most Christians are familiar with Herod the Great because he tried to put the child Jesus to death when He was in Bethlehem.* Certainly the attempt to kill the future king of Israel was a vicious act, and Herod was guilty of many other atrocities. As significant as this episode and Herod's bloodthirstiness are, there are a variety of reasons why he is important to secular and biblical history. He is known as a cunning politician, a successful military campaigner, but most of all a master builder.[1]

Herod was born in the late 70s BC of a wealthy Idumean father by the name of Antipater. His father was a favorite with the Romans and became *epistropos*, or overseer, of Judea in 47 BC. In time, Herod, with the assistance of his father, was appointed governor of Galilee and gained recognition for the subjugation of bandits there. This effectively gained him the attention of Rome, so that after the murder of his father, Herod was made king of Judea, a position that he held for 33 years, reigning from 37 to 4 BC.[2]

He was known as a ruthless ruler, but he was able to maintain his power

One of Herod's hilltop palaces overlooks the Dead Sea at Masada.

Herod's kingdom.

---

* The following discussions of Heord the Great, Pontius Pilate, and Caiaphas are adapted from material provided by Dr. H. Wayne House and are used by permission.

because of his effectiveness and the manner in which he ingratiated himself with various Roman rulers. In the changes within the Roman government, he seemed to know intuitively to whom to give allegiance. He also knew how to effectively use an army that he had trained to retain his power.*

The primary reason that Herod has gained the appellation "the Great" relates to his skill as a master builder. He built cities and temples in honor of Roman emperors and Roman gods. For example, Caesarea Maritima (on the Mediterranean Sea) was named after emperor Claudius, and Samaria was called Sebaste, the Greek name for Augustus. Herod

Herod's city known as the Herodium was a cone-shaped man-made fortress that featured internal tunnels to access the inner city structures. (Photo by Zev Radovan.)

These ruins of the Herodium are located in the cone atop Herod's fortress.

Professor Ehud Netzer. In addition to the location of Herod's tomb, the late Dr. Netzer, one of the leading Herodian archaeologists of our time, found a pottery shard at Masada with a Latin inscription that identified "Herod, King of Judea" and the date and type of wine he imported from Europe. These and other discoveries have removed all doubt about the historicity of Herod. (Photo by Zev Radovan.)

The Latin Herod inscription discovered at Masada. This sherd is part of a wine jug. (Photo courtesy of Randall Price.)

---

* "He was such a warrior as could not be withstood…fortune was also very favourable to him" (Josephus, *Wars of the Jews*, I, xxi, 13). See "Herod," newadvent.org (last visited November 18, 2011).

built an important harbor at Caesarea Maritima, including hippodromes and theaters[3]; he also built several fortresses (such as Masada, the Herodium, and Machaerus) to which he could flee in case of revolt.

In order to solicit the support of the Jewish people (he being despised by them as an Idumean, or Arab, ruler), he constructed the massive Temple foundation and retaining walls and rebuilt the Temple itself.

Death and Burial of Herod

The end of Herod's life reveals the essence of the character manifested throughout his life, in things such as the execution of his wives and sons, not to mention the killing of the infants in search of the Messiah in Bethlehem. Levine reports, "Realizing his end was imminent, Herod ordered that upon his death the men whom he had locked up in the Jericho hippodrome should be executed, thus ensuring general mourning at the time of his death (Ant 17 §173–75)." [4]

Herod's tomb located at the Herodium, prior to its excavation.

The existence and achievements of Herod the Great are not really challenged today, but there have been some questions surrounding his death and burial.[5] The question of where he was buried has now been answered to a large extent by the discovery in 2007 of his tomb at the Herodium,[6] one of his fortresses, by the recently deceased professor Ehud Netzer of Hebrew University.[7]

Pontius Pilate

Pontius Pilate (Greek Πόντιος Πίλατος) is one of the most well-known figures of ancient history, based almost entirely on his judgment of Jesus the Messiah as recorded in the New Testament. Jesus' appearance before Pontius Pilate is recorded by all four Gospels (Matthew 27:2; Mark 15:1-15; Luke 23:1-5; John 18:28–19:16), but information about him also occurs in the writings of Josephus, Tertullian, Eusebius, Philo, Tacitus, and Agapius of Hierapolis. For example, Tacitus says regarding Pilate,

> Christus, from whom the name had its origin, suffered the extreme penalty during the reign of Tiberius at the hands of one of our procurators, Pontius Pilatus, and a most mischievous superstition, thus checked for the moment, again broke out not only in Judaea, the first source of the evil, but even in Rome, where all things hideous and shameful from every part of the world find their centre and become popular.[8]

Pilate has been vilified by some and canonized by others*—considered as evil since

---

* A.N. Sherwin-White, "Pontius Pilate," *The International Standard Bible Encyclopedia*, revised, ed. Geoffrey W. Bromiley

he sentenced Jesus to death, and viewed by others as a Christian who influenced Tiberius to be favorable to Christianity.* As the fifth Roman governor of Judea, he had a troubled and less than lustrous (actually, undistinguished) career in that capacity. The date of his appointment and dismissal is subject to debate, but he is commonly thought to have been appointed governor in AD 26 or 27 and removed from office in AD 36. He is reported to have died by suicide.

Pilate had a rugged rule in Judea. Previous rulers there had respected Jewish customs and sensitivities, but he seems to have had little regard for them. He covertly brought in images of the imperial ensigns into Jerusalem at night, which he finally removed due to the protests of the Jews. He, first, threatened them with death, but afterward relented. At another time, he received a rebuke from Emperor Tiberius after he had irritated the Jews to insurrection when he set up gold-coated shields in Herod's palace; Tiberius had Pilate remove the shields to Caesarea and place them in the temple of Augustus.[9]

In another episode, Pilate was not so pliable. He had appropriated funds from the Temple treasury to pay for the construction of an aqueduct to carry water to Jerusalem. Josephus does not say that this action violated Jewish law, but he does say that the indignant Jerusalemites surrounded Pilate as he heard cases and protested angrily. Pilate, however, had taken the precaution of planting "plainclothes" soldiers among the crowd. At the appropriate moment he signaled for them to draw out clubs and beat the protesters. Josephus says that many Jews perished, either from the blows or from being trampled in the escape. Thus, under Pilate, the Jews were reduced to fearful silence.[10]

His last vicious act was to have his cavalry and infantry kill a number of Samaritans who went for religious purposes to Mount Gerizim.[11] After the Samaritans complained, the Roman governor of Syria, Vitellius, sent Pilate to Rome to explain himself to Tiberius, but before Pilate arrived, Tiberius had died.[12] The successor to Tiberius, Gaius Caesar Augustus Germanicus (Caligula), removed Pilate from his position and exiled him to Vienna-on-Rhone. He is believed to have committed suicide while in exile during the reign of Caligula.[†]

(Grand Rapids, MI: Wm. B. Eerdmans, 1988; 2002): "Origen described Pilate's wife as a convert, and the Coptic Church ultimately canonized Pilate himself." Coptic should probably be understood as Ethiopic. "The Coptic Church or the Abyssinian Coptic Orthodox Church referred to in this article is the Ethiopian church, but they are sometimes confused because of their origins in Egypt. The fourth or fifth century Gospel of Nicodemus (which contains the Acts of Pilate), does not make Pilate a Christian, but depicts him as more friendly toward Jesus than any of the canonical Gospels. Pilate was soon canonized by the Ethiopic churches. See "Questions and Answers," Coptic Orthodox Diocese of the Southern United States website, www.suscopts.org/q&a/index.php?qid=766&catid=446 (last visited November 8, 2011).

* See discussion in Philip Schaff, *The Nicene and Post-Nicene Fathers*, second series, vol. I (Oak Harbor, WA: Logos Research Systems, 1997), 105-106. Numerous stories arose regarding Pilate seeking to exonerate him or recognize him as a Christian. "For instance, the apocryphal Acts of Pilate recounts the trial showing that Pilate's decision was forced upon him. Colorful embellishments bring home the point: when Jesus enters Pilate's praetorium, the imperial standards miraculously bow down. Tertullian even speaks of Pilate as a 'Christian at heart' and contributes to the legendary conversion of both Pilate and his wife (who later gains the name Procula)" (Gary M. Burge, "Pilate, Pontius," in *Baker Encyclopedia of the Bible*, eds. Walter A. Elwell and Barry J. Beitzel [Grand Rapids, MI: Baker Book House, 1988], 1694-1695.

† The suicide is described by Eusebius (HE 2.7) as precipitated by his actions against the Samaritans, discussed by Arthur Cushman McGiffert, "The Church History of Eusebius," in Philip Schaff, *Nicene and Post-Nicene Fathers*, Second Series (Peabody, MA.: Hendrickson Publishers, Inc., 1995), 110 n13. According to Eusebius, "Pilate's downfall occurred in the following manner. A leader of the Samaritans had promised to disclose the sacred treasures which Moses was reported to

The Pontius Pilate Inscription

Though we have literary evidence for Pontius Pilate, no physical evidence existed until 1961, when archaeologist Antonio Frova and a team of other archaeologists discovered an inscription on a stone dated to the period from AD 26 to 37.[13] It was in secondary use as part of a stairway in the theater at Caesarea Maritima[14] on the coast of Israel, though "undoubtedly, the stone was first used as part of some important building called a Tiberium, possibly a temple, which was dedicated in honor of the emperor Tiberius."[15] Even though the stone is in poor condition, three of the four lines of the text may be partially reconstructed.

Pontius Pilate Dedication inscription discovered at Caesarea Maritima. (Photo by Zev Radovan.)

The inscription reads as follows:

[ ]S TIBERIEUM	(Tiberieum)
[PO]NTIUS PILATUS	(Pontius Pilate)
[PRAEF]ECTUS IUDA[EA]E	(Prefect of Judea)
[ ]	

Historians have often referred to Pilate as a procurator, but later governors after Emperor Claudius were so known; earlier governors like Pilate were known as prefects, as found in the inscription.*

have concealed upon Mount Gerizim, and the Samaritans came together in great numbers from all quarters. Pilate, supposing the gathering to be with rebellious purpose, sent troops against them and defeated them with great slaughter. The Samaritans complained to Vitellius, governor of Syria, who sent Pilate to Rome (36 A.D.) to answer the charges brought against him. Upon reaching Rome he found Tiberius dead and Caius upon the throne. He was unsuccessful in his attempt to defend himself, and, according to tradition, was banished to Vienne in Gaul, where a monument is still shown as Pilate's tomb. According to another tradition he committed suicide upon the mountain near Lake Lucerne, which bears his name" (McGiffert). Also see Geoffrey W. Bromiley, *The International Standard Bible Encyclopedia*, revised (Wm. B. Eerdmans, 1988; 2002). Eusebius, in *Ecclesiastical History*, 2.7, also comments, "It is worthy of note that Pilate himself, who was governor in the time of our Saviour, is reported to have fallen into such misfortunes under Caius, whose times we are recording, that he was forced to become his own murderer and executioner; and thus divine vengeance, as it seems, was not long in overtaking him. This is stated by those Greek historians who have recorded the Olympiads, together with the respective events which have taken place in each period" (Schaff, 110).

* For example, Pilate lived in Herod's palace, described by Philo as "the residence of the prefects" (see Philo, *Delegation to Gaius*, 38).

The life and career of Pontius Pilate has been known in literary sources since the days of the first century, but the inscription further substantiates the existence and position of this Roman who played a pivotal, though unfortunate, role in the plan of God for the Messiah Jesus.

Caiaphas

The Gospel accounts (Matthew 26:3,57; Luke 3:2; John 11:49; 18:13-14,24,28; Acts 4:6) indicate that Caiaphas (Greek, Καϊάφας) was the high priest in Jerusalem the year that Jesus died, serving between AD 18 and 36 (though his father-in-law, Annas,* retained the title).† The Gospel accounts refer to him only as Caiaphas, but his full title was Joseph, son of Caiaphas (Hebrew, קַיָּפָא בַּר יוֹסֵף, *Yosef Bar Kayafa*). He was son-in-law of Annas in the apostolic records, and was high priest by the appointment of Rome.‡ In AD 36, the Syrian governor Vitellius removed the prefect Pilate as well as Caiaphas.§

The Gospel writers view Caiaphas as the primary priestly opponent of Jesus, and he is especially known for his willingness to sacrifice Jesus for tranquility in Israel:¶

---

* "This Ananias was not the son of Nebedeus, as I take it, but he who was called Annas or Annanus the Elder, the 9th in the catalogue, and who had been esteemed high priest for a long time; and besides, Caiaphas his son-in-law had five of his own sons high priests after him, who were those of numbers 11, 14, 15, 17, 24, in the foregoing catalogue. Nor ought we to pass slightly over what Josephus here says of this Annas or Ananias, that he was high priest a long time before his children were so, he was the son of Seth, and is set down first for high priest in the foregoing catalogue, under number 9. He was made by Quirinus, and continued till Ismael, the tenth in number, for about twenty-three years; which long duration of his high priesthood, joined to the successions of his son-in-law, and five children of his own, made him a sort of perpetual high priest, and was perhaps the occasion that former high priests kept their titles ever afterwards; for I believe it is hardly met with before him" (*Antiquities*, 20.206).

† "Josephus often confuses the reader by speaking of various individuals as 'high priest' at the same time, or by calling someone high priest when he was no longer in office (for example, *Wars of the Jews* 2.441; *Antiquities of the Jews*, 20.205; *Life of Josephus*, 193). Yet the Bible and Josephus both insist that only one person can serve as high priest at one time. On closer examination, we realize that Josephus allows former high priests to retain the title and prestige of the office as long as they live. Perhaps this usage reflects his assumption that high priests ought to serve for life.

"In any case, we have a similar confusion in the Gospels and Acts. Luke 3:2 and Acts 4:6 mention several high priests (especially Annas and Caiaphas) as though they were current. More baffling yet, John 18:12-26 has Jesus interrogated by Annas (=Ananus I), who is first called "the father-in-law of the high priest" (18:13) but is then addressed as 'high priest' (18:15,19,22). And when Jesus' interview with the high priest is finished, He is sent in chains to 'Caiaphas the high priest' (18:24). If the authors of Luke and John made the same assumptions as Josephus, and expected their readers to do so, then their accounts become somewhat less puzzling. Ananus I was an extremely distinguished high priest in Josephus's view, for five of his sons followed him in office (*Antiquities of the Jews*, 20.197-198). So it makes sense that the Gospel authors would remember his name in conjunction with Caiaphas, the serving high priest at the time of Jesus' trial" (Steve Mason, *Josephus and the New Testament* [Peabody, MA.: Hendrickson Publishers, 1992]).

‡ Josephus says, "He [Nero] was now the third emperor; and he sent Valerius Gratus to be procurator of Judea, and to succeed Annius Rufus. (34) This man deprived Ananus of the high priesthood, and appointed Ismael, the son of Phabi, to be high priest. He also deprived him in a little time, and ordained Eleazar, the son of Ananus, who had been high priest before, to be high priest: which office, when he had held for a year, Gratus deprived him of it, and gave the high priesthood to Simon, the son of Camithus; (35) and when he had possessed that dignity no longer than a year, Joseph Caiaphas was made his successor" (*Antiquities of the Jews*, 18.31).

§ "Vitellius…deprived Joseph, who was called Caiaphas, of the high priesthood, and appointed Jonathan, the son of Ananus, the former high priest, to succeed him" (Josephus, *Antiquities of the Jews*, XVIII, iv, 3).

¶ Mason adds, "Josephus describes a coincidence of interest between Jewish chief-priestly circles and the Roman government. He presents the chief priests by and large as favoring cooperation with Rome, even in the face of severe provocation. Not only do these eminent citizens support the governors' harsh treatment of political terrorists and religious fanatics, they

"If we let Him *go on* like this, all men will believe in Him, and the Romans will come and take away both our place and our nation." But one of them, Caiaphas, who was high priest that year, said to them, "You know nothing at all, nor do you take into account that it is expedient for you that one man die for the people, and that the whole nation not perish" (John 11:48-50).

Among 12 ossuaries found in the Caiaphas family tomb in southern Jerusalem, this ossuary contains an inscription that bears Caiaphas's name. (Photo by Zev Radovan.)

The Caiaphas Ossuary

Not only do the canonical Gospels and the *Antiquities of the Jews* of Josephus provide evidence regarding the existence and position of Joseph, son of Caiaphas; contemporary archaeology also supports his existence. In November of 1990, while a work crew was building a road south of Abu Tor in southeast Jerusalem in what is called the Peace

---

also cooperate in removing such troublesome individuals. A particularly interesting case concerns one Jesus son of Ananias, a common peasant who predicted the fall of the temple four years before the outbreak of the revolt. For more than seven years, especially at festivals, he would cry, 'Woe to Jerusalem!' and 'A voice against Jerusalem and the sanctuary, a voice against the bridegroom and the bride, a voice against all the people.' The exasperated temple leaders punished him without success, and eventually passed him over to the Roman governor. As he would not answer any questions, he was flayed to the bone and released on grounds of insanity (*Wars of the Jews,* 6.300-309). This cooperation of the leading citizens with the Romans, when it came to a person who had disrupted the already tense festival periods in Jerusalem, fits with the general picture of political relations painted by Josephus. This picture in turn helps one to imagine some cooperation between the Jewish leadership and the Roman governor in the trial of Jesus" (Mason).

Forest, but on a hill traditionally called the Mount of Evil Counsel, the family tomb of Caiaphas was uncovered.

In the tomb archaeologists found an ornate ossuary with the inscription "Joseph, son of Caiaphas" in Aramaic. A few scholars question whether the inscription truly refers to Caiaphas the high priest, who condemned Jesus, especially since it does not mention his title, yet the ornate nature of the ossuary would indicate that the bones of the person placed inside are those of someone of considerable rank and wealth. One cannot argue with 100 percent certainty that the ossuary is that of the Caiaphas mentioned in the Gospels, but we know of no other Joseph, son of Caiaphas, in the first century who would be so identified and buried in an ossuary such as this.[16]

This ornate ossuary is believed to have belonged to the son of Caiaphas.

26

MORE FASCINATING FINDS RELATING TO THE NEW TESTAMENT

Sergius Paulus

On the apostle Paul's first missionary journey in the first century AD, he came to know the Roman proconsul (under the Emperor Claudius) who lived on Cyprus.* Of their time on Cyprus, Luke writes,

> When they had gone through the whole island as far as Paphos, they found a magician, a Jewish false prophet whose name was Bar-Jesus, who was with the proconsul, Sergius Paulus, a man of intelligence. This man summoned Barnabas and Saul and sought to hear the word of God. But Elymas the magician (for so his name is translated) was opposing them, seeking to turn the proconsul away from the faith. But Saul, who was also known as Paul, filled with the Holy Spirit, fixed his gaze on him, and said, "You who are full of all deceit and fraud, you son of the devil, you enemy of all righteousness, will you not cease to make crooked the straight ways of the Lord? Now, behold, the hand of the Lord is upon you, and you will be blind and not see the sun for a time." And immediately a mist and a darkness fell upon him, and he went about seeking those who would lead him by the hand. Then the proconsul believed when he saw what had happened, being amazed at the teaching of the Lord (Acts 13:6-12).

In the Roman Empire, provinces were divided under two different categories, those needing Roman troops and those that did not. The former were directly under the emperor, and the latter were governed by the senate and ruled by proconsuls. Cyprus, when Paul visited, was under the administration of a proconsul (ἀνθύπατος in Greek) from 22 BC until the time of the Emperor Hadrian.[1]

The proconsul is identified by Luke as an intelligent man and also one who was interested in the content of the message that Paul preached. The apostle, the record shows, had a confrontation with a magician by the name of Elymas, and when Paul brought a

---

* The following discussions of Sergius Paulus; city officials in the Acts of the Apostles; Gallio, proconsul of Achaia; and Erastus, city treasurer of Corinth were adapted from material provided by Dr. H. Wayne House and are used by permission.

351

judgment on him from God because of his activity, the proconsul embraced the gospel. The text indicates, however, that it was not only the miracle that brought him to Jesus, but also the teaching of the Lord.

Inscriptions Confirming Sergius Paulus

Is there evidence for this proconsul Luke mentions? There appear to be three inscriptions that refer to him, two in Cyprus and one in Rome.* The two in Cyprus are written in Greek and were discovered by General Louis di Cesnola.[2] One of them was discovered in 1877 on the northern coast of Cyprus, at Soli.[3] It mentions Paulus (*nomen*, name of clan) but does not have the *praenomen* (forename, personal name chosen by parents) or cognomen (third name, branch of clan) of the proconsul, so whether it refers to the Sergius Paulus in Acts is uncertain. The inscription reads,

An inscription displayed in the courtyard of the Yalvac Museum in Turkey. Clearly visible is the whole of "Paulli" and portions of "Sergii." The family of Sergius Paulus had large estates in the vicinity of Pisidian Antioch. The proconsul of Cyprus, Sergius Paulus, was converted to Christianity (Acts 13:7-12). It may have been that at that time Sergius Paulus requested Paul to travel to Pisidian Antioch to speak to other members of his extended family. (Photo used by permission of Carl Rasmussen/www.HolyLandPhotos.org.)

> Apollonius to his father...consecrated this enclosure and monument according to his family's wishes...having filled the offices of clerk of the market, prefect, town-clerk, high priest, and having been in charge as manager of the records office. Erected on the 25th of the month Demarchexusius in the thirteenth year [of the reign of Claudius—54 AD]. He also altered the senate by means of assessors during the time of the proconsul Paulus.[4]

The inscription does demonstrate that the family of Pauli was on the island of Cyprus.[5] The second Greek inscription is one found in Kythraia in northern Cyprus; it references Quintus Sergius Paulus in the time of Claudius,[6] which is the proper time period for the event given by Luke. Of the three inscriptions, this is probably the best evidence. In the opinion of Joseph Fitzmyer, Sergius Paulus may also be identified from a fragmentary dedicatory Greek inscription from Kythraia in northern Cyprus,[7] presently housed in the Metropolitan Museum of New York, which on line 10 may preserve part of his name, "Koïntou Serg[iou...]," after mentioning Claudius Caesar Augustus in

---

* David Williams mentions additional inscriptions that might relate to the family of Sergius Paulus. In addition, William Ramsay and John George Clark Anderson discovered in 1912 an inscription near Pisidian Antioch that mentions a "Lucius Sergius Paullus, the younger son of Lucius." In 1913 Ramsay discovered the woman's name "Sergia Paulla" on an inscription in the same region. These discoveries played an important part in his theory that the family of Sergius Paulus was Christians (see William Ramsay, *The Bearing of Recent Discovery on the Trustworthiness of the New Testament* [London: Hodder & Stoughton, 1915], pp. 150-72) (David J. Williams, *New International Biblical Commentary: Acts* [Peabody, MA: Hendrickson Publishers, 1990], 227-228).

the preceding line. Unfortunately the restoration is not certain, and the restored name is contested.[8]

The third inscription is written in Latin, reading "Lucius Sergius Paullus" (the Latin spelling of the name, in contrast to *Paulus* in the Greek), was discovered in Rome in 1887.[9] It was found on a boundary stone erected by Emperor Claudius. Ben Witherington III considers this inscription the most helpful because

> we have a clear reference to one Lucius Sergius Paulus, who was one of the curators of the Tiber River under Claudius. There is nothing in this inscription that would rule out the possibility that this Sergius Paulus was either at an earlier or a later date a proconsul on Cyprus, and in fact various classics scholars have been more ready than some New Testament scholars to identify the man mentioned in Acts 13 with the one in the Latin inscription.[10]

City Officials in the Acts of the Apostles

At one time, Luke, the companion of the apostle Paul, was viewed as an unreliable guide to the history and geography of the Mediterranean world. The writer of Luke and Acts often was alone in his use of terms, location of places, and mention of persons not known to scholarship. Such is no longer the case. He has been vindicated repeatedly, to the point that Sir William Ramsay, noted classical archaeologist, once a skeptic of the reliability of Luke, called him the greatest of historians, even above the Greek historian Thucydides.[11]

An example of the accuracy of Luke may be found in his mention of two types of officials in the ancient world, the *asiarch* and the *politarch*. Both of these titles were used by Luke in Acts, and both have been discovered on inscriptions in the Mediterranean world.

Asiarch

The word *asiarch* is a transliteration of the Greek word Ἀσιάρχης and is derived from the word Ἀσιά, the province of Asia, and the word ἄρχειν, meaning "to rule."[12] The Acts of the Apostles records an incident in which Paul the apostle was threatened by certain silversmiths in Ephesus, since his preaching of the gospel was causing them to lose business. Luke mentions that Paul had friends among the "asiarchs." Scholars formerly viewed Luke's usage as an anachronism, the only other example of the term being found in classical sources; namely, Strabo's *Geography*.[13] However, the word *asiarch* is also mentioned by the early church historian Eusebius in regard to the martyrdom of Polycarp:

> 26. And when this was proclaimed by the herald, the whole multitude, both of Gentiles and of Jews, who dwelt in Smyrna, cried out with ungovernable wrath and with a great shout, "This is the teacher of Asia, the father of the Christians, the overthrower of our gods, who teaches many not to sacrifice nor to worship."

27. When they had said this, they cried out and asked the Asiarch Philip to let a lion loose upon Polycarp. But he said that it was not lawful for him, since he had closed the games. Then they thought fit to cry out with one accord that Polycarp should be burned alive.[14]

Luke's care about historical accuracy lends credibility to his account in Acts 19:31, where he writes, "And even some of the Asiarchs, who were friends of his, sent to him and were urging him not to venture into the theater" (Acts 19:31 ESV). Paul had intended to go into the theater to speak for himself against the charges made by the silversmiths (specifically Demetrius), but certain asiarchs, possibly friends in view of their actions,* encouraged Paul not to do so. Whether they were friends or not is uncertain. Elwell and Beitzel say,

> Why there were a number of such officers in Ephesus at the time of the riot, or why the Asiarchs showed such concern for Paul, is not clear. Perhaps they were deputies of the "Commune of Asia," responsible to promote and protect the imperial cult (the worship practices of Rome and the emperor). The Asiarchs mentioned were evidently not adverse to a religious movement like Christianity, which embarrassed the prevailing pagan cult of Artemis. The long account in Acts 19 repeats one of Luke's themes, that Christianity was not subversive nor was Paul a political menace. Otherwise the Asiarchs would not have favored him in such a manner.[†]

The authenticity of this account in Acts chapter 19 is supported by Luke's firsthand knowledge of things at Ephesus.[15] Koester lists four items that support this thesis:[16] the use of the term "temple keeper" (verse 35) in respect to the cult of Artemis;[17] the

The above inscription containing the word *asiarch* was discovered in Miletus, a short distance from ancient Ephesus (Turkey). (Photo used by permission of Mark Wilson.)

---

* Paul's friendship with the asiarchs in Ephesians may provide understanding why Philip the Asiarch sought to convince the people in Smyrna against loosing a lion on Polycarp.

† Walter A. Elwell and Barry J. Beitzel, *Baker Encyclopedia of the Bible* (Grand Rapids, MI: Baker Book House, 1988), 217. Alexander Souter says similarly, "When we come to study the connexion of the Asiarchs with the Acts narrative, we are puzzled. It seems at first sight strange that men elected to foster the worship of Rome and the Emperor should be found favouring the ambassador of the Messiah, the Emperor's rival for the lordship of the Empire. This is only one, however, of a number of indications that the Empire was at first disposed to look with a kindly eye on the new religion. Christianity, with its outward respect for civil authority, seemed at first the strongest supporter of law and order. Artemis-worship, moreover, hulked so largely in Ephesus as perhaps to dwarf the Imperial worship. Thus St. Paul, whose preaching so threatened the authority of Artemis, may have appeared in a favourable light to the representatives of Cæsar-worship, as likely to create more enthusiasm in that direction" (Alexander Souter, "Asiarch," *Dictionary of the Apostolic Church* [2 vols.], ed. James Hastings [New York: Charles Scribner's Sons, 1916-1918].

fact that small silver shrines of Artemis were sold in Ephesus; the existence of asiarchs as local political persons (verse 31);[18] and the reference to the "scribe of the Demos"[19] as a very powerful Ephesian official (verse 35).

Who exactly were the asiarchs? There is some uncertainty regarding this, with some scholars saying that they were possibly high priests,[20] while others view them only as important and wealthy officials.[21] Strabo's account recognizes them as officials who were, according to one writer, "chosen from among the wealthiest and most aristocratic in the province. They were expected to finance public games and festivals and usually served one-year terms. Inscriptions attesting *Asiarchs* have been found in over 40 cities in Asia Minor."[22] There is evidence, also, that asiarchs, much like contemporary public officials, may have been retained in their capacities by private persons after they left office.[23]

Politarch

Greek city-states had local rulers similar to the archons of Athens who were also responsible to Roman provincial rulers to maintain order and suppress sedition against the empire. One of the officials mentioned by the writer Luke is the *politarch*. In Acts 17:6-8, he reports,

> When they did not find them [Paul and Silas], they *began* dragging Jason and some brethren before the city authorities, shouting, "These men who have upset the world have come here also; and Jason has welcomed them, and they all act contrary to the decrees of Caesar, saying that there is another king, Jesus." They stirred up the crowd and the city authorities who heard these things (Acts 17:6-8).

Recently, several politarch inscriptions were found within the ruins of ancient cities. Of the total number discovered, 19 of the 32 "politarch" inscriptions (like the one pictured here) come from the ancient city of Thessalonica, with 3 of these dating to the first century AD. (Photo © The Trustees of the British Museum.)

The charges against Paul and his fellow workers were that they were troublemakers and did things contrary to the decrees of the emperor by proclaiming another king, namely, Jesus—a very serious charge, were it proved.[24] This would have caused concern on the part of these city authorities to ensure that these Christians did not have seditious intentions and to calm the crowd.

The words "city authorities," in the Greek, are the term *politarchs* (Greek, τοὺς πολιτάρχας).* The word never occurs in Greek literature, though πολιτάρχας is used once by Aeneas Tacticus. In 1835 an inscription was discovered on an arch at Thessalonica, dated between AD 69 and 79, which begins πολειταρχούντων Σωσπάτρου ("politarchs Sosipater...") and then continues with the names of seven politarchs. Since that time many such examples in other Macedonian cities have been found.[25]

Though the historical accuracy of Luke has been questioned since the rise of historical skepticism about the Bible, his close familiarity with the world of his day and careful reporting should cause one to trust him when he speaks of persons, places, events, and other facts. As F.F. Bruce said, "When a writer's accuracy is established by valid evidence, he gains the right to be treated as a reliable informant on matters coming within his scope which are not corroborated elsewhere (Bruce 1985: 2578)."[26]

Gallio, Proconsul of Achaia

One of the Roman officials the apostle Paul encountered in his missionary travels was Gallio, whom Paul stood before in judgment at the *bema* in Corinth sometime in the years AD 51 to 53. According to Acts 18:12-13, he was brought before this Roman proconsul of Achaia for breaking the Jewish law. When Gallio heard that the charges regarded the Jewish law rather than actionable Roman law, he immediately dismissed them:

> While Gallio was proconsul of Achaia, the Jews with one accord rose up against Paul and brought him before the judgment seat, saying, "This man persuades men to worship God contrary to the law." But when Paul was about to open his mouth, Gallio said to the Jews, "If it were a matter of wrong or of vicious crime, O Jews, it would be reasonable for me to put up with you; but if there are questions about words and names and your own law, look after it yourselves; I am unwilling to be a judge of these matters." And he drove them away from the judgment seat. And they all took hold of Sosthenes, the leader of the synagogue, and *began* beating him in front of the judgment seat. But Gallio was not concerned about any of these things (Acts 18:12-17).

Junius Annaeus Gallio was the son of Marcus Annaeus Seneca, the rhetorician and

---

* Note that translations have tended not to use *politarch* but rather substitute a descriptive phrase, such as "city authorities" (NASB, ESV, NRSV), "rulers of the city" (KJV, ASV, NKJV), "city officials" (HSCB, NIV, NET), "city council" (NJB).

the brother of the famous philosopher, Lucius Annaeus Seneca. The latter spoke of Gallio highly: "No mortal is so pleasant to any one person as Gallio is to everybody."[27]

The existence of Gallio and his position is confirmed by an archaeological discovery made at Delphi in 1908, consisting of nine stone fragments. Adolf Deissman says regarding the discoveries that the inscription was a puzzle. Some years previous, four fragments had initially been unearthed, then three additional ones, and finally two more.[28] There was disagreement as to whether the pieces were part of different inscriptions, but finally scholars agreed that all nine fragments were from the same inscription.[29]

The inscription, dated to about AD 52, is a proclamation made by Emperor Claudius (AD 41–54) that mentions Gallio as the proconsul of Achaia (Greece). Gallio's position at Corinth helps to confirm Paul's time in that city between AD 51 and 53.[30] The pertinent part of the inscription reads (as reconstructed), "Gallio, my fr[iend] an[d procon]sul recently [reported to me]....":

The Gallio inscription, dating to AD 52, was discovered at the Temple of Apollo in Delphi, Greece, and has become an important artifact in forming a chronology of the life and ministry of Paul. (Photo by Todd Bolen/BiblePlaces.com.)

ΝΙΟΣ ΓΑΛΛΙΩΝ Ο Φ[ΙΛΟΣ] ΜΟΥ ΚΑ[Ι ΑΝΘΥ]ΠΑΤΟΣ [ΤΗΣ ΑΧΑΙΑΣ ΕΓΡΑΨΕΝ]

The entire inscription is thought to have read thus:

> Tiberius Claudius Caesar Augustus Germanicus, 12th year of tribunician power, acclaimed emperor for the 26th time, father of the country, sends greetings to [...]. For long have I been well-disposed to the city of Delphi and solicitous for its prosperity, and I have always observed the cult of the Pythian Apollo. Now since it is said to be destitute of citizens, as my friend and proconsul L. Iunius Gallio recently reported to me, and desiring that Delphi should regain its former splendour, I command you (singular) to invite well-born people also from other cities to come to Delphi as new inhabitants, and to accord them and their children all the privileges of the Delphians as being citizens on like and equal terms. For if some are transferred as colonists to these regions....[31]

Erastus, City Treasurer in Corinth

Three persons named Erastus are mentioned in the New Testament. One is mentioned alongside Timothy as among the helpers of Paul in Ephesus (Acts 19:22); another is said by Paul to have remained at Corinth (2 Timothy 4:20) when Paul continued his trip. Since Paul mentions him in his epistle, it is likely that Timothy knew him. Last of all, Paul sent greetings from a man known as Erastus to the recipients of the apostle's letter to the Romans: "Erastus, the city treasurer, and our brother Quartus, greet you" (Romans 16:23b ESV). Paul identified this person as the ὁ οἰκονομος τῆς (*ho oikonomos tes poleos*)—the treasurer, manager, or administrator of the city.[32] The first and second Erastus listed above very likely are the same person because of the nexus with Timothy, and persons two and three are likely the same because of the connection to Corinth. Consequently all three are probably the same person.[33]

The Erastus inscription is located in Greece within the ancient ruins of Corinth.

It has been argued that the latter Erastus may have been a city slave;[34] but the likelihood is that Erastus had an important enough status in Corinth to warrant Paul's mention of him as the οἰκονομος (*oikonomos*).[35] The Roman colony of Corinth would have had a Roman municipal structure, with the *oikonomos* as the Greek equivalent of the Latin office of *aedilis*.

One finds at Corinth a startling connection with Romans 16:23, in a grassy area not normally visited by tour groups today. At the head of a pavement is a long slab with reference to a person named Erastus. Scholars are in agreement that the inscription dates to the middle of the first century AD. The pavement is located east of the city theater. An *aedilis* was commissioned with the task to manage public markets. If indeed this builder of the pavement is the same person mentioned by Paul, then Erastus and Paul may have become acquainted while the former was about his duties of collecting rent or taxes.[36]

The inscription regarding Erastus reads, "Erastus laid this pavement at his own expense, in appreciation of his appointment as aedile."[37] Only two of the three slabs of the inscription have been found. The central slab was found in situ in April 1929; two portions of the right slab were found in March 1928 and then in August 1947, allowing a more complete reading. The extant text reads in Latin,

ERASTUS PRO AEDILITATE
S.P.* STRAVIT

---

* S.P. is a standard abbreviation for *sua pecunia*, "with his own money" (see J.H. Kent, *The Inscriptions 1926-1950*, vol.

This may be rendered, together with the likely wording of the missing first slab ("*Praenomen nomen*"), as follows: "Erastus in return for his aedileship laid [the pavement] at his own expense."[38]

More Archaeological Discoveries Supporting New Testament Reliability

Find	Description
Tomb of Lazarus 	On the east side of the Mount of Olives is the traditionally recognized tomb of Lazarus (John 11:38-44). It appears that by the second century AD the location had been identified with Lazarus. The church historian Eusebius says that the city was renamed the "Place of Lazarus" and that the tomb was being shown in his (Eusebius's) day. Currently, there is a mosque built over the site preventing access through the traditional entrance, though an alternative entrance was created.
Lithostrotos 	Located under the modern streets of Jerusalem near the Temple Mount, the *Gabbatha* (that is, place or seat of judgment) mentioned in John 19:13 and Matthew 27:27 is the location of Christ's judgment by Pontius Pilate. It was found at the Roman military headquarters known as the Tower of Antonia.
The Galilee Boat  (Photo by Zev Radovan.)	In 1986, a drought season revealed a 2,000-year-old boat (dated between the first century BC and the first century AD) in the sediment of the Sea of Galilee, offering an example of the kind of boats that sailed the sea during Jesus' time (Mark 4:37-41). It could accommodate over a dozen men, being over 26 feet long and more than 7 feet wide. An assortment of chemicals and foam were used to raise the fragile boat and transport it by sea to the Yigal Allon Museum (in Ginosar) on the shores of the Sea of Galilee.

VIII, "Corinth" [Princeton, NJ: Princeton University Press, 1966], #231, for a similar inscription celebrating a benefaction given *sua pecunia*).

Find	Description
Tyrannus Inscription	That the name *Tyrannus* was engraved on a stone pillar in Ephesus shows that the same name mentioned in Acts 19:9 (Tyrannus) was used in Ephesus during the first century AD; this find thus shows consistency with Luke's mentioning of the name when Paul visited Ephesus.
Luke's vocabulary in the Gospel and Acts	Luke, the writer of the Gospel of Luke and Acts, has in the past been faulted by some modern critics for alleged historical errors in his records. However, this view has been replaced by a much more favorable view of his accuracy in light of recent discoveries about the customs and language of Luke's time. In many cases, modern historians have had to revise their former opinions. Following are some of the points on which Luke's history in the book of Acts has been vindicated:* • Lycaonian as the correct language spoken at Lystra (14:11) • The proper form of the city name Troas (16:8) • Use of "politarchs" as proper designation of magistrates in Thessalonica (17:6) • Correct Athenian slang word for Paul as *spermologos* (17:18) • Uses *areopagite* as the proper title for a member of the Athenian court (17:34) • Proper title of *grammateus* for the chief executive magistrate ("clerk") in Ephesus (19:35) • Uses correct Roman authorized title of honor, *neokoros* (19:35) • Uses the plural *anthupatoi*, which could be referring to two men functioning as proconsuls at this time (19:38) • Uses precise term *bolisantes* for taking soundings and records the correct depth of the water near Malta (27:28) • Applies correct title *"first man of the Island"* (*protos tes nesou*) to Malta's leader (28:7) The precision of these historical details and others has led Roman historian A.N. Sherwin-White to remark, "For Acts the confirmation of historicity is overwhelming…But any attempt to reject its basic historicity even in matters of detail must now appear absurd. Roman historians have long taken it for granted."[†]

---

* See Colin J. Hemer, *The Book of Acts in the Setting of Hellenistic History* (Winona Lake, IN: Eisenbrauns, 1990).

† A.N. Sherwin-White, *Roman Society and Roman Law in the New Testament* (Oxford: Clarendon Press, 1963), 189.

Find	Description
Mamertine Prison (Rome) 	The Mamertine Prison is traditionally recognized as the place where Peter and Paul were incarcerated before being executed in Rome. Originally part of the ancient Roman Forum, today it is the location of two churches, San Giuseppe dei Falegnami and San Pietro in Carcere.
Bema seat 	A foundation platform of a "bema seat" was discovered in the early twentieth century in the ruins of ancient Corinth. It served as the place from which the city officials spoke to the citizens; there the apostle Paul was brought before the proconsul Gallio in Acts 18:12-17. It also may have been used to award competing athletes of the Isthmian games. In addition, Paul uses the Greek term *bema* to describe the "judgment seat" of Christ, where Christians will receive their heavenly rewards (2 Corinthians 5:10).
Jacob's Well  (Photo by Zev Radovan.)	Located in ancient Samaria within an unfinished Greek ortho-dox church is Jacob's Well (*bir ya'qub*), which is mentioned by Eusebius in the fourth century AD, as well as by John and the unnamed Samaritan woman (John 4:5,6,12; Genesis 33:18-19; 48:22). The well had been dug to over 200 feet deep in the seventh century AD (see John 4:11), and today it still produces fresh, cool water fed from underground. It lies a short distance from Mount Gerizim and the ruins of the Samaritan temple.

Find	Description
Capernaum Synagogue 	Excavations at the ancient city of Capernaum have revealed a fourth- or fifth-century AD synagogue that was most likely built over the black basalt foundation of an earlier first-century synagogue. The discovery of thousands of coins beneath the floors helped to securely date the later synagogue, while pottery remains and coins discovered under the black basalt foundation confirmed the date of the first-century structure. The earlier synagogue is most likely the same structure that John refers to (John 6:59) in which Jesus gave His lengthy sermon and said, "I am the bread of life" (Luke 4:33,38; John 6:35,48,59).
Peter's House 	From 1968 to 1998 archaeologists excavated an octagonal structure located in the ancient city of Capernaum near the shores of the Sea of Galilee, which they believe to be the house of Peter (Matthew 8:14; Mark 1:29; Luke 4:38). Early inscriptions venerating Christ as Lord, Most High, and God in various languages (Latin, Hebrew, Greek, Aramaic, and Syriac) scratched on the plaster walls of the dwelling may indicate that early Christians believed this was Peter's house. In the fifth century, Christians built an octagonal church over the first-century house. In 1990 the Roman Catholic Church honored the site by building the hexagonal Franciscan Chapel over the ruins of this same house church.
Zeus and Hermes in the account of Paul and Barnabas	In 1909, archaeologists unearthed several inscriptions and a temple near the ancient city of Lystra that identified Zeus and Hermes as the two most important gods, since they were believed to have visited the earth there. These gods were expected to return in the future, which helps scholars understand the reaction of the people when they acclaimed Barnabas and Paul as Zeus and Hermes (Acts 14:6-13). *

---

* H. Wayne House and Joseph M. Holden, "New Testament Archaeology," in *Charts of Apologetics and Christian Evidences* (Grand Rapids, MI: Zondervan, 2006), chart 44.

Find	Description
Nazareth Inscription	An inscription was discovered in Nazareth in 1878 forbidding the robbing of tombs, originating between the time of Augustus Caesar and Claudius Caesar. * Since Nazareth was such a small village, scholars have conjectured that the edict may have been issued in response to the rumor passed on by authorities in Israel regarding the robbing of the grave of Jesus, but there is no certainty that the inscription is attached to the resurrection of Jesus the Messiah.[†]
The Pool of Siloam 	In 2005, city workers excavating in the vicinity of the Gihon Spring accidentally unearthed the steps to the Pool of Siloam. Archaeologists have revealed that its shape is a trapezoid pool (corners greater than 90 degrees), surrounded by three descending sets of five stairs each. Ancient coins and masonry found at the site confirm this location as the first-century Pool of Siloam mentioned in John 9:7 as the place where Jesus healed the man born blind.
The Pool of Bethesda 	John 5:2-3 tells of a pool located by the Sheep Gate which had five porches where the sick and lame would wait for the stirring of the waters so they might be healed. The passage tells of Jesus healing a lame man who had been afflicted for 38 years. Excavations in the late 1800s uncovered such a pool, with remains that indicate it had several porches (porticoes), twin pool areas, and was fed by an underground water and lock (gate) system, which would result in the waters being disturbed on occasion. Eusebius mentions the Sheep Pool in the fourth century; this most likely refers to the Pool of Bethesda. Today, the pool may be visited at the site of the Church of Saint Anne, about 300 feet inside the Old City from Stephen's or the Lion's Gate (the ancient "Sheep Gate").

---

* House and Holden. Arguing for a date under Claudius of c. AD 50, see Jack Finegan, *Light from the Ancient Past: The Archaeological Background of the Hebrew-Christian Religion*, vol. II (Princeton, NJ: Princeton University Press, 1959), 299, while an early date in the time of Octavius Augustus Caesar is argued by Franz Cumont, "Un Rescrit Imperial sur la Violation de Sepulture," in *Revue Historique* (January-April, 1930): 241-266.

† House and Holden.

Find	Description
Absalom's Tomb Inscription	In 2003, on the east bank of the Kidron Valley, Emile Puech and Joe Zias found the oldest New Testament passage yet discovered, carved in stone on Absalom's Tomb. The passage contains Luke 2:25 and tells of Simeon, who in his old age finally saw the baby Jesus. It reads, "Now there was a man in Jerusalem, whose name was Simeon, and this man was righteous and devout, waiting for the consolation of Israel, and the Holy Spirit was upon him" (ESV).
Coins of the Bible	Throughout the New Testament various coins are mentioned in association with basic transactions and teaching illustrations. These include the widow's mite, the Tyre shekel, and the denarius, among others. Some coins contain inscriptions of rulers such as Herod Antipas and Herod Agrippa, King Aretas IV, and Emperor Claudius; the one pictured here is of Caesar Augustus.

Chart © Joseph M. Holden, 2013.

Information on this chart is drawn from Joseph M. Holden, *Archaeology and the Bible: A Pictorial Guide to the Amazing Discoveries of the Bible*, CD PowerPoint (Winchester, CA) © Joseph M. Holden 2007. All rights reserved.

This fourth- or fifth-century synagogue was built over the black basalt foundation of an earlier first-century synagogue—the place Jesus said, "I am the bread of life" (John 6:35,59). (Photo by Zev Radovan.)

Conclusion

The New Testament and its writers have proven themselves to be historically reliable, as is seen by the numerous extrabiblical sources and artifacts demonstrating as much. It appears that any effort to dismiss the New Testament as wholesale mythology or a compilation of embellishments can be met with an avalanche of evidence to the contrary. In view of the ever-growing body of archaeological data, it may be asserted with confidence that the New Testament is historically reliable.

GLOSSARY OF KEY TERMS

APPENDIXES

NOTES

SELECT BIBLIOGRAPHY

INDEX

See also the "Understanding Archaeological Terms" table in chapter 15.

Terminology	Definition
Alexandrian text-type	The type or family of Greek New Testament documents believed to be traceable back to Alexandria, Egypt. This group of manuscripts is believed to be the oldest and most reliable group of New Testament documents.
autograph (plural, *autographa*)	One of the original documents of the Bible.
biblical manuscript	An ancient copy of at least part of a biblical book or corpus.
bookhand	A more reformed style consisting of carefully written upright letters, separate from each other, written in a more fastidious fashion.
canon	The closed, definitive collections of writings inspired by God, which constitute authentic content of Scripture.
Caesarean text-type	The type or family of Greek New Testament documents believed to be traceable back to Israel.
codex (plural, *codices*)	An ancient version of what we today call a book which used leaved pages rather than a continuous scroll which was rolled up.
colophon	An ancient endnote, often indicating information about the manuscript to which it is attached.
consonantal text	The pre-Masoretic text containing only consonants with no vowels.
exemplar	An authoritative copy or archetype.
fair copy	The final draft of a manuscript after all revisions have been made.
final masora	An apparatus found in the second Rabbinic Bible at the end of each biblical book, which counts the number of letters, words, and verses in each biblical book.

Terminology	Definition
Jamnia, Scholars of	A rabbinic group that discussed, among other things, the canon of the Old Testament in AD 90.
Kethib-Qere	The *Kethib* (Aramaic for "written") referred to what was written in the text itself, whereas the *Qere* (Aramaic for "read") referred to the consonants in the margin with the vowels found in the text of the Kethib.
Nakdanim	A group of scribes whose name was derived from a word meaning "to point" and who were responsible for adding the vowel points and accents to the manuscript of the Hebrew Scriptures.
nomina sacra	Early Christian abbreviations within manuscripts that were usually used to abbreviate holy names (for example, *Jesus*) or theological words used quite frequently (for example, *man*).
Masora	"Tradition" that the Masoretes had received and usually transmitted in the margins of the Hebrew Bible.
Masoretes	The primary group of medieval scribes responsible for transmitting the pointed (vowelized) text of the Hebrew Bible along with significant apparatuses associated with the Hebrew text.
Masoretic Text	The group of Hebrew texts transmitted by a group of medieval scribes known as the Masoretes.
papyrus	A form of ancient paper created from the flattened, dried papyrus plant found in Egypt.
Pentateuch	*Penta-* (meaning five), Pentateuch refers to the first five books of the Old Testament, typically ascribed to the authorship of Moses.
pointing	The vowel markings found within the Hebrew text from the fifth century AD and after.
orthography	The system of writing used, including issues of script and handwriting.

Terminology	Definition
ostracon (plural, *ostraca*)	A piece of pottery or stone, usually broken off of a vase, pot, or other household item, on which an inscription is often found.
paleographers	Specialized historians who study ancient texts.
ruling hand	Also called "documentary hand," it was executed more quickly and less conscientiously than the bookhand.
scribe	A skilled copyist of the Scriptures.
scriptio plena	Semitic alphabet that contained vowel points.
scroll	A document used for recording written material that consisted of one continuous sheet that was compacted through rolling.
Septuagint (LXX)	The common designation used to refer to the numerous Greek translations of the Old Testament we find in the ancient world.
Sopherim	A group of scribes responsible for transmitting the consonantal text.
scriptio continua	Script that was connected without lapses or spaces between words or sentences.
scriptorium (plural, *scriptoria*)	A professional facility devoted to the copy and production of documents and books; a facility frequently used in the reproduction of New Testament manuscripts.
Syrian text-type	The type or family of Greek New Testament documents believed to be traceable back to Syria but which later dominated the Byzantine era. This text is largely believed to be the result of combining many other texts and is thought to be the least reliable of the manuscripts.
textual critic	A person who studies the textual traditions and individual manuscripts upon which the Bible was based.
textual families/types	A grouping of manuscripts based on geographical location and similar textual characteristics, such as having the same readings of particular verses in a given family.

Terminology	Definition
textual tradition	A group or family of manuscripts to which a particular manuscript is usually related.
uncial	Bookhand with larger and annular letters, found within the sixth and seventh centuries
version	An ancient translation of the Bible usually based on the original languages.
Vorlage	The source text underlying a text that is being used or translated.
Western text-type	The type or family of Greek New Testament documents believed to be traceable back to Rome.

NEW TESTAMENT MANUSCRIPT PAPYRI: A DESCRIPTIVE LIST

P⁵², Gr.P.457. The John Rylands Fragment is the oldest copy of any piece of the New Testament. The Alexandrian fragment is of John's Gospel, containing part of the five verses from John 18:31-33,37-38. It was discovered in Egypt among the Oxyrhynchus collection and dates back to the early days of the second century AD, most likely between 117 and 138 or even earlier. It is composed on papyrus and its origin is clearly from a codex, thus indicating to many paleographers that New Testament codices did indeed exist in the first century AD. (See photo in chapter 8.)

P¹⁰⁴. An impressive document, like the John Rylands fragment this papyrus was discovered in Egypt among the Oxyrhynchus collection. It dates into the early first half of the second century AD. It is the oldest extant text of Matthew, covering Matthew 21:34-37,43, and possibly verse 45. The textual character reflects the Alexandrian hand with distinctions of the Zierstil, or decorated rounded style, of handwriting.

P⁴⁶. Chester Beatty II/P.Mich.Inv.6238. The Chester Beatty Papyri II are dated to approximately AD 250. This is an excellent papyrus codex, demonstrating the duplication of an early-dated exemplar text. Although portions of this book have been lost (2 Thessalonians and parts of Romans and 1 Thessalonians), it still boasts Hebrews and the Pauline epistles of Romans, 1 Corinthians, 2 Corinthians, Ephesians, Galatians, Philippians, and Colossians. All of these books are embraced within the surviving 86 leaves of 11 by 6.5 inches, which are gathered in a single quire (collection of leaves, or *signature* in modern terminology). The text is large, with some scribal nuances of style. The original, without its lost pieces, was 104 pages of mostly Alexandrian and some Western text-type. There are 71 agreements and in contrast only 17 disagreements that make up the 88 units of variation in the text. Overall the textual fidelity of the scribal hand is admirable. (See photo in chapter 8.)

P⁶⁶. The Bodmer Papyri formed a single literary work containing six quires of most of John in just over one hundred leaves. This papyrus codex is dated at AD 200 or earlier. Again, it gives very early evidence for the circulation of John's Gospel. The codex pages measure about 6 by 5.5 inches and the text was written in the biblical uncial or biblical majuscule hand, medium sized, and displays both the Alexandrian and Western types. Four hundred and forty-four alterations have been made to the piece—mostly corrections from the scribe himself.

P⁸⁷. The Inv. Nr. 12 manuscript is small and contains Philemon verses 13-15 and 24-25. Its writing is very similar to P⁴⁶, thus dating it around the middle of the second century AD or possibly earlier. The craftsmanship of the scribe shows a clear *Roman uncial* hand. It is normal text and is classified as Alexandrian.

P⁴, P⁶⁴, P⁶⁷. The Chester Beatty II collection consists of fragments of papyri originally embodying all four of the Gospels. These fragments were first catalogued as texts belonging to separate works, P⁴ being discovered in a concealed jar in a home. After further review, they were finally recognized as belonging to the same codex in the single-quire form. They particularly display *out-denting* (where the Greek letter protrudes into the far outer left margin) and continuous text. They are recognized for their noteworthy agreement with P⁷⁵ in the Gospel of Luke.

P⁹⁸. The P.IFAO manuscript dates to the late second century AD. This fragment is housed in Cairo, Egypt, and consists of Revelation 1:13–2:1. It does not reveal the hand of a professional scribe but rather a common untrained hand.

P⁹⁰. P.Oxy. 3523. This papyrus fragment was discovered among the relics of Oxyrhynchus in Egypt. It has been dated to the later part of the second century AD. It bears John 18:36–19:7 and was likely intended for a church gathering, which is conveyed by the calligraphy—the size of the letters. It is more akin in textual comparison to P⁶⁶ than any other single manuscript. It is classified among the early papyrus fragments and was written in a *decorated rounded* hand.

P⁷⁷. P.Oxy. 2683 was discovered in Egypt and is dated to the period from the middle to the late second century AD. Of the Oxyrhynchus collection, this papyrus manuscript contains Matthew 23:30-39. It is proto-Alexandrian and may have been originally sourced from the same codex as P¹⁰³.

P¹⁰³. P.Oxy 4403. This manuscript of papyrus from Oxyrhynchus dates from the middle to late second century AD. It evidences Matthew 13:55-57 and 14:3-5 and likely stems from the same codex as P⁷⁷, exemplifying a proto-Alexandrian text-type.

P³². The P.Rylands 5 manuscript is dated from the middle to late second century AD. This reliable manuscript shows striking affinity in type of the text to Sinaiticus (aleph), Augiensis (F), and Boernerianus (G). It is the earliest manuscript of the pastoral epistles. It displays an informal hand with a decorated rounded style. It resides in England at the John Rylands University Library.

P¹⁰⁹. P.Oxy.4448 of the Oxyrhynchus collection, contains John 21:18-20, and 23-25. It has been speculated that it was intended for church reading. Its textual type is too difficult to label, due to the insignificant size of the papyri. It is dated from the middle to the late second century AD.

P¹⁰⁸. P.Oxy 4447 is a papyrus manuscript of the late second century. Discovered in Egypt, this document contains the text of John 17:23-24 and 18:1-5. It is recognized for its close affinity to Sinaiticus (aleph).

P¹. P.Oxy.2 dates from the middle to the third century AD from among the Oxyrhynchus collection. It consists of Matthew 1:1-9,12,14-20. Of the Alexandrian type, this papyrus shows remarkable agreement with Vaticanus (B) and was most likely copied from a respectable exemplar text.

P⁵. P.Oxy. was discovered in Egypt containing portions of John 1, 16, and 20. Among the great relics of Oxyrhynchus, this manuscript of papyrus dates within the early third century AD. It is recognized for its concurrence with Sinaiticus (aleph) and displays the distinct textual type of the Alexandrian order.

P¹³. P.Oxy.657+PSI 1292 dates within the first half of the third century AD. This papyrus includes portions of Hebrews 2–5 and 10–12. Its textual type agrees with Vaticanus (B), even providing text for where text is lacking. Originally discovered in Egypt it now resides in London at the British Library. This manuscript is written in a type of severe (slanted) style. Despite this manuscript being found with other manuscripts, such as P. Oxyrhynchus 654, that date back to the third century AD, some have dated this manuscript to the fourth century AD. This was based on comparable handwriting found in P. Oxyrhynchus 404. According to Comfort's analysis based on the handwriting form of comparable manuscripts, this text dates back to just after AD 200.[1] He compares this manuscript to that of P. Oxyrhynchus 852, in terms of its handwriting style, which has been dated back from the late second to the early third century AD because of the accounts that are documented on that manuscript to approximately the same time period. Comfort also finds striking resemblances between P¹³ and P. Oxyrhynchus 852 in terms of the formation of the characters and the overall appearance among other aspects. Its long-tailed swooping upsilon is also noted to be similar to P. Oxyrhynchus 2635, which is dated no later than AD 200.

P²³. P.Oxy.1229. One of the great manuscripts of Oxyrhynchus, this document contains James 1:10-12,15-18. Dated within the late second to early third century AD, it is noted for its textual likeness to Rescriptus (C), Sinaiticus (aleph), and Alexandrinus (A). This document has been dated based on an investigation of the letters of the manuscript. It has been noted by Philip Comfort that it displays small serifs in many of the characters, such as the Greek letters alpha, iota, lambda, mu, nu, with the absence of small omicrons, all of which are characteristic of the second century AD.

P²². P.Oxy.1228. Now residing in the University Library of Scotland, this papyrus manuscript preserves John 15:25–16:2,21-32. Dating to the middle of the third century AD, its textual type is eclectic, representing an independent text. It was uncovered in Egypt among the Oxyrhynchus manuscripts.

P³⁷. P.Mich.Inv.1570. This fragment upholds chapter 26, verses 19-52, of the Gospel of Matthew. It is dated at approximately AD 250. The textual character is free, with certain likenesses to P⁴⁵.

Papyrus 37 contains Matthew 26:19-52 and is housed in Ann Arbor, Michigan, at the University of Michigan. (Photo PD-Art.)

P³⁰. P.Oxy.1598. This papyrus manuscript was written in a relaxed biblical uncial script. It dates to the early third century AD and includes portions of 1 Thessalonians 4–5 and 2 Thessalonians 1–2. The similarities found between this document and other early third-century AD documents, such as P. Oxyrhynchus 867 and P. Oxyrhynchus 1398, would suggest that this manuscript dates to early third century AD. Among the documents of Oxyrhynchus, its textual character is recognized for its overall agreement with Sinaiticus (aleph).

P³⁸. P.Mich.Inv. 1571. This papyrus represents the book of Acts with various verses from chapters 18 and 19 (18:27–19:6,12-16). It is a fragment among the early documents dating to the early third century AD. The manuscript portrays the Western form. It is written in the *D-text*—the style of Codex Bezae Cantabrigiensis and Codex Claromontanus, primary exemplars of the Western text-type (see chapter 8 under the subheading "New Testament Codices"). Many comparable forms of this manuscript have been found in P. Oxyrhynchus 834 of the late second century AD and P. Oxyrhynchus 1607 from the late second to the early third century AD. An earlier stage of this form of handwriting can be seen in P. Oxyrhynchus 26, which dates back to the second century AD, while P. Oxyrhynchus 849 represents a later form. P. Oxyrhynchus 37, P. Oxyrhynchus 405, and P. Oxyrhynchus 406 from around the early third century AD display other comparable examples of the form of handwriting in this manuscript fragment.

P⁴⁵. The codex P⁴⁵ of the Chester Beatty collection contains text from all four of the Gospels and Acts. Of the approximately 220 leaves of papyrus, 30 still remain, which equates to approximately 14 percent of its original leaves. Its early date of AD 250 and the large portions of the Gospels and Acts make it a most valuable asset to the collection. After study of the text, some historians have critiqued the scribal liberties taken in its transcription, observing an emphasis on the copying of the idea of the text rather than the exact wording of it. Sir Frederic Kenyon notes particularities of the individual Greek characters, which display simplicity common to the Roman period. He notes that the lack of exaggeration found in the Greek letters upsilon and phi and the curves of the letters epsilon and sigma attest to its early date. But paleographers date this manuscript in the third century AD due to its severe (sloping) appearance. The text exemplifies the Caesarean, Alexandrian, and possibly the Western textual types. Philip Comfort notes calligraphic similarities with many comparable texts, comparing it to P. Michigan 3, P. Egerton 3, P. Oxyrhynchus 2082, P. Oxyrhynchus 1016, P. Oxyrhynchus 232, and P. Rylands 57. ²

P¹⁰⁶. P.Oxy.4445. This early papyri of the Oxyrhynchus manuscripts includes John 1:29-35,40-46. It was written within the first half of the third century AD and is mostly of the Alexandrian type.

P¹⁰⁷. P.Oxy 4446 was discovered in Egypt and dated from the early part of the third century AD. Of the Oxyrhynchus collection, this papyrus manuscript contains John 17:1-2,11. Its textual character is independent but is most agreeable with Washingtonianus (W).

P³⁹. P.Oxy.1780. Once among the relics in Egypt, this papyrus manuscript now resides in Rochester, New York, at the Ambrose Swabey Library. It contains John 8:14-22. Due to its agreement with P. Rylands 16 (dated from the late second to early third century AD) and P. Oxyrhynchus 25 (dated to the early third century AD) it is dated to the earlier half of the third century AD. Its penmanship shows that it was written by a professional scribe, who wrote in the biblical uncial script in its early form. It agrees with the Vaticanus (B), and is proto-Alexandrian in its textual type.

P²⁹. P.Oxy.1597. This papyrus fragment contains Acts 26:7-8,20 and was discovered in Egypt. This early third-century AD manuscript is too small to determine its character textually. But from what is available, the study of the characters of the manuscript, such as its square pi and epsilon and triangular theta, has shown that it shares similarities with P⁴⁵, which is a small portion of the book of Acts, and P. Oxyrhynchus 2949, an apocryphal Gospel. It has been suggested though that it may be connected to the Western text.

P¹¹¹. P.Oxy.4495 of the Oxyrhynchus collection contains Luke 17:11-13,22-23. Its textual type agrees with P⁷⁵. It is dated within the first half of the third century AD.

P⁴⁹. P.Yale 415 + 531. Dated to the middle of the third century AD, this manuscript contains Ephesians 4:16-29 and 4:31–5:13. Written on papyrus, this document shows the Alexandrian text-type. Paleographers have noted the striking familiarities between P⁴⁹ and P⁶⁵ in their letter formation, leading some to believe that they could very well be part of the same codex.

P⁶⁵. PSI XIV 1373. This papyrus manuscript holds 1 Thessalonians 1:3–2:1,6-13. Dated to around AD 250, this document clearly shows an Alexandrian distinction. It has also been hypothesized that P⁴⁹ and P⁶⁵ originated from the same codex.

P⁵³. P.Mich.Inv. 6652. Residing at the University of Michigan Library, this third-century AD papyrus contains Matthew 26:29-40 and Acts 9:33–10:1. The Acts portion clearly shows an Alexandrian-trained hand, whereas the Matthew portion displays no significant agreement.

P⁶⁹. P.Oxy.2383. Discovered among the manuscripts of Oxyrhynchus, this papyrus document bears scriptures from the Gospel of Luke (Luke 22:40,45-48,58-61). It is a free text with some D-text-style readings.

P⁸⁰. P.Barcelona 83. Dated at around AD 250, this papyrus fragment encompasses just one single verse from the Gospel of John (John 3:34). This fragment is not lengthy enough to correctly ascertain its textual character.

P⁹¹. P.Mil.Vogl.Inv.1224 + P.Macquarie Inv.360 contains selections from the second and third chapters of Acts: 2:30-37 and 2:46–3:2. Its text is most likely proto-Alexandrian.

P⁹. P.Oxy. 402. Housed in the Semitic Museum of Harvard University, this papyrus is too insignificant in length to determine its textual type. It is comprised of 1 John 4:11-12,14-17 and has been dated to the third century AD.

P²⁰. P.Oxy.1171. This manuscript provides a very reliable excerpt of the second and third chapter of James, accounting for 2:19–3:9. Discovered in Egypt in the Oxyrhynchus collection it displays an Alexandrian character. It is especially characteristic of Sinaiticus (aleph) and Vaticanus (B). Though some have dated this manuscript to around the late third century AD, no significant paleographic evidence has been provided to support this claim. This manuscript is similar to that of P. Oxyrhynchus 1230, which is a second-century AD document, as well as P. Oxyrhynchus 3830 of the same time period. P²⁰ possesses characteristics of a rounded, medium upright capital, with its informal appearance resembling that of P²⁷. Some suggest that the same scribe who produced P²⁰ may have also penned P²⁷.

P²⁴. P.Oxy.1355 contains portions of Romans 8–9. It is a third-century AD papyrus manuscript of the Alexandrian textual character.

P³⁵. PSI 1. Dated among the early manuscripts of antiquity, this third-century AD papyri is comprised of Matthew 25:12-15,20-23. Its textual affinity is distinctly to the Vaticanus (B).

P⁴⁰. P.Heidelberg G.645. This collection of papyrus fragments make up various portions of Romans 1–4, 6, and 9. It is among the Alexandrian documents of the third century AD.

P⁴⁸. PSI 1165. Preserved in the Biblioteca Medicea Laurenziana in Florence, Italy, this papyrus holds Acts 23:11-17,25-29. Though a small manuscript, it dates among the ancient documents of the third century AD since it displays the severe (slanted) style that was prominent during that time. The writing style found in P⁴⁸ can also be found in other manuscripts, such as P. Oxyrhynchus 223, P. Oxyrhynchus 852, P. Oxyrhynchus 2341, and P. Oxyrhynchus 2635. These comparable manuscripts solidify the third-century AD dating of P⁴⁸, which is in the D-text style.

P⁹⁵. PL II/31. This third-century AD manuscript contains John 5:26-29,36-38. It is too fragmentary to determine its textual character, but this papyrus does reflect a proto-Alexandrian text-type.

P¹⁰¹. P.Oxy.4401. Discovered in Egypt, this papyrus manuscript contains Matthew 3:10-12 and 3:16–4:3. It finds its place among the third-century AD Alexandrian texts.

P¹¹³. P.Oxy.4497. This papyrus contains only a few verses of Romans—2:12-13,19. It was found in Oxyrhynchus, Egypt, and dates to the third century AD. Its inadequate size makes it hard to determine its textual character.

P¹¹⁴. P.Oxy.4498 of the Oxyrhynchus collection contains Hebrews 1:7-12. It is a papyrus manuscript of the third century AD. Its textual type is too difficult to label due to its small size.

P¹⁸. P.Oxy.1079. Once among the relics of Egypt, these papyri are now housed in the British Library of London, England. This manuscript is a copy of Revelation 1:4-7 and dates from the middle to the late third century AD. Its text mostly agrees with Ephraemi Rescriptus (C), then Sinaiticus (aleph), and Vaticanus (B).

P⁴⁷. This papyrus manuscript of the Chester Beatty Collection once held the entire text of Revelation, but only about eight chapters (31 percent of its original text) survived, containing the text of Revelation 9–17. The manuscript reveals a documentary hand and dates from the middle to the late third century AD based on the formation of its letters. It was dated by Kenyon using his "test-letter" methodology, which is no longer used by paleographers, and he was unable to find any manuscripts that paralleled its handwriting from which to confirm its date. Comfort finds P. Tebtunis 268 a comparable manuscript to P⁴⁷. P. Tebtunis 268 is dated at approximately AD 220 and has been found to have many handwriting similarities with that of P⁴⁷, with its short, shallow strokes and their placement on a line. Although only 10 of the original 32 leaves of the codex have been preserved, these valuable papyri date to within 200 years of the autograph, marking its origin within the third century AD. The hand betrays the work of an untrained scribe and may even reveal that the codex was intended for private use. The text-type agrees with Alexandrinus (A), Ephraemi Rescriptus (C), and Sinaiticus (aleph). The omissions in the text are few (below 20) but outnumber the additions almost three to one.

P¹¹⁵. P.Oxy.4499. Of the great manuscripts of Oxyrhynchus, this manuscript contains large portions of Revelation and is dated to the mid to late third century AD. This document of papyrus is noted for its textual likeness to Alexandrinus (A) and Ephraemi Rescriptus.

P¹⁵/¹⁶. P.Oxy.108+109 was discovered in Egypt and is dated to the late third century AD. Of the Oxyrhynchus collection, this papyrus manuscript contains 1 Corinthians 7:18–8:4 and Philippians 3:10-17; 4:2-8. Its text-type is Alexandrian.

P¹⁷. P.Oxy.1078. This papyrus manuscript contains Hebrews 9:12-19. Discovered in Egypt, its late third-century text is in general accord with P⁴⁶.

P²⁴. P.Oxy.1230. Of the collection at Oxyrhynchus, this papyrus contains only eight verses from Revelation 5 and 6 (5:5-8; 6:5-8). It finds its place among the Alexandrian scripts of the late third century AD.

P²⁸. P. Oxy.1596. This late third-century AD manuscript contains John 6:8-12,17-22. The papyrus is of the Alexandrian type.

P⁵⁰. P.Oxy.1543 was discovered in Egypt. It contains Acts 8:26-32 and 10:26-31. Among the great relics of Oxyrhynchus, this papyrus manuscript dates within the late third century AD. Its textual type is decidedly of the Alexandrian order.

P⁷⁰. P.Oxy.2384+ PSI Inv. CNR 419, 420 date within the latter half of the third century AD. Among the artifacts of Oxyrhynchus, the papyri display Luke 22:40,45-48,58-61. Unfortunately, the text betrays the work of a careless hand, leaving its textual character uncertain.

P¹¹⁰. P.Oxy.4494. This independent text is of Matthew 10:13-15,25-27. It is part of the collection of papyrus manuscripts from Oxyrhynchus.

P²²⁰. MS 113. This manuscript dates to the late third century. It includes Romans 4:23–5:3,8-13. With the exception of Romans 5:1, its textual character agrees with Vaticanus (B) (see below).

P⁷². The P. Bodmer VII and VIII manuscript holds the oldest known texts of 1 Peter, 2 Peter, and Jude, dating to the late third century or early fourth century AD. It also contains apocryphal works. Its remarkably early date proves the use of 2 Peter among the Coptic Christians in Egypt during the 200s. Though debatable, the text-type has been recognized as normal text in 1 and 2 Peter and free in Jude, though both include textual idiosyncrasies. The codex, likely a private one, does reveal an Alexandrian influence and the hands of approximately four scribes. The variants within the text account for more omissions than additions.

P⁷⁸. P.Oxy.2684. From Egypt and now residing in England, this papyrus reveals four verses from Jude. It is a free text and distinctly represents Jude 4-5 and 7-8.

P⁹². P. Narmuthis 69.39a + 69.229a. This Alexandrian text is dated to the period from the late third century AD to the early fourth century AD. It contains Ephesians 1:11-13,19-21 and 2 Thessalonians 1:4-5,11-12.

P¹⁰⁰. P.Oxy.4449. Residing in the Ashmolean Museum in England, this papyrus manuscript contains James 3:13–4:4 and 4:9–5:1. Dated to the period from the late third to the early fourth century AD, it shows agreement with the Alexandrian witnesses.

P¹⁰². P.Oxy.4402. Dated around the late third to early fourth century AD, this papyrus fragment encompasses just four verses: Matthew 4:11-12,22-23. This fragment is not lengthy enough to adequately determine its textual character.

0162. P.Oxy.847. This Oxyrhynchus papyrus contains John 2:11-22. It is dated from the late third to the early fourth century AD. Its textual agreement is with P⁶⁶ and P⁷⁵ as well as Vaticanus (B).

033. This ninth-century AD piece is recognized for its great agreement with Codex Sinaiticus (aleph). This minuscule manuscript contains the Gospels, Acts, Paul's epistles, and the catholic (general) epistles. It is of the Alexandrian text-type.

081. Manuscript 81 is clearly one of the most valuable minuscule manuscripts. It was written in 1044 AD and exemplifies an Alexandrian text-type.

1739. Manuscript 1739 is a codex which was written in the tenth century AD. This document is substantially transcribed from an Alexandrian exemplar, with notations from the works of Origen, Basil, Clement, Irenaeus, and Eusebius.

Chart © Joseph M. Holden, 2013.

This minuscule manuscript (Gregory-Aland Codex 2882) dating from the tenth to twelfth century AD contains the entire Gospel of Luke (except for one missing leaf, Luke 22:5b-35) and an introduction to the Gospel of John written on parchment. This text can be viewed in the Turpin Library at Dallas Theological Seminary, Dallas, Texas. (The Center for the Study of New Testament Manuscripts [www.csntm.org] has granted permission for this image to be used.)

ASCERTAINING THE GEOGRAPHY OF THE
CITIES OF THE PLAIN: 40 POINTS

1. Storytellers and writers in the ancient Near East did not invent fictitious geographies, but used what was known from personal experience, shared (cultural) experience, or "traditional" geographical wisdom, that is, actual geography, whether phenomenological or formulaic.

2. Whether or not ancient stories—together with their characters—are factual or fictitious, they were "layered over" real-world geography and topography, whether phenomenological or formulaic.

3. The writer of the Sodom story likely had personal knowledge of the geography he utilized; perhaps intimate awareness based on experience.

4. Genesis 13:1-12 is the only narrative passage among the Sodom tales marking out the location of the cities of the plain by employing geographical data points and directions in a conscientious attempt to place them in a real-world context shared by the readers.

5. The Genesis passage in question contains both specific and approximate geographical quantities: (a) Egypt; (b) the Negev; (c) Bethel/Ai; (d) the place of the altar to Yahweh (hill between Bethel and Ai, Genesis 12:8); and (e) the *kikkar* (Hebrew) of the Jordan.

6. Outside the Old Testament, among the Semitic cognates and Egyptian, *kikkar/kakkar/kakkaru/kerker* is never used as a geographical referent, but means only a "talent, a flat, circular weight of metal" or "circular, flat loaf of bread"; in Egyptian there is also the meaning "to draw a circle in the sand with a stick."

7. *Kikkar* (disk, circle) in Old Testament Hebrew likewise refers (well over 50 times) to a talent of metal or a circular, flat loaf of bread; but these meanings never use the definite article, suggesting its general substantive, non-locative quality in such contexts.

8. The 13 rare geographical uses of *kikkar*, found exclusively in the Old Testamemt, 10 of which are in the Sodom tales, denote the disk-shaped southern Jordan Valley north of the Dead Sea (linguistically a phenomenological secondary referent—that is, from all angles the area looks like a disk, thus its name); of these 13 instances, 4 are constructed *kikkar hayarden* (disk of the Jordan, with the definite article), while the remaining 9 are *hakikkar* (the *kikkar*, with the definite article), suggesting a well-known geographical area (on a par with the Negev). There are many standard Hebrew terms (primary referents) for "plain" and "valley," but these are explicitly avoided when referring to the geographical region known as the *kikkar* and *kikkar* of the Jordan.

9. The *kikkar* of the Jordan is confined to the area north of the Dead Sea because (a) *hayarden* (the Jordan) never refers to anything other than the fresh water system of the Jordan River proper and the valley through which it flows; and (b) *hayarden* is never extended to include any part of the Valley of Siddim (Valley of the Dead Sea), but ends at "the mouth of the Jordan below Pisgah" (another known geographical quantity, easily documentable; cf. Numbers 34:12; Deuteronomy 3:17,27; 4:47-49; Joshua 15:5; 18:19).

10. Thus, the *kikkar* of the Jordan can only refer to the disk-shaped alluvial plain north of the Dead Sea which was well-watered (a) like the garden of Yahweh (streams, rivers, springs), and (b) like Egypt (annual river inundations depositing new layers of water-laden silt; indeed, hydrologically speaking, the Jordan is a "Nile in miniature").

11. The western Jordan Disk, the location of Jericho and little else, has reasonable perennial water resources plus the Jordan River and local wadis; the eastern Jordan Disk has far greater water resources than the western side, and sports numerous Bronze and Iron Age cities and towns, mainly along its eastern edge, just beyond the reach of the floodplain.

12. The text suggests that Lot viewed with his "unaided" physical eyes the entire Jordan Disk from the area east of Bethel/Ai (above and west-northwest of Jericho); the entire *kikkar* is, in fact, visible from the highland's edge east of Bethel/Ai (which I have personally viewed on many occasions).

13. Lot traveled eastward from Bethel/Ai, pitching his tent toward Sodom, one of the cities of the eastern Jordan Disk, while Abram remained "in Canaan"; that is, Lot went east of the Jordan River beyond the formulaic Canaan boundary, remaining north of the Dead Sea all the while, no doubt traveling along the convenient east/west trade route that passed near Jericho, then crossed the river to the cities on the far side of the alluvial plain—the cities of the *kikkar*.

14. Sodom was one of the cities of the plain (*kikkar* = disk). No city south of the mouth of *hayarden* would have been considered as belonging to the Jordan Disk or the cities thereof (see point 9 above). Any placement of Sodom (or any of the other *kikkar* cities) south of the mouth of the Jordan would force an unnatural meaning on the term *kikkar* that it simply will not bear.

15. As the writer mentally works his way through the geography of the passage, the cities of the *kikkar* are perceived to have existed on the eastern Jordan Disk, north of the Dead Sea, the formulaic order of which (Sodom and Gomorrah, Admah and Zeboiim), with its two doublets, is reminiscent of ancient "map lists," particularly those of ancient Egypt, indicating directionality (usually south-to-north for Transjordan routes).

16. The storyteller calculated or assumed that Sodom was the largest urban center on the eastern Jordan Disk as indicated by the fact that (a) it is the only *kikkar* city mentioned by itself; (b) it is always listed first when related cities are mentioned; and (c) the king of Sodom is the sole "spokesperson" for the *kikkar* cities coalition after the Kedorlaomer incident (Genesis 14:17-24).

17. The story of Abram and Lot, minimally, has roots in the Bronze Age (as viewed by most scholars) or, perhaps, in the early Iron Age (as suggested by some—a view in the extreme minority).

18. Biblical dating places Abram, Lot, and the Sodom tales—indeed, all the Genesis patriarchal narratives—squarely in the Middle Bronze Age, probably Middle Bronze II (an era of famines in Canaan when hordes of Semitic peoples migrated from the Levant to Lower Egypt; cf. Genesis 12:10; 26:1; 41:57ff).

19. Given a Middle Bronze Age date for Abram, Genesis 10 pushes the existence of the cities of the plain back well before the time of Abram, probably into the Early Bronze Age.

20. Sodom and the other cities of the Jordan Disk would, thus, have occupations dating from the Early Bronze Age into the Middle Bronze Age.

21. In Genesis 10, the mention of actual, known cities—such as Babylon, Erech (Uruk), Akkad, Nineveh, Sidon, Gerar, Gaza—and regions—such as Shinar, Assyria, Mizraim (Egypt), Caphtor—strongly suggests that Sodom, Gomorrah, Admah, and Zeboiim, in the same context, were also real cities in the true geographical sense.

22. Sodom, Gomorrah, Admah, and Zeboiim were known by the writer of Genesis 10 to mark the eastern extent of the Canaanite clans (Genesis 10:18-19), at the geographical and occupational "seat" of the Great Rift Valley, the best and most obvious natural boundary imaginable—real cities representing a real boundary.

23. The city of Sodom itself was fortified (Genesis 19:1).

24. Given a Middle Bronze Age date for Abram, archaeologically and geographically speaking, the largest fortified Bronze Age urban center on the eastern Jordan Disk would be a "most likely" candidate for biblical Sodom.

25. The presence of major Early Bronze Age, Intermediate Bronze Age, and Middle Bronze Age occupations at the "Sodom" urban center would make such a theory compelling.

26. An occupational hiatus of several centuries after a fiery Middle Bronze Age destruction would make that "Sodom" identification almost irresistible (in the time of Moses and Joshua the eastern Jordan Disk is called "the wasteland" below Pisgah—Numbers 21:20).

27. The presence of three or four nearby sites reflecting the "doublet" geographical configuration suggested in the text, and with the same occupational profile, would make the theory virtually irrefutable.

28. Given a Middle Bronze Age date for Abram, Tall el-Hammam satisfies every "Sodom" criterion embedded in Genesis 13:1-12 (points 20, 23-27).

29. Given virtually any other "date" for Abram, and if one assumes that the Sodom tales are etiological legends, the Bronze Age ruins of the eastern Jordan Disk would have provided geographical realism to the writer's narrative.

30. Southern Dead Sea sites, such as Bab edh-Dhra and Numeira, satisfy not a single "cities of the plain" criterion set forth in the Genesis 13 narrative (summarized in points 20, 23-27 above) because (a) they were destroyed at the end of the Early Bronze Age centuries before the time of Abram and Lot (given a Middle Bronze Age date for Abram); and (b) they are entirely in the wrong place (whether or not the tales are factual or etiological, and regardless of date!).

31. There are no archaeological sites with an Early Bronze Age to Middle Bronze Age occupational profile in the Dead Sea Valley south of the mouth of the Jordan River. Period. (This is as one might expect from the biblical chronology itself.)

32. Whether or not the Sodom tales are fact or fancy, the storyteller's urban landscape of the *kikkar* cities is real, and well-known to his readers.

33. Significant Early Bronze Age through Middle Bronze Age ruins would have been readily visible on the eastern Jordan Disk in antiquity, even after several of them were topped by smaller city/town occupations during Iron Age II (this is a reality at several eastern Jordan Disk sites including Tall el-Hammam and Tall Nimrin).

34. The writer penned his stories about the cities of the Jordan *kikkar* while ruins, more ancient still, dotted the eastern Jordan Disk, readily visible and well-known to anyone living in or near that region (whether he wrote during the Late Bronze Age or Iron Age!).

35. Had the author of Genesis 13:1-12 thought that southern Dead Sea sites like Bab edh-Dhra and Numeira were Sodom and Gomorrah, his clearly-written geography would have been constructed to incorporate the specificity of that location; it does not, by any stretch of the imagination.

36. The Sodom narrative carefully marks out a location for the cities of the *kikkar* north of the Dead Sea on the east bank of the Jordan River where, in fact, the ruins of significant Bronze and Iron Age cities exist. Such a high degree of correspondence between text and ground cannot be mere coincidence.

37. Given the extremely high degree of correspondence between the material evidence on the eastern Jordan Disk and a "literal" biblical chronology placing Abram in the Middle Bronze Age, one must ask whether or not such correspondence is actual or coincidental.

38. For the sake of argument, one is forced to admit that a "face-value" reading of the biblical text places the Patriarchal Period in the Middle Bronze Age, whereupon a remarkable level of correspondence exists between the Sodom tales and the material facts present on the eastern Jordan Disk; regardless of when the stories were codified—Late Bronze Age, Iron Age I, or Iron Age II.

39. If one assumes, for the sake of argument, that the Patriarchal Period either occurred much later—say, during the Late Bronze Age or early Iron Age—or such stories were predominantly works of pious fiction—say, seventh century BCE or later—then there is no historical correspondence between said narratives and the *kikkar's* archaeological record, compelling one to conclude that the Sodom tales are probably etiological in nature, but rising from the existence of multiple Bronze Age ruins on the eastern Jordan Disk.

40. Given the fact that the geography unequivocally places the cities of the *kikkar* north of the Dead Sea and east of the Jordan River, one must conclude that, whether the Sodom tales are authentically Middle Bronze Age in origin and date, or are late Iron Age etiological compositions, they are layered over the physical geography of the eastern Jordan Disk where multiple Bronze Age ruins provided the storyteller's readers with eloquent physical testimony of the destruction of a bygone civilization.

This chart adapted from Steven Collins, "40 Salient Points on the Geography of the Cities of the Kikkar," in *Biblical Research Bulletin,* vol. 7, no. 1: 2-5. Used by permission.

APPENDIX C

EXPERT WITNESS OPINIONS REGARDING THE AUTHENTICITY OF THE JAMES OSSUARY

Person	Expertise	Comments
Andre Lemaire	Epigrapher, ancient Hebrew and Aramaic inscriptions	Has no doubt that the entire inscription was ancient and inscribed in a single event. No reason to believe the contrary.
Ada Yardeni	Paleographer, researcher, Hebrew University of Jerusalem	Examined the inscription in 2002 and concluded that the entire inscription is of ancient origin and inscribed by a single individual. She also stated, "If this is a forgery, I quit."
Hagai Misgav	Member of the IAA Committee, expert in Hebrew and Aramaic ossuary inscriptions	Found no indication of forgery in the inscription.
Shmuel Ahituv	Member of the 2003 IAA Writing Committee to examine the authenticity of the inscription and expert on Hebrew inscriptions	Found no indication that the inscription is a forgery or is modern. The text and paleography make it difficult to rule out the authenticity of the inscription.
Yosef Naveh	Professor, prosecution witness	No indication the inscription is a forgery.
Y.L. Rahmani	Archaeologist, has published the corpus of IAA ossuary inscriptions in IAA's possession	After examining the inscription, found no indication that the inscription (or any part of it) was a forgery.

Person	Expertise	Comments
Esther Eshel	Prosecution witness	Cannot rule out the possibility that the entire inscription may be ancient.
Roni Reich	Jerusalem professor, archaeologist, and researcher	Ossuary inscription is ancient, there is no reason to doubt its authenticity, and most likely comes from the late Second Temple period.
Gabriel Barkay	Jerusalem archaeologist and professor	Ossuary is ancient; found no scientific evidence to doubt its authenticity.
Gideon Avni	IAA "Writing Committee" appointed to examine the paleography and inscription in 2003	Never testified against the authenticity of the inscription.
Orna Cohen	Senior antiquities conservator for the IAA and Israeli museums, archaeologist, chemist, and specialist in the conservation of ancient stone items	Based on her careful analysis of the patina within the letter grooves under various light conditions, she concluded with certainty the phrase "brother of Jesus" had been engraved in ancient times.
Wolfgang Krumbein	One of the world's leading experts (Oldenburg University, Germany) on the patination process, stone patina, geology, and bio-geology	Analyzed samples of patina taken from the ossuary letter grooves, and concluded that this patina would require 50 to 100 years to develop, and most likely reflect a development process of thousands of years. The patina in the letter grooves was consistent with the patina on the surface of the ossuary, whose antiquity has not been contested.

Person	Expertise	Comments
Shimon Ilani Amnon Rosenfeld	Experts in archaeometry (scientific testing of archaeological artifacts) at the Geological Survey of Israel in Jerusalem	After examination of the inscription in 2002, they identified natural bio-patina in all the letter grooves, thus demonstrating the inscription occurred prior to the scratches and patina forming. They have no doubt about the ancient origin of the entire inscription.
James Harrell	University of Toledo, Ohio, USA, expert in geology and stone of the ancient world	Found no indication that any part of the inscription was forged.
Dan Rahimi	Royal Ontario Museum of Toronto	Museum researchers tested the patina and found natural patina in the letter grooves under a granular substance that is consistent with detergent used by the IAA to formerly clean the ossuary.
Yuval Goren	Expert in petrography of potsherds and clay/silt, former member of IAA, and prosecution witness	Though Goren initially had submitted an opinion on the ossuary at the IAA's request in 2003 in which he denied any presence of natural patina in the letter grooves, he later contradicted this by reversing his finds. In 2007, after a reexamination of the inscription, he admitted to finding natural patina in the second half of the inscription.

Person	Expertise	Comments
Avnor Ayalon	Geochemist of the Geological Survey of Israel in Jerusalem and prosecution witness	He proposed to examine isotopic composition of the oxygen and carbon in carbonate patina, and compare it to the same found in stalactite caves in Jerusalem. Similar isotopic values would prove the carbonate patina on the ossuary may be natural, but a dissimilar value would demonstrate it is not natural and most likely a forgery. However, Ayalon's model has been demonstrated by others to be based on false assumptions and deemed inappropriate for examining ancient artifacts.
Elisabetta Boaretto	Expert in carbon-14 dating, prosecution witness	Found no evidence to support that the inscription is forged or new. Only signed the IAA petition against Golan because Goren (who later reversed his opinion) and Ayalon (whose model was subsequently shown to be mistaken) had previously asserted that they had found no patina, not due to her own analysis of the inscription.
Jacques Neguer	Chemist for the IAA and prosecution witness	Asserted the inscription had been cleaned (with detergent) in the past, but could not determine whether it was a forgery.
Israel Police Forensic Department (Mazap)	Forensics	Letters in the first half of the inscription (which are not contested), were engraved by the same individual who engraved the second half of the inscription.

Person	Expertise	Comments
Gerald B. Richards	Adjunct professor of forensic science at George Washington University, and senior consultant to the FBI	Conducted scientific tests of Oded Golan's photos (including infra-red and ultraviolet tests) of the ossu-ary, proving that the inscription had been engraved prior to 2002 since the photography (Kodak) paper used was discontinued in the 1980s. The indictment against Golan had claimed Golan had forged the inscription around 2002. This claim is now impossible to sustain.
Dan Bahat	State prosecutor in the case	Announced that the State would most likely dismiss the charges involving the ossuary and retract its claim that the ossuary inscription was a forgery had the bill of indict-ment not involved other charges.

Chart from Joseph M. Holden, "The James Ossuary: The Earliest Witness to Jesus and His Family?" in *Bible Translation Magazine: All Things Bible Translation* 13 (July 2012). (© Joseph M. Holden 2012. All rights reserved.) This chart is based on the summary of court proceedings offered by Oded Golan, "The Authenticity of the James Ossuary" (March 2011), 1-15.

NOTES

Chapter 1—The Masoretes and the Samaritans

1. Bibliography for the content up to this point: Philip Wesley Comfort, *The Origin of the Bible* (Wheaton, IL: Tyndale House Publishers, 2004); Brian Edwards, *Nothing but the Truth: The Inspiration, Authority and History of the Bible Explained* (Darlington, UK: Evangelical Press, 2006); Walter C. Kaiser Jr., *The Old Testament Documents: Are They Reliable & Relevant?* (Downers Grove, IL: InterVarsity Press, 2001); Page H. Kelley, Daniel S. Mynatt, and Timothy G. Crawford, *The Masorah of Biblia Hebraica Stuttgartensia: Introduction and Annotated Glossary* (Grand Rapids, MI: W.B. Eerdmans, 1998); Emanuel Tov, *Textual Criticism of the Hebrew Bible* (Minneapolis, MN: Fortress Press, 1992); Paul D. Wegner, *The Journey from Texts to Translations: The Origin and Development of the Bible* (Grand Rapids, MI: Baker Academic, 2004); Ernst Wurthwein, *The Text of the Old Testament: An Introduction to the Biblia Hebraica* (Grand Rapids, MI: W.B. Eerdmans Publishing Co., 1995).

2. See Tov, *Textual Criticism.*

3. Bibliography for this section: Comfort, *The Origin of the Bible*; Kaiser, *The Old Testament Documents*; Tov, *Textual Criticism*; Wegner, *The Journey from Texts to Translations.*

4. See Tov, *Textual Criticism.*

5. Tov, *Textual Criticism*; Wurthwein, *The Text of the Old Testament.*

6. Craig A. Evans, *Ancient Texts for New Testament Studies: A Guide to the Background Literature* (Peabody, MA: Hendrickson Publishers, 2005); Wurthwein, *The Text of the Old Testament.*

7. See Norman L. Geisler, *Baker Encyclopedia of Christian Apologetics* (Grand Rapids, MI: Baker Books, 1999).

8. Bibliography for this section: Comfort, *The Origin of the Bible*; Edwards, *Nothing but the Truth*; Geisler, *Baker Encyclopedia*; Norman L. Geisler, *Systematic Theology: Introduction and Bible*, vol. 1 (Minneapolis, MN: Bethany House, 2002); Norman L. Geisler and William E. Nix, *A General Introduction to the Bible*, rev. ed. (Chicago: Moody Press, 1968, 1986); Tov, *Textual Criticism*; Wegner, *The Journey from Texts to Translations*; Wurthwein, *The Text of the Old Testament.*

Chapter 2—The Dead Sea Scrolls and the Silver Scrolls

1. John C. Trever, "The Discovery of the Dead Sea Scrolls," *Biblical Archaeologist* 11 (September 1948), 55.

2. Norman L. Geisler and William E. Nix, *A General Introduction to the Bible*, rev. ed. (Chicago: Moody Press, 1968, 1986), 361-364.

3. Pliny the Elder, *Natural History*, 5:17,4.

4. Flavius Josephus, *Antiquities of the Jews*, 18:18-22.

5. Josephus, 13:5-9.

6. Dead Sea Scrolls, *Rule of the Community*, VIII.

7. Yitzhak Magen and Yuval Peleg offer an answer to the Essene theory in their recent report in Katharina Galor, Jean-Baptiste Humbert, and Jurgen Zangenberg, eds., *The Site of the Dead Sea Scrolls: Archaeological Interpretations and Debates* (Leiden, the Netherlands: Brill, 2006), 55-113.

8. Bibliography for this section: Philip Wesley Comfort, *The Origin of the Bible* (Wheaton, IL: Tyndale House Publishers, 2004); Brian Edwards, *Nothing but the Truth: The Inspiration, Authority and History of the Bible Explained* (Darlington, UK: Evangelical Press, 2006); Walter C. Kaiser Jr., *The Old Testament Documents: Are They Reliable & Relevant?* (Downers Grove, IL: InterVarsity Press, 2001); Page H. Kelley, Daniel S. Mynatt, and Timothy G. Crawford, *The Masorah of Biblia Hebraica Stuttgartensia: Introduction and Annotated Glossary* (Grand Rapids, MI: W.B. Eerdmans, 1998); Emanuel Tov, *Textual Criticism of the Hebrew Bible* (Minneapolis, MN: Fortress Press, 1992); Craig A. Evans, *Ancient Texts for New Testament Studies: A Guide to the Background Literature*

(Peabody, MA: Hendrickson Publishers, 2005); Wurthwein, *The Text of the Old Testament*; John L. Sharpe and Kimberly Van Kampen, eds., *The Bible As Book: The Manuscript Tradition* (London: British Library, 1998); Lawrence H. Schiffman and James C. VanderKam, eds., *Encyclopedia of the Dead Sea Scrolls* (New York: Oxford University Press, 2000); James C. VanderKam and Peter W. Flint, *The Meaning of the Dead Sea Scrolls: Their Significance for Understanding the Bible, Judaism, Jesus, and Christianity* (San Francisco: HarperSanFrancisco, 2002).

9. Gabriel Barkay, Marilyn J. Lundberg, Andrew G. Vaughn, Bruce Zuckerman, "The Amulets from Ketef Hinnom: A New Edition and Evaluation," *Bulletin of the American School of Oriental Research* 334 (May 2004), 41-70.

10. Barkay et al., 41-70.

Chapter 3—The Transmission of the Old Testament—Summary

1. Gleason L. Archer, *A Survey of Old Testament Introduction* (Chicago: Moody Press, 1994); Birger Gerhardsson, *Memory and Manuscript: Oral Tradition and Written Transmission in Rabbinic Judaism and Early Christianity* (Grand Rapids, MI: William B. Eerdmans Pub. 1998); Emanuel Tov, *Textual Criticism of the Hebrew Bible* (Minneapolis, MN: Fortress Press, 1992).

2. Millar Burrows, *The Dead Sea Scrolls* (New York: Random House, 1988), 304.

3. F.F. Bruce, *Second Thoughts on the Dead Sea Scrolls* (No city: Attic Press, 1986), 61-69.

4. Archer, *A Survey of Old Testament Introduction*, 19.

Chapter 4—Moses, the Pentateuch, and the Major Prophets

1. Gleason L. Archer, *A Survey of Old Testament Introduction* (Chicago: Moody Press, 1994), chapters 6-8.

2. William W. Hallo, *The World's Oldest Literature: Studies in Sumerian Belles-Lettres* (Leiden, the Netherlands: Brill, 2010), 677.

3. Meredith Kline, *The Treaty of the Great King* (Grand Rapids, MI: Eerdmans, 1963). See also Archer, *A Survey of Old Testament Introduction*, 253-262.

4. Charles Darwin, *The Origin of Species: A Facsimile of the First Edition* (Harvard University Press, 1964).

5. *American Scientist*, May/June 1997, 244.

6. *Discover Magazine*, May 1981.

7. Niles Eldredge, *Macroevolutionary Dynamics* (New York: McGraw-Hill, 1989), 22.

8. The *Washington Post*, May 15, 2005: D6.

9. Cited in H. Wayne House, ed., *Intelligent Design 101* (Grand Rapids, MI: Kregel, 2008), 218-219.

10. Sir Fred Hoyle, *Evolution from Space* (London: Dent, 1981), 77.

11. Mark Pagel, *Nature*, February 25, 1999.

12. Darwin, 189.

13. Richard Dawkins, *The Blind Watchmaker* (New York: Norton, 1996), 17-18, 116.

14. See Michael Behe, *Darwin's Black Box: The Biochemical Challenge to Evolution* (New York: Free Press, 1996, 2006); Stephen Meyer, *Signature in the Cell: DNA and the Evidence for Intelligent Design* (New York: HarperCollins Publishers, 2009); William Dembski and Jonathan Wells, *The Design of Life: Discovering Signs of Intelligence in Biological Systems* (Dallas, TX: The Foundation for Thought and Ethics, 2008).

15. Nelson Glueck, *Rivers in the Desert: A History of the Negev* (New York: Farrar, Strauss & Cudahy, 1959), 31, emphasis added.

16. Walter Kaiser, "Literary Form of Genesis 1-11," *New Perspectives on the Old Testament*, ed. J. Barton Payne (Waco, TX: Word, Inc., 1970), 59-60.

17. K.A. Kitchen, *Ancient Orient and the Old Testament* (Chicago: InterVarsity Press, 1966), 89.

18. See Alfred Rehwinkel, *The Flood: In the Light of the Bible, Geology, and Archaeology* (St. Louis, MO: Concordia, 1951).

19. Byron C. Nelson, *The Deluge Story in Stone* (Minneapolis, MN: Bethany Fellowship, 1968).

20. David Collins, "Was Noah's Ark Stable?" in *Creation Research Society Quarterly* 14 (September 1977), 86.

21. Collins, "Was Noah's Ark Stable?"

22. Flavius Josephus, *Antiquities of the Jews*, XX, ii, 2, in *The Works of Flavius Josephus*, 2 vols., tr. William Whiston (Philadelphia: J. Grigg, 1833), vol. II, 107; *Antiquities of the Jews*, I, iii, 5 and 6, in Whiston, vol. I, 17-18.

23. *Ad Autolycum*, book 3, chapter 19, tr. Marcus Dodds, in the *Ante-Nicene Fathers* (1885), vol. II, 117.

24. *Panarion*, I, i, 18, in John W. Montgomery, *The Quest for Noah's Ark*, 2nd ed. (Minneapolis, MN: Bethany Fellowship, 1974), 77.

25. John Chrysostom, "On Perfect Charity," in Montgomery, *The Quest*, 78.

26. Isidore of Seville, Etymologies, in "Scriptorum Classicorum Bibliotheca Oxoniensis" (1911), XIV, 8, 5, in Montgomery, *The Quest*, 80.

27. Montgomery, *The Quest*, 82-83.

28. Montgomery, *The Quest*, 93-94.

29. Adam Olearius, in *The Voyages and Travels of the Ambassadors*, tr. John Davies (London, 1662), Book IV, 187.

30. P.J. Wiseman, *Ancient Records and the Structure of Genesis* (Nashville, TN: Thomas Nelson, 1985), 74.

31. See Edwin Yamauchi, *The Stones and the Scriptures* (Philadelphia: J.B. Lippincott, 1972), 36; W.F. Albright, *The Archaeology of Palestine* (Baltimore: Penguin, 1949), 236; W.F. Albright, *The Biblical Period from Abraham to Ezra* (New York: Harper & Row, 1963), 1; K.A. Kitchen, *On the Reliability of the Old Testament* (Grand Rapids, MI: Eerdmans, 2003); Glueck, *Rivers in the Desert*; Wiseman, *Ancient Records*, 301-302. Also see the Amarna, Nuzi, Mari, and Ras Shamra tablets for cultural indicators, including civil and religious law codes.

32. Norman L. Geisler, *Systematic Theology: Introduction and Bible*, vol. 1 (Minneapolis, MN: Bethany House, 2002), 453.

33. Geisler, *Systematic Theology*, 454.

34. Kline, *The Treaty of the Great King*; see Archer, *Survey of Old Testament Introduction*, 253-262.

35. Wiseman, *Ancient Records*, 301-302.

36. Kitchen, *Ancient Orient and the Old Testament*, 379.

37. W.F. Albright, "Toward a More Conservative View," *Christianity Today*, January 1, 1963, 1329.

38. Jeffery L. Sheler, "Is the Bible True?" *U.S. News & World Report*, October 25, 1999, 52.

Chapter 5—Alleged Errors vs. Archaeological Discoveries

1. Norman L. Geisler and Thomas A. Howe, *The Big Book of Bible Difficulties* (Grand Rapids, MI: Baker, 1992); Walter C. Kaiser Jr., Peter H. Davids, F.F. Bruce, and Manfred Brauch, *Hard Sayings of the Bible* (Downers Grove, IL: InterVarsity Press, 1996); Gleason Archer, *Encyclopedia of Bible Difficulties* (Grand Rapids, MI: Zondervan Publishing, 1982); Ron Rhodes, *The Complete Book of Bible Answers* (Eugene, OR: Harvest House Publishers, 1997).

2. This list is based on Geisler and Howe, *The Big Book of Bible Difficulties*, chapter 1.

3. Bibliography and suggested reading for this section: Archer, *A Survey of Old Testament Introduction*; Gleason L. Archer, *Encyclopedia of Bible Difficulties* (Grand Rapids, MI: Zondervan Publishing, 1982); Roger Beckwith, *The Old Testament Canon of the New Testament Church and Its Background in Early Judaism* (Grand Rapids, MI. Eerdmans, 1986); Philip Wesley Comfort, *The Origin of the Bible* (Wheaton, IL: Tyndale House Publisher, MI, 2004); Brian Edwards, *Nothing but the Truth: The Inspiration, Authority and History of the Bible Explained* (Darlington, UK: Evangelical Press, 2006); Norman L. Geisler and Thomas A. Howe, *When Critics Ask: A Popular Handbook on Bible Difficulties* (Wheaton, IL: Victor Books, 1992); Laird Harris, *The Inspiration and Canonicity*

of the Bible (Grand Rapids, MI: Zondervan, 1957); Walter C. Kaiser Jr., *The Old Testament Documents: Are They Reliable & Relevant?* (Downers Grove, IL: InterVarsity Press, 2001); K.A. Kitchen, *On the Reliability of the Old Testament* (Grand Rapids, MI: Eerdmans, 2003).

4. See Paul Copan, *Is God a Moral Monster? Making Sense of the Old Testament God* (Grand Rapids, MI: Baker, 2011).

Chapter 6—The Canon of the Old Testament

1. Norman L. Geisler, *Baker Encyclopedia of Christian Apologetics* (Grand Rapids, MI: Baker Books, 1999), 233.

2. Roger Beckwith, *The Old Testament Canon of the New Testament Church and Its Background in Early Judaism* (Grand Rapids, MI: Eerdmans, 1986).

3. Josephus, *Against Apion*, 1.8.

4. Augustine, *City of God*, 18.36.

5. Josephus, *Against Apion*, 1.8.

6. *Tosefta Sotah* 13:2.

Chapter 7—The Transmission of the New Testament

1. Norman L. Geisler and William E. Nix, *A General Introduction to the Bible*, rev. ed. (Chicago: Moody Press, 1968, 1986), 387.

2. Bart Ehrman, *Misquoting Jesus: The Story Behind Who Changed the Bible and Why* (New York: HarperSanFrancisco, 2005), 89-90.

3. Ehrman, *Misquoting Jesus*, 55, emphasis added.

Chapter 8—The Manuscripts of the New Testament

1. D.C. Parker, *Codex Bezae: An Early Christian Manuscript and Its Text* (Cambridge, UK: Cambridge University Press, 1991), 280.

Chapter 9—The Accuracy of the New Testament Manuscripts

1. Bruce Metzger, *Chapters in the History of New Testament Textual Criticism* (Grand Rapids, MI: Eerdmans, 1963), 146.

2. Brooke Foss Westcott, Fenton John Anthony Hort, and W.J. Hickie, *The New Testament in the Original Greek* (New York: Macmillan Co., 1951), 2.2.

3. See B.B. Warfield, *An Introduction to Textual Criticism of the New Testament* (London: Hodder & Stoughton, 1886), 13-14.

4. A.T. Robertson, *An Introduction to the Textual Criticism of the New Testament* (London: Hodder & Stoughton, 1925), 22.

5. Bart Ehrman, *Misquoting Jesus: The Story Behind Who Changed the Bible and Why* (New York: HarperSanFrancisco, 2005), 55, emphasis added.

6. See Mariano Grinbank, "Bart Ehrman's Millions and Millions of Variants," part 1 of 2, posted September 16, 2010, at www.truefreethinker.com.

7. Frederick G. Kenyon, *The Bible and Archaeology* (New York/London: Harper, 1940), 288ff.

8. Philip Schaff, *A Companion to the Greek Testament and the English Version* (New York: Harper, 1883, 1903), 177, emphasis added.

Chapter 10—Historicity of the New Testament

1. Richard Bauckham, *Jesus and the Eyewitnesses: The Gospels as Eyewitness Testimony* (Grand Rapids, MI: Wm. B. Eerdmans Publishing Co., 2006), 506.

2. See Norman L. Geisler, *A Popular Survey of the New Testament* (Grand Rapids, MI: Baker Books, 2008), 85-86.

3. *Antiquities of the Jews*, 20.9.1.

4. Colin J. Hemer, *The Book of Acts in the Setting of Hellenistic History* (Winona Lake, IN: Eisenbrauns, 1990), 376-382.

5. See Craig Blomberg, *The Historical Reliability of the Gospels* (Downers Grove, IL: InterVarsity Press, 1987).

6. Simon Greenleaf, *The Testimony of the Evangelists* (Grand Rapids, MI: Baker Books reprint, 1984), 53-54.

7. Greenleaf, *The Testimony*, 46.

8. Nelson Glueck, *Rivers in the Desert* (Philadelphia: Jewish Publication Society of America, 1959), 31.

9. Jeffery Sheler, *US News & World Report* (October 25, 1999), 52.

10. W.F. Albright, "Toward a More Conservative View," *Christianity Today*, January 18, 1963.

11. Gary Habermas, *The Historical Jesus: Ancient Evidence for the Life of Christ* (Joplin, MO: College Press, 1996).

Chapter 11—Responding to Recent Criticisms of the Gospels

1. A.N. Sherwin-White, *Roman Society and Roman Law in the New Testament* (Oxford, UK: Clarendon Press, 1963), 27-28.

2. Bart D. Ehrman, *Jesus, Interrupted: Revealing the Hidden Contradictions in the Bible (and Why We Don't Know About Them)* (New York: HarperOne, 2009), 42.

3. Frederick W. Danker, Walter Bauer, and William Arndt, *A Greek-English Lexicon of the New Testament and Other Early Christian Literature* (Chicago: University of Chicago Press, 2000), 136.

4. Leon Morris, *The Gospel According to Matthew* (Grand Rapids, MI; Leicester, England: W.B. Eerdmans; Inter-Varsity Press, 1992), 228-229.

5. D.A. Carson, *The Gospel According to John* (Leicester, England: Inter-Varsity Press, 1991), 603-604.

6. C.K. Barrett, *The Gospel According to St John: An Introduction with Commentary and Notes on the Greek Text* (London: SPCK, 1978), 545.

7. See Josephus, *Antiquities*, XVI, 6, 2.

8. See A.T. Robertson, *Word Pictures in the New Testament* (Nashville, TN: B&H Publishing Group, 1973), vol. 4, 299.

Chapter 12—Criticisms of the Resurrection Accounts and the Epistles

1. Bart D. Ehrman, *Jesus, Interrupted: Revealing the Hidden Contradictions in the Bible (and Why We Don't Know About Them)* (New York: HarperOne, 2009), 48.

2. Michael R. Licona, *The Resurrection of Jesus: A New Historiographical Approach* (Downers Grove, IL: IVP Academic, 2010).

3. Licona's list of passages whose historicity can be doubted or denied also include 1) the account of the angels at the tomb, which is recorded in all four Gospels (Matthew 28:2-7; Mark 16:5-7; Luke 24:4-7; John 20:11-14) (Licona, *The Resurrection of Jesus*, 185-186); 2) the account of the mob falling backward at Jesus' claim "I am He" in John 18:4-6 (Licona, 306, note 114); and 3) the accuracy of the day of Jesus' crucifixion—in a debate with Bart Ehrman at Southern Evangelical Seminary in the spring of 2009, Licona asserted concerning the day Jesus was crucified that "I think that John probably altered the day in order for a theological—to make a theological point there. But that does not mean that Jesus wasn't crucified"; and 4) other New Testament passages, since he claims that the Gospel genre is Greco-Roman biography, which he says is a "flexible genre" in which "it is often difficult to determine where history ends and legend begins" (Licona, 34).

4. Licona, *The Resurrection of Jesus*, respectively, on pages 548 (compare 556) and 185-186.

5. Licona, *The Resurrection of Jesus*, 186.

6. After extensive criticism of this conclusion, Licona has weakened his certainty about it but has not denied the possibility of the Matthew text being legend.

7. All quotations after the previous note reference are from Licona, *The Resurrection of Jesus*, 552-553.

8. Licona, *The Resurrection of Jesus*, 553.

9. Frederick W. Danker, Walter Bauer, and William Arndt, *A Greek-English Lexicon of the New Testament and Other Early Christian Literature* (Chicago: University of Chicago Press, 2000), 257.

10. *Ellicott's Commentary*, vol. VI, 178.

11. See Colin J. Hemer, *The Book of Acts in the Setting of Hellenistic History* (Winona Lake, IN: Eisenbrauns, 1990).

12. Respectively, in *Epistles to the Trallians*, chap. 8, compare *Epistle to the Magnesians*, chap. 9; Fragment 28; *Against Celsus*, book II, chap. 33.

13. See Thomas Aquinas, *Catena Aurea [Commentary According to St. Matthew]*, vol. 1, 963-964.

14. Bart D. Ehrman, *Forged: Writing in the Name of God: Why the Bible's Authors Are Not Who We Think They Are* (New York: HarperOne, 2011), 95-96.

15. Donald A. Carson and Douglas J. Moo, *An Introduction to the New Testament* (Grand Rapids, MI: Zondervan, 2008), 556.

16. Bart D. Ehrman, *Misquoting Jesus: The Story Behind Who Changed the Bible and Why* (New York: HarperSan-Francisco, 2005), 7.

17. Ehrman, *Misquoting Jesus*, 64, 157, 159.

Chapter 13—The Canon of the New Testament

1. See F.F. Bruce, *Jesus and Christian Origins Outside the New Testament* (Grand Rapids, MI: Eerdmans Publishing Co., 1974).

2. Kurt Aland and Barbara Aland, *The Text of the New Testament: An Introduction to the Critical Editions and to the Theory and Practice of Modern Textual Criticism* (Grand Rapids, MI: W.B. Eerdmans Pub. Co., 1987), 50.

Chapter 14—Archaeology and the Bible

1. John D. Currid, *Doing Archaeology in the Land of the Bible* (Grand Rapids, MI: Baker Books, 1999), 16.

2. See Yosef Garfinkel, "The Birth and Death of Biblical Minimalism," *Biblical Archaeology Review*, May/June 2011, 46-53, 78.

3. K.A. Kitchen, "The Patriarchal Age: Myth or History?" *Biblical Archaeology Review*, March/April 1995, 48ff.

4. Kathleen Kenyon, *Digging Up Jericho* (London: Ernest Benn, 1957).

5. Bryant G. Wood, "Did the Israelites Conquer Jericho?" *Biblical Archaeology Review*, March/April 1990, 44-58.

Chapter 15—Keys to Understanding Archaeology in Biblical Lands

1. Dates adapted from John Witte Moore and Steven Collins, *A Geographical, Historical, and Archaeological Handbook for Travelers* (Albuquerque, NM: Trinity Southwest University Press, 2012); John D. Currid, *Doing Archaeology in the Land of the Bible* (Grand Rapids, MI: Baker Books, 1999), 19; and Alfred Hoerth and John McRay, *Bible Archaeology: An Exploration of the History and Culture of Early Civilizations* (Grand Rapids, MI: Baker Books, 2005).

Part Six—Archaeology of the Old Testament: Introduction

1. Edwin Yamauchi, *The Stones and the Scriptures* (Philadelphia and New York: J.B. Lippincott Company, 1972), 146-166.

2. Donald J. Wiseman, *Illustrations from Biblical Archaeology* (London: The Tyndale Press, 1958), 5.

3. See LaMoine F. Devries, *Cities of the Biblical World* (Peabody, MA: Hendrickson Publishers, 1997).

Chapter 16—Creation and Flood, the Tower of Babel, and the Cities of the Plain

1. James Pritchard, *Ancient Near Eastern Texts Relating to the Old Testament* (Princeton, NJ: Princeton University Press, 1969), 5.

2. Benjamin R. Foster, "Atra-Hasis," in William W. Hallo and K. Lawson Younger Jr., eds., *The Context of Scripture: Canonical Compositions from the Biblical World*, vol. 1 (Leiden, the Netherlands: Brill, 2003), I:451.

3. Foster, "Atra-Hasis," I:452.

4. Pritchard, *Ancient Near Eastern Texts*, 265.

5. Hallo and Younger, eds., *The Context of Scripture*, I:515

6. Thorkild Jacobsen, "The Eridu Genesis," *Journal of Biblical Literature*, vol. 100, no. 4 (December 1981), 513-529.

7. Charles J. Singer, *The History of Technology*, vol. 1 (Oxford, England: Clarendon Press, 1954), 250-254.

8. Thorkild Jacobsen, "Enmerkar and the Lord of Aratta," in William W. Hallo and K. Lawson Younger Jr., eds., *The Context of Scripture: Canonical Compositions from the Biblical World* (Leiden, the Netherlands: Brill, 2003), I:547-548.

9. Steven Collins, "40 Salient Points on the Geography of the Cities of the Kikkar," *Biblical Research Bulletin* VII:1, 5ff. Chart used by permission.

10. Steven Collins, "Where is Sodom?: The Case for Tall el-Hammam," *Biblical Archaeology Review*, March/April 2013.

Chapter 17—Exodus and Conquest

1. Brad C. Sparks paper presented to American Schools of Oriental Research annual meeting, Egyptology session, 2007, attended by the author (J.H.), citing the revised critical edition (1991) by Erik Hornung (with Gerhard Fecht) of the *Destruction of Mankind*, text of Seti I, KV 17, chamber Je, line 49.

2. Sparks, forthcoming.

3. For example, Ziony Zevit, "Three Ways to Look at the Ten Plagues," *Bible Review*, vol. 6, no. 3 (1990), pp. 18a, 19a.

4. Brad C. Sparks, "Red Algae Theories of the Ten Plagues" [Parts 1, 2, 3], *Bible and Spade*, vol. 16, no. 3 (Summer 2003) , 66-77; vol. 17, no. 1 (Winter 2004), 17-27; vol. 17, no. 3 (Summer 2004), 71-82.

5. See Manfred Bietak, *Avaris, the Capital of the Hyksos: Recent Excavations at Tell El-Dab'a* (London: British Museum Press, 1996); "Comments on the Exodus" in *Egypt, Israel, Sinai: Archaeological and Historical Relationships in the Biblical Period* (Tel Aviv: Tel Aviv University, 1987); Manfred Bietak, "Contra Bimson, Bietak Says Late Bronze Age Cannot Begin as Late as 1400 BC," *Biblical Archaeology Review* 15:4 (July/August, 1988); "Egypt and Canaan During the Middle Bronze Age," *Bulletin of the American School of Oriental Research*, 281 (1991).

6. Hershel Shanks, "When Did Ancient Israel Begin?" *Biblical Archaeology Review*, vol. 38, no. 1 (Jan/Feb 2012), 59-62, 67; Peter van der Veen, Christoffer Theis, and Manfred Görg, "Israel in Canaan (Long) Before Pharaoh Merneptah? A Fresh Look at Berlin Statue Pedestal Relief 21687," in *Journal of Ancient Egyptian Interconnections*, vol. 2 (2010), 15-25.

7. James Pritchard, *Ancient Near Eastern Texts Relating to the Old Testament* (Princeton, NJ: Princeton University Press, 1969), 378, emphasis added.

8. Pritchard, *Ancient Near Eastern Texts*, 378, fn18.

9. Sparks, forthcoming.

10. Bryant G. Wood, "Did the Israelites Conquer Jericho? A New Look at the Archaeological Evidence," *Biblical Archaeology Review*, 16:02 (March/April 1990), 44-58; online version at www.biblearchaeology.org/post/2008/05/Did-the-Israelites-Conquer-Jericho-A-New-Look-at-the-Archaeological-Evidence.aspx.

11. Wood, "Did the Israelites Conquer Jericho?"

12. Bryant G. Wood, "Researching Jericho," *Bible and Spade* (Summer 2009), online at www.biblearchaeology.org/post/2010/04/22/Researching-Jericho.aspx.

13. Bryant G. Wood, "Dating Jericho's Destruction: Bienkowski Is Wrong on All Counts," *Biblical Archaeology Review* 16:05 (September/October 1990), emphasis added.

14. Piotr Bienkowski, "Jericho Was Destroyed in the Middle Bronze Age, Not the Late Bronze Age," *Biblical Archaeology Review* 16:05 (September/October 1990).

Chapter 18—The Amarna Letters, the Hittites, and the City of Megiddo

1. Alfred Hoerth and John McCray, *Bible Archaeology: An Exploration of the History and Culture of Early Civilizations* (Grand Rapids, MI: Baker Books, 2005), 107.

Chapter 19—King David and His Dynasty

1. For a published discussion on this inscription see Aren M. Maeir, Aaron Demsky, Stefan J. Wimmer, and Alexander Zukerman, "A Late Iron Age I/Early Iron Age II Old Canaanite Inscription from Tell es-Safi/Gath, Israel: Paleography, Dating, and Historical-cultural Significance," in *Bulletin of the American Schools of Oriental Research*, no. 351 (August, 2008): 39-59.

2. Hershel Shanks, "Newly Discovered: A Fortified City from King David's Time: Answers and Questions at Khirbet Qeiyafa," *Biblical Archaeology Review* 35 (January/February 2009).

3. Shanks, "Newly Discovered."

4. Supporting this contention is Hershel Shanks, "Oldest Hebrew Inscription Found in Israelite Fort on Philistine Border," *Biblical Archaeology Review* 52 (March/April 2010).

5. Shanks, "Oldest Hebrew Inscription."

6. Emile Puech, Gershon Galil, Alan Millard, Yosef Garfinkel, and Saar Ganor.

7. Christopher A. Rollston, "What's the Oldest Hebrew Inscription?" in *Biblical Archaeology Review* 38:03 (May/June 2012).

8. See Haggai Misgav's analysis of the inscription in Hershel Shanks, "Prize Find: Oldest Hebrew Inscription Discovered in Israelite Fort on Philistine Border," in *Biblical Archaeology Review* 36 (March/April 2009).

9. Yosef Garfinkel, "A Minimalist Disputes His Demise: A Response to Philip Davies," *Biblical Archaeology Review* online article at www.bib-arch.org/scholars-study/minimalist-response-garfinkel.asp, accessed July 2, 2012. See Philip Davies, "The End of Biblical Minimalism?" in *Biblical Archaeology Review* online article at www.bib-arch.org/scholars-study/minimalist-response-davies.asp, accessed on July 2, 2012.

10. Garfinkel, "A Minimalist Disputes."

11. Garfinkel, "A Minimalist Disputes."

12. Alan Millard, "The Tell Dan Stele," in William W. Hallo and K. Lawson Younger Jr., eds., *The Context of Scripture: Canonical Compositions from the Biblical World*, vol. 1 (Leiden, the Netherlands: Brill, 2003), 2:161-162, emphasis added.

13. Andre Lemaire, "'House of David' Restored in Moabite Inscription," *Biblical Archaeology Review*, vol. 20, no. 03 (1994). The deconstructionist Philip Davies has rejected Lemaire's findings, while Anson Rainey has accepted the translation.

14. Lemaire, "'House of David' Restored."

15. Lemaire, "'House of David' Restored."

16. See the excellent work on stamp seals by Nahman Avigad in *Corpus of West Semitic Stamp Seals* (Jerusalem: Israel Academy of Sciences and Humanities; The Israel Exploration Society; Institute of Archaeology of the Hebrew University of Jerusalem, 1997).

Chapter 20—Nebuchadnezzar II and the Persian Kings

1. James Pritchard, *Ancient Near Eastern Texts Relating to the Old Testament* (Princeton, NJ: Princeton University Press, 1969), 322.

2. See the scholarly treatment and cataloguing of western Semitic seals by Nahman Avigad, *Corpus of West Semitic Stamp Seals* (Jerusalem: Israel Academy of Sciences and Humanities; The Israel Exploration Society; The Institute of Archaeology of the Hebrew University of Jerusalem, 1997).

3. Nigel Reynolds, "Tiny Tablet Provides Proof for Old Testament" (Telegraph Media Group, 2007).

4. Adapted from Joachim Marzahn, *The Ishtar Gate: The Processional Way; The New Year Festival of Babylon* (Mainz am Rhein, Germany: Philipp von Zaubern, 1995), 29-30. Also see D.J. Wiseman, *Nebuchadnezzar and Babylon* (Oxford, UK: Oxford University Press, 1985).

Chapter 22—Jesus and Other New Testament Persons in Non-Christian Sources

1. *Antiquities of the Jews*, 20.200, in *The Works of Flavius Josephus*, William Whiston, tr. (Peabody, MA: Hendrickson, 1987).

2. *Antiquities of the Jews*, 63.

3. Christopher Price, "Did Josephus Refer to Jesus? A Thorough Review of the *Testimonium Flavianum*" (2004, 2007), www.bede.org.uk/josephus.htm. Also see C.K. Barrett, *The New Testament Backgrounds, Selected Documents* (New York: Harper and Row, 1961), 196-201.

4. Gary R. Habermas, *The Historical Jesus: Ancient Evidence for the Life of Christ* (Joplin, MO: College Press Publishing Company, 1996), 192-196.

5. See Schlomo Pines, *An Arabic Version of the Testimonium Flavianum and Its Implications* (Jerusalem: Israel Academy of Sciences and Humanities, 1971).

6. See the helpful discussion offered by Habermas, *The Historical Jesus*, 192-196.

7. F.F. Bruce, *New Testament Documents: Are They Reliable?* (Grand Rapids, MI: Eerdmans, 1960), 108.

8. See Michael J. Cook, "References to Jesus in Early Rabbinic Literature," at www.bc.edu/research/cjl/meta-ele ments/text/cjrelations/resources/articles/cook_rabbis_and_jesus.htm.

9. Habermas, *The Historical Jesus*, 203.

10. Habermas, *The Historical Jesus*, 203.

11. Michael Grant, tr., *Tacitus: The Annals of Rome* (Baltimore: Penguin, 1989), 365-366.

12. Habermas, *The Historical Jesus*, 190.

13. Suetonius, "Claudius," 25:4, in *The Twelve Caesars*, tr. Robert Graves (Baltimore: Penguin, 1957), 202.

14. Suetonius, "Claudius," 221.

15. Tertullian, *Apology*, 2.5.7.

16. Eusebius, *Ecclesiastical History*, 4.9.

17. Cited from Habermas, *The Historical Jesus*, 208.

18. Julius Africanus, *Extant Writings*, 18, in Alexander Roberts and James Donaldson, eds., *Ante-Nicene Fathers*, vol. 6 (Grand Rapids, MI: Eerdmans, 1973), 130, as cited in Habermas, *The Historical Jesus*, 197; see Origen, *Against Celsus*, II.33, for confirmation of the same quotation.

19. Origen, *Against Celsus*, II.59, in Alexander Roberts, James Donaldson, et al., eds., *The Ante-Nicene Fathers*, accessed at www.earlychristianwritings.com/text/origen162.html.

20. Origen, *Against Celsus*, II.33.

21. Lucian of Samosata, "The Death of Peregrine," 11-13, in *The Works of Lucian of Samosata*, vol. 4.

22. Habermas, *The Historical Jesus*, 205.

23. Justin Martyr, *First Apology*, XXXV, accessed at www.earlychristianwritings.com/text/justinmartyr-firstapology .html.

24. Justin Martyr, *First Apology*, XLVIII.

Chapter 23—Jesus and Archaeological Sources

1. Everett Ferguson, *Backgrounds of Early Christianity* (Grand Rapids, MI: William B. Eerdmans Publishing Company, 1987), 475.

2. Orazio Marucchi, "Archæology of the Cross and Crucifix," *The Catholic Encyclopedia*, vol. 4 (New York: Robert Appleton Company, 1908) at www.newadvent.org/cathen/04517a.htmm accessed November 11, 2011.

3. Graydon F. Snyder, *Ante Pacem: Archaeological Evidence of Church Life Before Constantine* (Macon, GA: Mercer University Press, 1985), 27-28.

4. This has been suggested by Rodney Decker (Rodney J. Decker, "The Alexamenos Graffito," http://faculty.bbc.edu/rdecker/alex_graffito.htm).

5. Marucchi suggests a third-person singular, but this would need to be a present middle indicative third-person singular since the present active indicative third-person singular would be ει, not εται.

6. Tertullian, *To the Nations* 11.1-2, in Alexander Roberts et al., *The Ante-Nicene Fathers: Translations of the Writings of the Fathers Down to A.D. 325*, vol. III (Oak Harbor, WA: Logos Research Systems, 1997), 121; and Tertullian, *Apology* 16.1-2, in Roberts et al., *The Ante-Nicene Fathers*, vol. III, 30-31.

7. See David L. Balch and Carolyn Osiek, *Early Christian Families in Context: An Interdisciplinary Dialogue* (Grand Rapids, MI: William B. Eerdmans Publishing, 2003), 103, fn83.

8. Marucchi.

9. This section is an adapted reproduction of an article by Joseph M. Holden, "The James Ossuary: The Earliest Witness to Jesus and His Family?" in *Bible Translation Magazine: All Things Bible Translation* 13 (July 2012). (© Joseph M. Holden 2012. All rights reserved.)

10. Based on court transcripts and expert testimony summarized by Oden Golan, "The Authenticity of the James Ossuary and the Jehoash Tablet Inscriptions—Summary of Expert Trial Witnesses" (March 2011); also see arguments for authenticity put forth in Hershel Shanks and Ben Witherington III, *The Brother of Jesus: The Dramatic Story and Meaning of the First Archaeological Link to Jesus and His Family* (New York: Harper Collins, 2003).

11. Hershel Shanks, "'Brother of Jesus' Proved Ancient and Authentic" in *A Biblical Archaeology Press Release* (Washington DC: Biblical Archaeology Society, June 13, 2012); Hershel Shanks, "'Brother of Jesus' Inscription Is Authentic!" in *Biblical Archaeology Review* 38:04 (July/August 2012).

12. Golan, "The Authenticity of the James Ossuary," 13-15.

13. Shanks, "'Brother of Jesus' Inscription Is Authentic!"

14. Paul L. Maier, "The James Ossuary," Issues, Etc., at www.mtio.com/articles/bissar95.htm, accessed November 13, 2011.

15. Shanks, "'Brother of Jesus' Inscription Is Authentic!"; also see the record of the defense's cross-examination of Joe Zias in the Hebrew court transcript at http://bib-arch.org/pdf/trial-hebrew-transcript.pdf.

16. "Joe Zias: 'Hershel Has No Sense of Humor,'" *Biblical Archaeology Review* 38:03 (May/June 2012).

17. Golan, "The Authenticity of the James Ossuary," 13, referring to p. 11,462 of the Hebrew language court transcript.

18. This can be seen on several fronts, such as by comparing earlier and later court documents, and by comparing the later Golan, "The Authenticity of the James Ossuary" (2011) with earlier accounts of IAA witnesses recorded in Shanks and Witherington, *The Brother of Jesus*.

19. Golan, "The Authenticity of the James Ossuary," 10.

20. http://orthodoxwiki.org/Church_of_the_Holy_Sepulchre_(Jerusalem), accessed November 18, 2011.

21. The following list is from H. Wayne House and Timothy Demy, "Where did Jesus die and rise again?" *Answers to Common Questions about Jesus* (Grand Rapids, MI: Kregel, 2011), 25. Also see topographical description of the region of Golgotha, Basilica of the Anastasis, www. holyland.ccreadbible.org/holysepulchre/, accessed November 18, 2011.

22. House and Demy. Their book says the Garden Tomb satisfies item 8, but this is an error. The Garden Tomb is

a First Temple tomb, used in the eighth century BC. A case for the Garden Tomb may be found at The Resurrection Garden, www.oxfordbiblechurch.co.uk/pages/books/mount-moriah-golgotha-the-garden-tomb/chapter-4a.php, accessed November 18, 2011. But see W. Harold Mare, "The Place of Christ's Crucifixion and Burial," *Associates for Biblical Research, Bible and Spade*, vol. 3 (Ephrata, PA: Associates for Biblical Research, 1974; 2005).

23. "Jerusalem Report: Israeli Scholars Date Garden Tomb to the Israelite Monarchy," *Associates for Biblical Research, Bible and Spade*, vol. 11 (Ephrata, PA: Associates for Biblical Research, 1982).

24. For more on the long and important history of the site and the Church of the Holy Sepulchre, see Martin Biddle, *The Tomb of Christ* (Stroud, UK: Sutton Publishers, 1999). See also Dan Bahat, "Does the Holy Sepulchre Church Mark the Burial of Jesus?" *Biblical Archaeology Review* 12:3 (May-June 1986): 26-45.

25. This section is adapted from Joseph M. Holden, "Is Jesus' Hometown (Nazareth) a Myth?" (© Joseph M. Holden, 2012. All rights reserved), http://normangeisler.net/articles/Bible/Reliability/2012-IsNazarethAMyth.htm, accessed June 20, 2012.

26. Craig A. Evans, *Jesus and His World: The Archaeological Evidence* (Westminster John Knox Press, 2012), 13-14. See also Bellarmino Bagatti, *Excavations in Nazareth: Vol. 1, From the Beginning till the XII Century*, 2 vols. (Jerusalem: Franciscan Printing Press, 1969), 174-218.

27. "First Jesus-era house discovered in Nazareth," CBC News (Technology & Science), December 22, 2009, www.cbc.ca/news/technology/story/2009/12/22/tech-archeology-nazareth.html, accessed on September 5, 2012.

28. Stephen J. Pfann and Yehudah Rapuano, "On the Nazareth Village Farm Report: A Reply to Salm," *Bulletin of the Anglo-Israel Archaeology Society*, vol. 26 (2008), 106.

29. Pfann and Rapuano, "On the Nazareth Village Farm Report."

30. Pfann and Rapuano, "On the Nazareth Village Farm Report."

31. Pfann and Rapuano, "On the Nazareth Village Farm Report," 107-108. Salm has charged that there are "substantial different claims" between a surface survey report (1997) and Pfann and Rapuano's report. However, these charges have been answered in the above cited work (see pages 105-106). Also see criticisms of Salm's work in Ken Dark, "Nazareth Village Farm: A Reply to Salm" in *Bulletin of the Anglo-Israel Archaeology Society*, vol. 26 (2008), 109-111.

32. For an archaeological refutation of several of Salm's ideas present in liberal scholarship, including the notion that there were no synagogues in Israel (or in particular Galilee) prior to AD 70, see Craig A. Evans, *Jesus and His World: The Archaeological Evidence* (Louisville, KY: Westminster John Knox Press, 2012). For textual reliability see Bruce M. Metzger, *The Transmission of the New Testament Text: Its Transmission, Corruption and Restoration*, 3rd ed. (New York: Oxford University Press, USA, 1992); Norman Geisler and William E. Nix, *From God to Us: How We Got Our Bible*, rev. ed. (Chicago: Moody, 2012); and Joseph Holden and Norman Geisler, *The Popular Handbook of Archaeology and the Bible* (Eugene, OR: Harvest House, 2013); Norman Geisler and Frank Turek, *I Don't Have Enough Faith to Be an Atheist* (Wheaton, IL: Crossway, 2004).

Chapter 24—The Temple Mount

1. *Antiquities of the Jews*, 8.50-55.

2. Hershel Shanks, "The 'Three Shekels' and 'Widow's Plea' Ostraca: Real or Fake?" *Biblical Archaeology Review*, May/June 2003; for confirmation see Pierre Bordreuil, Felice Israel, and Dennis Pardee, "Deux Ostraca Paleo-Hebreux de la Collection Sh. Moussaieff," *Semitica* 46 (1997), p. 49. Shanks consulted several other paleographers, such as Frank Moore Cross, P. Kyle McCarter, and André Lemaire, who also confirmed the ostracon as genuine.

3. Josephus, *Antiquities of the Jews*, 15.380.

4. *Wars of the Jews*, 4.582.

5. *Sukkah*, 5.5.

6. Eusebius, *Church History*, 3.5.3.

7. See the *Smithsonian Magazine* web article by Joshua Hammer, "What Is Beneath the Temple Mount?" www.smithsonianmag.com/history-archaeology/What-Is-Beneath-the-Temple-Mount.html#ixzz1bId9y8h0.

8. Respectively, *Antiquities of the Jews*, 15-20, and *Wars of the Jews* 5, 8; *Middot* 2.1 and 1.3.

9. Leen Ritmeyer, *The Quest: Revealing the Temple Mount in Jerusalem* (CARTA Jerusalem & the LAMB Foundation, 2006), 146. See pages 146-164 where Ritmeyer evaluates 12 prominent nineteenth- and twentieth-century theories as well as the proposals of Asher Kaufman and David Jacobson.

10. Ritmeyer, *The Quest*, 165-167.

11. Ritmeyer, *The Quest*, 246.

12. Ritmeyer, *The Quest*, 273.

13. Ritmeyer, *The Quest*, 273.

14. See Josephus, *War of the Jews*, 6.124-126, where he refers to this *soreg* and the Jews' power to execute trespassers; Ritmeyer, *The Quest*, 346-347; *Middot* 2.1ff.

Chapter 25—Herod, Pilate, and Caiaphas

1. See the article by L.I. Levine in David Noel Freedman, *The Anchor Yale Bible Dictionary* (New York: Doubleday, 1996).

2. See the interesting study by Steinmann, in which he argues that Herod reigned from 39–1 BC. Andrew Steinmann, "When Did Herod the Great Reign?" *Novum Testamentum* 51 (2009) 1-29.

3. Josephus, *Antiquities of the Jews*, XV, viii, 1; *Antiquities of the Jews*, XVI, v, 1; *Jewish Ward*, I, xxi, 1, 5.

4. L.I. Levine.

5. Judy Siegel, "US physician unlocks mystery of King Herod's death," *The Jerusalem Post*, January 27, 2002.

6. See article by Ehud Netzer, "Herodium," *The Anchor Yale Bible Dictionary*.

7. The Hebrew University of Jerusalem, News Release, "Tomb of King Herod discovered at Herodium by Hebrew University archaeologist" (Jerusalem, May 8, 2007).

8. Cornelius Tacitus, *Annals* 15.44, quoted from *Early Christian Writings*, www.earlychristianwritings.com/tacitus.html, accessed November 8, 2011.

9. Philo, *On the Embassy of Gaius*, Book XXXVIII, 299-305. See the translation of this event in Charles Duke Yonge, *The Works of Philo: Complete and Unabridged* (Peabody, MA: Hendrickson, 1996), 784. See also Paul L. Maier, "The Episode of the Golden Roman Shields at Jerusalem," *Harvard Theological Review* 62 (1969): 109-121.

10. Josephus, *Antiquities of the Jews*, 18.3.2; Josephus, *Wars of the Jews*, 2.177. See the following for discussion of this and other acts of Pilate in Steve Mason, *Josephus and the New Testament* (Peabody, MA.: Hendrickson Publishers, 1992).

11. Josephus, *Antiquities of the Jews*, 18.4.1.

12. Josephus, *Antiquities of the Jews*, 18.4.1.

13. Antonio Frova, "L'Iscrizione di Ponzio Pilato a Cesarea," *Rendiconti dell'Istituto Lombardo* 95 (1961), 419-34, as quoted in Alan Millard, "The Knowledge of Writing in Iron Age Palestine," *Tyndale Bulletin*, vol. 46 (Cambridge: Tyndale House, 1995), 214.

14. Alan Millard, "The Knowledge of Writing," 206-214.

15. John McRay, *Archaeology and the New Testament* (Grand Rapids, MI: Baker Book House, 1991), 204.

16. Helen K. Bond, *Caiaphas: Friend of Rome and Judge of Jesus?* (Louisville, KY: Westminster John Knox Press, 2004), x-220; Bond says that most of the objections have been met, and that it is most likely the tomb of Caiaphas; see also Zvi Greenhut, "Burial Cave of the Caiaphas Family," *Biblical Archaeology Review* 18/5 (1992), 28-36, 76; and Ronny Reich, "Caiaphas Name Inscribed on Bone Boxes," *Biblical Archaeology Review* 18/5 (1992), 38-44, 76. But see the caution of W. Horbury, "The 'Caiaphas' Ossuaries and Joseph Caiaphas," *Palestine Exploration Quarterly* 126 (1994), 32-48; and W.D. Davies and Dale C. Allison, *A Critical and Exegetical Commentary on the Gospel According to Saint Matthew* (London, New York: T&T Clark International, 2004), 438-439.

Chapter 26—More Fascinating Finds Relating to the New Testament

1. David J. Williams, *New International Biblical Commentary: Acts* (Peabody, MA: Hendrickson Publishers, 1990), 227-228. See discussion by Philip and David Schley Schaff, *History of the Christian Church*, vol. 1 (New York: Charles Scribner's Sons, 1882), 733-734.

2. *The Encyclopedia Britannica*, 11th ed., vol. 7 (Cambridge, England: University Press, 1910), 700; Louis Palma di Cesnola, Find a Grave, www.findagrave.com/cgi-bin/fg.cgi?page=pv&GRid=4011, accessed November 9, 2011. See Philip Schaff and David Schley Schaff, *History of the Christian Church* (Oak Harbor, WA: Logos Research Systems, Inc., 1997).

3. Schaff and Schaff, 734.

4. T.B. Mitford, *Annual of British School at Athens* 42 (1947), 201-206, as quoted in "Sergius Paulus," www.bible history.net, accessed November 11, 2011.

5. Ben Witherington III, *The Acts of the Apostles: A Socio-Rhetorical Commentary* (Grand Rapids, MI: Wm. B. Eerdmans Publishing Co., 1998), 399-400. See Witherington's discussion of Ramsay's discoveries in former Asia Minor (modern Turkey) in the region of Pisidian Antioch.

6. www.pleaseconvinceme.com/index/The_New_Testament_Is_Verified_Archeologically, accessed November 11, 2011.

7. *IGRR* 3.935 = *SEG* 20.302 (*SEG Supplementum epigraphicum graecum*).

8. Joseph A. Fitzmyer, *The Acts of the Apostles: A New Translation with Introduction and Commentary* (New Haven, CT; London: Yale University Press, 2008), 501-502.

9. Fitzmyer, *The Acts of the Apostles*.

10. Witherington, *The Acts of the Apostles*, 399-400.

11. Sir William Ramsay, *St. Paul the Traveller and the Roman Citizen*; Sir William Ramsay, *The Bearing of Recent Discovery on the Trustworthiness of the New Testament*.

12. A. Souter, "Asiarch," *Dictionary of the Apostolic Church* (2 vols.), ed. James Hastings (New York: Charles Scribner's Sons, 1916–1918).

13. Steven J. Friesen, "Asiarchs, "*Zeitschrift für Papyrologie und Epigraphik*, Bd. 126 (1999), 275-290.

14. Eusebius of Caesarea, *Ecclesiastical History*, book IV, chap 15, 26-27.

15. Witherington, *The Acts of the Apostles*, 584-585.

16. Helmut Koester, "Ephesos in Early Christian Literature," in Helmut Koester, ed., *Ephesos, Metropolis of Asia* (Boston: Harvard Divinity School, 2004).

17. On this see Steven J. Friesen, *Twice Neokoros: Ephesus, Asia and the Cult of the Flavian Imperial Family* (Leiden, the Netherlands: Brill Academic Publishing, 1993), 55-56.

18. They are widely attested in Ephesian inscriptions. See Colin J. Hemer, *The Book of Acts in the Setting of Hellenistic History* (Winona Lake, IN: Eisenbrauns, 1990), passim.

19. See Koester, "Ephesos in Early Christian Literature," 130, n42.

20. Friesen, "Asiarchs," 275-290.

21. Thomas Kelly Cheyne, *Encyclopaedia Biblica, A Dictionary of the Bible*, vol. 1: A-D (London: Adam and Charles Black, 1899), 341.

22. John McRay, *Archaeology and the New Testament* (Grand Rapids, MI: Baker Book House, 1991), 255.

23. Michael Cart, "Archiereis and Asiarchs: A Gladiatorial Perspective," www.duke.edu/web/classics/grbs/FTexts/44/Carter, 66, accessed September 26, 2011.

24. Witherington, *The Acts of the Apostles*, 507.

25. Colin J. Hemer, *The Book of Acts in the Setting of Hellenistic History* (Winona Lake, IN: Eisenbrauns, 1990), 115, especially fn35.

26. Associates for Biblical Research, *Bible and Spade*, vol. 12 (Associates for Biblical Research, 1999; 2003), 55.

27. Seneca, *Natural Questions*, iv. a; preface 11.

28. Adolf Deissmann, *St. Paul: A Study in Social and Religious History*, tr. Lionel R.M. Strachan (New York: Hodder and Stoughton, 1912), 238.

29. Gardner Gordon, "Paul, Dating, and Corinth: The Gallio Inscription and Pauline Chronology," www.reformed perspectives.org, accessed November 18, 2011.

30. See the detailed arguments in Gordon, "Paul, Dating, and Corinth," regarding the reign of Claudius, the ascendancy of Seneca to tutor of Nero, and the appointment of Gallio and the impact of these on the dating of Paul's work at Corinth.

31. See the Greek text and translation in Hans Conzelmann, "Acts of the Apostles," *Hermeneia* (Philadelphia: Fortress, 1987), 153-154.

32. BDAG Greek lexicon defines οἰκονόμος as "public treasurer, treasurer" and ὁ οἰκονομος τῆς πολεῶς as "the city treasurer" (SIG 1252 πολεῶς Κῶων ὁ οἰκονομος; other examples in P. Landvogt, *Epigr. Untersuchungen über den ὁ οἰκονόμος*, diss. Strassburg 1908; H. Cadbury, *Journal of Biblical Literature* 50, 1931, 47ff), Romans 16:23 (Frederick W. Danker, Walter Bauer, and William Arndt, *A Greek-English Lexicon of the New Testament and Other Early Christian Literature* [Chicago: University of Chicago Press, 2000], 698).

33. G.A. Lee in Geoffrey W. Bromiley, *The International Standard Bible Encyclopedia*, rev. ed. (Wm. B. Eerdmans, 1988, 2002).

34. David Noel Freedman, *The Anchor Yale Bible Dictionary* (New York: Doubleday, 1996).

35. Gerd Theissen, *The Social Setting of Pauline Christianity: Essays on Corinth*, tr. John H. Schuetz (Philadelphia: Augsburg Fortress Publishers, 1982).

36. Jerome Murphy-O'Connor, "The Corinth That Saint Paul Saw," *Biblical Archaeologist* 47 (September 1984), 147-159.

37. A.F. Walls, in D.R.W. Wood and I. Howard Marshall, *New Bible Dictionary*, 3rd ed. (Leicester, England; Downers Grove, IL: InterVarsity Press, 1996), 332.

38. For a more complete study of Erastus and the Erastus inscription, see Andrew D. Clarke, *Secular and Christian Leadership in Corinth: A Socio-Historical and Exegetical Study of 1 Corinthians 1-6* (Leiden, the Netherlands: E.J. Brill, 1993), 46-57.

Appendix A — New Testament Manuscript Papyri: A Descriptive List

1. Philip Wesley Comfort, *Encountering the Manuscripts: An Introduction to New Testament Paleography and Textual Criticism* (Nashville, TN: Broadman & Holman, 2005), 168.

2. Comfort, *Encountering the Manuscripts*, 173, 176.

SELECT BIBLIOGRAPHY

Archaeological Study Bible (NIV). Grand Rapids, MI: Zondervan Publishing, 2005.

Archer, Gleason. *Survey of Old Testament Introduction*. Chicago: Moody Press, 1994.

Avigad, Nahman (rev. and completed Benjamin Sass). *Corpus of West Semitic Stamp Seals*. Jerusalem: The Israel Academy of Sciences and Humanities; The Israel Exploration Society; The Institute of Archaeology, The Hebrew University of Jerusalem, 1997.

Bienkowski, Piotr, and Alan Millard, eds. *Dictionary of the Ancient Near East*. Philadelphia: University of Pennsylvania Press, 2000.

Bruce, F.F. *Jesus and Christian Origins Outside the New Testament*. Grand Rapids, MI: Eerdmans, 1974.

Collins, Steven, and Latayne C. Scott. *Discovering the City of Sodom: The Fascinating, True Account of the Discovery of the Old Testament's Most Infamous City*. New York: Howard Books, 2013.

Coogan, Michael D., ed. *The Oxford History of the Biblical World*. New York: Oxford University Press, 1998.

Currid, John D. *Doing Archaeology in the Land of the Bible: A Basic Guide*. Grand Rapids, MI: Baker Books, 1999.

The Dead Sea Scrolls: Study Edition, vols. 1-2. Florentino Garcia Martinez and Eibert J.C. Tigchelaar, eds. Grand Rapids, MI: William B. Eerdmans Publishing Company, 1997.

DeVries, LaMoine F. *Cities of the Biblical World*. Peabody, MA: Hendrickson Publishing, 1997.

Edwards, Brian, and Clive Anderson. *Through the British Museum with the Bible: Day One*. Leominster, England: Day One Publications, 2004.

Evans, Craig A. *Jesus and His World: The Archaeological Evidence*. Louisville, KY: Westminster John Knox Press, 2012.

Fagan, Brian M., ed. *The Oxford Companion to Archaeology*. Oxford, UK: Oxford University Press, 1996.

Flusser, David. *Judaism of the Second Temple Period: Qumran and Apocalypticism*, vol. 1. Grand Rapids, MI: William B. Eerdmans Publishing Company, 2007.

Free, Joseph P., and Howard F. Vos. *Archaeology and the Bible History*, rev. Grand Rapids, MI: Zondervan Publishing, 1992.

Geisler, Norman, and William E. Nix. *From God to Us: How We Got Our Bible*, rev. ed. Chicago, IL: Moody Publishers, 1974, 2012.

Geisler, Norman, and William C. Roach. *Defending Inerrancy: Affirming the Accuracy of Scripture for a New Generation*. Grand Rapids, MI: Baker Books, 2012.

Habermas, Gary. *Ancient Evidence for the Life of Jesus*. Nashville, TN: Thomas Nelson, 1984.

———. *The Historical Jesus: Ancient Evidence for the Life of Christ*. Joplin, MO: College Press, 1996.

Hallo, William W., and K. Lawson Younger, Jr., eds. *The Context of Scripture*. Vol. 1, "Canonical Compositions from the Biblical World." Leiden/Boston: Brill, 2003.

———. *The Context of Scripture*. Vol. 2, "Monumental Inscriptions from the Biblical World." Leiden/Boston: Brill, 2003.

———. *The Context of Scripture*. Vol. 3, "Archival Documents from the Biblical World." Leiden/Boston: Brill, 2003.

Hannah, John D. *Inerrancy and the Church*. Chicago: Moody Press, 1984.

Hemer, Colin J. *The Book of Acts in the Setting of Hellenistic History*. Winona Lake, IN: Eisenbrauns, 1990.

Hoerth, Alfred J. *Archaeology and the Old Testament*. Grand Rapids, MI: Baker Publishing Group, 2009.

Hoerth, Alfred J., and John McRay. *Bible Archaeology: An Exploration of the History and Culture of Early Civilizations*. Grand Rapids, MI: Baker Books, 2005.

Hoffmeier, James K. *The Archaeology of the Bible*. Oxford, UK: Lion Hudson, 2008.

Kaiser, Walter C., Jr. *The Old Testament Documents: Are They Reliable & Relevant?* Downers Grove, IL: InterVarsity Press, 2001.

Kenyon, Frederic. *The Bible and Arcaheology*. London: George G. Harrap & Co. Ltd., 1949.

Kitchen, K.A. *On the Reliability of the Old Testament*. Grand Rapids, MI: William B. Eerdmans Publishing Company, 2003.

Lightfoot, Neil R. *How We Got the Bible*. Grand Rapids, MI: Baker Books, 1972.

Magness, Jodi. *The Archaeology of Qumran and the Dead Sea Scrolls*. Grand Rapids, MI and Cambridge, UK: William B. Eerdmans Publishing Company, 2002.

McRay, John. *Archaeology and the New Testament*. Grand Rapids, MI: Baker Academic, 1991.

Metzger, Bruce M. *Manuscripts of the Greek Bible: An Introduction to Greek Paleography*. New York: Oxford University Press, 1981.

———. *The New Testament: Its Background, Growth, and Content*. New York: Abingdon Press, 1965.

———. *The Text of the New Testament: Its Transmission, Corruption, and Restoration*. New York: Oxford University Press, 1968.

The New Encyclopedia of Archaeological Excavations in the Holy Land. Volumes 1-5. Ephraim Stern et al., eds. Jerusalem: The Israel Exploration Society and Carta; New York: Simon and Schuster, 1993-2008.

Pritchard, James B., ed. *Ancient Near Eastern Texts Relating to the Old Testament with Supplement*. Princeton University Press, 1950, 1955, 1969, 1978.

Ramsay, William M. *St. Paul: The Traveler and Roman Citizen*, updated and rev. ed. Mark Wilson, ed. Grand Rapids, MI: Kregel Publications, 2001.

Reich, Ronny. *Excavating the City of David: Where Jerusalem's History Began*. Jerusalem: Israel Exploration Society and Biblical Archaeology Society, 2011.

Ritmeyer, Leen. *The Quest: Revealing the Temple Mount in Jerusalem*. Jerusalem: CARTA Jerusalem and The LAMB Foundation, 2006.

Sherwin-White, A.N. *Roman Law and Roman Society in the New Testament: The Sarum Lectures 1960-1961*. Grand Rapids, MI: Baker Book House/Oxford University Press, 1963.

VanderKam, James, and Peter Flint. *The Meaning of the Dead Sea Scrolls: Their Significance for Understanding the Bible, Judaism, Jesus, and Christianity*. New York: Harper San Francisco, 2002.

Wilson, Clifford A. *Rocks, Relics, and Biblical Reliability*. Grand Rapids, MI: Zondervan Publishing House, 1977.

Yamauchi, Edwin. *Persia and the Bible*. Grand Rapids, MI: Baker Books, 1990, 1996.

———. *The Stones and the Scriptures*. Philadelphia: J.B. Lippincott, 1972.

INDEX

A

Acropolis, 136
Adam and Eve, 61-62, 64-66, 68-70, 78, 86, 145, 155, 407
Aedilis, 358
Ahaz, 260, 262, 264, 267, 283
Al-Aqsa Mosque, 263, 274, 285, 324, 327-28, 333
Albright, William, 33, 70-71, 76, 139, 179, 214-15, 397, 399
Aleppo Codex, 22, 25-29, 53
Alexamenos Graffito, 304, 308-09, 404
Alexandrinus, Codex, 116, 121, 375, 380
Alleged errors, 9, 77-79, 81, 83, 85, 397
Amarna Letters, 10, 231, 239-41, 243-45, 247, 254, 397, 402
Amphitheater, 292
Apocrypha, apocryphal, 33, 37, 39, 52, 90-93, 114, 116, 165, 346, 377, 381
Apologetics, 1-2, 15-16, 53, 129, 291, 362, 395, 398
Arabic, 100, 114, 122, 124, 297, 323, 328, 335, 403
archaios, 177
Arch of Titus, 326-27, 330, 333
Archaeological ages, 191
Archaeological terms, 193
Archer, Gleason, 51, 57-58, 396, 397, 409
Ark of the Covenant, 89, 337
Artaxerxes I, 93, 202, 247, 280-84
Asiarch, 353-55, 407
Atrahasis Epic, 68, 207
Augustine, 90-92, 175, 313, 398
Augustus Caesar, 144, 147, 153, 295, 303, 363-64
Avaris, 228, 401
Azekah, 83, 250, 270, 272, 286

B

Bab edh-dhra, 70, 214, 215-16, 219-20, 386-87
Babel, 9, 68-69, 82, 203, 205, 207, 209, 211, 213-15, 217, 219, 279, 401
Babylonian Chronicles, 266, 271, 286-87, 333
Balaam, 200, 202, 229-30, 257, 284
Barkay, Gabriel, 46-48, 202, 263, 273, 285, 333, 390, 396
Baruch Seal, 75, 202, 262, 273, 284, 334
Behistun, 280, 284, 287
Belshazzar, 82, 139, 185, 202, 270-71, 276, 277-79, 284
Bema, 356, 361
Bethlehem, 34, 36, 147, 149, 320, 343, 345
Beth-Shan, 81, 194, 202
Ben Asher, 21, 24-25, 27, 29-30
Bezae, Codex, 117, 121, 376, 398
Biblia Hebraica, 22, 25, 29-30, 395
Bietak, Manfred, 228-29, 401
Shalmaneser III, 81-83, 182, 259
Botta, Paul, 81, 179
Bruce, F.F., 51, 135, 140, 297, 356, 397, 400, 403
Bulla(-ae), 195, 260-64, 268, 273, 283-89, 334

C

Caiaphas, 10, 303, 343, 345, 347-50, 406
Cairensis, Codex, 22, 29
Cairo Geniza, 22, 29
Canaanite(s), 71, 84, 191, 200, 216, 240-41, 244-46, 248, 250-53, 255, 259-60, 385, 402
Capernaum, 292, 319-21, 362

Carson, D.A., 135, 151, 167, 399-00
Census, 147, 153-54, 324
Chrestus/Christus, 299, 345
Church of the Holy Sepulchre, 315-18, 404-5
Cities of the Plain, 10-11, 203, 205, 207, 209, 211, 213-15, 217, 219-20, 383, 385-87, 401
City of David, 199, 202, 259-61, 265, 273, 410
Claudius Caesar, 352-53, 357, 363-64, 403
Code of Hammurabi, 231-32
Codex Alexandrinus, 116, 121, 375, 380
Codex Cairensis, 22, 29
Codex Leningradensis, 22, 25-26, 33
Codex Sinaiticus, 50, 52, 114-15, 121, 375-76, 378-81
Codex Vaticanus, 116-17, 121, 375, 377-79, 381
Collins, Steven, 1, 70, 202, 215-19, 387, 400, 409
Copper Scroll, 38
Coptic, 122-24, 346, 381
Cyrus II (the Great), 83, 202, 270, 278-80, 284, 326

D
Darius the Great, 202, 247, 264, 280-82, 284, 326
Darwin, 62-64, 67, 396
Dead Sea Scrolls, 9, 19, 25, 27-28, 31-37, 39-43, 45-49, 51-52, 58, 82, 90, 276, 292, 395-96, 409-11
De Vaux, Father Roland, 35, 38, 202
Decapolis, 81
Diatessaron, 122, 126, 163
Didache, 126, 175
Dittography, 107
Dome of the Rock, the, 324, 327-28, 335-37
Dynasty, 9, 182, 192, 204, 223, 249, 251, 253, 255, 257, 260, 270, 276-77, 402

E
Early citations of the New Testament, 125
Ebla Tablets, 86
Ecofacts, 195
Ehrman, Bart, 79, 97, 106, 127-28, 143-59, 163, 165-70, 398-400
Ekron Inscription, 48, 83, 252, 267
Enomizeto, 155
Enuma Elish, 203-05, 247
Epic of Gilgamesh, 68, 206-07, 247-48
Erastus Inscription, 303, 358-59, 408
Eridu Genesis, 68, 208, 211, 213, 401
Essenes, 37, 41-42
Eusebius, 125, 163, 175, 300, 314, 331, 345-47, 353, 359, 361, 363, 382, 403, 405, 407
Evolution, theory of, 58, 60, 62-64, 67, 180, 396

F
Finkelstein, Israel, 182, 238, 244, 249, 252-53
Forgeries, 165-66, 194
Franz, Gordon, 46
Frova, Antonio, 347, 406

G
Galilee Boat, 359
Gallio, 136, 292, 304, 356-57, 361, 408
Gath, 83, 201-02, 250-53, 285, 402
Garden Tomb, 315-18, 404-05
Gennao, 157
Genealogy(-ies), 60-61, 67, 145, 154-58, 177, 249
Gezer, 202, 230-31, 241, 244, 246, 248, 253
Golan, Oded, 311-13, 315, 392-93, 404
Gothic, 122, 124
Greenleaf, Simon, 138-39, 399

H
Habermas, Gary, 135, 140, 297, 298-99, 399, 403, 409
Hadley, Judith, 46

Hammurabi Code, 231-32

Harmonization, harmony (of events and texts), 59, 108, 161, 213

Hazor, 86, 202, 241, 244, 246, 248, 253

Hemer, Colin, 135, 137, 173, 399, 400, 407, 410

Herod, 10, 144, 147, 149, 152-54, 200, 292, 303-05, 319, 323, 326-32, 335, 339, 343-47, 364, 406

Herod Jug Inscription, 304, 344

Herodium, 304, 344-45, 406

Herod's Tomb, 304, 344-45, 406

Hezekiah's Broad Wall, 265-66, 268, 286

Hezekiah's Water Tunnel, 246, 260, 266, 286

Hittites, 10, 239-45, 247, 402

Holy of Holies, 336-38

Homer, 103, 126-27, 129

Homoeoteleuton, 107

House of God Ostracon, 289, 325

I

Immer bulla, 75, 263, 269, 274, 285-86, 333-34, 404

Ipsissima verba/vox, 79, 148

Ipuwer Papyrus, 11, 73, 222-24, 238

Irenaeus, 125-26, 136, 165, 172-75, 382

Ishtar Gate, 270, 272, 275-76, 287, 403

J

Jacob's Well, 361

James Ossuary, 10-11, 304, 310-15, 389, 391, 393, 404

JEDP, 57-58

Jehoiachin Ration Record, 270, 272, 285-86

Jericho, 38, 177, 183, 192, 202, 216, 234-38, 241, 345, 384, 400-02

Jerome, 91, 92, 123, 136, 165, 175, 297, 408

Jerusalem, 21, 26-29, 32, 34, 39, 41-42, 46, 48, 74-75, 82, 84-86, 137, 153, 160, 162, 169, 175, 185, 192, 201-02, 216, 240-41, 246, 249-50, 252-55, 259-61, 264-68, 270-71, 273-74, 279, 281-82, 286, 291-

92, 299, 310-11, 313-14, 316-18, 320, 323-27, 330-31, 333-35, 337, 341, 346, 348-49, 359, 389-92, 402-06, 409-11

Jesus, 8, 10-11, 16, 23, 60, 66, 69, 76-77, 81, 88, 91-93, 95, 107-08, 113, 128, 133-57, 159, 161-67, 169, 171-72, 176, 202, 211, 241, 291, 293, 295-305, 307-21, 328-31, 339, 343, 345-46, 348-52, 355-56, 359, 362-65, 370, 390, 393, 396, 398-400, 403-06, 409, 411

John Rylands Fragment, 112, 118, 373

Josephus, 30, 41, 68, 89, 93, 136-37, 140-41, 148 152-54, 172, 177, 229, 274, 295-97, 303-05, 311, 313-14, 319, 321, 325-26, 329-30, 333, 335, 337, 344-46, 348-49, 395, 397-99, 403, 405-06

Julius Africanus, 301, 403

Julius Caesar, 78, 129, 192

Justin Martyr, 125, 172-73, 175, 301-02, 403

K

Kaiser, Walter, 9, 13-14, 66, 395-98, 410

Kenyon, Kathleen, 183, 202, 235-37, 400

Ketef Hinnom Silver Scrolls, 33, 46, 48

Khirbet Qeiyafa, 182, 252-55, 264, 402

Khirbet Qumran, 19, 33-45

Kikkar, 215-16, 218-20, 383-87, 401

Kurkh Monolith, 81, 283

L

Lachish Letters, 271, 285

Lapp, Paul, 215

Layard, Austen, 81-82, 179

Lazarus Tomb, 359

Leningradensis, Codex, 22, 25-26, 33

Lewis, C.S., 15, 205

Licona, Michael, 77, 163-64, 399-400

Lucian (of Samosata), 141, 172, 295, 300-01, 304, 403

M

Machaerus, 304, 345

Madaba Map, 85, 185, 220, 303

Maeir, Aren, 202, 250-51, 402

Mahabharata, 127

Mamertine Prison, 361

Masada, 26, 42, 304, 343-45

Masoretes, 9, 21-24, 29, 49, 370, 395

Masoretic, 19, 21-27, 29, 31-32, 36, 43-46, 48, 50-51, 58, 198, 369, 370

Maximalism(-ist), 186

Megiddo, 10, 86, 191, 194, 202, 206, 239, 241, 243-48, 261, 304, 307, 402

Merneptah Stele, 72, 192, 197, 230-31, 401

Messianic Testimony (4Q175), 45

Metzger, Bruce, 105, 127, 135

Middot, 335, 339, 405-06

Minimalism(-ist), 13, 48, 139-40, 182-84, 254-55, 400, 402

Mishnah, 21, 38, 89, 304, 330, 333, 335, 337

Mesha Stele (Moabite Stone), 182, 197, 258, 283-84, 287-89

Moo, Douglas, 135, 167, 400

Moses, 9, 21, 25, 27, 29-30, 32, 37, 41, 48, 53, 55, 57, 59-61, 69, 71-73, 76, 84-85, 87, 89, 94, 182, 186, 192, 197, 204-05, 217, 221, 224, 228, 231-32, 238, 240, 265, 337, 346, 370, 386, 396

N

Nebuchadnezzar II, 10, 83, 192, 202, 269-75, 277-78, 287, 325, 402-03

Nabonidus, 82, 139, 270, 276-77, 279, 284

Nag Hammadi, 33 166, 292

Nash Papyrus, 49, 52

Nazareth, 145, 149, 155, 295, 304, 315, 319-22, 363, 405

Netzer, Ehud, 344-45, 406

Nuzi, 71, 85, 232, 397

O

Oikonomos, 358

Old Testament Persons Confirmed by Archaeology, 10-11, 283

Origen, 91, 118, 122, 125, 136, 165, 175, 296, 301, 346, 382, 403

Ossuary, 10-11, 195, 303-04, 309-15, 318, 349-50, 389-93, 404

Ostracon(-ca), 196, 257, 325, 371, 405

P-Q

Palestine, 190, 397, 406

Papyrus(-ri), 11, 52, 105, 112-13, 373-75, 377, 379-81

Paraskeue, 151

Parchment, 28, 36-37, 43, 90, 100, 113-16, 382

Pentateuch, 9, 30-32, 36, 51, 53, 57-59, 74, 89-90, 231, 238, 370, 396

Peter's house, 362

Petrie, Sir William Flinders, 179, 230, 239

Pedaiah Seal, 263-64, 273, 288

Pella ruins, 81, 331

Persepolis, 278-84

Philippi, 169, 202, 292

Phlegon, 141, 172, 295, 300, 301

Pilate Inscription, 200, 292, 305, 347-48

Pliny the Younger, 129, 295, 299, 304

Politarch, *politarcho*, 187, 353, 355-56, 360

Pontius Pilate, 140, 200, 292, 295, 298-99, 302, 305, 320, 345-48, 359

Pool of Bethesda, 292, 363

Pool of Siloam, 202, 266, 292, 316, 363

Postmodern, 13

Protos, 154, 360

Pseudepigrapha, 37, 90

Quirinius, 154, 292, 305

R

Ras Shamra Tablets, 71-72, 84, 397

Rast, Walter, 215

Red Algae/Red Mud Theory, 11, 225-27, 401

Reuchlin, 22, 30

Resurrection, 9, 11, 77, 135, 138-41, 150, 159, 160-61, 163-65, 167, 169, 171, 300-01, 316-18, 363, 399, 400

Ritmeyer, Leen, 1, 202, 334-41, 405-06, 411

Robertson, A.T., 127, 398-99
Rock of Binding (*Es-Sakhra*), 336
Rosetta Stone, 178-79
Royal bricks, 83, 275-76, 280
Royal Steward Inscription, 74, 82, 260, 288

S
Salm, Rene, 319-22
Samaritan Pentateuch, 30-32, 36, 53, 89
Samaritans, 9, 21, 23, 25, 27, 29-32, 81, 89, 346-47, 395
Samuel, Mar Athanasius, 34
Sarsekim (Tablet), 75, 274, 288
Schaub, Thomas, 215
Seal Impressions, 11, 195, 246, 260-61, 273, 334
Seneca, 356-57, 407-08
Sennacherib, 81, 83, 202, 252, 265, 266-68, 286-88
Septuagint, 23, 32, 37, 45, 89-90, 114-15, 192, 371
Sergius Paulus, 292, 305, 351, 353, 407
Shema Seal, 246, 248, 261
Siloam Inscription, 260, 266
Sinaiticus, Codex, 50, 52, 114-15, 121, 375-76, 378-81
Slavonic, 122, 124
Sodom, 11, 70, 177, 191, 195, 202, 214-20, 383-87, 401, 409
Solomon, 80, 155-56, 186, 192, 200, 202, 217, 231, 243-48, 251, 254-55, 259, 270, 277, 323, 324-26, 334, 335-38
Suetonius, 129, 140-41, 295, 299, 303-05, 403
Sukenik, E.L., 34, 74, 261
Synagogue, 27-29, 51, 356, 362, 365
Syriac, 52, 122-24, 163, 297, 362

T
Tacitus, 129, 140-41, 172, 295, 298-99, 303-05, 345, 403, 406
Tall el-Hammam, 1, 70, 191, 193, 215-20, 386, 401

Talmud, 21, 93, 140-41, 172, 295, 297-98, 304, 319, 321
Tell Dan Stele, 52, 122-24, 163, 297, 362
Tel es-Safi, 201, 250-52, 264, 402
Temple Mount, 10, 202, 259, 263, 273-74, 285, 304, 316, 323-35, 337, 339-41, 405, 411
Temple Warning, 339
Tertullian, 125, 136, 175, 300-01, 309, 345-46, 403-04
Thallus, 140-41, 295, 300-01
Thanksgiving Scroll, 34
Thanksgiving hymns, 37
Thomas, Gospel of, 166
Three Shekels Ostracon, 12, 405
Tiberius Caesar, 299, 301, 305, 346
Tischendorf, Constantin von, 115
Toledoth Jesu, 141, 301, 304
Tower of Babel, 10, 20, 68-69, 82, 203, 205, 207, 209, 211, 213-15, 217, 219, 401
Transposition, 107
Trumpeting Stone, 330
Tyrannus Inscription, 136, 360

U-V
Utnapishtim, 207
Uzziah, 74-75, 157, 230, 261, 287, 289
Vaticanus, Codex, 116-17, 121, 375, 377-79, 381
Vulgate, 52, 91, 123

W-X-Y-Z
Weld-Blundell Prism, 84
Western (Wailing) Wall, 331-32, 334-35, 337
Wood, Bryant, 183, 192, 202, 215, 235-37, 400, 401-02
Wurthwein, Ernst, 29, 46, 395-96
Xerxes I, 202, 247, 280-83
Yadin, Yigael, 34, 40, 202, 244-45, 248, 252
Yehohanan ben Hagkol, 309-10
Ziggurat, 68, 82, 211-12, 275

ABOUT THE AUTHORS

Joseph M. Holden is the president and cofounder of Veritas Evangelical Seminary in Murrieta, California. He earned his BA from Western Illinois University and his MDiv with a concentration in apologetics from Southern Evangelical Seminary in Charlotte, North Carolina. He also holds a PhD in theology from the University of Wales in Lampeter, Wales. In addition to his service as president of Veritas Evangelical Seminary, he is a member of various adjunct faculties, including that of Azusa Pacific University's graduate school of theology, where he teaches theology and ethics.

Dr. Holden has published or contributed to several books on Christian apologetics, including *Living Loud: Defending your Faith* (2002); *Charts of Christian Apologetics and Evidences* (2007); and *The Apologetics Study Bible for Students* (2010). He has also produced the documentary *Archaeology and the Bible: The Top 10 Amazing Discoveries* (2009). He has traveled throughout the United States and also abroad, speaking, hosting conferences, and offering courses on apologetic issues relating to the Christian worldview. His research in and travel to Europe and the Middle East, as well as his involvement in archaeological excavation, have made him familiar with the relationship between the archaeology of biblical lands and the Bible. Dr. Holden resides in southern California with his wife, Theresa, and two sons, David and Ian.

Norman Geisler holds the Norman L. Geisler Chair of Christian Apologetics as the Distinguished Professor of Apologetics and Theology at Veritas Evangelical Seminary in Murrieta, California. He earned his PhD in philosophy at Loyola University in Chicago and is a prolific author, veteran professor, speaker, lecturer, traveler, philosopher, apologist, evangelist, and theologian.

Dr. Geisler has authored or coauthored over 80 books and hundreds of articles on various topics including apologetics, Bible, theology, and philosophy. In addition to pastoring at several churches, he has taught theology, philosophy, and apologetics on the college or graduate level for more than 50 years. He has also served as a professor at some of the finest seminaries in the United States, including Trinity Evangelical Seminary, Dallas Theological Seminary, and Southern Evangelical Seminary. Dr. Geisler resides in Charlotte, North Carolina, with his wife, Barbara.

In 2012, Veritas Evangelical Seminary's graduate apologetics program was rated among the top 10 such programs in the country by *TheBestSchools.org*, as well as being rated "best newcomer." The mission of Veritas Evangelical Seminary is to equip Christian men and women to evangelize the world and defend the historic Christian faith. To accomplish this mission, all graduate instruction will emphasize the formation of a Christ-centered and biblical worldview based on God's truth as revealed in the Bible.

As a community of learners devoted to the mission of Jesus Christ and the furtherance of His Church, we seek to proclaim Christ's death and resurrection in a classical, biblically based environment. As our name suggests, we seek to create an educational atmosphere that characterizes and fulfills our mission by:

Veritas (Truth): Discovering truth in both general and special revelation, teaching the truth of the Bible as the inspired, inerrant, and infallible Word of God, defending the truth, and longing to cultivate a Christian worldview within all students who will in turn communicate these truths to others.

Evangelical (Biblical/Redemptive): Proclaiming the good news of Jesus Christ's redemptive power through His death and resurrection, instilling within our students a passion and desire to evangelize through clear and winsome biblical exposition, outreach, and mission service.

Seminary (Community): As an academic institution we seek to draw together a community of learners who can encourage, challenge, and interact with others of like mind, including their instructors, who seek to refine and expand their spiritual and intellectual foundation in Christ. Our goal is to educate the whole student within a Christian environment, realizing that God works through our peers to the benefit of all (Luke 2:52; Matthew 22:37). Therefore, the seminary environment serves as a means to cultivating our whole person to the cause of Christ, and thereby, serving God to the fulfillment of the great commission (Matthew 28:19-20).

ALSO BY NORMAN GEISLER

Conversational Evangelism
How to Listen and Speak So You Can Be Heard
Norman and David Geisler

With a passion for people, Norman and David
Geisler offer an engaging, conversational approach
to evangelism as they address

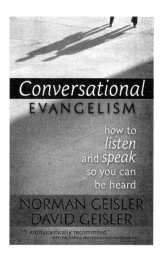

- what makes old models of witnessing ineffective
  in today's culture

- why evangelism must start with relational
  pre-evangelism

- how to ask questions, listen attentively, and
  understand what someone believes

- how to identify the real barriers to belief in order to build a bridge to truth

You will discover how God can use your everyday encounters for life-changing
purposes when you switch from trying to witness effectively to effectively being
a witness through communication and compassion. You'll never again think the
same about your conversations with your nonbelieving friends.

"I enthusiastically recommend."
RAVI ZACHARIAS
Author and international speaker, scholar, and evangelist

The Popular Encyclopedia of Church History
The People, Places, and Events That Shaped Christianity
Ed Hindson and Dan Mitchell

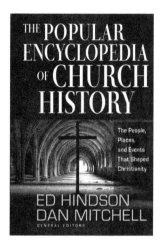

*A Comprehensive Panorama of Church History
in One Volume*

A lot has happened in 2000 years of church history, and this clear, user-friendly guide is an ideal resource for getting to know the key people, places, and events that have shaped Christianity.

The Popular Encyclopedia of Church History combines expert scholarship with popular accessibility, offering concise summaries of essential high points every Christian should know. More than 220 articles give you...

- a comprehensive overview of church history and its key turning points from Acts 2 to today
- a sense for how the church and its teachings have developed over the centuries
- fascinating biographies and details about the men and women, movements, and ministries that have influenced the church and the world around it

This book will enrich your appreciation for the wonderful heritage behind your faith.

The Popular Encyclopedia of Apologetics
Surveying the Evidence for the Truth of Christianity
Ed Hindson and Ergun Caner

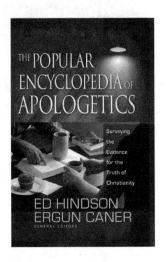

With more than 175 articles and 55 expert contributors (including Christian converts from some of the belief systems discussed within), *The Popular Encyclopedia of Apologetics* provides the most current essentials you need to know about a wide variety of apologetic concerns, including...

- critical issues related to God, Christ, the Spirit, and the Bible
- scientific and historical controversies (including creationism and biblical inerrancy)
- ethical matters (including abortion, stem cell research, and homosexuality)
- a Christian response to major world religions and cults
- a Christian response to major worldviews and secular philosophies

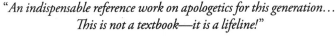

*"An indispensable reference work on apologetics for this generation...
This is not a textbook—it is a lifeline!"*

JOSH MCDOWELL
International apologist and author

To learn more about Harvest House books and
to read sample chapters, log on to our website:

www.harvesthousepublishers.com